D1451974

# Jay and Ellsworth,
# The First Courts

# ABC-CLIO SUPREME COURT HANDBOOKS

*The Burger Court,* Tinsley E. Yarbrough
*The Stone Court,* Peter G. Renstrom
*The Warren Court,* Melvin I. Urofsky
*The Fuller Court,* James W. Ely, Jr.
*The Hughes Court,* Michael E. Parrish
*Jay and Ellsworth, The First Courts,* Matthew P. Harrington
*The Rehnquist Court,* Thomas R. Hensley
*The Taft Court,* Peter G. Renstrom
*The Taney Court,* Timothy S. Huebner
*The Vinson Court,* Michal R. Belknap

Forthcoming:
*The Marshall Court,* Robert L. Clinton and Christopher B. Budzisz

**Peter G. Renstrom, Series Editor**

ABC-CLIO SUPREME COURT HANDBOOKS

# *Jay and Ellsworth, The First Courts*

## Justices, Rulings, and Legacy

Matthew P. Harrington

*Universite de Montreal*

ABC-CLIO

Santa Barbara, California • Denver, Colorado • Oxford, England

Copyright © 2008 by ABC-CLIO

Library of Congress Cataloging-in-Publication Data
Harrington, Matthew P.
    Jay and Ellsworth, the first courts : justices, rulings and legacy / Matthew P.
Harrington.
      p. cm.
    Includes bibliographical references and index.
    ISBN 978-1-57607-841-9 (hard copy : alk. paper) — ISBN 978-1-57607-842-6 (ebook)
1. United States. Supreme Court—History   2. Constitutional law—United States.
3. Jay, John, 1745-1829.   4. Ellsworth, Oliver, 1745-1807.   5. Judges—United
States—Biography.   I. Title.

    KF8742.H368 2008
    347.73'2609—dc22
                                                2008009349

09  08  07  06      10  9  8  7  6  5  4  3  2  1

This book is also available on the World Wide Web as an e-book. Visit
http://www.abc-clio.com for details.

ABC-CLIO, Inc.
130 Cremona Drive, P.O. Box 1911
Santa Barbara, California 93116–1911

*For Susan*

# Contents

# *Series Foreword*

There is an extensive literature on the U.S. Supreme Court, but it contains discussion familiar largely to the academic community and the legal profession. The ABC-CLIO Supreme Court series is designed to have value to the academic and legal communities also, but each volume is intended as well for the general reader who does not possess an extensive background on the Court or American constitutional law. The series is intended to effectively represent each of fourteen periods in the history of the Supreme Court with each of these fourteen eras defined by the chief justice, beginning with John Jay in 1789. Each Court confronted constitutional and statutory questions that were of major importance to and influenced by the historical period. The Court's decisions were also influenced by the values of each of the individual justices sitting at the time. The issues, the historical period, the justices, and the Supreme Court's decisions in the most significant cases will be examined in the volumes of this series.

ABC-CLIO's Supreme Court series provides scholarly examinations of the Court as it functioned in different historical periods and with different justices. Each volume contains information necessary to understand each particular Court and an interpretative analysis by the author of each Court's record and legacy. In addition to representing the major decisions of each Court, institutional linkages are examined as well—the political connections among the Court, Congress, and the executive branch. These relationships are important for several reasons. Although the Court retains some institutional autonomy, all the Court's justices are selected by a process that involves the other two branches. Many of the significant decisions of the Court involve the review of actions of Congress or the president. In addition, the Court frequently depends on the other two branches to secure compliance with its rulings.

The authors of the volumes in the ABC-CLIO series were selected with great care. Each author has worked extensively with the Court, the period, and the personalities about which he or she has written. ABC-CLIO wanted each of the volumes to examine several common themes, and each author agreed to work within certain guidelines. Each author was free, however, to develop the content of each volume, and many of the volumes advance new or distinctive conclusions about the Court under examination.

Each volume will contain four substantive chapters. The first chapter introduces the Court and the historical period in which it served. The second chapter examines each of the justices who sat on the particular Court. The third chapter represents the most significant decisions rendered by the particular Court. Among other things, the impact of the historical period and the value orientations of the individual justices will be developed. A fourth and final chapter addresses the impact of each particular Court on American constitutional law—its doctrinal legacy.

Each volume contains several features designed to make the volume more valuable to those whose previous exposure to the Supreme Court and American constitutional law is limited. Each volume has a reference section that will contain brief entries on some of the people, statutes, events, and concepts introduced in the four substantive chapters. Entries in this section are arranged alphabetically. Each volume also contains a glossary of selected legal terms used in the text. Following each of the four chapters, a list of sources used in the chapter and suggestions for further reading will appear. Each volume also has a comprehensive annotated bibliography. A listing of Internet sources is presented at the end of the bibliography. Finally, there will be a comprehensive subject index and a list of cases (with citation numbers) discussed in each volume. ABC-CLIO is delighted with the quality of scholarship represented in each volume and is proud to offer this series to the reading public.

Permit me to conclude with a personal note. This project has been an extraordinarily rewarding undertaking for me as series editor. Misgivings about serving in this capacity were plentiful at the outset of the project. After tending to some administrative business pertaining to the series, securing authors for each volume was the first major task. I developed a list of possible authors after reviewing previous work and obtaining valuable counsel from several recognized experts in American constitutional history. In virtually every instance, the first person on my list agreed to participate in the project. The high quality of the series was assured and enhanced as each author signed on. I could not have been more pleased. My interactions with each author have been most pleasant, and the excellence of their work will be immediately apparent to the reader. I sincerely thank each author.

Finally, a word about ABC-CLIO and its staff. ABC-CLIO was enthusiastic about the project from the beginning and has done everything necessary to make this series successful. I am very appreciative of the level of support I have received from ABC-CLIO. Alicia Merritt, senior acquisitions editor, deserves special recognition. She held my hand throughout the project. She facilitated making this project a reality in every conceivable way. She encouraged me from the beginning, provided invaluable counsel, and given me latitude to operate as I wished while keeping me on track at the same time. This project would not have gotten off the ground without Alicia, and I cannot thank her enough.

Peter G. Renstrom
Series Editor

# *Preface*

The Supreme Court of the United States occupies a special place in the American political system. Relying on John Marshall's famous assertion that "[i]t is emphatically the province and duty of the judicial department to say what the law is," Americans have generally come to regard the Supreme Court as the final arbiter of constitutional questions. Thus, when it comes to resolving disputes between the political branches of government or the interpretation of the Constitution's various provisions guaranteeing fundamental liberties, the American people seem confident that the Court will provide well-reasoned, impartial resolutions of even the most difficult questions. It is rather obvious that the Supreme Court occupies a special place in the political system because it has built up a large reservoir of respect among the public at large. When pollsters ask Americans which of the three branches of the federal government they trust the most, the Supreme Court routinely tops the list. Although the precise level of this support often varies in response to particular decisions, it is clear that the Court remains one of America's most respected public institutions.

This has not always been the case, however. The road to popular acclaim has not been an easy one. Indeed, in the early years of its history, the Supreme Court was often regarded with far less equanimity. James Madison's assertion that the judiciary was the "least dangerous branch" was more true than he realised when it first uttered it. For, in its early years, the Court had to constantly struggle to gain the respect of both the public and political leaders. While this was true of the new federal government as a whole, the Court was especially in danger of sinking into irrelevancy. In its early years, after all, there was often not very much work for the justices to do. Because of the way in which Congress chose to order the judiciary in the Judiciary Act of 1789, the volume of cases was low, and much of the justices' time was spent presiding over routine civil or criminal trials in the circuit courts, rather than hearing appeals of great constitutional questions. The difficulties of riding circuit, combined with the Supreme Court's rather limited subject matter jurisdiction, made service on the Court rather onerous. Indeed, in those early years, a number of very prominent men either refused to serve or resigned their seats in order to take more prestigious positions in the own state governments.

In time, however, the volume of business increased, thus creating numerous opportunities for the Supreme Court to find itself at the centre of political and constitutional controversy. Decisions such as *Chisholm v. Georgia*, in which the Court held that states were amenable to suit in federal courts, *Ware v. Hylton*, in which the Court permitted Americans to be sued by British creditors for pre-Revolutionary War debts, and *Hayburn's Case*, in which the justices refused to give effect to an act of Congress, forced the Court to confront the pretensions of both Congress and the state governments. By the end of the decade, the controversy over certain justices' efforts to enforce the Alien and Sedition Acts created a widespread impression that the members of the Court were mere tools of an overbearing national government intent on subverting the rights of the states.

One source of the difficulties was the justices more activist approach to the project of government. In the modern era, most justices have taken pains to avoid the appearance of entanglement with other branches of the federal government. The justices of the Jay and Ellsworth courts were not so fastidious, however. On the contrary, the members of the early Supreme Court regarded themselves as "federal officers" whose duty it was to support and defend the national government to the extent it was possible to do so in the context of their judicial capacity. Thus, many justices freely gave advise to members of the president's cabinet, while others used their grand jury charges to educate the public on the virtues or wisdom of particular government policies. Perhaps most striking is the fact that both of the first two chief justices took a leave from the Court to lead foreign diplomatic missions. Chief Justice Jay went to England to negotiate a commercial treaty, while Chief Justice Ellsworth led a peace mission to France during the Quasi-War.

At the same time, however, the justices of the early Supreme Court had precious little with which to work. Aside from the traditions of English and colonial judicial practise, the early justices were forced to create an institution with very little guidance or support from either the Constitution or the Congress. They had to create rules of practise and determine procedure. More importantly, they given the duty of interpreting an entirely new frame government, one which was revolutionary in its scope and entirely untried anywhere else on earth. Being first, every one of their decisions created a precedent and had the potential to shape the development of government at all levels. In short, the Jay and Ellsworth Courts occupied a very different place in the American political edifice. The justices of this era were, in effect, pioneers given the task of creating a judicial institution out of whole cloth. How they went about this task is the subject of work which follows.

# The Supreme Court
# in the Early Republic

The history of the Supreme Court in the early years of the American Republic is, in fact, a history of the founding of the nation itself. This is so because in no other time does it seem that the Supreme Court has played as integral a role in the domestic and international affairs of the nation as in the period between 1789 and 1801. While the Court itself was only in its infant stages, it must be remembered that the federal government of which it was a part was also little more than an experiment. At the time the Supreme Court met for its first session in 1790, the American nation was but a few years old. Moreover, the years between the Peace of Paris, which ended the Revolution in 1783, and the ratification of the Constitution in 1789 had not been kind. The country was racked by sectional strife, the Congress was derided as ineffective by critics both at home and abroad, and it often looked as though the Union forged in necessity after Lexington and Concord would crumble into two, and possibly three, different confederacies.

The new government created by the Constitution was controversial from the start. A long and contentious ratification debate did little to allay the fears of those who believed the national government would trample individual rights and subvert the powers of the state governments. Consequently, a large segment of the American public still had not yet been reconciled to the new order when the federal government opened for business in New York in the spring of 1789. No one, after all, was quite sure whether a country as vast and diverse as the United States could be governed from a single capital. Meanwhile, those who held political power in the various states were unwilling to permit the national government to encroach upon their prerogatives. Upon taking their places, therefore, the justices of the first Supreme Court understood the precarious nature of the federal system. They knew that their every word and deed would be scrutinized by both supporters and opponents of the new Constitution. At the same time, they also knew that they were integral to the success of the enterprise, and that the way in which they went about fulfilling their duties would have a tremendous impact on the very survival of the government itself.

Over the ensuing twelve years, therefore, the Supreme Court often found itself at the center of political controversy. However, unlike today, when the pronouncements of the Court are treated with a deference borne of two hundred years of tradition, the first justices could never be sure that anyone would care what they had to say. Thus, while the members of the Court were certain of the necessity of their place in the constitutional scheme, they were cognizant that they had to tread carefully. The Supreme Court was designed to be a mediating body between the political branches of the federal government itself, as well as the primary arbiter of disputes between the federal government and the various states, which retained elements of sovereignty under the Constitution.

As a result, every step the court took had the potential to alienate or enrage some segment of the body politic. Nevertheless, the justices found their way over time, often tentatively but with conviction. Indeed, they did their work so well that in that first decade they were able to lay the groundwork that made the modern Supreme Court what it is today. How the Court went about this task is the story of this book.

## *Creating the Court*

The convention that gathered in Philadelphia during the summer of 1787 was given a momentous task. It was charged with recommending revisions to the Articles of Confederation, a document that was itself largely a compact between thirteen independent sovereigns (Jensen, 109–10). The defects of the Articles had been apparent for some time. Although they enabled Congress to wage a war and conclude a peace treaty with Great Britain, the Articles were deeply flawed (Jensen, 243). Under the Articles, Congress was dependent on the good will of the states, for each state retained "its sovereignty, freedom and independence." This meant that Congress could not actually enact legislation that was binding on the states. Instead, it was forced to "recommend" that the states take action. Thus, Congress could negotiate treaties, but it could not force the states to comply with their terms. Congress could borrow money, but it could not levy the taxes to repay the loans. Perhaps most serious of all, given the economic dislocations of the 1780s, Congress had no power over the management of interstate or international trade. As one observer noted, "the revolutionaries who wrote the Articles were so concerned about preventing tyranny and not replacing King George with a monarch that they created a government that was incapable of action" (Urofsky & Finkelman, 84).

As a result, although the Philadelphia Convention was convened "for the sole and express purpose of revising the Articles of Confederation," it was not long before the delegates jettisoned any hope of correcting the defects in the Articles and set about creating an entirely new frame of government. Their aim was to establish a government that would be "adequate to the exigencies of the Union," which meant that certain powers had to be vested in the national government, including the power to wage war, to conduct foreign relations, and to regulate trade (3 Farrand 14).

Shortly after the Convention opened, Virginia's Edmund Randolph introduced a plan for a new national government. This so-called "Virginia Plan" called for the creation of a tripartite frame of government, consisting of a bicameral legislature, a "national executive," and a "national judiciary." (1 Farrand, 18–23) Much of the Convention's time was thereafter spent in debating the composition of the legislative and executive branches. In the end, the delegates agreed to establish a bicameral legislature, composed of a House of Representatives apportioned on the basis of population and a Senate made up of two representatives from each state. They also agreed that the executive power would be vested in a president who served as the nation's chief magistrate and commander in chief of the armed forces.

When it came to determining the outlines of the judiciary, the delegates started from the proposition that the national courts had to be given some degree of independence from the other branches of the national government, as well as from the states themselves. At the same time, however, the framers, ever wary of concentrating power in the hands of a few, did not want to give the judges too much independence. The task, therefore, was to find some means of providing a degree of freedom for the judiciary while still ensuring that the judges would be subject to popular control. The Convention solved the problem of independence by giving federal judges life tenure, at fixed salaries, during good behavior (2 Farrand 428–35). It then required that judges be nominated by the president subject to the "advice and consent" of the Senate, thereby making sure that the people, through their elected representatives, would have a voice in the composition of the judiciary.

Another problem confronting the delegates was the relationship between the courts created by the new constitution and those of the states. Many delegates worried that creating an extensive national judiciary would result in friction between the state and national courts. Indeed, some observers feared that creating an extensive federal court system would ultimately result in the elimination of the state courts altogether. As a result, the framers considered two different solutions to this problem. The first was a proposal to create a supreme federal tribunal for appeals only. This would have left the trial of most cases to the state courts, leaving an appeal to the national judiciary only in cases where some matter of national interest was at stake. A second proposal would have created an extensive system of national trial and appellate courts with power to hear and determine cases affecting the national government, albeit with a limited jurisdiction. The debate over these two proposals was ultimately to have far-reaching effects on the structure and jurisdiction of the federal judiciary.

## What Kind of Court?

The original Virginia Plan called for the creation of "one or more supreme tribunals" along with an extensive system of lower courts distributed throughout the nation and empowered to try all "questions which may involve the national peace and harmony." (1 Farrand 20, 21–22). This idea was quickly accepted, and the Convention tentatively voted to create "one supreme tribunal, and one or more inferior tribunals." A short time later, however, several members of the Convention moved to reconsider this proposal. They suggested that state courts should try all cases in the first instance. National interests could be protected by allowing an appeal to the supreme national tribunal. This would, it was argued, save the national government the expense of having to create a set of federal courts that would essentially duplicate the work of the state courts.

James Madison took the lead in opposing this suggestion. He argued that when it came to considering the interests of the states in opposition to those of the national government, state court judges would naturally favor the rights of the states. Madison also argued that the Supreme Court alone could not be an effective check on biased state court decision making. This was so because unless the Supreme Court was willing to rehear the case in its entirety, it would be forced to return the matter to the state courts for a new trial whenever it determined that state court judges had acted improperly. The very same state court judges would then be given control over the case a second time.

At issue in this debate was whether the state or national judiciary would best be able to fairly balance the interests of the respective governments. Opponents of an extensive national judiciary argued that creating a large number of federal courts would result in federal judges encroaching upon the rights and powers of state courts. Proponents of federal courts countered that without a system of national courts, federal interests could not be adequately protected. In the end, the Convention decided to compromise: rather than require the creation of lower federal courts, the Constitution would provide that "[t]he Judicial Power of the United States, shall be vested in one supreme Court and such inferior Courts as the Congress may from time to time ordain and establish." The effect of the compromise was to put the question off to another day. Upon ratification, there would be a Supreme Court, but whether other courts would be created was a decision to be left to the new Congress. The delegates obviously expected that a duly elected Congress would be better suited to determine whether lower courts were necessary.

## Federal Court Jurisdiction

Having decided to give Congress the power to create lower federal courts, the delegates to the Convention next considered the kinds of cases federal courts should be allowed to hear. The possibility that Congress might establish an extensive system of federal courts at some point in the future made it imperative that the courts' jurisdiction be carefully prescribed. A broad jurisdiction would give rise to the possibility that federal judges would infringe on the prerogatives of the state courts. Too narrow a jurisdiction, on the other hand, would severely hamper the federal courts' ability to protect national interests. It was clear, therefore, that some balance had to be struck.

The original Virginia Plan provided that federal courts would have jurisdiction over admiralty, revenue, and impeachment cases, as well as cases involving citizens of different states or foreigners, and "questions which may involve the national peace and harmony" (1 Farrand, 22). However, the possibility that the national courts would be given this extensive jurisdiction excited fears in many delegates. For example, Maryland's Luther Martin complained that a new set of federal courts would "create jealousies [and] oppositions in the State tribunals, with the jurisdiction of which they will interfere." Massachusetts' Nathaniel Gorham responded by arguing that federal courts with a broad jurisdiction were "essential to render[ing] the authority of the Natl. Legislature effectual." In the end, the proponents of a broad jurisdiction won out. In its final form, Article III, the Constitution's judiciary article, provided as follows:

> Section 1. The judicial Power of the United States, shall be vested in one supreme Court, and in such inferior Courts as the Congress may from time to time ordain and establish....
>
> Section 2. The judicial Power shall extend to all Cases, in Law and Equity, arising under this Constitution, the Laws of the United States, and Treaties made, or which shall be made, under their Authority;—to all Cases affecting Ambassadors, other public Ministers and Consuls;—to all Cases of admiralty and maritime Jurisdiction;—to Controversies in which the United States shall be a Party;—to Controversies between two or more States;—between a State and Citizens of another State;—between Citizens of different States;—between Citizens of the same State claiming Lands under Grants of different States, and between a State, or the Citizens thereof, and foreign States, Citizens or Subjects.
>
> In all Cases affecting Ambassadors, other public Ministers and Consuls, and those in which a State shall be a Party, the supreme Court shall have original Jurisdiction. In all other Cases before mentioned, the supreme Court shall have appellate Jurisdiction, both as to Law and Fact, with such Exceptions, and under such Regulations as the Congress shall make.

It is important to note that Article III represented a series of compromises. In the first place, it is clear that proponents of an extensive national judiciary eventually triumphed, at least insofar as they succeeded in leaving open the question of whether lower federal courts would be established. Moreover, while all the delegates seemed to agree that a Supreme Court ought to be established, and that this court had to have the final say on matters affecting national interests, the Court's jurisdiction was carefully circumscribed. In general, the Supreme Court was given power to hear cases involving foreign relations and controversies between the several states, but other aspects of its jurisdiction were limited to ensure that the Court would not become an overwhelming force. Thus, Article III gave the Supreme Court "original jurisdiction"—which is to say the power to conduct trials in the first instance—over cases involving diplomats from foreign countries and cases where two or more states were parties. However, the Court was only given "appellate jurisdiction," or the power to hear appeals, over other cases of national interest. Among these were cases of admiralty or maritime jurisdiction, "diversity" and "alienage" cases, and cases in which the U.S. government was a party. In limiting the Court's appellate power in this way, the Convention apparently believed that the new Congress would provide for some means by which the bulk of federal litigation would take place in courts located in the various states. Whether these would be federal or state courts was, of course, left to be determined another day.

Admiralty cases were thought to be of national import because they frequently involved the rights of foreigners as well as questions of international law. Often, such cases arose in the context of suits for "prize" in which a vessel captured by a "privateer" in wartime was declared to be forfeit to the captors who were then entitled to sell the ship and retain the proceeds. Admiralty cases also involved violations of the navigation and customs laws. Ships involved in smuggling or which violated the trade laws were sued *in rem* in the admiralty courts, where they were "condemned" and sold for the payment of fines due the government. Entrusting these sorts of cases to federal courts prevented the possibility that state court judges or juries would render judgments in favor of local plaintiffs to the detriment of the claims of foreign citizens.

Concerns of bias were also at issue in the grant of "diversity" and "alienage" jurisdiction. Diversity jurisdiction is the power to try cases involving citizens of different states. Alienage jurisdiction allows courts to hear cases involving citizens of foreign countries. Providing a federal forum for these cases was one means of ensuring that these out-of-state plaintiffs would be able to receive a fair trial. This was particularly important to the vast numbers of British subjects who were owed money by American citizens for debts due before the Revolution. Many British merchants had long complained about their inability to recover judgment on debts due them because of the bias of state court juries. Members of the Philadelphia Convention recognized the difficulties for foreign relations caused by these complaints and thus sought to provide some means by which foreigners and out-of-state plaintiffs might be able to receive redress of their claims. Finally, cases in which the U.S. government itself was a party were also within the Supreme Court's appellate jurisdiction. Quite naturally, this jurisdiction ensured that the federal government would always have a right of appeal to the national tribunal whenever it was a party to an action in any court. Such a jurisdiction was obviously thought necessary to ensure that the interests of the national government were protected in the last resort.

It is important to note that the Supreme Court was not necessarily entitled to all the jurisdiction provided for in the judiciary article. On the contrary, Article III merely provided that the Supreme Court would have original jurisdiction in only two definite classes of cases: those involving foreign diplomats and those in which a state was a party. In all other cases, Article III provided that the Supreme Court would have appellate jurisdiction subject to "*such Exceptions, and under such Regulations as the Congress shall make.*" Presumably, this clause meant that Congress could distribute the judicial power in almost any way it saw fit. Congress might, for example, allow state or lower federal courts to try admiralty, diversity and alienage cases, leaving appeals to go to the Supreme Court. Conversely, Congress might allow such cases to be tried in state courts and allow appeals to a federal court other than the Supreme Court. Congress might even create two different kinds of federal courts, one set with original jurisdiction over Article III cases, and another with appellate jurisdiction. Whatever the configuration, however, it was clear that the Constitution did not require that the Supreme Court have all the appellate jurisdiction provided for in Article III (Collins, 1515–23).

## The Ratification Debates

The Constitution's judiciary article was the subject of vigorous debate throughout the ratification process. Opponents of the Constitution, who were soon to be labeled "antifederalists," quickly seized on Article III's provisions as evidence that the delegates to the Philadelphia Convention were engaged in a plot to subvert popular government.

Among the charges leveled against the judiciary article was the allegation that the framers had abolished the right to trial by jury. The jury, after all, had a long and storied history in Anglo-American jurisprudence. Beginning in the 17th century, the jury was credited with being a bulwark against tyranny. Requiring juries in criminal cases meant that government officials could not use the criminal justice system to oppress their opponents because a jury would always be ready to acquit those falsely accused. Likewise, in civil cases, juries were useful in that they were available to assess damages against government officers who abused their power or violated the rights of citizens. Yet, while Article III required the use of juries in criminal cases, it did not contain any provision for jury trials in civil cases. Antifederalists noted this omission and argued that a valuable protection for rights of the citizenry had thereby been eliminated (Main, 159–160). Antifederalists also pointed to that portion of Article III that gave the Supreme Court appellate jurisdiction over law and fact. They charged that allowing the Supreme Court to have jurisdiction over fact would be to vest the Court with the power to overturn the findings of juries even in those few cases in which juries were used ("Brutus," November 1, 1787).

Critics also claimed that the broad grant of jurisdiction to the federal courts would leave the state courts with very little to do. Of particular concern in this regard was the Constitution's grant of diversity and alienage jurisdiction. Antifederalists argued that most diversity or alienage cases involved routine questions of state law, which should be tried in state courts. Moreover, to sue a defendant usually required that the suit be brought in the county in which the defendant resided. Since it was not expected that federal courts would be created in every county in every state, out-of-state or foreign plaintiffs would be able to drag defendants many miles to a court located far from their homes. In such a case, many small farmers or poor defendants would be unable to defend themselves because they would be unable to bear the costs of litigation in a distant place ("Brutus," February 7, 14, 1788).

Federalists attempted to rebut these arguments. With respect to jury trials, they argued that the Constitution did not prohibit juries from being used in civil cases. Rather, it merely left Congress free to determine the circumstances under which juries should be used in any particular case. This was necessary, federalists said, because the rules for empaneling juries in the various states differed so much that it was impossible for the members of the Philadelphia Convention to devise a general rule. As a result, the Convention intended to leave to Congress the question of when juries would be used in federal trials. As for the concerns about the Supreme Court's appellate jurisdiction over law and fact, federalists argued that the power to review facts did not necessarily mean that the Supreme Court would simply ignore the facts found by juries. Instead, the Supreme Court might simply empanel a new jury to rehear the case in its entirety. In any event, said the federalists, the vast majority of both civil and criminal cases would still be tried in state courts, where the right to jury trial would be preserved as before.

When it came to dealing with the objections about the broad jurisdiction given the federal judiciary, federalists argued that diversity and alienage jurisdiction were necessary to safeguard national interests. Experience during the confederation period showed that state courts could not be trusted to protect the rights of foreigners. As for jurisdiction over cases between two or more states, Alexander Hamilton contended that state courts could not be expected to be impartial, and reminded his listeners that "[n]o man ought certainly to be a judge in his own cause" (The Federalist No. 80). Putting these cases in the Supreme Court was the only way to prevent private wars from breaking out between the states themselves.

In spite of these and other antifederalist objections, the Constitution was eventually ratified by eleven states by the summer of 1788. The Confederation was thus dissolved and a new union formed.

# *The First Judiciary Act*

The Constitution itself provided only the barest outlines of a judicial system. As noted earlier, Article III vested the "judicial power" in a Supreme Court and such other courts as Congress might itself create. Judges were to hold office during "good behavior," and their salaries could not be diminished while in office. In addition, the courts were given a relatively broad jurisdiction subject to Congress's power to make certain exceptions.

Beyond these limited requirements, however, the Constitution gave Congress very little guidance on precisely how the judiciary ought to be structured. This was mainly because the delegates to the Philadelphia Convention could not agree among themselves on what the national judiciary should look like. For example, while Article III provided for the creation of a Supreme Court, it did not specify the number of judges that would make up the court, how they would be selected, or what their precise duties should be. Similarly, while the Constitution allowed Congress to create lower federal courts, the dispute over the extent of federal jurisdiction in the Convention prevented any consensus on the size, number, or nature of other federal courts. This was in spite of the fact that the Constitutional Convention spent a great deal of time defining the limits of legislative and executive power in great detail. When it came to the federal courts, however, the Convention decided to leave to Congress the problem of solving many of the disputes that surrounded the creation of the federal courts. As a result, Congress's first session was devoted, in part, to establishing a functioning judiciary.

The work of creating the courts commenced in earnest shortly after the first Congress convened in New York on March 4, 1789. The task of bringing in a judiciary bill was left to the Senate, which formed a committee for the purpose. Another Senate committee was created to draft a crimes code, while the House of Representatives set about the work of drafting a revenue bill.

The Senate judiciary committee, like the Senate itself, worked in secret, with the result that very little of the committee's deliberations were made public. What little is known is not surprising, however. To a large degree, the debate in the Constitutional Convention over the wisdom of creating an extensive federal judiciary was recreated in the Senate. It appears that most, if not all, of the members of the judiciary committee favored creating some lower federal courts, but there was a great deal of disagreement on the precise extent of the jurisdiction these courts would be given. The committee had to find a consensus between those who favored a very limited jurisdiction for federal courts and those seeking the establishment of a strong national judiciary. Connecticut's Oliver Ellsworth led the supporters of a strong judiciary and sought to vest the lower federal courts with power over diversity, alienage, and federal question cases. Virginia's Richard Henry Lee, who was equally determined to confine federal judicial power within very narrow limits, led the opposition. Like many in the Philadelphia Convention, Lee preferred to use state courts as the primary trial courts for resolving Article III disputes, leaving the Supreme Court to hear appeals only.

The committee eventually reported a bill to the full Senate on June 12, 1789. This bill provided for a three-tiered judicial system. At the bottom of the pyramid were the district courts. These were to be established in every state and presided over by a single district judge. They were to have jurisdiction over admiralty and revenue cases, in addition to minor criminal offenses. The judiciary bill also provided for a circuit court in each state, designed to function as the federal judiciary's primary trial court. The circuit courts were to have jurisdiction over diversity and alienage cases, as well as major criminal offenses. In addition, the circuit courts would hear criminal and civil appeals from the district courts.

At the apex of the system was the Supreme Court. It was to be composed of six justices, who would meet twice each year, in February and August. As provided in Article III, the Supreme Court would have original jurisdiction over cases involving ambassadors and other "public ministers," as well as suits in which states were a party. The judiciary committee took advantage of Congress's power to make "exceptions" to the Supreme Court's appellate jurisdiction, however. Its bill provided that the Supreme Court would have jurisdiction over appeals in civil cases only. The Court would have no jurisdiction over appeals in criminal cases. Nonetheless, the provisions of the judiciary bill were hotly debated in the full Senate. Among those aspects of the bill that generated most debate were the clauses granting the Supreme Court jurisdiction to hear appeals in admiralty cases, the provision allowing federal courts to determine cases arising in equity, and the availability of jury trials (Maclay's Journal 91–110).

That federal courts should have jurisdiction over admiralty cases was probably the least controversial provision in the entire judiciary bill. This is because almost every senator recognized the fact that admiralty cases involved important issues of international law and trade. Moreover, during the Revolutionary War, the Continental Congress was frequently involved in controversies with foreign governments over the decisions of state admiralty courts, which condemned property belonging to neutral countries and even allies contrary to the provisions of maritime law. As a result, vesting some federal court with admiralty jurisdiction seemed the most effective means of ensuring that the rights of foreigners were respected. In addition, admiralty courts had long been the primary forums for adjudicating seizures under the revenue and customs laws. Admiralty jurisdiction was, therefore, important to protecting the new nation's revenue, since most of the new nation's taxes were expected to come from customs and excise fees.

Yet, while there was general agreement on the need to vest federal courts with admiralty jurisdiction, there was continuing concern about the right to jury trial. After all, admiralty courts had long tried cases without juries, and given the concerns about jury trials already raised during the course of the ratification debates, there was some concern that federal courts sitting in admiralty would contrive to deprive the citizenry of the right to a jury trial. The drafters of the judiciary bill attempted to address this concern through what has since become known as the "savings clause." This clause gave federal courts jurisdiction over traditional admiralty cases involving important points of international law or commerce, such as cases of prize or piracy, while leaving other routine maritime disputes to be heard in state courts if the common law was able to give a remedy.

The Supreme Court's equity jurisdiction was also a subject of some debate. Equity courts were traditionally associated with the royal prerogative, an association that made them suspect in the minds of many erstwhile revolutionaries. Moreover, equity court procedure was controversial. Like admiralty courts, equity courts did not use jury trials. In addition, equity courts often took testimony in writing without witnesses actually being examined in open court. Also, suits in equity were notorious for being very expensive and time consuming, and some had been known to last for many years (Maclay's Journal 108–109).

During the course of the debates over the judiciary bill, therefore, several attempts were made to restrict the federal courts' equity jurisdiction. In the end, the best that opponents could muster was a provision prohibiting federal courts from sitting in equity in any case where "a plain, adequate and complete remedy may be had at law." On its face, this provision was designed to prevent federal judges from using their equity powers to avoid trying cases to juries. The full Senate also included a provision requiring all testimony in federal courts to be given orally in open court unless the witness was outside the jurisdiction of the court.

As was the case during the ratification debates, some Senators complained that the judiciary bill did not contain adequate protections for the right to a jury trial in other cases as well. The judiciary committee attempted to address some of these concerns by providing for juries in both civil and criminal cases, something the Constitution itself had not done explicitly. The primary exceptions to this rule were admiralty and equity cases, which would continue to be tried without juries as was the case in England. A few senators urged the inclusion of a provision requiring juries in all federal trials, but this motion was successfully defeated by the full Senate.

Far more troubling for some, however, was a provision giving the Supreme Court power to "redetermine" facts on appeal. The original judiciary bill required circuit courts "to cause the evidence exhibited" at the trial of admiralty and equity cases to be reduced to writing. Some senators suspected that the purpose of this provision was to allow the Supreme Court to review the entire record of the lower court and redetermine the facts if it believed the trial court had been in error. After a great deal of debate, however, the provision was altered to require merely that the facts on which the decree was based to be put in writing, thus allowing the Supreme Court to see the factual basis for the ruling below. In this way, the trial court's traditional right to determine facts would be preserved, while the Supreme Court would still have the ability to review the decision for errors in law.

The fate of the judiciary bill was intimately tied to a series of amendments to the Constitution put forward in the House of Representatives by James Madison on June 8, 1791. Fears about the extensive powers given the federal courts in Article III led to over 200 different amendments being proposed by the various state ratifying conventions (Main, 158–59). Among these were proposals that would have required jury trials in civil cases as well as limitations on the federal courts' diversity and alienage jurisdiction. In distilling these various proposals for consideration by Congress, Madison attempted to allay the concerns of those who feared the powers of an extensive federal judiciary while refraining from making any dramatic alterations in the Constitution until such time as it had been subjected to a fair trial. As a result, Madison's proposed amendments included several changes to Article III, and were designed to guarantee the right to a jury trial in civil cases, as well as limiting the power of federal courts to review facts found by a jury. Madison also proposed something akin to a bill of rights guaranteeing, among other things, freedom of religion, of the press and the right to keep and bear arms.

Madison's proposed amendments moved through Congress at almost precisely the same time as the judiciary bill. To some extent, therefore, the limitations on the judiciary contained in the judiciary bill went a long way toward lessening concerns about the powers of an extensive national court system. In the end, therefore, most attempts to alter Article III were defeated, and only amendments guaranteeing a right to a jury in civil cases, as well as a jury of the vicinage in criminal cases, made it through the amendment process. The House eventually passed the judiciary bill on September 17, 1789, and the Judiciary Act was signed into law by President Washington on September 24, 1789. The new courts were now ready for business.

## Opening for Business

The final version of the Judiciary Act created thirteen federal judicial districts. Each of the eleven states then in the Union comprised a district. Separate districts were also created for Maine, which was then a part of Massachusetts, and Kentucky, then a part of Virginia. A district court was established in each district to be presided over by a district judge.

The act also divided the country into three circuits. New Hampshire, Massachusetts, Connecticut and New York comprised the Eastern Circuit. New Jersey, Pennsylvania, Delaware, Maryland, and Virginia made up the Middle Circuit. South Carolina and Georgia formed the Southern Circuit. (Because the volume of business in these districts was expected to be low, Maine and Kentucky were not included as part of any circuit. Instead, the district court judge in those states was empowered to hear cases that might otherwise have been within the jurisdiction of the circuit court.) A circuit court was to be held in each district twice every year. This circuit court was to be convened by the district judge of the state in which the circuit court was held along with two members of the Supreme Court. Using Supreme Court justices in this fashion was largely a device to save money. Rather than creating a separate set of federal judges to preside over the circuit courts, Congress decided to use Supreme Court justices to do the work. After all, it was not expected that the Supreme Court would have much to do for some time after the federal judiciary was established, and many in Congress had reservations about creating large numbers of federal judges who would have tenure at fixed salaries for life.

The Judiciary Act required the Supreme Court to meet twice each year, in February and August, in the seat of government. The first session of the Court was held in New York in February 1790. Of the six members of the Court, only four, Chief Justice Jay and Justices Wilson, Cushing, and Blair were present. Justices Rutledge and Harrison did not attend. Harrison had resigned his commission a few weeks earlier because of failing health. No one knows why Rutledge failed to show. As might be expected, there were no cases for the Court to hear that term. This is because the Supreme Court was primarily designed to be a court of last resort, and would be, for the most part, concerned with hearing appeals from the district and circuit courts. At this point, however, the lower federal courts had only been in business a very short time. Few cases had, therefore, been tried or taken up on appeal by the circuit courts. As a result, the justices spent the bulk of their time that first term organizing the Court and admitting lawyers to the bar.

The August 1790 term was also held in New York. The Court's newest justice, North Carolina's James Iredell, was appointed to replace Harrison and arrived in town. The other five justices were in New York as well, but in the end, only five actually appeared for the opening of the term. Justice Rutledge remained at his lodgings because he was afflicted with gout. In the end, however, this second term, like its predecessor, passed without the justices being required to take up any cases.

It was not until February 1791, when the federal government had moved to Philadelphia, that the first case, *Van Staphorst v. Maryland*, was placed on the docket. This case was eventually settled without the Court having to take any action on it. The Supreme Court's first oral argument was not to take place until August 1791, in *West v. Barnes*. The specific question before the Court that term was whether the particular writ of error bringing the case before the Court was valid. The Court eventually decided it was not and dismissed the appeal. A total of only thirteen cases were filed in the Supreme Court between 1791 and 1794. However, business gradually picked up, so that by the middle of the 1790s, the Supreme Court sat for approximately one full month in each term hearing cases and issuing opinions.

In addition to sitting twice each year in the seat of government, the members of the Supreme Court were also required to "ride circuit." As noted earlier, in drafting the first Judiciary Act, Congress devised a system by which members of the Supreme Court would actually sit as trial judges in the circuit courts to be held in each state. Every spring and fall, therefore, the justices set out on horseback or by coach to attend the sessions of the various circuit courts. Since two sessions of the circuit courts were to be held in each state, the rigors of circuit riding quickly became a source of great hardship and discontent. No sooner had the justices finished their work in Philadelphia than they were required to move with some dispatch to be on time for the opening of the various circuit courts.

During the Supreme Court's first session, the justices divided the circuits among themselves. The primary concern in doing so seemed to be residence, as the allocation usually allowed each justice to preside over the circuit closest to his home state. Thus, Chief Justice Jay (New York) and Justice Cushing (Massachusetts) were assigned the eastern circuit. Justices Wilson (Pennsylvania) and Blair (Virginia) took the middle circuit. Justice Rutledge (South Carolina) and, later, Justice Iredell (North Carolina) were assigned to ride the southern circuit.

Circuit riding could be arduous. Once they set out on the road, the justices had to hurry in order to make the opening of each circuit court on time. For example, attending the spring term of the eastern circuit meant that the justices would have to leave Philadelphia and be in New York by April 4. Thereafter, they headed north to be in New Haven on April 22, Boston on May 3, Portsmouth, New Hampshire, on May 20, and then back south to be in Newport, Rhode Island, by June 4. They then had to head north again to attend the Vermont circuit court on June 17. After a few weeks' rest, the justices were required to return to Philadelphia for the Supreme Court's August term. Once that was over, they started out on circuit all over again.

Delays caused by weather, illness, and missed transport often meant that many circuit courts were either delayed or cancelled altogether because the justices could not make it on time. Moreover, traveling hundreds of miles over bad roads in all kinds of weather put a great strain on the justices' emotional and physical health. As a result, over the years, the justices repeatedly appealed to Congress to relieve them of circuit duty, presenting several petitions to Congress urging changes in the system. But, while Congress made minor alterations in the times and places for holding the various courts, it refused to eliminate this aspect of the justices' duties until well into the 19th century.

## The Federalist Era

The justices of the first Supreme Court often found themselves at the center of the political storms that wracked the early republic. Disputes over states' rights, the powers of the national government, and the role of the government in the economy found their way into the lower courts and eventually to the Supreme Court. Added to the domestic difficulties was the fact that, as a new nation, the United States was forced to walk a very fine line in the conduct of foreign affairs, constantly trying to avoid being dragged into the midst of the almost century-long conflict between the great European powers. In fulfilling their responsibilities, therefore, the members of the Supreme Court were often forced to consider the political as well as legal aspects of the controversies that came before them.

## Domestic Tensions and the Rise of Political Parties

Among the agencies of the federal government created in that first year were the Treasury and State Departments. As is the case today, the State Department was primarily responsible for the conduct of foreign relations, while the Treasury was charged with managing the national revenue, which included administering the customs and excise laws. As heads of these departments, President Washington appointed Alexander Hamilton at Treasury and Thomas Jefferson at State. Jefferson was, of course, well known at this point in his career. Widely credited with being the principal drafter of the Declaration of Independence, Jefferson played an important role in the conduct of American foreign policy throughout the Revolution, serving as Minister to France. Alexander Hamilton had served as Washington's aide-de-camp during the war, and had a successful law practice in New York. That he was one of the primary authors, with James Madison and John Jay, of *The Federalist* was known to very few, although Washington himself was surely aware of the fact.

From the outset, Hamilton took upon himself to establish the tone and character of the new government. Hamilton had long been an advocate of a strong central government and repeatedly expressed the view that the union had more to fear from encroachments by the states than from the activities of the national government. Once in office he had two concerns: The first was the need to raise revenue sufficient to carry on the normal activities of the government. The second was the need to find some way to retire the enormous debt incurred by both the states and Congress during the Revolution. Paying off the national debt was widely recognized as both a moral obligation as well as good economic policy. Of the estimated $50 million outstanding in continental securities, approximately $11 million was owed to foreign governments and lenders, while the remaining $40 million was owed to citizens of the several states (Chernow, 295–301).

Although few thought the government ought to default on the debt, there was a great deal of disagreement on precisely how the debt should be repaid. Almost everyone understood that the nation's ability to borrow in the future would be hampered if the United States did not repay the foreign portion of the debt. That part of the debt owed to American citizens was more problematic, however. In the first place, by 1790, very few of the certificates evidencing the debt were in the hands of the original holders. These certificates had been issued to soldiers in lieu of pay or to tradesmen or merchants in exchange for supplies given to the army. Over time, these original holders had despaired of receiving any payment from the increasingly weak and ineffective Continental Congress and so were persuaded to sell their certificates to speculators for pennies on the dollar (Chernow, 297–98). As a result, many in Congress thought that some sort of discrimination would be in order. They argued that original holders, who had borne the brunt of the fighting and the burden of supporting the government during the heat of battle, should be entitled to be paid in full with interest. On the other hand, speculators, who purchased the certificates of destitute soldiers or tradesmen, should not be rewarded for their scheming, and so should receive some discounted payment (Chernow, 297–98).

In October 1789, Congress directed Secretary Hamilton to come up with a plan for dealing with the debt. Hamilton responded with a *Report on the Public Credit*, which he submitted to Congress in January 1790. Hamilton's *Report* was immediately controversial. In it, he proposed that the federal government repay the continental debt at par without discrimination between original holders and speculators. "Funding" the debt in this way was essential, Hamilton said, to ensure that future creditors would be willing to lend to the national government. Discriminating between holders of continental securities on equitable grounds would diminish confidence in government securities.

In addition to the funding scheme, Hamilton also proposed that the national government assume the debts of the states. In essence, Hamilton sought to use the "assumption plan" as a means of weakening the public's attachment to the state governments. By taking on the state debts, Hamilton believed that he would be able to strengthen the attachment between the commercial classes and the national government. He expected that converting holders of state certificates into owners of federal securities would create a whole new segment of society interested in ensuring the success of the new Constitution. In addition, by taking upon itself the obligation to repay the entire public debt, the national government would relieve the states of having to levy extensive taxes. In Hamilton's view, if the state governments were deprived of the need to raise revenue, they would eventually whither away (Chernow, 298–99).

Hamilton's report provoked a firestorm. Advocates of discrimination between original holders and speculators attacked the funding plan on the grounds that paying all debts at face value violated basic principles of equity (Chernow, 303–05). The assumption plan was even more controversial because it seemed to discriminate between the states themselves. Many states had made great strides reducing the size of their outstanding debts, while others had done very little. In calling for the federal government to take over all outstanding state debts, Hamilton seemed to be penalizing those states that had been diligent in paying their debts. For example, between 1783 and 1790, Virginia had succeeded in paying down almost half its outstanding debt, while other states, such as New York, had not done as much. Led by Thomas Jefferson and James Madison, Virginians vehemently objected to assumption (Chernow, 321–24).

Hamilton's plan practically split the Congress in two. States with large debts tended to support assumption, while those with small debts were opposed. After months of wrangling and horse trading, the deadlock was broken. However, the rancor generated during the debate over Hamilton's plan revealed a growing rift between the northern and southern states. Many southerners believed that the northern speculators were the largest beneficiaries of Hamilton's plan. Virginians, in particular, were convinced that they paid more than their fair share of federal taxes, while receiving very little in return. As a result, during the course of the debates, the Virginia legislature sent a protest to Congress declaring that assumption of state debts was "repugnant to the Constitution" and the funding system "dangerous to the rights and subversive of the interests of the people."

Later that same year, Hamilton created more controversy with the submission of a report recommending the creation the Bank of the United States. Hamilton intended the bank be the primary depository of federal funds and the central regulator of state-chartered banks. He also proposed that the bank be authorized to issue bank notes backed up by the credit of the United States. These notes would circulate throughout the economy as a means of currency (Chernow, 347–48).

The bank proposal excited the ire of the agrarian faction in Congress. Some of this hostility sprang from the traditional rural suspicion of banks as tools of moneyed interests (Chernow, 349–50). Many others, however, opposed the idea because they believed the Constitution did not authorize Congress to charter a bank. In making this argument, James Madison, who became a leader of the opposition to Hamilton's policies, relied on the theory of "enumerated powers," and asserted that the federal government could only do those things that were specifically granted to it in the Constitution. Hamilton responded to this charge by relying on the "necessary and proper" clause contained in Article I of the Constitution. The clause permitted Congress to "make all Laws necessary and proper" for carrying into execution the authority granted to it elsewhere in the Constitution. A bank was necessary, Hamilton said, to collect taxes, regulate trade, and provide for the common defense. In the end, Hamilton won this debate and the bank was established. However, the arguments over the extent of federal power under the necessary and proper clause were to reverberate throughout the course of American history (Chernow, 351–55).

The battle over Hamilton's economic plan and the Bank of the United States accelerated the creation of two different factions, one led by the treasury secretary and the other by Secretary of State Jefferson. The differences between Hamilton and Jefferson were obvious from the outset of the administration. Jefferson was very much the agrarian, cautious about the merits of industrialization, and always skeptical about the extent of the federal government's power. Hamilton, on the other hand, believed that the future of the United States lay in the development of commerce and industry and was interested in ensuring that the national government did all it could to encourage the growth of trade and manufactures. Adding to their disagreements on economic matters was a profound divergence of opinion on the nature of popular government. Ever the nationalist, Hamilton believed that only national-minded men could be trusted to govern properly. More importantly, he was fearful of an "excess of democracy," and thus strongly believed that only men of means and standing in the community could be trusted with the reigns of government. For his part, Jefferson believed that Hamilton and his followers were committed to the overthrow of the republic and the imposition of a monarchy. There was no difference in his mind between "stock-jobbers and king makers," and he was sure that Hamilton was at the head of a "monarchical conspiracy." Unlike Hamilton, Jefferson did not fear "the good sense of the people." On the contrary, Jefferson often argued that there was nothing wrong with the United States that could not be cured with good newspapers and sound schoolmasters.

By 1792, the differences between Hamilton and Jefferson widened into the creation of two distinct political parties representing the United States's two dominant economic interests. Jefferson's followers, now called "Republicans," generally represented planter-farmer interests in the south and west. Hamilton's "Federalists," on the other hand, represented commercial and shipping interests dominant in the northern states (Elkins & McKitrick, 263–70).

In the early part of the 1790s, the Federalist party was in the ascendent, mainly as a result of its control of federal offices. And, although President Washington attempted to steer clear of party involvement, he generally came down on the side of Hamilton's Federalist policies in shaping his administrative program. As for Congress, the House was almost evenly divided between Hamilton's and Jefferson's supporters, although the Senate remained in Federalist hands through most of the decade. Most of the judges appointed to the federal bench in the period were strong Federalists as well.

As time progressed, however, Republican strength increased. Opposition to Federalism's centralizing tendencies and the departure of the revered George Washington from the political stage combined to bring new converts to the Republican cause. Throughout the remainder of the period, therefore, the two parties fought a pitched battle in both the halls of government and in the press. Newspapers in every state soon took sides in a vicious press war. Federalist editors such as William Cobbett, publisher of *Porcupine's Gazette,* and Benjamin Bache, the staunchly Republican editor of *The Aurora,* gave voice to the parties' respective platforms. Almost every aspect of economic and political affairs became a matter of party controversy, so much so that the battle between Hamilton and Jefferson soon began to affect the conduct of the United States's foreign policy.

## Foreign Relations

By the time the Supreme Court held its first session in February 1790, France and Great Britain had been at war on and off for almost a century. As a new nation with no navy and an army smaller than that of any of its potential foes, the United States was forced to tread very carefully so as not to be sucked into the continuing conflict in Europe. Consequently, both Presidents Washington and Adams spent a large part of their time attempting to steer American foreign policy clear of "entangling alliances" that might result in the nation becoming an unwilling participant in war.

In the early years of the 1790s, the United States's main difficulties were with Great Britain. This was in spite of the fact that the two nations had very close trade relationships with each other. In 1789, almost 75 percent of the United States's exports went to ports in the United Kingdom , while 90 percent of its imported goods came from England (Elkins & McKitrick, 68–74). This close trade relationship provided the opportunity for a great deal of friction between the two countries. Foremost among these was the ongoing conflict over the provisions of the Definitive Treaty of Peace between England and the United States, which brought an end to the Revolution in 1783.

Under Article 4 of the treaty, the United States was required to ensure that British creditors who were owed money on debts due prior to the Revolution "should meet with no lawful Impediment to the Recovery of the full Value in Sterling Money." Throughout the confederation period, Congress was unable to induce the states to open their courts to the recovery of British debts. Even in those states in which British creditors were successful in bringing actions, state court juries routinely refused to give judgment or limited the creditor's recovery. British government officials repeatedly complained about the United States's failure to honor its obligations under the peace treaty, and they used this failure as the justification for England's refusal to evacuate forts on the United States's northern and western frontier. Holding on to the forts allowed Britain to retain control of the lucrative fur trade. Americans on the frontier also complained that the forts gave English officers a base from which to incite the Indians to attack American settlements (DeConde, Entangling Alliance, 66–100).

Relations with the French were little better. The same year, which saw the inauguration of the new American regime, also witnessed the start of the French Revolution. Within a few months after fall of the Bastille in 1789, American conservatives began to worry about the course of events in France. As time passed, the excesses of that revolution horrified Federalist leaders, particularly as reports of mass executions, riots, and attacks on the aristocracy made their way to the American continent. By August 1790, many Federalists pointed to the chaos in France as proof of the dangers that resulted from a surfeit of democracy. Indeed, President Washington himself asserted that the unrest in Europe was proof of the problems that might result from "too great eagerness in swallowing something so delightful as liberty."

Nonetheless, while the Republicans were unsettled by the execution of the French king and the Reign of Terror, Jefferson believed that the excesses to which the revolution gave rise would end in the triumph of order and liberty (Miller, 127). Moreover, while he expressed some regret at the level of bloodshed, Jefferson remained convinced that the revolution must take its course. In a letter some years later, he argued that "[t]he liberty of the whole earth was depending on the issue of the contest, and ... rather than it should have failed, I would have seen half the earth devastated." Jefferson was convinced that the vast majority of Americans supported the revolution in France, asserting that ninety-nine percent of the people were on the side of the French revolutionaries. He attributed this attachment to the fact that many Americans believed that French help during the United States's struggle against Great Britain was largely responsible for ensuring American independence.

In time, therefore, Americans began to divide into two camps. On one side were those who feared that French sympathizers in the United States would seek to subvert the American system of government and engineer a reprise of the worst excesses of the Reign of Terror in the new world. On the other side, however, were those who believed that Federalist opposition to France was further evidence of a secret plan to establish an aristocratic, if not monarchical, government in the United States. When in 1793, France proclaimed itself a republic and declared war on Great Britain, the American political establishment was rent asunder.

Domestic tensions were further exacerbated with the arrival of Citizen Edmund Genet, the new French minister to the United States. Almost immediately upon landing, Genet used his position to fan the flames of American hostility toward England and bring the United States into the war on the French side. Genet began by demanding that the American government honor its commitments under the Treaty of Alliance between France and the United States. This treaty required the United States to help protect French possessions in the West Indies, as well as to open its ports to French privateers. As might be expected, however, President Washington and his cabinet feared that complying with the terms of the treaty would have the effect of drawing the United States into war with Great Britain, as that country would surely regard any aid to the French as a violation of American neutrality. Much to Citizen Genet's consternation, therefore, Washington issued a proclamation in April 1793, declaring the United States's intention to pursue "a conduct friendly and impartial towards the belligerent powers." The proclamation also prohibited American citizens from engaging in any act that would threaten American neutrality (DeConde, Entangling Alliances, 204–34).

Washington's neutrality proclamation was controversial for several reasons. For those who believed that Americans owed France a debt of honor for the latter's help during the War of Independence, the proclamation represented a betrayal of a trusted friend and ally. For others, however, the proclamation represented an even more sinister development. Critics contended that in undertaking to position the country between two warring powers, Washington had gone beyond his authority as president (Deconde, Entangling Alliances, 188–90). Writing under the pseudonym, *Helvidius*, James Madison argued that the power to conduct foreign relations was vested in Congress alone, and the president was limited to merely executing policies set by the legislative branch. Although Madison favored a policy of neutrality, he believed that such a proclamation could come from Congress alone.

The issuance of the neutrality proclamation did little to dampen the ardor of Genet or his American supporters, however. In the ensuing months, the French envoy worked to evade the restrictions on American assistance to the French cause, by seeking funds to arm expeditions against British territory and outfitting privateers to undertake attacks on British shipping. By the summer of 1793, the federal courts were the scene of a number of trials of American citizens accused of violating the neutrality proclamation. Genet added to the controversy by creating a series of consular courts on American soil. These courts were presided over by French officials who were authorized to determine whether British ships taken on the high seas could lawfully be considered prize. When several British warships were captured by French privateers and brought into American ports, the British government vehemently complained that allowing French courts to act in American territory was a violation of the United States's professed policy of neutrality. These and other matters relating to the war in Europe soon placed the Supreme Court at the center of the storm.

While Genet's ability to manipulate lingering American hostility toward Great Britain certainly caused problems for Washington's administration, the English government persisted in creating a number of other problems on its own. The most serious of these involved British seizures of American shipping. In the fall of 1793, England dispatched a fleet of warships to conquer the French West Indies. In an effort to support this venture and disrupt French supply lines, an Order in Council authorized British commanders to seize all neutral vessels engaged in transporting supplies to those islands or carrying their produce. To ensure that the tally of seized ships would be as large as possible, the order was kept secret until December 1793, which meant that many vessels that had put to sea prior to that time were caught unawares. As a result, over 250 American vessels were taken by British warships and condemned in British vice-admiralty courts (Miller, 141).

The seizure of so many American ships in so underhanded a fashion inflamed American public opinion. Adding to the controversy was the fact that the British government refused to permit American ships to enter ports in the British West Indies, thus cutting off a trade that had been so profitable before the Revolution. Britain also refused to enter into discussions for a commercial treaty with the United States, which meant that American exports to England and her empire were subjected to extremely high tariffs. British intransigence on this point only encouraged Republican members of Congress to argue for retaliatory measures, the imposition of which would likely have resulted in the outbreak of war between the two countries (Bemis, 100–101).

As a result, by the time the Order in Council was repealed in January 1794, war with Great Britain seemed a foregone conclusion. British restrictions on American trade, her refusal to evacuate the forts on the frontier, and her continuing attempts to incite the Indians to attack American settlements raised the ire of Americans to fever pitch. Among the United States's political leaders, only Alexander Hamilton seemed to hold out hope for some kind of reconciliation (Bemis, Diplomatic History, 101). With his backing, President Washington eventually agreed to send a minister plenipotentiary to Great Britain to negotiate a resolution of all the United States's outstanding grievances. Among the items to be taken up were compensation for vessels seized in the West Indies, the evacuation of the forts on the frontier, compensation for slaves carried away during the Revolution, and the negotiation of a commercial treaty.

Although most people assumed that Hamilton would be given the post, President Washington believed that the treasury secretary was too controversial a figure for the job. Instead, Washington appointed Chief Justice John Jay. While Jay's appointment was somewhat problematic, in that it implicated concerns about dual office holding, the fact remained that the chief justice had a long and distinguished career as a diplomat. During the Revolution, Jay served as ambassador to Spain and was one of the commissioners appointed to negotiate the treaty of peace between England and the United States. Upon his return to the United States in 1783, Jay was appointed Secretary of Foreign Affairs by the confederation congress, a post he held until Thomas Jefferson became Secretary of State in the new federal government. Given this background, Jay seemed an obvious choice.

On arriving in England, Jay found the British government generally receptive to the American overture. Jay himself characterized the dispute between Britain and the United States as a family quarrel, which should have been made up long ago, while at the same time, the English seemed to realize that war was in neither their economic nor political interest. Economic considerations loomed large, for as one British minister noted, the Americans "are so much in debt to this country that we scarcely dare to quarrel with them." Meanwhile, Lord Grenville, Britain's Foreign Secretary, seemed desirous of ensuring the current American administration be supported. After all, he noted, the Federalist party seemed to be the only real barrier to the "Torrent of Jacobin Principles" in the United States.

With this as a basis on which to work, Jay succeeded in obtaining an agreement with the British government. Under the terms of the treaty which was eventually to bear his own name, Britain agreed to surrender the forts on the western frontier by June 1796. Britain also agreed to enter into a commercial alliance by which American ships were granted the privilege of trading with India and the West Indies. The price of these concessions was rather high, however. In exchange for these rather modest gains, Jay was forced to abandon the United States's previous commitment to the principle of freedom of the seas. As a maritime nation without a large navy, the United States was a strong and early proponent of the idea that "free ships make free goods." Simply put, this principle permitted neutrals to trade with belligerents so long as they did not carry war materiel or supplies. In addition to agreeing to abandon the freedom of the seas, Jay was also forced to agree that the United States would no longer allow the French to outfit privateers in its ports and to ban the sale of seized British vessels by the French consular courts (DeConde, Entangling Alliances, 100–140).

Jay's treaty was bound to be controversial, and it was. On his return, the administration decided to keep the terms of treaty secret until the Senate had time to consider it. However, details of the agreement were leaked to the Republican press, which used the opportunity to denounce Jay in the harshest terms. The Boston town meeting condemned the treaty, and in New York City, Alexander Hamilton was pelted with stones for attempting to speak in its favor. In July 1795, Senator Charles Coatesworth Pinckney rose in the Senate to demand Jay's impeachment. Jay himself was sanguine about it all, once remarking that he could have found his way across the country by the light of his burning effigies. In the spring of 1795, Jay was elected governor of New York. He thereupon resigned the office of Chief Justice and avoided the specter of a long and bitter impeachment struggle. The Senate eventually ratified the treaty by a vote of twenty to ten, but only on the condition that the commercial agreements be eliminated (Bemis, Diplomatic History, 103–104).

The controversy over Jay's Treaty and the continuing party strife took its toll on President Washington, with the result that he decided not to seek reelection to a third term in 1796. In fact, Washington appears to have decided long before Jay returned that he would retire to Mount Vernon at the end of his second term. He had, after all, spent over twenty years in the service of his country and was looking forward to a quiet retirement with his wife Martha. The vitriol of the Republican press no doubt confirmed him in this decision, however; and so it was that in September 1796, Washington delivered his farewell address.

The address was the product of many hands, besides Washington's own. James Madison wrote an early draft about four years before, while Alexander Hamilton and John Jay appear to have offered comments and suggestions on the final product. The bulk of the address was devoted to domestic affairs, especially the difficulties caused by the rise of political parties. In this respect, Washington urged his countrymen to avoid party strife and do everything they could to preserve the union. The remainder focused on foreign policy. Washington encouraged Americans to cultivate friendship and commerce with all nations, but he also warned them to avoid "entangling alliances" with other countries. Washington allowed that short-term military treaties might be necessary, but he pointed to the French attempt to manipulate the Franco-American alliance as evidence of the dangers that come from failing to pursue an independent course in foreign affairs (Bemis, Diplomatic History, 108–109).

Washington's retirement left John Adams and Thomas Jefferson as the primary candidates for the presidency. After a bitterly fought campaign, Adams emerged successful—but barely—winning a total of seventy-one electoral votes to Jefferson's sixty-eight. Adams's election and the ratification of Jay's Treaty precipitated the next crisis in foreign affairs. In 1796, the French government notified James Monroe, the American ambassador, that the Treaty of Alliance of 1778 was abrogated and that customary relations between the two nations were at an end. Under orders from the Directory, French warships soon undertook widespread seizures of American vessels and impressed American seamen. When the French government rebuffed an American peace mission until it offered to pay a bribe in the so-called "XYZ affair," the breach between the two nations was complete (DeConde, Quasi-War, 36–73). Throughout 1797 and 1798, therefore, the United States prepared for war with France. Congress appropriated money for the building of ships and increased the size of the army. Commercial relations between the two countries came to an end, and although there was no actual declaration of war, by the summer of 1778, the United States and France found themselves engaged in open hostilities on the high seas. For the next two years, American legal and political events unfolded against the background of what was to become known as the "Quasi-War" (DeConde, Quasi-War, 109–41).

The Quasi-War itself generated a number of controversies that found their way into the federal courts. These primarily included prize cases, in which important principles of maritime law were established. At the same time, however, the context of the prize cases was such that the justices of the Supreme Court were often called upon to determine a number of significant constitutional questions relating to Congress's power to declare war and the power of the president to conduct foreign relations. The Quasi-War also set the stage for further domestic tensions, the effects of which were to be felt on presidential politics for years to come. The source of this controversy is to be found in the ongoing war of words between Republican newspaper editors and the Federalist administration.

## The Alien and Sedition Acts

Although Republican support for the French cause had long been the subject of criticism by Federalist writers and politicians, war with France made Republicans appear to be unpatriotic. Indeed, many Federalists accused Republicans of being French agents intent on undermining the union. As a result, in addition to taking steps to increase the size of the army and navy, Congress also sought to eliminate the perceived domestic threat posed by "Jacobins" who sought to overthrow the American government. Into this category went not only native-born members of the Republican party, but increasing numbers of Irish immigrants who came to this country with a healthy dose of contempt for the "aristocratic" elements of the Federalist party. These "United Irish" were said to constitute part of the growing network of French sympathizers in the United States. Irish immigrants then compounded the supposed error of their ways by tending to vote Republican.

The Federalist response to these threats was the passage, in 1798, of four different acts of Congress, which have since come to be referred to collectively as the Alien and Sedition Acts. They included the Alien Enemies Act, the Alien Friends Act, the Naturalization Act, and the Sedition Act.

The Alien Enemies Act authorized the president to arrest, detain, and deport foreign nationals from countries at war with the United States. The Alien Friends Act gave the president similar powers with respect to any alien whom he determined posed a danger to the public, regardless of whether a state of war existed between the United States and the nation of which the alien was a citizen (Elkins & McKitrick, 591). While the alien acts were never enforced, they did cause substantial discomfort for noncitizens residing in the United States. Indeed, it is commonly believed that the two acts were responsible for the departure of large numbers of French citizens and caused some foreign-born Republican newspaper editors to take out citizenship papers.

The Naturalization Act might reasonably be regarded as a direct assault on new immigrants in general and the Republican party in particular. It raised the residency requirement for citizenship from five to fourteen years, after some in Congress argued that restraining immigration was necessary to prevent the American character from being polluted by foreign elements. According to one such congressman, Americans themselves were doing a good job of populating the country, so there was no need "to invite hordes of wild Irishmen, nor the turbulent and disorderly of all parts of the world, to come here with a view to distract our tranquillity, after having succeeded in the overthrow of their own Governments" (3 *Annals of Congress*, 1023). The effect of the Naturalization Act was not merely to make it more difficult for immigrants to become citizens; it also had the additional benefit of cutting off the Republican party's supply of new voters (Miller, Crisis, 47).

By far, however, the most famous, and in some ways most draconian, part of the Federalist's legislative package was the Sedition Act of 1798. The act made it a crime for any group of people to "unlawfully combine or conspire together" to oppose any measure of the government or to prevent any government official from carrying out his assigned duties. The second section made it unlawful for any person to "write, print, utter or publish ... any false, scandalous, or malicious writing" against the President or any member of Congress.

While it might seem unusual to us today, few people in the latter part of the 18th century questioned the federal government's ability to pass an act punishing sedition. For the Federalists, the Sedition Act was merely one piece of a comprehensive defense program. It was, they said, a measure designed to ensure that French sympathizers would be prevented from causing chaos and confusion. As for claims that the Sedition Act of 1798 violated the First Amendment's guarantee of freedom of speech and press, Federalist supporters argued that "[i]t was never intended that the right to side with the enemies of one's country in slandering and vilifying the government, and dividing the people should be protected under the name of Liberty of the Press." As proof of the legitimacy of the act, Federalist supporters noted that every state in the union allowed the prosecution of sedition either by statute or common law rule.

To Republicans, on the other hand, the passage of the Naturalization and Sedition Acts only confirmed basic suspicions. Federalists, they said, were bent upon the destruction of liberty and the imposition of an aristocratical, if not monarchical, government. Indeed, some Virginians openly asserted that the Federalist administration was "an enemy infinitely more formidable and infinitely more to be guarded against than the French Directory" (Miller, Federalist Era, 237). With some justification, Republicans saw the passage of the Alien and Sedition Acts as part of a concerted plan to destroy the Republican party by denying it the ability to attract new voters and to prevent Republican newspapermen from criticizing the government. That the Sedition Act, by its own terms, was to expire shortly after the presidential election in 1800 was proof that the Alien and Sedition Acts were more about electoral politics than national security.

Between 1798 and 1800, the government sought a total of fifteen indictments under the Sedition Act (Ferling, 122). Of these, ten resulted in conviction. As might have been expected, Republican newspapers were the primary targets of these prosecutions, and three of the most prominent Republic editors, James Callender, Thomas Cooper, and William Duane, were convicted of sedition. The prime mover behind many of the prosecutions was Secretary of State Timothy Pickering, an ardent New England Federalist. Pickering was aided, however, by Supreme Court Justice Samuel Chase, whose aggressiveness in presiding over sedition trials while on circuit made him an object of contempt to Republicans and eventually served as the basis for the first attempt to impeach a Supreme Court justice (Presser, 120–28).

The passage of the Alien and Sedition Acts provoked something of a mild revolt in Virginia. Led by Thomas Jefferson and James Madison, Virginians recoiled at what they saw as the increasing accumulation of power in the national government. The federal government's extensive use of its power to tax to support the creation of a large standing army, the increasing use of federal courts to try common law crimes, and the suppression of free speech represented by the Sedition Act itself, convinced good Republicans in the South that resistance to the federal government was necessary if the liberties of the people were to be preserved. In their view, the increasing powers of the federal government would eventually result in the destruction of the states themselves.

In response to these provocations, Jefferson and Madison collaborated to produce the Virginia and Kentucky Resolutions (1798), which amounted to a stunning declaration of the rights of the states. In Jefferson and Madison's view, the union was little more than a compact between sovereign states, each of which gave up only a limited amount of their power to the central government. As the primary locus of sovereignty, the states were entitled to judge for themselves when an act of the federal government endangered the rights of the people, and the states were thus entitled to prevent such a law from coming into force (Elkins & McKitrick, 720–21). This so-called "compact theory of government" was later to find fuller expression in the works of John C. Calhoun and the southern successionists in the years leading to the Civil War. That James Madison was one of the prime authors of one of its earliest statements is truly one of the great ironies of history. The Virginia and Kentucky Resolutions called for the other states to join in seeking repeal of the Alien and Sedition Acts. In response, however, seven other states passed resolutions noting that the Supreme Court was the only body vested with the power to decide upon the constitutionality of an act of Congress.

## The Election of 1800 and the End of an Era

In the fall of 1800, President John Adams took up residence in the new national capital located on the Potomac River on land ceded by Virginia and Maryland. A few weeks later, he was joined by the members of Congress, who found themselves convening amidst a collection of rude huts hardly worth describing as a village, let alone the "federal city." Under construction since 1791, the new capital was barely habitable when the government arrived. The president's house was still not complete, so much so that the present East Room was used to hang the Adams's laundry. The Capitol also remained unfinished, and workers were still engaged in cutting down trees in the middle of Pennsylvania Avenue. New York's Senator, Gouverneur Morris, wryly noted that the federal city would be perfect, except for the lack of "houses, cellars, kitchens, well informed men, amiable women, and other little trifles of this kind." After the comfort and excitement of

Philadelphia, President Adams and many members of Congress clearly felt they had moved to the heart of a desolate wilderness. In the end, however, the Federalists move to the wilderness was to become more than physical. As the election of 1800 drew closer, it became clear that the Republican party would soon have the capacity to drive the Federalist party into the political wilderness as well (Ferling, 135–66).

By the fall of 1799, the Federalist party was in trouble. Although President Adams had successfully negotiated an end to hostilities with the French, the popularity of his administration was on the wane. Calling out the army to suppress Fries's Rebellion, the imposition of heavy taxes to support the new defense establishment, and the passage of the Sedition Act gave credence to Republican charges that Federalists were planning to subvert democracy. The following year, things looked even worse. Republicans had made substantial gains in the various state legislatures, especially New York and Pennsylvania. And, in most states, it was the legislature that chose the presidential electors.

When the campaign began in earnest in the latter part of 1800, John Adams and Charles Coatsworth Pinckney were again selected to be the Federalist standard-bearers. Adams, of course, had the advantage of incumbency, and Pinckney's choice was designed to shore up support in the South. For their part, the Republicans were led by Vice President Thomas Jefferson and New York's Senator Aaron Burr. After a hard fought and sometimes vicious campaign, the electoral vote was tied. In a surprising twist, the two Republicans, Jefferson and Burr, were in the lead with seventy-three votes each. Adams was third with sixty-five electoral votes, and Pinckney came in just behind with sixty-four. Former Chief Justice John Jay came in fifth with one vote (Ferling, 164).

The Constitution provided that the House of Representatives would elect the president in the event of a tie in the Electoral College, but the House was not scheduled to convene until March 4, 1801, leaving the nation in suspense for over three months. Complicating matters even further was the fact that in deciding presidential elections, the Constitution required the House to vote by states. Thus, although the Federalists had a slight numerical advantage in members, the state delegations were almost evenly divided. Six state delegations had a majority of Federalists, while the Republicans controlled six. The remaining two states' delegations were divided.

Although Republicans had always expected Jefferson to be president and Burr to be vice president, Burr had a change of heart once the final electoral count was in. As a result, the battle in the House was not merely whether the Republican candidate would be able to oust President Adams. On the contrary, the more interesting question was which Republican, Jefferson or Burr, would emerge with the prize. The intervening three months thus saw all sides attempt to cajole, manipulate, and threaten these members of Congress whose votes might be altered. Burr and Jefferson's partisans sought to work behind the scenes to secure victory for their candidate.

When it became clear that Adams could not obtain the necessary votes, the Federalists then began to consider which of the two Republicans would be the least dangerous. In the end, Jefferson was elected on the thirty-sixth ballot (Ferling, 175–204).

The Federalist administration had come to an end, but there was one last scene to be played. In February 1801, the lame-duck Congress passed the Judiciary Act of 1801. The act was long in the making and was designed to remedy a number of defects in the federal judiciary. Chief among these was the problem of circuit riding. As noted earlier, the justices of the Supreme Court complained bitterly throughout the first decade of the rigors of riding circuit each fall and spring. In response to these complaints, the Judiciary Act of 1801 created a whole new series of circuit judges who were to hold the circuit courts instead of the Supreme Court justices.

The Judiciary Act of 1801 was doomed from the start, however. Republicans regarded the Act with a great deal of suspicion. After all, its primary effect was to expand the size and scope of the federal judiciary, and as a result, many Republicans promised to make repeal one of the first items on the new Congress's agenda in March. Republican hostility was further inflamed, however, when President Adams used the waning days of his administration to fill the newly created judgeships with loyal Federalists. As Thomas Jefferson later observed, the Federalists "retired into the Judiciary as a stronghold ... and from that battery all the works of Republicanism are to be beaten down and erased." Jefferson's accusation was not far off the mark. President Adams and his supporters no doubt expected the appointment of Federalist judges would be the primary means to counter Republican control of the political branches of government. The Federalist judiciary would, in effect, serve as a check on Jefferson and the "Jacobins."

Among the other appointments Adams made that winter, was that of a new Chief Justice. Upon his return from France in 1800, Chief Justice Oliver Ellsworth resigned his seat on the court and returned home to Connecticut. Adams used this opportunity to nominate his own Secretary of State, John Marshall, to Ellsworth's post in January 1801. Marshall went on to lead the Court for almost thirty-five years. In the event, the Republicans were true to their word. Within a year, they succeeded in repealing the Judiciary Act of 1801. In so doing, they precipitated one of the most significant controversies ever to find its way to the Supreme Court, *Marbury v. Madison*, the opinion in which was delivered by Chief Justice Marshall, and which opened a whole new chapter in the history of the Supreme Court.

## References and Further Reading

*Annals of the Congress of the United States* (Washington, D.C.: Gales & Seaton 1834–1856).

Bemis, Samuel Flagg. *A Diplomatic History of the United States* (New York: Henry Holt & Co. 1936).

_____. *Jay's Treaty: A Study in Commerce and Diplomacy* (Westport, CT:1975).

Bernstein, Richard B., and Thomas Jefferson (New York: Oxford University Press 2003).

Chernow, Ron, and Alexander Hamilton (New York: Penguin Press 2004).

Collins, Michael G. "The Federal Courts, The First Congress, And The Non-Settlement Of 1789," *Virginia Law Review* 91 (2005): 1515.

Deconde, Alexander. *Entangling Alliance: Politics & Diplomacy Under George Washington* (Westport, CT: Greenwood Press 1974).

_____. *The Quasi-War: The Politics and Diplomacy of the Undeclared War With France 1797–1801* (New York: Scribner's 1966)

Elkins, Stanley, and Eric Mckitrick. *The Age of Federalism* (New York: Oxford University Press 1993).

Farrand, Max. *The Records of the Federal Convention of 1787* (New Haven, CT: Yale University Press 1937).

Ferling, John. *Adams V. Jefferson: The Tumultuous Election of 1800* (New York: Oxford University Pres 2004).

Hamilton, Alexander, John Jay, and James Madison. *The Federalist* (Bernard Bailyn Ed., Washington, D.C.: Library of Congress 1978).

Harrington, Matthew P. "The Economic Origins of the Seventh Amendment," *Iowa Law Review* 87 (2001): 145.

Jensen, Merrill P. *The Articles of Confederation* (Madison, Wisconsin: University of Wisconsin Press 1970).

Maclay, William. *The Journal of William Maclay, United States Senator from Pennsylvania, 1789–1791*. Edgar S. Maclay, Ed. New York: D.A. Appleton 1890.

Main, Jackson Turer. *The Antifederalists: Critics of the Constitution* (New York: Norton 1961).

Miller, John C. *The Federalist Era* (New York: Harper1960).

_____. Crisis in Freedom: The Alien and Sedition Acts (Boston, Little Brown 1951).

Presser, Stephen B. *The Original Misunderstanding: The English, The Americans and the Dialectic of Federalist Jurisprudence* (Chapel Hill, NC: University of North Carolina Press 1991).

Smith, James Morton. *Freedom's Fetters: The Alien and Sedition Laws and American Civil Liberties* (Ithaca, NY: Cornell University Press 1956).

Slaughter, Thomas P. *The Whiskey Rebellion: Frontier Epilogue to the American Revolution* (New York: Oxford University Press 1986).

Urofsky, Melvin I. and Paul Finkelman. A March of Liberty: A Constitutional History of the United States (New York: Oxford University Press 2002).

Wilson, David A. *United Irishmen, United States: Immigrant Radicals in the Early Republic* (Ithaca, NY: Cornell University Press 1998).

# *The Justices*

## *George Washington's Appointments*

President George Washington had an opportunity to do something no other president has ever been able to do: appoint an entire federal bench. On the very same day he signed the Judiciary Act into law, Washington nominated six men to serve on the Supreme Court. For the post of Chief Justice, Washington selected New York's John Jay. Washington then nominated five other men to serve as associate justices. These included William Cushing of Massachusetts, James Wilson of Pennsylvania, Robert H. Harrison of Maryland, John Blair of Virginia, and John Rutledge of South Carolina. Washington's choices met with widespread approval, for the president had taken great pains to ensure that his selections were men of skill and substance. Indeed, Connecticut merchant David Humphreys wrote Washington that his travels through North Carolina and Virginia convinced him that the president's selections had met with "almost universal approbation," so much so that Humphreys was certain that the Supreme Court would become "the first Court in the world in point of respectability."

## *Washington's Selection Criteria*

Washington paid careful attention to the composition of the Supreme Court, for he believed that the proper administration of justice was "the strongest cement of good government." Putting the judiciary on a sound footing, he said, was "essential to the happiness of our Citizens, and to the stability of our political system." Consequently, Washington did not want the court to become populated with political hacks. Instead, it was "an invariable object of anxious solicitude" for him to select "the fittest Characters to expound the laws and dispense justice."

Washington appears to have considered a number of factors in selecting the first justices. Among the characteristics that seem to have been most important were the nominee's support for the Constitution, service in the Revolution, and active participation in the political life of his state.

Although Washington never explicitly stated that support for the Constitution factored into his consideration of appointments, the inference is certainly strong that it did. Washington believed that the Supreme Court was integral to ensuring the stability of the new government. Appointing an antifederalist would, therefore, have been inconceivable, as it would have created an unacceptable diversity of opinion on the Court. As a result, with the exception of Robert H. Harrison, Washington's first set of nominees were staunch supporters of the Constitution. Although, Jay's authorship of several numbers of *The Federalist* was probably not public knowledge at the time, both Hamilton and Madison no doubt made Washington aware that Jay had played an important role in New York's ratification debate. James Wilson was the foremost advocate for ratification in the Pennsylvania state ratifying convention, holding the floor for days at a time. John Rutledge was a strong advocate for ratification in South Carolina, as was Virginia's John Blair. Similarly, James Iredell's advocacy for the Constitution in North Carolina, a state that originally refused to ratify, was legendary.

Service in the Revolution did not necessarily mean military service. For example, neither John Rutledge nor James Wilson served in the continental army. Instead, Wilson served the cause as member of Congress from Pennsylvania, while Rutledge was governor of South Carolina. Moreover, while being a Tory would obviously have been a disqualifier, it is also clear that those who remained neutral were passed over as well.

Although prior judicial experience was desirable, it seems not to have been a necessary qualification for Washington's nominees. On the contrary, Washington believed that the new Court required statesmen more than lawyers. Thus, while Rutledge, Cushing, Harrison, and Blair had extensive experience on their states' highest court, Chief Justice Jay had only a brief tenure as New York's chief justice. James Wilson had no service as a state court judge, although he did hear a few prize cases as a member of the Continental Congress' ad hoc Committee on Appeals. Similarly, Justice James Iredell had less than six months service on the North Carolina Superior Court when he was chosen to replace Robert H. Harrison.

Finally, cognizant of the need to ensure that the Court was representative of the nation's diverse constituencies, Washington also took geography into consideration, ensuring that northern, middle, and southern states were all represented on the Court. In addition to this broad regional approach, Washington also seems to have ensured that certain states were always represented on the Court. Thus, when John Rutledge resigned his seat in 1790, Washington first sought to replace Rutledge with another South Carolinian. It was only after both Edward Rutledge and Charles Coastworth Pinckney declined nomination that Washington selected Maryland's Thomas Johnson. James Iredell's selection was motivated by similar concerns. When Robert H. Harrison refused to serve, Washington looked toward North Carolina for a replacement because no major federal officeholder had yet come from that state. Perhaps the most important of Washington's geographic rules was his subsequent refusal to appoint two justices from the same state. Thus, after Virginia's Blair resigned his seat in 1795, Washington replaced him with a Marylander, Samuel Chase. He later explained that the vacancy caused by Blair's departure "could not be filled from Virginia without giving two judges to that state, which would have excited unpleasant sensations in other states."

The geographic test, combined with the requirement that nominees have been supporters of the Constitution, evidences Washington's expectation that the Supreme Court would have a political as well as a legal function. Selecting nominees with a view toward geographic considerations helped engender support for the national government throughout the union. Limiting his choices to those who were advocates of the new Constitution ensured that the Court would be able to speak with one voice on most matters and would not be distracted by larger debates over the legitimacy of the constitutional enterprise.

# The Justices

## John Jay (1789)

Nominated as the first Chief Justice, John Jay was born in New York City on December 12, 1745. As the son of Peter Jay and Mary Van Cortlandt, John Jay was connected to two of the most important families in the province. Jay's grandfather, Augustus Jay, was a French Huguenot refugee who amassed a sizeable fortune in trade and then added connections to that fortune through his marriage to Anna Maria Bayard, who was herself related to the Van Cortlandt, Van Rensselaer, and Schulyer families. His mother's connections allowed Peter Jay to strengthen the family alliance with his marriage to Mary Van Cortlandt, who was the granddaughter of the first lord of the manor of Philipsburg.

Shortly after his birth, Jay's family moved to Rye, New York, where he remained until sent to a grammar school in New Rochelle. When he turned eleven, Jay returned home to Rye and continued his education under the direction of a tutor, George Murray. In August 1760, Jay enrolled at King's College (now Columbia University) in New York City. There his course of study included Greek, Latin, philosophy, science, and some law.

After graduating from King's in 1764, Jay went to study law in the office of New York lawyer Benjamin Kissam. However, his clerkship was interrupted by the lawyers' protest over the Stamp Act and the subsequent closure of the courts. With no work to do, Jay returned to the family home in Rye and spent the winter of 1765–1766 reading the classics. Using this study as a foundation, Jay eventually returned to King's and received his Master of Arts degree in 1767. He then took up his clerkship in Kissam's office and was admitted to the bar two years later. By 1774, John Jay was one of the most successful lawyers in New York. In a very short time after his admission, Jay had appeared before the Supreme Court of Judicature, the Court of Chancery and the Mayor's Court of New York, as well as the county courts in most of the surrounding counties (Vanburkleo, 29–30).

Jay's prominence at the bar and in New York's society allowed him to assume positions of importance in other areas as well. With other graduates of King's College, Jay founded the Debating Society of New York City. He also helped organize the "Moot," a society devoted to debating important questions of law. Perhaps most interesting, Jay's position as manager of the Dancing Assembly of New York City allowed him to exert a great deal of influence over the conduct of New York's social season.

On April 28, 1774, Jay married Sarah Van Brugh Livingston, a cousin of Robert Livingston, then his law partner. From a social perspective, it was a brilliant match, for the Livingstons were among New York's finest families, and the bride's father, William Livingston, was arguably the most prominent member of the New York bar. Together, John and Sarah Jay had six children, two of whom, Peter Augustus and William, followed their father into the law.

Increasing tensions between the colonies and the mother country gradually drew Jay toward the center of political controversy. In 1774, Parliament ordered the closure of the port of Boston in response to the dumping of the tea. New York City's merchant community responded by forming the Committee of Fifty-One to maintain contact with similar groups in other colonies. John Jay was appointed to a subcommittee of this group to draft a response to the Boston Town Meeting's call for a nonimportation agreement among the colonies until the Boston Port Act was repealed. The subcommittee eventually called for a meeting of delegates from each of the colonies to meet at a congress the following year.

New York's delegation to the First Continental Congress, which met at Philadelphia in September 1774, consisted of John Alsop, Philip Livingston, James Duane, and John Jay. By and large, Jay attempted to steer a middle course in the dispute with Parliament. He supported James Galloway's plan of union and urged his fellow delegates to seek some compromise that would avoid further conflict with the mother country. At the same time, however, Jay signed on to the Continental Association, which called for an economic boycott against England. He also authored "An Address to the People of Great Britain" in which he appealed directly to the British public to help reverse what he claimed was a plot by the king's ministers to subvert the rights of the colonists.

On his return to New York, Jay became even more deeply involved in politics. He was quickly elected to serve on the Committee of Sixty, an extra-legal group charged with enforcing the terms of the nonimportation agreement. The following year, he was sent as one of New York's delegates to the Second Continental Congress, where he continued to be a tireless advocate for reconciliation. Along with Benjamin Franklin, John Dickinson, Thomas Johnson, and John Rutledge, Jay was appointed to a committee responsible for drafting the "Olive Branch Petition," which was designed to be one final attempt to assure Parliament of America's desire to avoid conflict.

On his return to New York in April 1776, Jay was elected to the state's provincial congress. While there, he played a crucial role in the drafting of New York's 1777 constitution, and upon its adoption was elected chief justice of New York's Supreme Court of Judicature. His judicial tenure was relatively brief, however, for within a year of his election, he was again made a member of New York's delegation to the Continental Congress. Three days after he arrived in Philadelphia, he was elected president of Congress when South Carolina's Henry Laurens resigned in a dispute over the censure of Silas Deane, a member of the American mission to France. Jay's service in Congress was marked by a series of controversies over difficulties in supplying the army and in managing the United States' chaotic fiscal and monetary policy.

In March 1779, Jay was appointed minister plenipotentiary to Spain. In making this appointment, Congress hoped that Jay would be able to negotiate a treaty of alliance akin to that made with France the year before. Congress also hoped that Jay would obtain a loan from the Spanish government to prop up the United States' precarious financial position. Jay arrived in Cadiz in January 1780, and then spent the next two and one-half years working to negotiate the alliance and loans. On June 13, 1781, Jay was appointed one of the commissioners charged with negotiating a peace treaty with England. The other commissioners were Benjamin Franklin, John Adams, Henry Laurens, and Thomas Jefferson. Although five commissioners were named, only Franklin was actually in Paris at the time. Adams was detained in the Netherlands attempting to negotiate a treaty with the Estates General, and the ship carrying Henry Laurens was captured by a British cruiser while en route. For his part, Jay remained in Spain for almost another year working to negotiate the Spanish alliance. He did not depart for Paris until May 1782, after receiving a specific request from Benjamin Franklin. Adams later joined Jay and Franklin in Paris in October 1782.

Jay, Adams, and Franklin were ultimately successful in negotiating a treaty with England. This treaty guaranteed American independence as well as the possession of a vast tract of land between the Atlantic seaboard and the Mississippi River. At the same time, however, the treaty contained several provisions that were to cause a great deal of difficulty for Jay when he eventually assumed his seat as chief justice. One of these required the United States to ensure that British creditors who were owed money on debts due prior to the Revolution "should meet with no lawful Impediment to the Recovery of the full Value in Sterling Money." Unfortunately, however, Congress was unable to induce the states to open their courts to the recovery of British debts once hostilities had ended. Moreover, in those states in which British creditors were successful in bringing actions, state court juries routinely refused to give judgment or limited the creditor's recovery. Throughout the 1780s, British government officials repeatedly complained about the United States' failure to honor its obligations under the peace treaty, and Britain used this failure as the justification for its refusal to evacuate forts on the northern and western frontier. Holding on to these forts allowed Britain to retain control of the lucrative fur trade. Americans on the frontier also complained that the forts gave British officers a base from which to incite the Indians to attack American settlements. As a result, the issues arising from the provisions of the peace treaty were to plague the conduct of American foreign policy throughout the remainder of the confederation period. More importantly, the simmering dispute over the interpretation of the treaty was to form the background of a number of cases that eventually made their way to the Supreme Court in the 1790s.

Jay returned to the United States in the summer of 1784. Upon his arrival, he learned that Congress had voted to appoint him secretary of foreign affairs while he was still at sea. For the next five years, therefore, Jay struggled to gain respect for the new nation among the great powers of Europe. Of particular concern was the continued refusal of the states to open their courts to British debts and the consequent refusal of the British government to evacuate the forts in the Northwest territories. Meanwhile, Spain's refusal to allow American access to the Gulf of Mexico via the Mississippi greatly restricted trade with the west and was a continuing source of complaint by settlers in the trans-Appalachian region. Jay thus attempted to negotiate a treaty with Spain to give American vessels the right to transit the Mississippi through New Orleans.

His service as a diplomat convinced Jay that a stronger national government was needed if the new nation was to survive. Throughout the latter part of the 1780s, therefore, he was a tireless advocate for the drafting of a new frame of government. In 1788, Jay collaborated with Alexander Hamilton and James Madison to write a series of essays urging ratification of the Constitution. These essays, which are now known as *The Federalist*, were instrumental in winning support for the Constitution in New York. Writing under the pseudonym, *Publius*, Jay authored four papers, Numbers 2–5, demonstrating that the United States' current form of government weakened its position in foreign affairs and exposed it to great danger. He wrote a later essay, Number 64, in which he defended the Constitution's allocation of executive and legislative power in the making of treaties.

Jay's service as secretary of foreign affairs did not come to an end with the ratification of the Constitution in 1788. Instead, he remained in that post until September 24, 1789, when President Washington nominated him to be Chief Justice. Nevertheless, although now a member of the judiciary, John Jay continued to serve as secretary of state *ad interim* until Thomas Jefferson took office in March 1790.

John Jay's service on the bench was colored by his by his political and economic conservatism. As noted earlier, Jay was something of a reluctant patriot and maintained a dim view of the prospects of success for republican government. He was not optimistic about the ability of the weak and fragmented confederation governments to combat the increasingly self-destructive elements of democratic rule. In the words of one biographer, Jay bemoaned the fact that "republicans everywhere seemed to embrace or tolerate moral degeneracy, demagoguery, disdain for law, ëlevelling,' disastrous logjams in Congress the fettering of diplomats, drifts of worthless paper currency, and tooth-and-nail competition among the states for trading privileges" (Vanburkleo, 31). As the nation's first chief justice, therefore, Jay sought to determine how the national judiciary might best provide "due support to the national government" (Vanburkleo, 32).

Jay believed that the Supreme Court was uniquely positioned to provide that support. In his view, the Court provided the means by which domestic order and economic stability might be established. Jay sought to do so by taking advantage of the federal courts' extensive subject matter jurisdiction. At the same time, Jay also believed in necessity of a "working alliance" between the executive and judiciary (Vanburkleo, 46). Such an alliance was desirable as a means of providing a counterbalance to the legislative branch, which he always feared would be too responsive to popular passion. It was for this reason that Jay repeatedly offered informal political and legal advice to President Washington and the cabinet. In both 1789 and 1790, Jay advised the president on several matters affecting foreign relations and the judiciary. He also consulted repeatedly with Treasury Secretary Hamilton on subjects as varied as Indian relations, the building of federal facilities, currency regulation, and the best means to subdue the Whiskey Rebellion. At the same time, however, Jay refused to allow the formal boundaries between the executive and judicial branches to be ignored completely. Thus, in 1793, he led the other members of the Supreme Court in declining President Washington's request for an advisory opinion during the neutrality crisis. Similarly, in *Hayburn's Case* (1792), Jay and his colleagues on the New York circuit refused to enforce the Invalid Pensioners' Act because the act allowed the decisions of the federal courts to be reviewed by executive branch officials.

Jay strongly believed that the new nation could not long survive unless the national government was able to exercise unfettered power in those areas delegated by the Constitution to it. In 1793, he got the chance to advance this view most forcefully in *Chisolm v. Georgia*. The case involved a suit by a citizen of South Carolina against the State of Georgia seeking enforcement of a contract. When Chisolm filed suit in the federal court, Georgia claimed sovereign immunity and refused to appear. For Jay, the problem was not merely one of forcing a state to submit to federal power, for if Georgia could not be forced to comply, the nation's reputation at home and abroad would suffer. Jay clearly believed that foreign governments would be reluctant to enter into future treaties if they could not be certain that the federal government would ever be able to obtain compliance from the states. In the end, therefore, the Supreme Court voted overwhelmingly to require Georgia to appear.

The decision in *Chisolm* generated a storm of controversy. Even before the Court's decision was announced, the Georgia legislature voted not to abide by any adverse decision. After the decision came down, the Massachusetts General Court began a drive to amend the Constitution to effectively overrule the Supreme Court's decision, while the Virginia assembly formally condemned Jay for breaching the principle of state sovereign immunity. The states' greatest fear was that they would be dragged into federal court to defend against numerous claims by British creditors or loyalists whose claims or property were confiscated by the states during the Revolution. Jay was not deterred. Within a few months of the decision in *Chisolm*, the Supreme Court allowed suit to be initiated against New York, Virginia, and Massachusetts. State fears were thus quickly realized, with the result that in a few months, three-fourths of the states approved the Eleventh Amendment, which provided that the "Judicial Power of the United States shall not be construed to extend to any Suit in Law or Equity, commenced or prosecuted against one of the United States by Citizens of another State or by Citizens or Subjects of any foreign State."

With his attempt to assert federal judicial power effectively thwarted, Jay apparently looked for the exit. After 1793, the federal courts were effectively closed to claims arising from breaches of the peace treaty, at least where the states themselves were concerned. Jay was clearly disappointed with the limited role of the Supreme Court after passage of the Eleventh Amendment. Rather than being an integral player in the creation of a strong central government, the federal courts were destined, in Jay's view at least, to play a minor role on the national stage. For his part, Jay had no desire to immerse himself in the tedious ritual of creating domestic common law (Vanburkleo, 51). As a result, when President Washington sought to appoint a diplomat to negotiate a treaty of amity and commerce with Great Britain, Jay eagerly accepted the post.

Jay's mission was to secure a resolution of the dispute over British debts and obtain the evacuation of the forts on the western frontier. Jay was also instructed to seek commercial concessions, particularly the reopening of ports in the British West Indies to American vessels. These ports, which had been closed since the Revolution, had long been an important source of trade for American merchants and carriers. Jay's efforts culminated in the Treaty of Amity and Commerce and was signed on November 19, 1794. The agreement quickly became the object of scorn on the part of many who thought that Jay had agreed to give away too much in return for very few real concessions from the British. "Jay's Treaty," as it was soon to become known, provoked a great deal of controversy and further exacerbated the growing party strife between Federalist supporters of the administration and the Republican opposition.

Upon his return from England in May 1795, Chief Justice Jay learned that New York's Federalist party nominated him as its candidate for governor, and on June 5, 1795, his election was made official. Consequently, Jay resigned his commission as chief justice on June 29, 1795, and returned home to New York. He served as New York's governor until the spring of 1801, when he declined to run for another term. In a rather strange twist, however, President Adams again nominated Jay to serve as chief justice to replace Oliver Ellsworth, who had resigned in October 1800. Although the Senate immediately confirmed the nomination, Jay refused the commission. In a letter to President Adams, Jay expressed his continuing regret that Congress had so far refused to make the improvements he had urged so many times before, particularly with respect to the obligation ride circuit. Such improvements, Jay said, were necessary in order "to place the judicial Depart[ment] on a proper Footing." Without them, Jay almost despaired of the Court's future. He reminded the president that he had "left the Bench perfectly convinced that under a System so defective, it would not obtain the Energy[,] weight and Dignity which are essential to its affording due support to the national Govern[ment]; nor acquire the public Confidence and Respect, which, as the last Resort of the Justice of the nation, it should possess." Congress' inattention to the organization of the judiciary in the years since he left only convinced Jay his return would only reward Congress for its "neglect and Indifference." Jay thus retired to his estate where he spent the next twenty-eight years in quiet retirement until his death in 1829.

## John Rutledge (1789)

John Rutledge was born in Charleston, South Carolina, in 1739. He was the son of Dr. John Rutledge and Sarah Hext, one of the state's wealthiest heiresses. Rutledge's early education was supervised by his father until the latter's death in 1750. Thereafter, he was tutored by an English clergyman, and was later enrolled in a school run by David Rhind.

Rutledge did not attend university. Instead, he began to read law under his uncle, Andrew Rutledge, once the speaker of the South Carolina legislature. Upon Andrew's death in 1755, Rutledge continued his studies under the tutelage of James Parsons of Charleston. Two years later, he sailed for England to study at the Middle Temple, and was called to the bar in 1760. On returning to South Carolina in December 1760, Rutledge gained admission to the South Carolina bar in January 1761, where his mother's social connections allowed him to quickly establish himself as one of the foremost members of the bar. Between 1761 and 1774, Rutledge handled more cases in the South Carolina Court of Common Pleas than any other lawyer in the colony.

Rutledge also became involved in politics. He was elected a member of the South Carolina assembly in March 1761, where he became a leader of the "country party." Like his uncle Andrew, the former speaker, John Rutledge was a firm defender of local rights and the prerogatives of the legislature in numerous clashes with the royal governor.

Rutledge also opposed the Stamp Act and Townshend duties, although he refrained from becoming involved in extra-legal political activity. Indeed, like most members of his class, Rutledge did not immediately embrace the radical position. Rather, he believed that Parliament had the power to manage the trade of the empire, but lacked the power to levy "internal" taxes on the colonies (Haw, 71). Rutledge's leadership on this issue resulted in his being elected a member of the South Carolina delegation to the Stamp Act Congress, where he chaired the committee that drafted a petition to the House of Lords requesting repeal of the act.

In 1774, Rutledge was elected a delegate to the First Continental Congress. In Congress, Rutledge, like John Jay, was a reluctant revolutionary. He was hesitant about severing all ties with Great Britain and thus supported the Galloway plan of union rather than Patrick Henry's drive for a complete break. In time, however, Rutledge came to support the cause of independence, especially after the outbreak of hostilities at Lexington and Concord. By October 1775, Rutledge had come to believe that the various colonies needed to form new governments based on popular sovereignty. As a result, when South Carolina's Second Provincial Congress met in February 1776, Rutledge found himself a member of the committee appointed to draft a new constitution for the "Republic of South Carolina."

With the formation of a new state government in 1776, Rutledge was elected the South Carolina republic's first president. As governor, he was widely credited with helping to mount a successful defense against a British invasion of Charleston in June 1776, and protecting the western frontier against attack by the Cherokee Indians. Rutledge resigned as governor two years later when the assembly approved a new state constitution. This new frame of government provided for the disestablishment of the Anglican church, the elimination of the governor's veto over legislative acts, and the popular election of members of the state senate. Rutledge believed that the new state constitution abandoned the safety of a mixed government in favor of one that tended too much toward unfettered democracy. Like many of his day, Rutledge firmly believed that "democratic" (as opposed to "republican") governments were too easily susceptible to manipulation by demagogues (Haw, 73).

Rutledge's absence from the political arena was relatively brief, however. The invasion of South Carolina by British troops in 1779 caused so much turmoil that the legislature eventually elected Rutledge governor with almost unlimited powers of government. The legislature clearly hoped that Rutledge would be able to provide the same measure of stability and leadership that allowed the state to resist the first invasion in 1776. Unfortunately, local Continental forces were too weak to withstand the British assault. Charleston surrendered in May 1780, forcing Rutledge to retreat to North Carolina where he remained at the head of a government-in-exile until the summer of 1781. Upon restoration of civil government in 1782, Rutledge was elected to the Continental Congress, where he served until November 1783. While in Congress,

Rutledge worked to shore up the nation's shaky finances as well as to ensure that the eventual peace treaty with Great Britain would provide a western boundary for the United States on the Mississippi River.

Upon his return to South Carolina, Rutledge devoted a large part of his time to restoring his family's ailing financial situation. As was the case with many Southern farms, the war had taken a heavy toll on the Rutledge plantation. Crop failures in 1784 and 1785, combined with the collapse in old trading patterns, left planters like Rutledge in dire straits. Nevertheless, Rutledge might have supplemented his income by returning to his law practice, but he chose instead to serve as the Chief Judge of the South Carolina Court of Chancery. His desire to maintain position and influence ensured that Rutledge would remain on the brink of financial ruin (Haw, 74).

By the end of the 1780s, therefore, John Rutledge was well acquainted with the numerous difficulties facing the new nation. As a member of the South Carolina assembly, he fought against the various paper money and debtor protection schemes designed to relieve the economic burden on farmer and artisan alike. As governor, he was intimately familiar with the inability of Congress to obtain the necessary support for the war and thus provide for the common defense. As a farmer, he knew all too well the havoc caused by the closure of the West Indies trade and the instability of the currency. Thus, when the South Carolina assembly elected him a delegate to the Constitutional Convention, Rutledge went to Philadelphia determined to find some means by which the central government would have the ability to effectively provide for the national defense and manage the nation's commerce (Haw, 74–75).

John Rutledge's work at the Philadelphia Convention "reflected a political outlook grounded in traditional Anglo-American Whig thinking, adapted to the circumstances of the South Carolina lowcountry gentry" (Haw, 75). In general, Rutledge had great faith in the theory of mixed government, which in England meant rule by a Parliament composed of king, lords, and commons. While unfettered democracy was attractive on the surface, Rutledge believed that the effects of democracy had thus far been found to be "arbitrary, severe and destructive." For Rutledge, therefore, the American situation required a republican government built on a "mixed" model. American governments should be composed of a strong executive and a legislature consisting of two houses, one of which would be elected by the people and the other having some insulation from popular passion. Such a structure would provide ample protection for the rights of property, and in the South Carolina context, preserve the rights and position of Lowcountry planters against the excesses of a government controlled by small farmers and tradesmen from the interior (Haw, 75).

At the Constitutional Convention, Rutledge and the rest of the South Carolina delegation originally opposed popular election of either house of the national legislature. Instead, they argued for the creation of a Congress with a lower house elected by the state legislatures and an upper house chosen by the members of the lower.

Such a scheme would ensure that the members of the national assembly would be insulated from popular passion. In addition, Rutledge argued for extensive property qualifications for federal office holders and suggested that members of the national legislature ought not to receive salaries for their service. Rutledge expected that requirements like these would ensure that only men of property or substance would be able to serve.

The Convention rejected South Carolina's proposals for the national legislature. Instead, the delegates agreed to popular election of the House of Representatives. As a result, when attention turned to the problem of how to apportion members of the House, Rutledge argued that apportionment of members in the Congress ought to be based on the amount of taxes paid by each state. This formula would give South Carolina and the southern states an advantage because taxes were generally levied on property and not people. Thus, while states like South Carolina and Georgia had far fewer people than Massachusetts or Connecticut, they had a great deal more property when measured in terms of land or slaves. A system based on property taxes would, therefore, have given the states of the deep South a great deal of leverage in the new Congress. The proposal was also rejected, however.

Although Rutledge was a member of the committee formed to draft a compromise between the large and small states, he opposed the Great Compromise on the floor. The Compromise provided for a lower house apportioned on the basis of population and an upper house in which each state would have equal representation. Rutledge thought that this manner of apportioning representation would result in newly created states in the west eventually having the upper hand. Because he expected these new states to be populated by wild frontiersmen, Rutledge worried that the rights of property would become less secure. To his credit, however, Rutledge helped keep the Convention together after it approved the Great Compromise.

When it came time to consider the composition of the national judiciary, Rutledge opposed the creation of lower federal courts. He believed that lower courts would infringe on the rights and powers of the state courts. As a result, he argued that cases arising under federal law should be tried in state courts in the first instance. Thereafter, an appeal could be brought to the Supreme Court. As was noted in Chapter 1, this proposal, too, was rejected and the Convention eventually agreed to allow the national legislature to determine whether lower federal courts ought to be established. Notwithstanding his opposition to an extensive federal judicial system, Rutledge supported giving federal judges lifetime tenure as a means of ensuring that they would be immune from political pressure.

Rutledge was not entirely happy with the final version of the Constitution. Nonetheless, while he thought it had many defects, he became a strong advocate for its ratification. In his view, the new Constitution was a vast improvement on the old Articles of Confederation. The new frame of government was clearly a compromise in many respects, but it was a compromise that, on the whole, protected South Carolina's interests while still providing a degree of energy to the national government.

Shortly after passage of the Judiciary Act, President Washington nominated Rutledge to be the senior associate justice. Although Rutledge accepted the appointment, he was disappointed that Washington had not offered him the office of chief justice. Rutledge believed that his education and judicial experience made him far better qualified to be chief justice than John Jay.

Rutledge's unhappiness in this regard seems to be reflected in the fact that he did not actually attend any of the Supreme Court's sessions. He was absent when the Court met for its first session in February 1790, but no one really knows what kept him away. Although he was present in New York when the Court met for its second session in August 1790, illness prevented Rutledge from attending this session as well. Since no cases had been docketed, Rutledge's absence posed no great difficulty for the Court. Rutledge did attend the meetings of circuit courts in both the spring and fall 1790 terms, although most of the early business of those courts was taken up with admitting attorneys and establishing rules of procedure.

In March 1790, Rutledge resigned his seat on the Supreme Court to accept an appointment as chief justice of South Carolina's Court of Common Pleas. It may be that his disappointment at not having been chosen as chief justice began to take its toll. He was, after all, used to high office, having been both governor and chief judge of South Carolina's chancery court. Service in a junior capacity could not, therefore, have been very attractive to him. At the same time, however, Rutledge's resignation is also evidence of the fact that the Supreme Court did not, at least in its early years, offer the sort of prestige and position that it does today. Although he was only fifty-five years old at the time, Rutledge no doubt found the difficulties of riding circuit too high a cost to bear in order to retain federal office. For many jurists of the day, a position on the states' highest courts offered more lucrative and prestigious employment than service as a member of a federal court that offered little to do and rigorous circuit duty.

Rutledge returned to South Carolina in the spring of 1791 to take up his seat on the state court bench. For the better part of a year, he performed his duties ably. The following year, however, Rutledge began to evidence signs of severe depression. The death of both his mother and wife within the space of six months was a serious blow to his mental health. Adding to these difficulties was his own declining physical health and continuing financial pressures. By 1795, his behavior became so erratic that one observer was led to remark that Rutledge's "mind was frequently so much deranged, as to be in a great measure deprived of his senses."

Upon John Jay's election to the New York governor's office in June 1795, Rutledge assumed that Jay would soon resign his seat on the Supreme Court. In anticipation of that event, he wrote President Washington offering to replace Jay as chief justice. Jay's resignation and Rutledge's letter reached Washington on the very same day. Obviously unaware of Rutledge's emotional difficulties, Washington decided to accept the offer. Washington wrote Rutledge and advised him that the he would receive a temporary commission because the Senate was out of session until December.

In the meantime, Rutledge made a fatal mistake—at least as far as his career was concerned. On June 26, 1795, he attended a meeting in Charleston called to protest the terms of Jay's Treaty. Rutledge attacked the treaty in the most vehement and intemperate language because he and other South Carolinians believed that the treaty was far too favorable to British interests. Indeed, Rutledge went so far as to declare, "he had rather the president die, dearly as he loves him, than he should sign that treaty." Unfortunately for him, news of the speech spread rapidly. Supporters of the treaty were outraged and demanded that Washington rescind Rutledge's appointment, but Washington refused. John Adams expressed the sentiments of many, commenting rather dryly that "C[hief] Justices must not go to illegal Meetings and become popular orators in favour of Sedition." Federalist newspapers and politicians used the six months between Rutledge's speech in June and the time when the Senate reconvened in December to drum up opposition to the permanent appointment. Outraged supporters of the treaty castigated Rutledge for being "deranged in his mind" and frequently drunk.

In spite of the controversy surrounding his appointment, Rutledge behaved with great dignity when he went to Philadelphia to preside over the August 1795 term of the Supreme Court (Haw, 87). He participated in two decisions having tremendous importance for the conduct of foreign relations. In *Talbot v. Jansen* (1795), Rutledge joined the other justices in releasing a Dutch vessel that had been seized by an American ship sailing under a French letter of marque. In so doing, the Court upheld the Washington administration's policy of neutrality by preventing the French government from using American ports to arm vessels for use in the war with England and her allies. At the same term, Rutledge led the majority in *United States v. Peters* (1795), holding that a French vessel could not be detained in an American court for having taken prizes on the high seas. Whether the French vessel acted lawfully or not, Rutledge wrote, was a matter for French courts alone to decide. Together, these two decisions helped keep the federal courts, and by extension the United States itself, from being drawn into the widening conflict in Europe.

Rutledge attended the fall 1795 southern circuit. After presiding over the South Carolina Circuit Court in late October, he journeyed to Georgia to open the circuit court in that state. The session was cancelled, however, because the district court judge failed to appear and the clerk of court had died. Rutledge then headed to North Carolina, but took ill along the way. He appears to have suffered a further bout of depression and twice attempted suicide by drowning. On December 28, 1795, Rutledge wrote the president and resigned his commission. The letter was a mere formality, however. Unbeknownst to Rutledge, the Senate had voted two weeks earlier to reject his appointment as chief justice. The 14 to 10 vote was almost the same margin by which the Jay Treaty had been approved, indicating that it was Rutledge's opposition to the treaty, more than any concerns about his qualifications, which sealed his fate (Haw, 87–88). Rutledge spent the remaining five years of his life in retirement and died in Charleston on July 18, 1800.

## William Cushing (1789)

William Cushing was born in Scituate, Massachusetts, on March 1, 1732. Cushing was descended from very distinguished, although not very wealthy, New England stock. As the son of Mary Cotton Cushing, he was a direct descendent of the great New England preacher, Cotton Mather. His father, on the other hand, was a distinguished Massachusetts judge, serving as both a member of the provincial council and the Supreme Court of Judicature. In fact, John Cushing was one of the judges who presided over the trial of the British soldiers involved in the Boston Massacre.

William began his education at a local Latin school in Scituate until his admission to Harvard College in 1747. After graduation in 1751, Cushing served as a preceptor at a grammar school in Roxbury. His career as a schoolteacher was brief, however, for Cushing returned to Harvard in 1752 on a fellowship to study divinity. Two years later, he quit this as well and left the university to study law in the offices of Jeremiah Gridley, a prominent Boston lawyer. After four years riding circuit and managing Gridley's office, Cushing was admitted to the bar in February 1758. He then opened his own law practice in Scituate, Massachusetts, but did not remain there long. With the organization of Maine into separate counties in 1760, Cushing set off with his younger brother, Charles, to seek new opportunities there, and they arrived in Pownalborough, (now Dresden), Maine, later that year. A short time thereafter, Charles was named sheriff of the newly created Lincoln County, while William was appointed probate judge and justice of the peace.

Pownalborough did not offer lucrative employment for a young lawyer, but William Cushing was often the only educated member of the bar for many miles around. As a result, he frequently served as acting attorney general in the absence of the king's attorney. He also represented a number of land companies, the most prominent of which was the Kennebec Proprietors. It was in representing the interests of these land speculators that Cushing became associated with John Adams, who was engaged in similar work. In 1771, William's father, John, resigned his seat on the Massachusetts Supreme Court of Judicature, although not before reaching an agreement with the lieutenant governor to appoint his son in his place. A few weeks later, William left Maine for Boston to claim his father's seat.

As a judge of the province's highest court, William Cushing labored mightily to avoid being drawn into the growing controversy between England and her colonies. For example, while on the bench, he refused to take a position on the question of whether Massachusetts' judges ought to be paid by the Crown or the legislature. It was only when faced with impeachment that he eventually agreed that judges ought to answer to the assembly rather than the executive. Although this choice earned him the hostility of the royal government, he angered many radicals by being the only Massachusetts judge to continue to ride circuit in the year prior to the outbreak of the war.

Cushing remained on the bench after the start of the Revolution. In 1774, he exchanged his royal commission for one issued by the commonwealth after the revolutionary council of state reorganized the courts. Thereafter, Cushing was appointed to the Superior Court of Judicature, along with John Adams, and became chief justice of that court upon Adams' resignation. While serving in that capacity, Cushing presided over the trials of many of the rebels involved in Shays' Rebellion. Cushing's involvement in the trials of the Shaysites convinced him that the United States needed a stronger national government.

Cushing was not a delegate to the Constitutional Convention in Philadelphia, but he was instrumental in securing ratification by the Massachusetts convention. As chief justice of Massachusetts, Cushing delivered a series of grand jury charges designed to educate the public about the need for a new national government. Later, as vice president of the ratifying convention, Cushing presided over most of the sessions of the convention when it met in Boston in January 1788 (Gerber, 101).

President Washington nominated Cushing to the Supreme Court on September 24, 1789, and the Senate confirmed the nomination two days later. Cushing is often criticized as an ineffective justice. Critics point out that he authored a total of only eighteen opinions, although he served for over two decades on the Court. In addition, critics note that those opinions Cushing did write are often superficial and almost devoid of any in-depth legal analysis (Gerber, 106). Of the eighteen Cushing opinions, two cases in particular, *Chisholm v. Georgia* (1793) and *Ware v. Hylton* (1796), are significant because they reveal the early Court's struggle with the problem of what is now called "textualism," which is essentially the problem of trying to determine what weight to give the plain meaning of the constitutional text in light of the intentions of the document's drafters.

As noted earlier, *Chisholm* involved an attempt by a citizen of South Carolina to sue the State of Georgia in the federal court. In their opinions, most of the other justices, especially Justice Iredell, primarily addressed the political aspects of the case, trying to determine what the impact of the suit would be for federal–state relations. Justice Cushing, on the other hand, insisted on treating the matter as simply one of textual interpretation. He noted that the Constitution gave the federal courts jurisdiction over controversies "between a state and citizens of another state." A plain reading of the text led to the inescapable conclusion that the suit was cognizable. If the Framers had intended to include exceptions to the suability of states, Cushing said, they would have included such a provision in the constitutional text. Moreover, Cushing noted, the Constitution allowed foreign nations to be sued in federal courts. Clearly, the Constitution intended to abrogate the principle of sovereign immunity, otherwise, one would have to conclude, rather improbably, that "we may touch foreign sovereigns but not our own" (Gerber, 110).

Cushing's opinion in *Ware v. Hylton* (1796) took a similar tack. *Ware* involved the constitutionality of a Virginia statute that "sequestered" debts owed to British citizens arising before the Revolution. On its face, the statute conflicted with the terms of the Treaty of Paris, which provided that British citizens would meet with "no lawful impediment" to the recovery of the value of their debts. The specific question before the Supreme Court was whether ratification of the Constitution, which contained a provision making treaties the "law of the land," had the effect of annulling the Virginia statute. As he had in *Chisholm*, Cushing decided the case on the basis of a strict reading of the Constitution and the text of the treaty. He began by noting that the Constitution made treaties with foreign powers superior to the laws of the states, and thus, the "plain and obvious" meaning of the treaty of peace was to "nullify ab initio" any law that had the effect of preventing a creditor from obtaining payment on debts owed before the Revolution.

Cushing made other contributions to constitutional theory as well. Among the most important was his efforts to strengthen the Court's power of judicial review. While many constitutional theorists trace the origins of judicial review to John Marshall's opinion in *Marbury v. Madison* (1803), it appears that in at least two cases, William Cushing helped lay the groundwork for Marshall's later assertions. The first of these was *Hayburn's Case* (1792), which came before Chief Justice Jay, Justice Cushing, and District Judge William Duane at the spring 1792 New York circuit court. Although the judges upheld the federal statute at issue, they nevertheless recognized the power of federal courts to declare acts of Congress unconstitutional. Similarly, in *Cooper v. Telfair* (1800), a case that came before the full Supreme Court, challenging the constitutionality of a Georgia statute, Cushing declared that the Supreme Court had "the same[] power that a court of Georgia would possess[] to declare a law void" (Gerber, 113–14).

In addition to his normal duties as an associate justice, Cushing also served as acting chief justice during John Jay's mission to England in 1794 and 1795. Upon Jay's resignation as chief justice and the Senate's failure to confirm John Rutledge's nomination to that post, President Washington nominated Cushing to serve as chief justice on January 26, 1796. The Senate confirmed Cushing's appointment the following day. In the event, however, Cushing declined to serve as chief justice. In a letter to Washington on February 2, 1796, Cushing complained that his declining health made it impossible for him to assume the chief justice's duties on a permanent basis, and he returned the commission to Washington. Cushing's claims of ill health did not prevent him from serving a total of twenty-four years on the Supreme Court. He died on September 13, 1810, the last of George Washington's original nominees to leave the bench.

### Robert H. Harrison (1789)

Robert Hanson Harrison may arguably be the least known of George Washington's nominees to the federal bench. Born in Charles County, Maryland, in 1745, Harrison's father, Richard, was a member of the local gentry and a justice of the peace. His mother, Dorothy Hanson Harrison, was a member of one of Maryland's most prominent families. The details of Harrison's upbringing and education are largely a mystery, although it is clear that sometime before August 1765, Harrison moved to Fairfax County, Virginia, where it is believed that he had several relatives.

By 1768, Harrison had become a prominent member of the local bar. In the early 1770s, he joined Fairfax County neighbors George Washington and George Mason in pushing for greater rights for the American colonies. Harrison served as the clerk of a meeting presided over by Washington in Alexandria in 1774, which resulted in the drafting of the Virginia Resolves. Harrison later joined the Alexandria militia, and was subsequently commissioned a lieutenant in the Third Virginia Regiment. On November 6, 1775, Washington asked Harrison to serve as one of his aides-de-camp, another of whom was Alexander Hamilton. During the war, Harrison served as Washington's military secretary and handled negotiations for prisoner exchanges with the British army.

Harrison returned to Maryland after the Revolution and accepted appointment as chief judge of the Maryland General Court and served in this capacity from 1781 until 1790. Harrison was obviously considered a skilled jurist, for over the years he was repeatedly called upon to serve in a variety of judicial and quasi-judicial roles, most of which he turned down. For example, in 1785, he declined an appointment to serve on a special commission created by Congress to resolve a dispute between Massachusetts and New York over title to western lands. In October 1789, Harrison refused appointment to serve as Maryland's chancellor. In the interim, he also declined to serve as a member Maryland's delegation to Congress. While little is known about the precise reasons for his refusal to take up these posts, it appears that Harrison was reluctant to spend too much time away from his family and farm.

On September 24, 1789, President Washington made Robert Harrison one of his original nominees to the Supreme Court. Unfortunately for Washington, it does not appear that he made inquiries as to whether Harrison would accept the post before submitting the nomination to the Senate. Washington enclosed a personal note with Harrison's commission urging his old aide to accept the appointment. One month later, however, Harrison wrote Washington a letter declining the position and returning the commission. Harrison offered two reasons to justify his refusal. First, he expressed disappointment with the structure of the Supreme Court under the terms of the first Judiciary Act. He noted that the duties required of the justices would be "extremely difficult and burdensome to perform." Harrison complained that the requirements of riding circuit would be difficult for those who lived at the seat of government, but for those who did not, and wanted to return home at the end of each term, circuit riding would be next to impossible. Perhaps more important to Harrison was the realization that the duties required of a Supreme Court justice would interfere with certain family obligations, foremost among them the obligation to care for his recently deceased brother's children.

At first, Washington refused to take no for an answer. He admitted that the duties of Supreme Court justices under the current scheme would indeed be onerous but suggested that Congress was in the process of considering amendments that would permit Harrison "to pay as much attention to your private affairs as your present situation does." Washington enclosed the original commission and urged Harrison to take more time to investigate for himself the possibility that changes in the judiciary would be forthcoming. Washington's letter to Harrison was followed a few days later by one from his old friend Alexander Hamilton, praying that Harrison reconsider his refusal. "If it is possible," Hamilton wrote, "give yourself to us. We want men like you. They are rare in all times."

Apparently, Harrison was swayed by these entreaties. On January 14, 1790, he set out for New York in hopes of attending the Supreme Court's first session in February. He never made it. On January 21, Harrison wrote Washington explaining that he had gotten as far as Bladensburg, Maryland, before he was taken ill. He decided to return to his home, where he died three months later.

## John Blair, Jr.

John Blair, Jr., was born in Williamsburg in 1732, to one of the first families of Virginia. His great uncle, James Blair, was a member of the Provincial Council for over fifty years and the founding president of the College of William and Mary. His father, John Blair, Sr., was a member of the council for twenty-five years and was four times an acting governor of the colony (Holt, 156). The younger Blair graduated from William and Mary in 1754, and moved to England to study law at the Middle Temple.

Soon after being called to the bar in 1757, Blair returned to his native Virginia, where he became active in colonial politics. In 1765, he was elected a member of the House of Burgesses to represent the College of William and Mary. While there, Blair joined other conservatives in opposing Patrick Henry's Stamp Act Resolutions, arguing that they were far too radical and provocative. In time, however, Blair's views changed. After the dissolution of the House by Virginia's governor in 1769, Blair helped draft the Virginia nonimportation agreement. At the fifth Virginia Convention held in May 1776, Blair served on a committee charged with drafting a declaration of rights and a new frame of government for the commonwealth. After ratification of the Virginia Constitution, Blair became a member of the Governor's Council.

Blair's judicial career began in January 1776, when the Virginia Convention named him as one of the judges of the state's admiralty court. After the legislature reorganized the judiciary the following year, Blair was appointed one of five judges of the General Court. Two years later, he became chief justice of that court, and the following year became chancellor of Virginia's High Court of Chancery. His appointment to the latter court meant that Blair sat *ex officio* as a member of the state's highest court, the Court of Appeals. While sitting as a judge of the latter court, Blair participated in *Commonwealth v. Caton* (1784), a case that may be rightfully regarded as a milestone in the development of the doctrine of judicial review (Holt, 159–61).

Blair was a delegate to the Constitutional Convention in Philadelphia, where he supported the creation of a stronger national government. There is no record of John Blair having made any speech on the floor of the Convention, although it appears that he opposed several of James Madison's ideas while in committee (Holt, 162). After affixing his signature to the new Constitution, Blair returned to Virginia and was elected a delegate from York County to that state's ratifying convention. Here again, however, it appears that Blair did not take a very active role in the convention debates. Instead, it seems Blair's activities in the cause of ratification "must have been done, in the tradition of gentry politics, in the halls, in church and at the dinner table" (Holt, 162).

After ratification of the Constitution in 1789, President Washington nominated John Blair to serve on the U.S. Supreme Court. As a member of the Court, Blair's opinions reflected a cautious brand of federalism. Convinced that the new federal system of government offered the best hope for the future of the republic, Blair sought to use the authority of the Court to defend the powers of the central government. At the same time, however, he recognized the necessity of treading carefully so as not to provoke antifederalist elements in the states. Throughout the decade, Blair and the other justices used their grand jury charges to trumpet the power and goodness of the federal government. In their actual opinions, however, those same justices often hesitated to push too hard, fearing that widespread opposition from the states would cause the entire federal edifice to collapse.

Shortly after the Supreme Court opened for business, Blair was assigned to ride the southern circuit. Among the most vexing problem facing the judges in the first few years was what to do about the British debt cases, which had languished on state court dockets for years, because state judges repeatedly refused to schedule trials on the claims. Many Virginians, in particular, believed that Britain's conduct during the war obviated the need for American debtors to repay prewar debts. British troops were accused of having taken slaves in large numbers from Virginia's planters without compensation and wantonly destroying plantations and property without purpose. In addition, the failure of the British to evacuate the forts on the western frontier remained a continuing sore point, especially since many Americans believed that British army officers in the west were inciting the Indians to attack settlers on the frontier.

The fear that the new federal courts would take jurisdiction over the long-stalled British debts cases was one reason that many antifederalists opposed giving the courts the power to hear diversity and alienage cases. These fears were quickly realized when the new courts opened for business in the spring of 1790. Almost immediately, British creditors flooded the courts with claims for prewar debt, exciting a great deal of consternation on the part of debtors who had thus far been able to avoid having to pay their creditors. The controversy surrounding the British debt cases was no doubt a factor in the Supreme Court's decision to assign Justice Blair, a prominent Virginian, to preside over the first few sessions of Southern circuit.

The first case raising the debt question, *Jones v. Walker*, came before the Virginia circuit court in the fall of 1791. *Jones* itself was chosen as a test case because it raised all the important issues arising from the debt controversy. Both debtors and creditors eagerly anticipated the circuit court's disposition of the case, for it was thought that a decision one way or the other would finally put an end to a controversy that had raged for almost a decade. The courtroom was packed when the litigants appeared for argument on November 24, 1791. Appearing on behalf of the debtors was none other than Patrick Henry, the great revolutionary orator. His defense of the debtors' position captivated the audience for almost three full days. Indeed, so many prominent members of the Virginia establishment attended the session that the general assembly itself shut down for lack of a quorum (Holt, 170). But, whether Henry's oration was ultimately persuasive is hard to tell. Unfortunately, Justice Blair left the bench the day before the trial began to attend the funeral of his son. In his absence, Justice Thomas Johnson of Maryland, and District Judge Cyrus Griffin of Virginia, finally refused to rule, and ordered the case to be retried next term. Creditor interests were outraged.

The inability of one or more judges to attend subsequent sessions of the Virginia circuit court prevented a rehearing of *Jones v. Walker* until the spring of 1793. The death of the plaintiff resulted in a substitution of parties so that the case continued under a new name, *Ware v. Hylton*. The primary issue before the court was the whether Virginia's 1777 sequestration law violated that part of the peace treaty between Britain and the United States that provided that British subjects should meet with "no lawful impediment" to the repayment of their debts. The sequestration act was a wartime measure designed to deprive Britain of hard currency with which to fight the war. The law allowed Virginia debtors to discharge debts owed to British subjects by paying the balance owed to the state treasurer in depreciated paper currency. In *Ware*, British creditors contended that the sequestration act conflicted with the treaty provisions and thus could not act as a bar to repayment of prewar debts. The Virginia circuit court originally held that the sequestration act was a valid bar to Ware's claim. On appeal, however, the Supreme Court reversed, opening the way for the backlog of British debt cases to proceed in the circuit court.

As a result, the next two sessions of the Virginia circuit court were almost entirely devoted to reducing the backlog of debt cases. Justice Blair sat patiently through weeks of jury trials. Blair's service in this regard was significant because his presence on the circuit court bench apparently lessened the backlash that might have accompanied the reopening of the courts to cases, which had tremendous political and economic consequences. As a Virginian, Blair was able to shepherd the debt cases through the docket without provoking widespread hostility to the court.

Blair's "cautious federalism" was evidenced in a several other cases in the circuit courts. The first of these, *Penhallow v. Doane*, arose while Blair was presiding over the New Hampshire circuit court in the fall of 1793. The case arose after a ship owned by Elisha Doane was seized in 1775 by a New Hampshire privateer commanded by John Pennhallow. Doane claimed that the vessel was American-owned, but a New Hampshire jury twice declared the ship a lawful prize. Doane appealed to the congressional Court of Appeals in Cases of Capture, which reversed the state court decree. New Hampshire refused to honor the reversal, and Congress took no steps to obtain compliance from the state. Therefore, the matter remained until the new federal courts were established.

In 1789, Doane filed suit in the New Hampshire circuit court seeking enforcement of the congressional court's order. Penhallow argued that the federal court did not have power to give effect to the decrees of the congressional court. Justice Blair held that Congress had plenary power over admiralty matters, which was inherent in its power to wage war. Blair then held that the congressional court's admiralty power was transferred to the newly created federal courts, thus giving them the power to put the former court's decrees into effect. The decision in *Penhallow* was a ringing affirmation of federal power. In upholding the broad scope of the federal courts' inherent admiralty jurisdiction, Blair succeeded in protecting the courts' power in an area of jurisdiction of significant importance to the nation's commercial development.

Blair's willingness to defend federal power was made even more explicit in his opinion in *Chisholm v. Georgia*. As noted earlier, *Chisholm* involved an attempt by a citizen of South Carolina to sue the State of Georgia in an action for debt. Georgia refused to appear in the case, claiming the right of sovereign immunity. Justice Blair joined with Chief Justice Jay and Justices Cushing and Wilson in upholding the federal courts' power to hear Chisholm's suit. Unlike Jay and Wilson, both of whom wrote rather elaborate treatises on the relationship between the states and the national government, Justice Blair adopted a rather straightforward approach to the problem. He began by rejecting the idea advanced by some that the Constitution permitted federal jurisdiction only when states were plaintiffs. This idea stemmed from the wording of Article III, which provided that the judicial power would extend to controversies "between a State and Citizens of another State." For Blair, however, such a reading made little sense. "A dispute between A. and B.," he said, "is surely a dispute between B. and A." Moreover, Blair noted, Article III's grant of jurisdiction over "Controversies between two or more States" and between "a State and foreign States" was a clear indication that states could be made defendants without their consent.

Justice Blair's position in *Chisholm*, like his opinion in *Penhallow*, demonstrates his concern that the states were not completely sovereign. On the contrary, he believed that they had to be subordinate to federal power; otherwise the nation would be in danger of splintering. Blair was thus unique among the southerners on the first Supreme Court in consistently defending federal power against the centrifugal forces of states' rights.

Yet, while it is clear that he could be counted on to defend the powers of the national government against encroachment by the states, Blair also showed that he was quite prepared to defend the powers of the judiciary against erosion by the other branches of the federal government. In 1792, Congress passed a statute designed to resolve the numerous claims for pensions made by veterans of the Revolution. The act required a person claiming a pension to file an application with the circuit court of the district in which he resided. Thereafter, the judges of the circuit court were to examine the claimant and prepare a list recommending or denying the claim, which was to be forwarded to the Secretary of War for final approval.

The justices were concerned about the structure of the Pension Act. By and large, they believed that the act was unconstitutional to the extent it permitted an executive branch official to review the decisions of a federal court. As a result, when the Pennsylvania circuit court met in Philadelphia in the spring of 1792, Justice Blair joined Justice Wilson and District Judge Richard Peters in refusing to hear any pension claims. On April 18, 1792, the judges wrote a letter to President Washington expressing the view that the circuit court could not proceed in the manner directed by the act because to do so would mean that its judgments might "have been revised and controlled by the legislature, and by an officer in the executive department." Such revision, they declared, would be "radically inconsistent with the independence of that judicial power which is vested in the courts" alone.

The Pennsylvania circuit court's opinion provoked a firestorm of controversy when made public. Federalist members of Congress were particularly outraged. Massachusetts congressman Fisher Ames expressed the opinion of many when he complained that the judges had given aid and comfort to the enemies of the federal government. "At best," Ames wrote, "our business is all up hill, and with the aid of our law courts the authority of Congress is barely adequate to keep the machine moving; but when [the federal courts] condemn the law as invalid, they embolden the State and their courts to make many claims of power, which otherwise they would not have thought of." In the end, the Pension Act came before the Supreme Court in *Hayburn's Case* (1792). Before the matter could be finally resolved, however, Congress resolved to amend the act rather than face the prospect of having it struck down. The opinion of the Pennsylvania circuit court in the pension cases is significant because it was the first time the members of the Supreme Court took upon themselves to question the constitutional validity of an Act of Congress. While many scholars point to *Marbury v. Madison* (1803) as the source of the federal courts' power of judicial review, it is clear that the groundwork for Chief Justice Marshall's opinion in *Marbury* was first laid in the Pennsylvania circuit court's letter to George Washington.

Justice Blair suffered frequent bouts of illness while on the Court. In the spring of 1795, he was forced to leave the southern circuit and missed the August 1795 term of the Supreme Court. Finally, on October 25, 1795, he wrote President Washington and resigned his commission. He retired to his home in Williamsburg and died on August 31, 1800.

## James Wilson

James Wilson was born in Scotland in 1742, the eldest son of a small farmer. Unlike the rest of Washington's original appointees, Wilson's family was neither prominent nor wealthy. Wilson's parents wanted him to become a minister and so worked hard to gather sufficient funds to send him to the local parish school, where he studied Greek, Latin, mathematics, and rhetoric. Upon graduation, he earned a scholarship to the University of St. Andrews, and after four years of further study in the classics, Wilson enrolled in St. Mary's College, the school of divinity at St. Andrews (Smith, 3–16).

Wilson never completed his theological education, however. A short time after beginning his religious training, his father died, and as the oldest son, James had to return home to provide for his mother and his six brothers and sisters. On his return, Wilson became a tutor, and supported the family until his younger brothers were able to take over the farm. In the spring of 1765, James moved to Edinburgh, where he took up bookkeeping and accounting, although it was not long before he realized that the key to his future lay in America. Thus, by the autumn of 1765, James Wilson sailed for Philadelphia to seek his fortune (Smith, 17–21).

Wilson's university education allowed him to secure an appointment as a tutor at the College of Philadelphia, now the University of Pennsylvania. In time, however, he decided that the study of law offered greater advantages, and so with some help from a cousin, he began to read law in John Dickinson's office in Philadelphia in 1766

(Smith, 21–24). A year later, Wilson left Philadelphia to open his own law practice in Reading, the seat of Berks County. Soon thereafter, Wilson was admitted to the bar of neighboring Lancaster County, and in 1769, he was admitted to the bar of the Supreme Court of Pennsylvania (Smith, 29–42).

In the fall of 1770, Wilson decided to move his office to Carlisle, in Cumberland County, the most important town in what was then western Pennsylvania. His practice thrived and he soon became involved in local politics. In July 1774, Wilson was appointed head of the Carlisle Committee of Correspondence and was elected a delegate to the provincial convention at Philadelphia. That same year, he published a treatise entitled, *Considerations on the Nature and Extent of the Legislative Authority of the British Parliament*, in which he asserted that Parliament had no right to exercise legislative authority over the king's North American colonies. Wilson's treatise catapulted him to fame. On May 6, 1775, he was elected a delegate to the Second Continental Congress, and, after a long struggle within the Pennsylvania delegation, voted for independence (Smith, 51–61). Wilson's tenure in Congress came to an end after he vigorously, but unsuccessfully, opposed ratification of Pennsylvania's radical 1776 constitution. After one or two false starts, the state legislature succeeded in punishing Wilson for his opposition by recalling him from Congress the following year (Marcus, 46).

Sensing that his political and business interests would prosper more in Philadelphia, Wilson moved his practice to that city in the summer of 1778. During the next several years, he became involved in a number of speculative commercial ventures. In 1780, along with Robert Morris and Thomas Willing, Wilson helped create the Bank of Pennsylvania. Although the bank failed the following year, Wilson and Morris convinced Congress to establish a national bank, the Bank of North America (Marcus, 46). Wilson was also involved in land speculation on a grand scale. He borrowed heavily from the Bank of North America and used the proceeds to obtain large tracts of land on the western frontier, which he then divided and hoped to resell to settlers at a profit. Unfortunately for Wilson—and many others similarly engaged—these land sales were on credit, with the result that those to whom Wilson sold the land often either failed or refused to pay while other tracts remained unsold.

Wilson's land speculation served as the impetus for an intense desire to foster the development of the interior. In 1782, Pennsylvania's Supreme Executive Council appointed Wilson to serve on a committee to resolve conflicting claims between Pennsylvania and Connecticut over lands in the western part of the state. The following year, the Pennsylvania assembly reappointed Wilson to Congress. For the next several years, therefore, Wilson used his position in Congress to argue for a stronger national government, one that would be capable of tightening the bonds between the states, more effectively manage trade, and provide for the development of the western frontier (Smith, 187–214). In 1787, the Pennsylvania assembly appointed Wilson one of the state's delegates to the Constitutional Convention. While there, he participated in every one of the most important debates, and is notable for speaking more times than any other member except Governor Morris. Indeed, it has been asserted that Wilson's influence in the Convention was second only to that of James Madison (Hall, 129).

James Wilson went to the Convention firmly convinced of the need to establish a stronger central government. He believed that the national government ought to be supreme, and that the state power should be severely restricted. At the same time, however, Wilson was "the most democratic member of the Convention," consistently arguing that every aspect of government be founded on the principle of popular sovereignty. As a result, from the outset of the Convention, Wilson advocated the broadest possible franchise, including the direct, popular election of both houses of the national legislature as well as the national executive (Hall, 130). He also opposed property qualifications on voters and opposed limits on the admission of new states.

Although firmly convinced of the need to ensure rule by the people, Wilson was well aware of the need to provide some mechanism to restrain popular passion. He, therefore, supported the Constitution's system of checks and balances as a means of preventing both the tyranny of the majority as well as of the minority (Hall, 130). As one part of this system of checks and balances, Wilson urged the creation of an extensive national judiciary composed of both a supreme court and a number of lower federal courts. Wilson also believed that the Supreme Court ought to have the power of judicial review. In his view, the members of the court would be in the best position to decide on the constitutionality of legislative acts because they would be both well trained in legal complexities and insulated from popular passions (Holt, 131). Wilson avoided the counter-majoritarian implications of this theory by asserting that the Court would use its power sparingly, and then only to strike down patently unconstitutional laws. Even then, however, Wilson recognized that judicial review would only be a temporary deterrent, for a majority determined to pass an unjust law would not be constrained by judicial pronouncements. For Wilson, therefore, the purpose of judicial review was to restrain the execution of unconstitutional laws until the people could be made to recognize them as such (Hall, 132).

After the Convention finished its work, Wilson was elected a member of the Pennsylvania ratifying convention, where he served as the primary advocate for ratification. The following year, he led the effort to revise the radical Pennsylvania constitution of 1776 and was largely responsible for the drafting of a new one along the lines of the federal model (Marcus, 47).

James Wilson made no secret of his desire to be appointed chief justice of the United States. In the spring of 1789, he wrote President Washington suggesting that he might be an appropriate choice for chief justice. Washington replied rather coolly, however, declaring his intention to enter upon his office "without the constraint of a single engagement." His eventual nomination as an associate justice must, therefore, have come as something of a disappointment (Marcus, 47).

In the early years of his tenure, Wilson was a dedicated jurist, attending every session of the Supreme Court and performing his circuit riding duties with great efficiency. At the same time, Wilson undertook other activities as well. In 1790, he was appointed the first professor of law at the College of Philadelphia, and a series of lectures he delivered during the winters of 1790 and 1791 later proved to be an important milestone in American legal thought, although they were not published in his lifetime.

In time, however, Wilson's declining financial affairs began to take their toll. By late 1796, Wilson was forced to devote ever-larger amounts of time to keeping his creditors at bay. He missed several sittings of the circuit court in order to return to Philadelphia to attend to personal business. The pressures of impending financial collapse also began to affect his health. (McCloskey, 94–5). By the spring of 1797, Wilson was forced to flee Philadelphia for Bethlehem, Pennsylvania, to avoid being arrested for debt. He moved on to Burlington, New Jersey, but was arrested upon his arrival. Although Wilson was able to secure his release from jail after payment of the debt in question, he was soon forced to run south. Unfortunately, creditors awaited him there as well. Justice Wilson was finally arrested in North Carolina on a claim of debt owing to former Senator Pierce Butler in the amount of $197,000 (Marcus, 48). Wilson's son, Bird, was able to secure his father's release, but the end was near. Talk of impeachment began to be heard in Philadelphia, and Wilson himself was forced to live in hiding in a tavern. Finally, in July 1798, he contracted malaria and suffered a stroke a few weeks later. James Wilson died on August 21, 1798 (Smith, 383–87). He was buried in North Carolina because his family was too poor to have the body returned to Philadelphia.

## James Iredell (1789)

James Iredell was born in England on October 5, 1751, the son of an impoverished Bristol merchant. Although little is known about his schooling, Iredell appears to have been reasonably well educated, in spite of his family's limited resources. His prospects were improved when a wealthy cousin purchased a position in the customs service for young James. At the age of seventeen, therefore, James Iredell set sail for North Carolina to assume the post of comptroller of the customs. The lot of a customs officer was not a happy one in America at this time. By 1768, colonial hostility toward the British navigation acts was approaching fever pitch. American mobs routinely attacked customs officials and interfered with their work. Iredell was responsible for collecting customs duties at Port Roanoke in Edenton, North Carolina. As it happens, however, Iredell seems to have escaped much of the hostility directed at most colonial customs officials. This is probably because his cousin, Henry E. McCulloh, was one of the largest landowners in the colony. (Marcus, 60).

Once in North Carolina, Iredell became friendly with Samuel Johnson, a leading figure in the colony's political affairs. In time, Iredell began to read law in Johnson's chambers. He was admitted to practice before the inferior courts of North Carolina in 1770, and the following year admitted to the Superior Court. From there, Iredell's career began to take off. In 1774, he was made collector of customs for Edenton, as well as deputy king's attorney for Hertford, Perquimans, and Tyrrell Counties.

Iredell's official positions did not prevent him from adopting the colonists' cause in the dispute with Great Britain. In 1774, he wrote an essay entitled, *To the Inhabitants of Great Britain*, in which he argued that Parliament had no jurisdiction over the colonies because the colonies belonged to the Crown alone. Iredell advocated a commonwealth system, in which each part of the British Empire would be united under one monarch with its own, independent legislature. Iredell was not a radical, however. Although he sided with the colonists, he did so only reluctantly. After all, he was English by birth, and he had a great many friends and family at home. In addition, Iredell knew that his support for the colonies would result in the loss of an inheritance from a rich uncle in Jamaica. Nonetheless, by July 1776, Iredell had closed up his customs office and publicly supported independence (Marcus, 62).

In 1776, the North Carolina provincial congress appointed Iredell to a committee to revise the state's laws. The following year, he was elected one of three judges of the North Carolina Superior Court, although he resigned this post after serving a mere six months because he detested the obligation to ride circuit. He remained in private life for only a year, however, for in 1779, Iredell was appointed the state's attorney general, and served in that office until 1781, when he returned to private practice (Marcus, 62). Shortly thereafter, Iredell became involved in a number of high profile legal cases, the most notable of which was *Bayard v. Singleton* (1787), which presented the question of whether judges had the power to strike down acts of the legislature that were not in conformity with the written constitution. Iredell was a firm believer in the power of a written constitution and the power of judicial review. In 1783, he argued that judges must have fixed salaries while in office to ensure that they would be independent. This independence would allow them to serve as "guardians and protectors" of the Constitution, which he asserted was superior to ordinary legislation.

In 1788, Iredell was elected to serve in the North Carolina ratifying convention, held at Hillsborough. He was a vocal advocate for ratification and authored an important refutation of George Mason's *Objections to the Constitution* (1787). In spite of Iredell's efforts, the North Carolina convention refused to ratify primarily because the Philadelphia Convention had not included a Bill of Rights in the Constitution. As a result, North Carolina remained outside the union when the new government was formed in the spring of 1789. The state was now in a precarious position, for with respect to the other states, North Carolina was a foreign country. Iredell thus devoted his efforts to securing ratification. He spent the next several months engaged in a vigorous public relations campaign, arranging for the publication of the debates of the Hillsborough convention and authoring newspaper articles in support of ratification. His efforts eventually paid off when North Carolina's second convention, held at Fayetteville, finally ratified the Constitution on November 21, 1789.

Iredell's efforts on behalf of ratification brought him national prominence. Upon the resignation of Robert H. Harrison, President Washington nominated Iredell to serve as associate justice on February 8, 1790. At thirty-eight, Iredell was the youngest of the justices; but he was to serve for only ten years. He died at his home in Edenton on October 20, 1799.

## *Thomas Johnson (1791)*

Thomas Johnson was born in Calvert County, Maryland, on November 4, 1732. Johnson's father, also named Thomas, was a member of the minor gentry, and had served for some years in the Lower House of Assembly. Johnson received his education at home, but eventually found his way to Annapolis, where he secured a position as a scrivener in the office of the clerk of the Maryland Provincial Court. In time, Johnson began to read law in the offices of Stephen Bordley, one of Maryland's leading lawyers. He was admitted to the bar of the Annapolis Mayor's Court in 1756, and the Maryland Provincial Court in 1759. Three years later, Johnson was elected to the Lower House of Assembly where he served for over twelve years.

While in the assembly, Johnson became a strong advocate for the rights of the American colonies. In 1774, he was elected to the Annapolis Committee of Correspondence and then to the Continental Congress. In Congress, Johnson became friendly with John Adams, but did not immediately support independence from England. In time, however, Johnson and the Maryland delegation gradually embraced the calls for independence from England. Johnson did not remain in the Congress long, however. Instead, he left Congress a few weeks before the Declaration of Independence was adopted to raise money and munitions to support Washington's army. In late 1776, Johnson was appointed commander of the Maryland militia, and a few months later, he and the militia marched to New Jersey to assist General Washington. On arriving there in February 1777, however, Johnson found that he had been elected governor of Maryland, and thus immediately hurried back to Annapolis to assume his new office. He served two terms as governor and, when unable to run for the third term, was elected to the House of Delegates.

After the war, Johnson retired from public life. He spent the years between 1782 and 1786 engaged in a variety of projects designed to spur commercial development in his native state. He later served on a committee charged with preparing legislation to create a state court of admiralty, and was also one of the judges responsible for resolving a land dispute between New York and Massachusetts. In 1785, Johnson joined with George Washington and others to establish the Potomac Company, a land development company interested in encouraging navigation along the Potomac River.

Johnson returned to public service in 1786, when he was again elected a member of the House of Delegates. Although he did not serve in the Philadelphia Convention, Johnson was a tireless advocate for adoption of the new Constitution as a member of the Maryland ratifying convention. President Washington sought to appoint Johnson to a federal office. Washington was concerned, however, that Johnson would not accept a post that would require him to leave Maryland. Consequently, on September 24, 1789, Washington nominated Johnson to be the district judge for the district of Maryland, and the Senate confirmed the appointment two days later, although Johnson declined the office.

Upon John Rutledge's resignation from the Supreme Court in 1791, Washington approached Johnson again inquiring whether he would consent to serve in Rutledge's place. This time, Johnson's reply was somewhat equivocal. Rather than accept the post outright, Johnson inquired as to whether he would have to ride the southern circuit, the most arduous of the three circuits. If so, he informed Washington, he would have to decline the office. Washington consulted the remaining justices one night while at dinner, and they agreed the Johnson might be excused from having to ride the southern circuit, at least in the first instance. As a result, Washington issued a temporary commission to Johnson on August 5, 1791, thus making Thomas Johnson the first recess appointment in Supreme Court history. The Senate confirmed Johnson's appointment on November 7, 1791.

In any event, Johnson did find his duties too difficult, and after little more than a year on the Court, he resigned his commission. In a letter to Washington, Johnson wrote Washington that he accepted appointment to the Supreme Court on the expectation that Congress would make changes in the justices' circuit riding duties. To Johnson, the Judiciary Act appeared to be "an Essay" and he had "no Doubt but that there would have been an Alteration as soon as the Attention of Congress could be again drawn to the Subject." However, Congress' continued inaction made it impossible for him to continue. Consequently, Johnson wrote Washington that "I cannot resolve to spend six Months in the Year of the few I may have left from my Family, on Roads at Taverns chiefly and often in Situations where the most moderate Desires are disappointed: My Time of Life[,] Temper and other Circumstances forbid it."

After he left the Court, Washington appointed Johnson to serve as a commissioner of the new capital city, but he declined subsequent appointments as Secretary of State in 1795, and as chief judge of the newly created circuit court for the District of Columbia in 1801. He died at his home in Frederick, Maryland, on October 26, 1819.

## William Paterson (1793)

William Paterson was born in County Antrim, Ireland, on December 24, 1745. At the time of his birth, Paterson's parents had only recently emigrated to Ireland from Scotland. They did not remain there long, for in 1747, the Paterson family moved to America, arriving first in New Castle, Delaware. The Patersons moved about for some time, but finally settled in Princeton, New Jersey, where William's father, Richard, hoped to establish a tin plate manufactory. This venture was not a success, however, and in the end, Richard set up a grocery store (Wood, 1–3).

William began his education at a local grammar school and entered Princeton University in 1759, at the age of thirteen. After graduating in 1763, he began to read law in the office of Richard Stockton, a prominent Princeton lawyer. He also worked part time in his father's grocery store (O'Connor, 8–15). In the beginning, Paterson found his legal education to be rather boring, and likened it to "being entangled in the cobwebs of antiquity." In time, however, his views changed, and he excelled in his studies. Paterson was admitted to the New Jersey bar in 1768, and the following year, he moved to the nearby village of New Bromley to open his own law practice (Wood, 12–16). A short time later, he was appointed a provincial surrogate, an office that allowed him to represent the state in the administration of decedents' estates, but provided him with only a modest income. In time, however, Paterson became dissatisfied with life in New Bromley and moved to Raritan, in Somerset County, where he joined his brother in establishing a general store (O'Connor 33–34; Wood, 16–17).

Although Paterson continued to practice law in Raritan, his caseload was rather small. Between 1769 and 1774, he averaged only five cases per year. However, Paterson's difficulties in setting up a law practice do not appear to be the result of incompetence. On the contrary, there is every indication that he was an accomplished and talented lawyer. Instead, the problem, as one biographer noted, was that Paterson "chose to sit back where the action wasn't and wait for clients and status to seek him out" (O'Connor, 43). All this changed, however, with the outbreak of hostilities between England and her American colonies.

A month after Lexington and Concord, the freeholders of Somerset County elected William Paterson to serve in New Jersey's provincial congress. He soon became that body's secretary and in 1776, he was appointed the state's attorney general (O'Connor, 68–89). In 1780, Paterson was elected to serve in the Continental Congress, but he declined the position on the grounds that his duties as attorney general would not allow him to attend.

Paterson's law practice soon kept pace with his growing prominence. Between 1775 and 1782, his caseload increased dramatically. Clients flocked to Paterson's office both because of his position as attorney general and because a number of prominent loyalist attorneys fled the province (O'Connor, 108–109). By 1787, Paterson was firmly established as a leader of the New Jersey bar, with an income of over £1,000 per year. He also attracted a growing number of eager students willing to read law with him, including Aaron Burr, the future Vice President of the United States, Robert Troup, a future federal district court judge, and Andrew Kirkpatrick, a future chief justice of the New Jersey Supreme Court (O'Connor, 118–121).

In 1787, the New Jersey legislature appointed Paterson to serve as a delegate to the Constitutional Convention in Philadelphia. During the course of the Convention, the delegates became bogged down over a dispute between the large and small states over how seats in the national legislature were to be apportioned. Led by William Paterson, small states, such as New Jersey, Delaware, and Connecticut, feared that a Congress whose members were apportioned on the basis of population would be dominated by the larger states, such as Virginia or Pennsylvania. Under such an arrangement, the small states feared that the large states would dominate the legislative agenda and ignore the small states' concerns. On July 15, therefore, William Paterson introduced what has since become known as the "New Jersey Plan." This plan attempted to restrain the large states' power by retaining the current system of voting in Congress, wherein each state had one vote. Although Paterson's plan was not adopted, the principle of equal representation for the states was eventually incorporated into the Constitution in the apportionment of representation in the Senate (Rossiter, 186–89).

Paterson left the Convention in mid-July, but not because he was unhappy with the final draft of the document. Rather, the press of business called him home to New Jersey. Paterson supported ratification of the new Constitution and was elected one of New Jersey's first U.S. Senators. Upon his arrival in the Senate, Paterson was appointed to the judiciary committee, which was then engaged in drafting a bill establishing the federal courts. Although Connecticut's Oliver Ellsworth is generally—and rightly—assumed to have been the primary architect of the judiciary bill, it is clear that William Paterson played an important part in the bill's construction. Several sections of the judiciary committee's version are believed to have been in his hand, and he was a tireless advocate for its adoption before the full Senate. Shortly after the bill was passed, Paterson resigned his Senate seat when he was elected governor of New Jersey after the death of William Livingston in 1790.

Justice Thomas Johnson's resignation in 1793 prompted President Washington to look for another southerner to fill the vacancy. He considered three Marylanders, a Georgian, and William Paterson of New Jersey. Attorney General Edmund Randolph was assigned to investigate the qualifications of the prospective nominees, and eventually reported the only two deserving of consideration were Paterson and Senator Richard Potts of Maryland. Of the two, Randolph thought Paterson the better qualified and urged Washington to appoint Paterson to the bench. In offering this advice, Randolph was motivated by the desire to ensure that only men of the highest caliber and reputation be appointed to the nation's highest court. A few weeks earlier, the Attorney General had argued the case of *Chisholm v. Georgia* (1793), which involved the question of whether the states were able to be sued in federal courts without regard to their traditional sovereign immunity. The Court concluded that they were, which generated a great deal of controversy, especially in the south. In recommending Paterson, Randolph wrote, "many decisions [of the Court] must be very grating to the states [and] that the dissatisfaction will be increased by a distrust of the abilities of some of our judges." It was important, therefore, that only the best men be appointed to the Court. Although Washington probably preferred to appoint another Marylander to replace Johnson, he took Randolph's advice, and selected Paterson "notwithstanding his local situation."

Paterson remained on the Court until his death in 1806.

## Samuel Chase (1796)

Samuel Chase was born in Somerset County, Maryland, on April 17, 1741, the son of an Anglican minister. He was educated at home by his father until the age of eighteen, when he began to read law in the offices of two Annapolis lawyers, John Hammond and John Hall. After two years of training, Chase was admitted to the Annapolis Mayor's Court in 1761; and in 1764, he was elected to the Maryland General Assembly, where he soon became a leader of the opposition to the proprietary governor.

Unlike most other members of the early Supreme Court, Samuel Chase was not a reluctant revolutionary. On the contrary, Chase was an early adherent to the cause of independence. As a member of the Sons of Liberty, in 1765, Chase is alleged to have led a mob to the home of Zechariah Hood, an Annapolis man who had obtained a commission to collect the Stamp Act taxes. The mob paraded Hood's effigy about the town before burning it. A few days later, the mob returned and tore down a storehouse on which Hood had been working. Although there is no evidence Chase had any part in the latter incident, the Annapolis aldermen condemned Chase as a "busy restless Incendiary ____ a Ringleader of Mobs ____ a foul mouth'd and inflaming son of Discord and Faction ____ a common Disturber of the public Tranquillity, and a Promoter of the lawless excesses of the multitude." Chase was unbowed, however, and responded that his accusers were a bunch of "despicable Pimps and Tools of Power, emerged from Obscurity and Basking in proprietary Sunshine." The vitriolic response to the aldermen's criticism was characteristic of Chase's public persona. Throughout the course of his public life, he found himself at the center of angry exchanges with government officials and political opponents. This tendency was to cause a great deal of controversy when he eventually took his seat on the Supreme Court.

Chase's reputation as a vigorous opponent of government oppression grew during the Revolution. In 1774, he was elected to the Maryland Committee of Correspondence and the Maryland provincial congress. Later that year, Chase was sent to Philadelphia as a member of Maryland's delegation to the first Continental Congress. While in Congress, Chase acted with some degree of restraint, refusing the radicals' call for a complete break with England. Instead, he worked to keep the colonies within the British Empire, although he did support an economic boycott (Haw, 43–47).

In the spring of 1776, Chase accompanied Benjamin Franklin and Charles Carroll of Carrollton on a mission to Canada designed to secure an alliance with Canada in the fight against England. The mission failed, but, on his return to Philadelphia, Chase discovered that the Maryland legislature had instructed its congressional delegation to oppose independence. Chase left the city for Annapolis where he worked with other patriots to convince the legislature to change its mind. In the end, his efforts were successful, although Chase himself was not able to return to Philadelphia in time to cast his vote on July 2. He did, however, sign the Declaration of Independence on August 2 (Haw, 58–68).

In 1778, Chase's public career came to a crashing halt. In the spring of that year, Congress voted to procure large quantities of flour to supply the troops. Using this "inside" information, Chase began to corner the market in flour. Unfortunately for him, however, the scheme was discovered and made public. Chase was denounced as a war profiteer and widely criticized in newspapers throughout the country. The Maryland legislature responded by refusing to reappoint Chase to another term in Congress, and after fourteen years of public service, Samuel Chase was returned to private life (Haw 105–109). Chase spent the next several years fighting to restore his reputation. Finally, in January 1782, the Maryland House of Delegates voted to dismiss charges that he abused his office for personal gain (Haw, 108–115). His exoneration by the legislature did not put an end to all his troubles, however. During the Revolution, Chase's law practice continued to thrive, but he began to involve himself in a number of speculative business ventures. These soon failed, and Chase found himself sinking rapidly in debt. In 1787, his finances were such that he was forced to petition the Maryland legislature for bankruptcy relief (Haw, 143).

The following year, Chase embarked on a new career, when Governor William Smallwood appointed him to a seat on the newly formed Court of Oyer and Terminer and General Gaol Delivery of Baltimore County. Chase held the seat for only two years. In 1790, he resigned ostensibly on the grounds that a judge's salary did not provide him with an adequate income. In reality, however, Chase believed that his ability to perform his duties had been compromised by a campaign in the press criticizing his judicial abilities and temperament. (Haw, 162–63) This turned out to be but the first of many such episodes in which Samuel Chase antagonized large numbers of political opponents.

Unlike Washington's other appointees, Samuel Chase did not support the Constitution when first proposed. Writing under the pseudonym, "Caution," he attacked the Constitution as a device for enriching the well-connected few to the detriment of the working man. Supporters of the Constitution were outraged by Chase's activities, so much so that one staunch federalist derided him as an "Arch Fiend of Hell" for "playing the Devil in Town [with] his D—d anti nightly meetings" (Marcus, 108). Ratification of the Constitution brought an end to Chase's tirades, and he gradually became a supporter of the new government. His conversion to the cause of federalism was speeded by events occurring after his reappointment to the state court bench in Baltimore County.

In 1791, Governor John Eager Howard appointed Chase to two different judgeships. First, in August, Howard appointed Chase chief judge of the Maryland General Court. In December, Howard appointed Chase chief justice of the Baltimore County criminal court. These appointments were immediately controversial and made Chase an easy target for his political opponents. Matters came to a head when a group of French sympathizers were arrested at Fells Point, in Baltimore. Chase convened the criminal court and jailed the defendants when they refused to post a bond for their good behavior. For this, he was subjected to threats by supporters of the jailed men, but neither the county sheriff nor the town's leading citizens came to his aid. When Chase convened a grand jury to investigate the disturbance at Fells Point, the grand jury did not indict the rioters. Instead, it returned a presentment against Judge Chase for holding two judicial offices at the same time. It issued a second presentment against the governor for having appointed Chase to the two courts. Chase responded by challenging his critics to seek his removal from the legislature (Haw 168–74). The legislature rejected the petitions to remove Chase from office, but Chase's victory was short lived. The following year, the legislature abolished the criminal court entirely, thus eliminating one of Chase's judgeships.

The disturbances in Maryland combined with concerns over the outbreak of the Whiskey Rebellion in Pennsylvania gradually caused Chase to rethink his opposition to the national government. By the spring of 1795, he had become an ardent supporter of the Washington administration, mainly because he believed that only the federal government could be trusted to keep law and order. Chase's conversion allowed his friend, James McHenry, to approach President Washington to obtain a federal appointment for Chase. At first, Washington considered Chase as a candidate for attorney general, but eventually rejected that idea because of concerns about "impurity in his conduct." McHenry's efforts on Chase's behalf were ultimately successful, for on January 26, 1796, Washington nominated Samuel Chase to replace the retiring Justice John Blair.

Chase's fiery personality created even more difficulties for him once he took his seat on the Supreme Court. He quickly gained a reputation as a federalist partisan, delivering grand jury charges that inflamed members of the Republican party and the press. Indeed, Chase's conduct on the bench during the trial of several newspaper editors charged under the Sedition Act eventually led to efforts to impeach him. In January 1803, the House of Representatives formed a committee to review Chase's judicial conduct. Within a short time, the House voted articles of impeachment, and the Senate convened a trial. The most serious allegations against Chase concerned his conduct of during the trials of John Fries and James Callender. The Senate trial lasted almost three months. Chase put up a spirited defense and in the end was acquitted of the charges.

Chase remained on the Court until his death on June 19, 1811.

## Oliver Ellsworth (1796)

Oliver Ellsworth was born in Windsor, Connecticut, on April 29, 1745. Marked for a career in the ministry, Ellsworth began his education in the home of the Reverend Joseph Bellamy, a well-known follower of the great New England preacher, Jonathan Edwards. In 1762, Ellsworth enrolled at Yale to study divinity, but he did not succeed in impressing his teachers with his devotion or piety, for he was expelled from the college two years later. Apparently, Ellsworth was a rather fun-loving character who flouted a number of college rules, including violating curfew, creating a disturbance in the college yard, and participating in a raucous drinking party with his friends (Lettieri, 10–11). Ellsworth made his way to the College of New Jersey (now Princeton), where he seems to have reformed his ways and become a dedicated theological student.

After graduating from Princeton in 1766, Ellsworth returned to Connecticut where he undertook further theological study under the tutelage of the Reverend John Smalley of New Britain. Apparently, the two men did not get along, and Ellsworth moved on after only a year (Lettieri, 11). He eventually gave up his theological education and took up the study of law. He began his legal education in the office of Matthew Griswold, a prominent member of the Connecticut bar, but left after a short time, apparently because he could not afford Griswold's fees. He completed his studies in the office of Jesse Root and was admitted to the Connecticut bar in 1771 (Lettieri, 12–14).

Two years later, Ellsworth entered Connecticut politics and was elected a member of the General Assembly, and the following year, he was appointed a justice of the peace. In April 1775, Ellsworth was appointed a member of the Committee of the Pay Table, an assembly committee charged with overseeing the state's military expenses. The importance of this committee's work brought Ellsworth some prominence and in 1777, he was appointed attorney general for Hartford County. Two years later, Ellsworth was appointed to the Connecticut Committee of Safety and in April 1780, he was elected to the Governor's Council, the state's most powerful political body.

Meanwhile, in late 1777, the General Assembly appointed Ellsworth a member of Connecticut's delegation to Congress. Ellsworth did not immediately set off for Philadelphia, however. Instead, he remained in Hartford attending to personal business (Lettieri, 15–21). As a result, Ellsworth did not arrive in Philadelphia until the fall of 1778, almost a year after he was appointed. While in Congress, Ellsworth served on a number of committees. One of these, the Committee on Appeals in prize cases, was charged with hearing appeals of cases originally heard in the various state admiralty courts. Throughout its existence, the congressional committee repeatedly had difficulty enforcing its decrees. This experience helped convince Ellsworth that some form of national judicial tribunal was needed. As a result, he helped draft a report that proposed the establishment of the Court of Appeals in Cases of Capture (Lettieri, 52–53). Ellsworth left Congress in 1783, and the following year, he became a member of Connecticut's Supreme Court of Errors, and later became a member of the Superior Court.

In 1787, Ellsworth was appointed a delegate to the Constitutional Convention. While in Philadelphia, he was a strong supporter of the rights of the small states in the discussions over the composition of the federal legislature. As time went on, he became increasingly alarmed at the possibility that the Convention might break up because of differences between the large and small states over the problem of representation in the national assembly. As a result, Ellsworth submitted a proposal for a bicameral legislature composed of lower house whose seats would be allocated on the basis of population and an upper house in which the states would have equal representation. This proposal was to form the basis of what has since been called, the "Great Compromise," and which broke the logjam over representation on July 16, 1787 (Rossiter, 186–91). Although he supported the Constitution in its final form, Ellsworth left the Convention before it adjourned in order to attend to judicial business back in Connecticut. He was an ardent defender of the Convention's work during the ratification debates, and in November 1787, he published a series of essays in support of the Constitution under the pseudonym, "A Landholder." He was then elected a member of the Connecticut ratifying convention, where he led the federalist faction. As a result of his efforts, Connecticut became the first New England state to ratify the Constitution on January 9, 1788.

Ellsworth's leadership in the ratification effort led to his election as one of Connecticut's first U.S. Senators. Shortly after his arrival at the seat of government in New York, Ellsworth was appointed to the judiciary committee. As has been noted in Chapter 1, it is clear that Ellsworth was the prime mover in the efforts to establish a national judiciary. His proposals for the creation of a multilayered court system, as well as an extensive federal jurisdiction, served as the model for the judiciary committee's draft of the judiciary bill, and many of Ellsworth's ideas eventually found their way into the final text.

The Senate's rejection of John Rutledge to be chief justice in 1796, forced President Washington to make another nomination. Washington first proposed to elevate associate justice William Cushing. Cushing was nominated and confirmed, but he declined the commission when offered apparently because he felt the administrative burden too onerous. As a result, Washington turned to Ellsworth, the architect of the federal judiciary, to fill the vacancy, and the Senate confirmed Ellsworth's nomination on March 4, 1796.

Ellsworth took office at a time of increasing tension with the two most important European powers. Throughout his tenure, therefore, the Court Ellsworth found himself at the center of the American efforts to avoid being drawn into war with France. In 1799, in one final effort to avoid war with France, President Adams decided to send a peace mission to Paris and chose Oliver Ellsworth to lead the delegation. Ellsworth arrived in Paris in March 1800, and was ultimately successful in helping to negotiate the Treaty of Mortefontaine, which brought an end to the "Quasi-War" with France. Unfortunately, service abroad was injurious to Ellsworth's health. While still in Paris, Ellsworth wrote President Adams on October 16, 1800, and resigned his commission. He returned a few months later and retired to his estate in Windsor, Connecticut, where he died on November 26, 1807.

## John Adams Appointments

The election of 1796 was among the most bitter contests ever fought for the presidency. The eventual winner, Vice President John Adams, took office at a time of great danger for the young republic. Tensions with France were on the rise, and the American economy remained in deep recession. Even Thomas Jefferson, the man Adams defeated for the presidency, expressed some relief at his own defeat. President Washington, he said, was "fortunate to get off just as the bubble is bursting," and that his "departure will mark the moment when the difficulties begin to work." As a result, Jefferson said, "no man will bring out of [the presidency] the reputation which carries him into it" (Ellis, 165–66). In Jefferson's view, John Adams had actually lost the election of 1796.

Jefferson's assessment of the dangers confronting the new president proved to be quite accurate, and Adams' appointments to the Supreme Court reflected these concerns. To a large extent, Adams seems to have continued Washington's practice of appointing only strong federalists to the courts, although he later denied that he had any litmus test for judicial appointments.

### Bushrod Washington (1798)

Bushrod Washington was born on June 5, 1762, in Westmoreland County, Virginia, the son of Augustine Washington, the first president's brother, and Hannah Bushrod Washington. Bushrod's earliest schooling was obtained from a tutor in the home of Richard

Henry Lee. Thereafter, he entered the College of William and Mary at the age of thirteen and graduated in 1778. Washington then left Williamsburg for a short time, but
returned in 1780, to attend a series of lectures on the law given by George Wythe,
William and Mary's first professor of law (Marcus, 124).

In 1781, Washington enlisted in Colonel John Mercer's cavalry. He later fought at
the battle of Green Springs and was present at Cornwallis' surrender at Yorktown.
After the war, Washington left Virginia for Philadelphia, and began to read law in the
office of James Wilson. He remained in Philadelphia until 1784, when he returned to
Virginia and opened his own law practice (Marcus, 124).Washington was elected to the
Virginia House of Delegates in 1787, and the Virginia ratifying convention in 1788.
Later in 1788, Washington moved to Alexandria to devote his energies to his law practice. A few years later, Washington moved again, this time to Richmond, and it was
here that his practice began to prosper. Between 1792 and 1796, he appeared as counsel in almost one-fourth of all the cases heard by the Virginia Court of Appeals. He kept
detailed notes of the court's proceedings and later published his *Reports of Cases
Argued in the Court of Appeals of Virginia* (Marcus, 124).

Washington returned to politics in 1798, running for a seat in Congress. Apparently,
he did so reluctantly, having been persuaded by his uncle that Virginia needed strong federalist representation in the House of Representatives. In the event, Washington's congressional career never materialized. Upon Justice James Wilson's death in August 1798,
President Adams sought to appoint a Virginian to the Supreme Court, because the Court
was without a member from that state at the time. Consequently, Adams wrote Secretary of State Timothy Pickering instructing him to ascertain whether John Marshall or
Bushrod Washington would accept the nomination. While Adams expressed a mild pref-
erence for Marshall, Pickering did not think that Marshall would accept, for, in Pickering's words, "there is little hope that an eminent lawyer, in the full tide of practice at the
bar, and receiving eight or ten thousand dollars a year, will relinquish it for the meager
reward of thirty five hundred dollars, a large part of which must be expended in traveling expenses." Pickering's assessment turned out to be correct for Marshall did decline
the appointment. As a result, the President issued a temporary commission to Bushrod
Washington on September 29, 1798. The Senate confirmed the recess appointment the
following December. Washington went on to serve a total of thirty-two years on the
Court, and died on November 26, 1829, while attending the Pennsylvania circuit court.

## Alfred Moore (1799)

Alfred Moore was born on May 21, 1755, in Brunswick County, North Carolina. He
received his early education in Boston, but returned to North Carolina to study law. He
was admitted to the bar in 1775.

The start of Moore's legal career was interrupted by the outbreak of the Revolution. On September 1, 1775, he was elected a captain in the First North Carolina Regiment. After two years' military service, Moore resigned his commission so that he might return home and take care of his family, although he did accept command of the local militia. Unfortunately, Moore's service in the militia brought about the destruction of his plantation. When it became known to the local British commander that Moore led the militia unit harassing his forces, the British marched on Moore's plantation and burned it down. Moore remained in the militia, however, and eventually served as North Carolina's judge advocate (Marcus, 137).

After the war, Moore embarked upon a political career. In 1782, he was elected a member of the state senate for Brunswick County, and in May of that same year, he was elected to succeed James Iredell as attorney general, a position in which he served for nine years. During the course of his service as attorney general, he prosecuted numerous cases of fraud. On case, however, stands out. In *Bayard v. Singleton* (1787), Moore represented the defendant in an action brought by the heirs of a landowner who had fled North Carolina for England. Under a statute passed by the North Carolina General Assembly, the state commissioners of forfeited estates were authorized to sell abandoned lands, and owners of lands who contested the transfer were denied the right to a jury trial. The North Carolina Superior Court eventually struck down the statute on the grounds that it violated the state constitution's guarantee of a jury trial. *Bayard v. Singleton* is, thus, often cited as an early example of the use of the power of judicial review (Marcus, 137).

Moore served on the national level as well. In 1786, the North Carolina legislature appointed him as one of the state's delegates to the Annapolis Convention, although illness prevented him from attending. In 1788, Moore sought election as a delegate to the first North Carolina ratifying convention, but was defeated. That convention refused to ratify the Constitution ostensibly because of the lack of a bill of rights. The following year, however, Moore joined James Iredell as a delegate to the Fayetteville convention, which did ratify the Constitution on November 21, 1789 (Marcus, 138).

Apparently, Moore decided to leave politics in 1791. That year, he resigned as attorney general after the legislature created a solicitor general for the state. Moore believed that the new solicitor's powers would infringe on his constitutional prerogatives. He may also have wanted to spend more time attending to his family and managing his plantation. Moore's retirement from the political stage was relatively brief, however. In 1792, he was elected to the state legislature, and in 1795, he failed to win election to the United States Senate by only one vote (Marcus, 138–39).

It was not until 1798 that Moore began his judicial career. On December 7th of that year, the state legislature appointed him to fill a vacancy on the North Carolina Superior Court. Barely a year later, on December 4, 1799, President Adams appointed Moore to fill the vacancy on the U.S. Supreme Court caused by the death of James

Iredell, a fellow North Carolinian. Moore did not attend the February 1800 term of the Supreme Court in Philadelphia. Instead, he waited until April 21, 1800, before taking the oath of office at the Georgia circuit court in Savannah (Marcus, 139).

Moore remained on the Supreme Court for only four years. In 1804, he resigned his commission on the grounds of failing health and returned home. He spent the remainder of his days working to establish a university for his native state, and his efforts culminated in the creation of the University of North Carolina. Alfred Moore died at his home in Brunswick County on October 15, 1810.

## Nominations and Appointments

| Nominee | Appointed | Confirmation | End of Term |
|---------|-----------|--------------|-------------|
| John Jay | September 24, 1789 | September 26, 1789 | Resigned June 29, 1795 |
| John Rutledge | September 24, 1789 | September 26, 1789 | Resigned March 5, 1791 |
| William Cushing | September 24, 1789 | September 26, 1789 | Died September 13, 1810 |
| Robert H. Harrison | September 24, 1789 | September 26, 1789 | Declined to serve |
| James Wilson | September 24, 1789 | September 26, 1789 | Died August 21, 1798 |
| John Blair, Jr. | September 24, 1789 | September 26, 1789 | Resigned October 25, 1795 |
| James Iredell | February 8, 1790 | February 10, 1790 | Died October 20, 1799 |
| Thomas Johnson | August 5, 1791 | Recess appointment | Resigned January 16, 1793 |
| William Paterson | March 4, 1793 | March 4, 1793 | Died September 9, 1806 |
| John Rutledge (CJ) | July 1, 1795 | Recess appointment | Nomination Rejected December 15, 1795 |
| William Cushing (CJ) | January 26, 1796 | January 27, 1796 | Declined to serve |
| Samuel Chase | January 26, 1796 | January 27, 1796 | Died June 19, 1811 |
| Oliver Ellsworth (CJ) | March 3, 1796 | March 4, 1796 | Resigned December 15, 1800 |
| Bushrod Washington | September 29, 1798 | Recess appointment | Died November 26, 1829 |
| Alfred Moore | December 4, 1799 | December 10, 1799 | Resigned January 26, 1804 |
| John Jay (CJ) | December 18, 1800 | December 19, 1800 | Declined to serve |

## References and Further Reading

William Garrott Brown, *The Life of Oliver Ellsworth* (New York: Macmillian, 1905).

Robert R. Bair and Robin D Coblentz, "The Trials of Mr. Justice Samuel Chase," *27 Maryland Law Review* 368 (1967).

Joseph J. Ellis, *American Sphinx: The Character of Thomas Jefferson* (New York: Knopf, 1997).

Scott D. Gerber, "Deconstructing William Cushing," in Scott Douglas Gerber, *Seriatim: The Supreme Court Before John Marshall* 97 (New York: New York University Press 1998).

Mark D. Hall, *James Wilson: Democratic Theorist and Supreme Court Justice*, in Scott Douglas Gerber, *Seriatim: The Supreme Court Before John Marshall* 126 (New York: New York University Press 1998).

James Haw, et al., *Stormy Patriot: The Life of Samuel Chase* (Baltimore: Maryland Historical Society, 1980).

James Haw, *John Rutledge: Distinction and Declension*, in Scott Douglas Gerber, *Seriatim: The Supreme Court Before John Marshall* 70 (New York: New York University Press 1998). Wythe Holt, *John Blair: "A Safe and Conscientious Judge,"* in Scott Douglas Gerber, *Seriatim: The Supreme Court Before John Marshall* 156 (New York: New York University Press 1998). Ronald J. Lettieri, *Connecticut's Young Man of the Revolution: Oliver Ellsworth* (Deep River, CT: New Era Printing, 1978).

Robert G. McCloskey, "James Wilson," in *The Justices of the United States Supreme Court 1789–1969: Their Lives and Major Opinions*, ed. Leon Friedman and Fred L. Israel, 4 vols. (New York: R.†R. Bowker 1969-19780)

Maeva Marcus, *The Documentary History of the Supreme Court of the United States* (New York: Columbia University Press 1985-2007

John E. O'Connor, *William Paterson: Lawyer and Statesman, 1745–1806* (New Brunswick: Rutgers University Press, 1979).

Clinton G. Rossiter, *1787: The Grand Convention* (New York: Macmillan, 1966).

Charles Paige Smith, *James Wilson: Founding Father, 1742–1798* (Chapel Hill: University of North Carolina Press, 1956).

*The Papers of James Iredell*, Raleigh, NC: Division of Archives and History, Department of Cultural Resources, 1976)

Sandra Francis Vanburkleo, *"Honour, Justice, Interest:" John Jay's Republican Politics and Statesmanship on the Federal Bench*, in Scott Douglas Gerber, *Seriatim: The Supreme Court Before John Marshall* 26 (New York: New York University Press 1998). Gertrude Sceery Wood, *William Paterson of New Jersey, 1745–1806* (Fair Lawn, NJ: Fair Lawn Press, 1933).

# 3

# *Cases and Controversies*

Perhaps the most important feature of the early Supreme Court was the requirement that the justices ride circuit in addition to hearing cases at the seat of government. This meant that in the first few years of the court's existence, most of the justices' time was spent presiding over trials in the circuit courts, rather that hearing appeals in the Supreme Court. One rather intriguing consequence of this arrangement was that the justices were often placed in the position of hearing appeals of decisions they themselves had rendered in the lower courts. Another consequence was that some of the most significant judicial decisions in the history of the early Republic were actually authored by the justices while on circuit rather than in the Supreme Court itself.

The breadth of the federal courts' jurisdiction meant that the early Supreme Court was confronted with a wide variety of cases having important consequences for the very survival of the new nation. Indeed, within a few short months of its creation, the Supreme Court was forced to defend its independence from what it perceived to be unwarranted interference from both the executive and legislative branches. Thereafter, the court found itself embroiled in controversies over the proper relationship between the state and federal governments, the conduct of America's foreign policy, and the power of the national government to prosecute criminal offences. In each case, the court was not only required to make new law, but was forced to do so in an environment in which its every move was met with a healthy dose of suspicion and even outright hostility.

## Securing Judicial Independence

### *The Circuit Riding Controversy*

The Constitution provided only the broad outlines of a judicial system. Article III declared that the "judicial power" would be "vested in one supreme Court" and in "such inferior Courts as the Congress may from time to time ordain and establish." It also provided that judges were to have life tenure during good behavior and that their salaries could not be diminished while in office. In addition, the courts were to have jurisdiction over a wide range of cases, subject to "such Exceptions, and under such Regulations as the Congress shall make." Yet, although Article III provided for the creation of a "supreme Court," it left the precise details of how that court would be structured to Congress. The number of justices, the rules of procedure, and the precise extent of the Supreme Court's jurisdiction were all matters left to be determined when the first Congress met in New York in the spring of 1789.

After months of drafting and debate, Congress eventually enacted a judiciary bill, which was signed into law by President Washington on September 24, 1789. The Judiciary Act of 1789 created a three-tiered system of federal courts. At the apex of the structure was the Supreme Court. Section One of the Judiciary Act provided that the Supreme Court would be composed of a chief justice and five associate justices. The court was to have two sessions annually at the seat of government, meeting on the first Monday in February and August. The country was then divided into districts, with each state comprising a single district. (Kentucky, which was then a part of Virginia, and Maine, which was then a part of Massachusetts, were also separate districts.) The district courts primarily had jurisdiction over minor criminal matters, as well as revenue and admiralty cases. The Judiciary Act also provided for the creation of three circuits, called the Eastern, Middle and Southern Circuit. The Eastern Circuit originally comprised the states of Massachusetts, New Hampshire, Connecticut, and New York. The Middle Circuit consisted of New Jersey, Pennsylvania, Delaware, Maryland, and Virginia. The Southern Circuit comprised the states of South Carolina and Georgia. Rhode Island and Vermont were subsequently added to the Eastern Circuit after their admission as states, while North Carolina was later added to the Southern Circuit.

The circuit courts had original jurisdiction over most major criminal cases, including capital offences such as piracy, murder, or treason against the United States. They also had original jurisdiction in "diversity cases," or cases involving citizens of different states, where the amount in controversy exceeded the sum of five hundred dollars. In addition, they had jurisdiction over cases brought by aliens against American citizens, if the jurisdictional amount of five hundred dollars was satisfied. In years to come, the diversity and alienage provisions were to be the source of some of the Supreme Court's most important decisions.

In addition to creating the courts, the Judiciary Act created two sets of judges. Section One of the act provided that the Supreme Court would be composed of a chief justice and five associate justices. Section Three provided for the appointment of a district judge to preside over the district court in each state. The Judiciary Act did not create judges to preside over the circuit courts, however. Instead, the circuit courts were to be presided over by two justices of the Supreme Court and the judge of the district in which the circuit court was sitting. The decision to have members of the Supreme

Court ride circuit was obviously designed to save the salaries that would be associated with the creation of a set of circuit court judges. Yet, in attempting to render justice on the cheap, Congress wound up creating a variety of other problems. On a practical level, the requirement that the justices ride circuit meant that many sessions of the various circuit courts were often delayed or cancelled when travel difficulties prevented the justices from keeping to the schedule Congress set for the opening of the courts. On a more theoretical level, having the justices preside over a lower federal court meant that the Supreme Court would be hearing appeals from decisions rendered by its own members. While there was precedent for this type of arrangement in England, it was not long before many justices became concerned about the apparent conflicts of interest that the circuit riding system created.

Two circuit courts were to be held annually in each district, one in the spring and the other in the fall. Twice each year, therefore, the justices of the Supreme Court were required to attend the Supreme Court's session in the nation's capital; and then almost immediately thereafter, they set off to hold the various sessions of the circuit courts. The schedule set by Congress was quite ambitious. For example, the justices assigned to the Eastern Circuit had to be in New York City to open the New York Circuit Court on April 4, and in New Haven to open the Connecticut court on April 22. After that, they were to travel up the Connecticut River and overland to Boston to preside over the Massachusetts Circuit Court on May 3. From there, the justices went north to hold the New Hampshire court on May 20, and then south to preside over the Rhode Island Circuit Court in Newport on June 4. Once that court was adjourned, the justices had to travel north again to Vermont to open that state's circuit court on June 17. At the conclusion of the spring circuit, the justices might head home for a brief vacation, but they had to be back at the seat of government on the first Monday in August to be on hand for the opening of the Supreme Court's next term. While the Middle Circuit was slightly more compact, the Southern Circuit was a traveler's nightmare, requiring the justices to cover over 1,100 miles in the space of six weeks.

The obligation to ride circuit was a constant source of complaint, and several justices ultimately stepped down rather than spend the bulk of their judicial career traveling bad roads and lodging at inns far from home. For example, Justice Thomas Johnson resigned his seat on the Court after less than two years because he found the job of riding circuit too arduous. In a letter to President Washington, Johnson complained that he could not continue "to spend six Months in the Year of the few I may have left from my Family, on Roads at Taverns chiefly and often in Situations where the most moderate Desires are disappointed: My Time of Life[,] Temper and other Circumstances forbid it." John Jay resigned as chief justice in 1795, partly because he detested the duty to ride circuit and refused reappointment as chief justice in 1800 because Congress had failed to make alterations in the system.

Adding to the controversy over the duty to ride circuit was the allocation of the circuits. Congress did not provide any mechanism in the Judiciary Act by which the justices would be assigned to circuit riding duty. Instead, it left the division of labor to be decided by the justices themselves. As a result, when the Court met for its first term in February 1790, the justices agreed to assign circuit-riding duties on the basis of residence. Thus, Chief Justice John Jay (New York) and Justice William Cushing (Massachusetts) were assigned to the Eastern Circuit. Justice Wilson (Pennsylvania) and John Blair (Virginia) took the Middle Circuit. Justices Rutledge (South Carolina) and Iredell (North Carolina), neither of whom was in attendance that first session, were assigned the Southern Circuit. (Rutledge missed the session because he was ill, and Iredell did not receive his commission until after the Court's term began.)

While traveling over poorly developed roads was difficult for all the justices, those assigned to the Southern Circuit bore the heaviest burden. Intense heat, combined with inadequate transportation facilities, made the journey through the Deep South an ordeal. As a result, when the justices met again in August 1790, Justice Iredell expected that the members of the Court would agree to a rotation of the circuits. To his dismay, however, the rest of the Court decided to make the original assignments permanent. Condemned to suffer the greatest hardship, Iredell appealed to Congress to relieve him from what he perceived to be a great injustice. Congress responded to Iredell's appeal with the passage of an act providing that "no judge, unless by his own consent, shall have assigned to him any circuit which he hath already attended, until the same hath been afterwards attended by every other of the said judges." The circuits would, therefore, be rotated among the justices in turn.

Throughout the 1790s, the justices made repeated attempts to secure some relief from the hardships of riding circuit. Beginning in the fall of 1790, the members of the Supreme Court drafted petitions to both the President and Congress urging that the system be revised. In general, they made two arguments. First, they contended that the system was unworkable. They complained that the schedule for holding the courts set by Congress was too ambitious and posed a danger to their health. Second, they contended (albeit gently) that the obligation to ride circuit was unconstitutional. The justices began their campaign with a letter to President Washington in August 1790, pointing out their belief that the appointment of the same people to hold office as circuit judges and Supreme Court justices violated the Constitution's prohibition on dual office holding. While nothing concrete seems to have come of this letter, Attorney General William Randolph took up the justices' cause in his *Report on the Judicial System*, issued in December 1790. Although Randolph ignored the constitutional question in his report, he argued that circuit riding ought to be abolished because it prevented the justices from having the time to reflect and acquire "proficiency" in their capacities as justices of the nation's highest court. Randolph's report failed to convince, however, and the circuit riding system remained in effect.

By the spring of 1792, the justices formulated a plan of their own. They agreed that each justice would accept a reduction in salary of $500 in exchange for being relieved of circuit duty. They hoped to convince Congress to use the money thus saved to create a set of circuit judges. In the end, the plan was never sent to Congress out of fear that it would insult the members. Instead, later that year, the justices presented another petition, this time downplaying the constitutional argument and emphasizing the hardship of circuit riding. President Washington responded to this petition by urging Congress to consider reform of the judiciary. Congress did so by passing the Judiciary Act of 1793, which provided that the circuit courts would henceforth be presided over by only one justice and the district judge. Although this statute did not eliminate the duty to ride circuit, it had the effect of reducing the time the justices spent on the road by half.

Vacancies and the absence of several members of the Supreme Court on other business added to the difficulties of circuit riding. Chief Justice Jay's mission to Great Britain threw the assignment of the spring and fall 1794 circuits into utter confusion. Jay's continued absence meant that only five members of the Supreme Court were available for circuit duty in the fall of 1795. Several justices now considered resigning their commissions, and Justice Iredell summed up the mood of the Court despairing that "[i]t is impossible I can lead this life much longer." By 1797, therefore, the justices were becoming desperate. They took matters into their own hands and drafted a statute altering the schedule for holding the circuit courts, which resulted in the passage of the Judiciary Act of 1797. While this new rotation promised some relief, the duty to ride circuit remained.

It was not until passage of the ill-fated Judiciary Act of 1801 that the justices were to be relieved of circuit-riding duties. This act dramatically altered the structure of the federal judiciary by creating an entire new set of federal judges to preside over the circuit courts. Unfortunately, the act became a casualty of the ongoing struggle between the Federalist and Republican parties. After passage of the act, President Adams decided to appoint a number of staunch federalists to fill these new judgeships in the waning days of his term. Incensed by what they believed to be a blatant attempt at "court packing," the new Republican majority in Congress made repeal of the Judiciary Act of 1801 a priority. Scarcely a year passed, therefore, before the justices were again condemned to ride circuit, a duty they were forced to undertake for another one hundred years. Circuit riding was finally abolished in 1891.

## *Advisory Opinions*

Long experience with royal government during the colonial period had taught Americans that a combination of government powers in one set of hands often leads to tyranny. As a result, political theorists of the revolutionary period argued that a clear separation of powers among the branches of government was necessary to prevent oppression. In spite of this consensus, however, it seems that a number of delegates to the Constitutional Convention argued that the justices of the Supreme Court ought to play some rule in the drafting of law and policy. Some thought that this might be accomplished by creating a "Council of Revision," composed of members of both the executive and a "convenient number" of the judiciary with power to veto unwise or unconstitutional legislation. Others thought that the President ought to have the ability to call upon the judiciary to render legal advice, and argued for the inclusion of an "advisory opinion" process in the Constitution. While both these proposals were ultimately rejected at the convention, the extent to which the justices might be involved in the making of policy became a source of some concern very early in the life of the new government.

Although nothing in the constitutional text allowed judges to give advisory opinions, no provision seems to prohibit their doing it. Thus, the decade of the 1790s is remarkable for the frequency with which members of the Supreme Court were called upon to render advice to the President and various cabinet officials. Even more remarkable is the ease with which members of the Court were willing to offer that advice. Throughout their terms, Chief Justices Jay and Ellsworth drafted lengthy opinions on a wide array of political and legal problems, including foreign affairs, criminal law, and constitutional questions. The fact that many of the matters in which the justices gave these opinions might eventually be the subject of litigation in the Supreme Court did not seem to trouble their authors. Rather, ironically, however, although the justices seemed quite willing to offer advice on an ad hoc basis, the Supreme Court as a whole precipitated one of the nation's earliest constitutional crises, when, citing the doctrine of separation of powers, it refused to respond to a formal request for advice by President Washington. Apparently, the justices believed that rendering individual opinions did not result in an improper mingling of executive and judicial branch functions, but feared that formally establishing a process by which the president would have the right to demand advice from the court would unduly limit the court's independence.

The earliest example of the use of advisory opinions appears to have occurred in the spring of 1790, after a Spanish military expedition attacked a British trading post on the Nootka Sound of Vancouver Island. The British government threatened to go to war with Spain unless the latter agreed to abandon any claim to the region and provide compensation. Although the dispute was largely between two foreign powers, President Washington worried about the possibility that Britain might ultimately retaliate by attacking Spanish interests in North America. As a result, Washington wrote a letter to his cabinet and the chief justice asking advice on how to respond in the event Great Britain requested permission to march its troops over American soil to launch an attack on Spanish colonies in Louisiana or Florida. He also asked for advice on the proper course of action should the British enter upon American territory without permission. Chief Justice Jay responded to Washington's request with a lengthy letter analyzing both the political and legal aspects of the problem. Jay's advice was ultimately unnecessary because Spain agreed to Britain's demands and war between the two great powers was averted.

Some commentators believe that Washington's conduct during the Nootka Sound incident demonstrated the president's belief that he had the right to call upon members of the judiciary for advice. And, to some extent, this opinion is justified by the fact that the president wrote a single letter to both the cabinet and chief justice soliciting their advice. It may also be the case, however, that Washington had simply become used to asking Jay's advice on foreign affairs. After all, Jay had served as secretary of foreign affairs in the confederation government and was acting secretary of state from September 1789, until Thomas Jefferson returned from France in the spring of 1790. Whatever the motivation behind Washington's request for advice, however, Chief Justice Jay seems to have had no hesitation in providing it.

President Washington was not the only one to call upon the members of the Supreme Court for advice. A number of cabinet officers also appear to have assumed that members of the Court were available for consultation on matters of political or legal policy. For example, when Great Britain and France went to war in the spring of 1793, President Washington sought some way to keep the United States from being drawn into the conflict. After consulting with his cabinet, in April 1793, Washington decided to issue a proclamation declaring American neutrality. Treasury Secretary Alexander Hamilton wrote Chief Justice Jay soliciting his advice on the neutrality question and asking Jay to draft an appropriate proclamation. Jay responded by providing a detailed legal analysis of the diplomatic situation. He also enclosed a draft of neutrality proclamation. This document professed American neutrality and warned American citizens against taking any steps to aid either of the belligerent powers. Perhaps more striking, however, is the fact that Jay also recommended that violators be "prosecuted & punished in an Exemplary manner." The fact that such prosecutions would be commenced in the circuit courts over which Jay would likely preside did not seem to trouble the chief justice. Moreover, while there is no concrete evidence that Washington or the cabinet used Jay's draft as the basis of the final neutrality proclamation, the document issued by President Washington bore a strong similarity to Jay's draft and included the recommendation that criminal prosecutions be commenced against those who violated its terms.

The issuance of the neutrality proclamation did not put an end to America's difficulties, however. Two weeks before the proclamation was issued, Edmund Genet, the new French minister, arrived in the United States and immediately began to take steps to enlist American aid in his country's struggle against Great Britain. Drawing on the vast well of public support for the French revolutionary cause, Genet issued commissions to American citizens authorizing them to seize British vessels as prize on behalf of the French government. He then began to arrange for a number of ships in American ports to be fitted out as privateers to prey on British shipping. The British government reacted by demanding that the Washington administration put an end to Genet's activities. In a series of notes to Secretary of State Thomas Jefferson, Britain's ambassador complained that allowing American citizens to assist the French war effort was a violation of American neutrality.

Fearful of being drawn further into the conflict, Washington consulted his cabinet, and together they agreed that Genet's activities were improper. Nonetheless, the cabinet decided to seek an opinion from the Supreme Court on America's responsibilities under the law of nations and the treaties then in force. This request, which was perfectly consistent with traditional English and state court practice, set the stage for the Supreme Court's first formal assertion of the principle of judicial independence. As a result, on July 18, 1793, the Secretary of State submitted a request to the justices seeking their advice on the legal merits of the controversy. Jefferson began by advising that the Court that he was acting on behalf of the president and requesting "to know, in the first place, [the justices'] opinion, whether the public may, with propriety, be availed of their advice on these questions." He then set forth a list of twenty-nine specific questions concerning the intricacies of neutrality and the law of nations. In urging the Court to provide its advice, Jefferson noted that, while important in themselves, the questions dealt with matters which are often "not presented under circumstances which give a cognizance of them in the tribunals of the country." Nonetheless, he said, the consideration of them were "so little analogous to the ordinary functions of the executive, as to occasion much embarrassment and difficulty to them."

A few weeks later, the justices formally rejected the Jefferson's request. In a letter to the Secretary of State, the Court explained that giving advisory opinions to the executive branch would tend to erode the independence of the judiciary:

> The Lines of Separation drawn by the Constitution between the three Departments of government—their being in certain Respects checks on each other—and our being Judges of a Court in the last Resort—are Considerations which afford strong arguments against the Propriety of our extrajudicially deciding the questions alluded to; especially as the Power given by the Constitution to the President of calling on the Heads of Departments for opinions, seems to have been purposely as well as expressly limited to the executive Departments.

In refusing to give an opinion, the justices established two significant precedents: First, they declared that the Constitution does not authorize the president to require the Supreme Court to provide advice. Second, they declared their belief that the Court should not, as a prudential matter, render advice to the executive (Casto 1995, 79).

The justices made the constitutional point through means of a negative inference. They noted that Article II of the Constitution gives the president the power to require the opinion of the heads of the various cabinet departments on any subject relating to their duties. However, the fact that no other officer was mentioned in this provision led the justices to conclude that the President's power to demand advice was "expressly limited" to cabinet officers. While arguments from silence can be difficult to sustain, it appears that in making this inference, at least three justices, Blair, Wilson, and Paterson, may have been drawing on their experiences as members of the Constitutional Convention. During the Convention, South Carolina's Charles Pinckney specifically proposed giving the executive the power "to require the opinions of the supreme Judicial Court upon important questions of law" (2 Farrand, 340–41). This proposal was rejected, however, and it appears that the Court relied on this bit of history to limit presidential authority and preserve judicial independence (Casto 1995, 80).

The justices' jurisprudential point was more subtle. Even if the president was prohibited from demanding that the Supreme Court provide an advisory opinion, nothing in the Constitution would seem to have prevented the Court from doing so had it desired. After all, Chief Justice Jay had already issued advisory opinions on several subjects prior to the cabinet's formal request to the full Court. The Court's refusal to provide a response to Jefferson's letter was simply a function of the fact that most justices appeared to believe that the Supreme Court was designed to serve as a check on the actions of the other branches. Clearly, they were worried about the possibility that advice rendered publicly today would prejudice their participation in a future legal proceeding involving a challenge to executive branch action in which they had participated, albeit indirectly. Although Jefferson had attempted to foreclose this possibility by noting that the matters in question would not normally arise in the context of legal proceedings, the justices obviously thought the risk too great.

It is important to note that the Supreme Court's refusal to render a formal advisory opinion in the neutrality controversy did not prevent members of the Court from continuing to give advice about matters of public policy, international affairs, and criminal prosecutions in years to come. For example, just a few days after he became chief justice in 1796, Oliver Ellsworth wrote a lengthy advisory opinion on the legality of the House of Representatives' demand that the President produce papers relevant to the negotiation of the Jay Treaty. Although the opinion was written to Connecticut Senator Jonathan Trumbull, it seems likely that Ellsworth expected its contents to be revealed to President Washington (Casto 1995, 98). There is also evidence that Chief Justice Ellsworth regularly advised Secretary of State Timothy Pickering on the use of the federal courts to advance the nation's foreign policy aims (Casto 1995, 116). Similarly, in

1798, Justice William Paterson authored an opinion to Tench Coxe, the Commissioner of Revenue, on the question of whether an attempt to bribe a federal official could be prosecuted in the absence of an applicable statute. Later that same year, Chief Justice Ellsworth wrote an extensive letter to Secretary Pickering expressing his opinion that the Sedition Act was constitutional. The fact that Ellsworth might be called upon to preside over cases brought under the act in the circuit court did not seem to trouble the chief justice. Indeed, so widespread was the practice of giving informal advice that even the most mundane matters might have elicited an advisory opinion. Chief Justice Jay once wrote an opinion to the Sinking Fund Commission on the legality of a proposal to repurchase some of the public debt, while Justice Chase rendered an opinion on the president's authority to appoint a public printer. In reviewing this activity, one is tempted to draw a line between formal opinions issued by the Supreme Court as an institution and informal opinions rendered by individual justices. Yet, the justices themselves never seem to have made such a distinction, and it is difficult to articulate a clear line between the two. Perhaps the most that can be said of the Court's refusal to render a formal opinion to the cabinet in the neutrality controversy is that it was a tactic designed to ensure that the decision to render advisory opinions would forever remain with the justices alone.

## Judicial Review and the Separation of Powers

As noted earlier, there were several discussions during the Constitutional Convention about integrating the judiciary into the legislative process. The original Virginia Plan called for the creation of a "council of revision" made up of "the Executive and a convenient number of the National Judiciary" with the power to veto acts of Congress and the state legislatures. Many delegates opposed this idea, however, believing instead that judges exercising the power of judicial review would have the ability to prevent the operation of laws that were in conflict with the Constitution.

Supporters of the proposal to create the council of revision argued that the power of judicial review would be an inadequate remedy against legislative over reaching. As James Wilson explained:

> It had been said that the Judges, as expositors of the Laws would have an opportunity of defending their constitutional rights. There was weight in this observation; but this power of the Judges did not go far enough. Laws may be unjust, may be unwise, may be dangerous, may be destructive; and yet not be so unconstitutional as to justify the judges in refusing to give them effect. Let them have a share in the Revisionary power, and they will have an opportunity of taking notice of these characters of a law, and of counteracting, by the weight of their opinions the improper views of the Legislature.

For Wilson, therefore, a judicial veto of legislation encompassed more than review of the constitutionality of legislation. Rather, as members of the council of revision, the judges would have a hand in determining whether a particular statute was "unwise," "dangerous," or "destructive." In essence, they would have the power to determine whether a statute was good public policy.

Opponents of the council thought that vesting such power in members of the judiciary would be going too far. Massachusetts' Elbridge Gerry asserted that it is "quite foreign from the nature of the [judges'] office to make them judges of the public policy measures." Luther Martin agreed, noting "[a] knowledge of mankind, and of Legislative affairs cannot be presumed to belong in a higher degree to the Judges than to the Legislature" (1 Farrand, 76, 97–98). In the end, the proposal for a council of revision was rejected, perhaps because the majority of delegates thought "the Judges ought never to give their opinion on a law till it comes before them." Instead, it was thought that to be truly independent "Judges ought to be able to expound the law as it should come before them, free from the bias of having participated in its formation" (2 Farrand, 80, 98).

As we have seen, however, defeat of the council of revision did not prevent the justices of the Supreme Court from giving advice on matters of public policy. Yet, what is most revealing about the debate over the council was the apparent widespread expectation that members of the judiciary would have the power to strike down legislation that was contrary to the terms of the federal Constitution. This consensus was revealed in more detail during the course of the ratification debates. For example, in defending the provisions of the Constitution giving federal judges life tenure, Alexander Hamilton argued that the "complete independence of the courts of justice is peculiarly essential in a limited Constitution." Because the Constitution was a government of limited powers, it was important to have some means by which the legislature could be kept within its proper bounds. That task, Hamilton said, fell to the judiciary (The Federalist 78). During the Connecticut ratifying convention, Oliver Ellsworth made the same point:

> If the general legislature should at any time overleap their limits, the judicial department is a constitutional check. If the United States go beyond their powers, if they make a law which the Constitution does not authorize, it is void; and the national judges, who to secure their impartiality are to be made independent, will declare it to be void.

Opponents of ratification often agreed that the Constitution gave the federal judiciary the power of judicial review. They did not agree, however, that this was necessarily a good thing. *Brutus*, the author of a series of letters written during the course of the New York ratification debate, argued that the power of judicial review would become the source of a great deal of abuse because there was no constitutional mechanism to control the judges when exercising it. Once the Supreme Court declared a statute unconstitutional, he said, neither the president nor the Congress had the power to reverse the decree. For *Brutus*, therefore, the "opinions of the Supreme Court, whatever they may be, will have the force of law; because there is no power provided in the constitution, that can correct their errors, or control their adjudication."

Two distinct problems were to confront the justices of the Supreme Court in their exercise of the power of judicial review. The first question facing the members of the Supreme Court was the extent to which federal judges had the power to strike down acts of Congress. As noted earlier, there appears to have been some expectation that the federal courts would have that power, at least during the ratification debates. A far more difficult question, however, was the extent to which federal judges might have the ability to invalidate acts of the various state legislatures. Such a power obviously had explosive consequences for state–federal relations, and so it is natural that supporters of the Constitution would seek to avoid too detailed an analysis of this aspect of judicial review. As might be expected, however, it was not long before the justices of the Supreme Court found themselves at the center of controversy over their attempts to exercise the power of judicial review over both federal and state legislation.

## Judicial Review of Federal Legislation

The first test came in 1792, after Congress passed the Invalid Pensions Act. This statute was designed to provide a mechanism for resolving the numerous claims for pensions by veterans of the Revolutionary War. It required that soldiers or sailors injured during the war apply to the circuit court for the state in which they resided to be put on the government's pension list. The judges of the circuit court were to examine the applicant and determine the amount of the pension to be awarded. At the end of every term, the circuit court was to forward a list of eligible pensioners to the Secretary of War, who would have the power to delete names where he suspected some "imposition or mistake."

The justices of the Supreme Court immediately expressed reservations about the act. Most believed that the provisions of the act allowing the decisions of the circuit court to be reviewed by an executive branch official was unconstitutional. As a result, when the New York Circuit Court met for its spring 1792 session, Chief Justice Jay, Justice Cushing, and District Judge James Duane expressed the opinion that they could not perform the duties required of the statute without doing damage to the principle of separation of powers. Nonetheless, the judges were sensitive to the importance of the act in relieving the suffering of aging veterans, and did not want to provoke a controversy with Congress. As a result, they agreed to hear pension claims, but only as "commissioners" appointed by "official rather than personal designation." The judges, therefore, adjourned the circuit court, and prepared the pension list in their capacity as commissioners. In so doing, Jay, Cushing and Duane avoided creating the spectacle of a conflict between two branches of the federal government within a very short time after its organization.

Other justices were not so hesitant, however. When the Pennsylvania circuit court met a few weeks later, Justices Wilson and Blair joined District Judge Richard Peters in refusing to hear any pension claims. On April 18, 1792, they addressed a letter to President Washington expressing their belief that the power given to the Secretary of War to revise the judgments of the circuit court was "radically inconsistent with the independence of that judicial power which is vested in the courts." They, therefore, adjourned the circuit court without preparing the pension list. Among those denied a pension because of this action was one William Hayburn. Unable to get the circuit court to fulfill its duties under the Pension Act, Hayburn petitioned Congress for redress. Members of Congress reacted with horror to the Pennsylvania court's decision. Some talked of impeachment, and the House of Representatives convened a committee to consider a response. The House ultimately took no action against the judges and Hayburn's petition went ignored by Congress.

Some time later, the North Carolina Circuit Court, presided over by Justice Iredell and District Judge Stigreaves, weighed in on the subject. This court, too, refused to act on pension claims, expressing the opinion that "no decision of any court of the United States can, under any circumstances ... agreeable to the constitution, be liable to a revision, or even a suspension, by the legislature itself, in which no judicial power of any kind appears to be vested." Iredell and Stigreaves also rejected the solution adopted by the New York court and refused to act as commissioners. By October 1792, Justice Thomas Johnson had joined the fray. While sitting on the South Carolina circuit court, Johnson, along with District Judge Thomas Bee, declared that the court could not "constitutionally take Cognixance" of pension claims.

As a result, by the fall of 1792, every justice of the Supreme Court had expressed the opinion—albeit on circuit—that an act of Congress was constitutionally infirm. Meanwhile, Attorney General Edmund Randolph, acting on behalf of William Hayburn, filed a petition in the Supreme Court seeking a writ of mandamus to compel the Pennsylvania circuit court to hear Hayburn's claim for a pension. In doing so, Randolph sought to force the Supreme Court to formally consider whether the Pension Act was valid. At first glance, it is not entirely clear why Randolph would have wanted to provoke this controversy, since by the time he filed Hayburn's petition in August 1792, the justices had already expressed the view that the Act was unconstitutional. That they had done so in letters to the President, rather than in a formal judicial opinion, hardly made Randolph's case stronger. For their part, however, the justices obviously wanted to avoid a direct conflict with Congress. Thus, when *Hayburn's Case* came before the

Court for argument, the justices questioned whether Randolph had standing to appear on behalf of Hayburn, and postponed consideration of the matter for several months. Sensing that a confrontation would not be beneficial to the new government, Congress amended the Pension Act in early 1793, and removed the circuit courts from the process. *Hayburn's Case* was made moot.

Although the Supreme Court never officially rendered an opinion as to the constitutionality of the Pension Act, it is clear that its willingness to do so caused members of the other branches a great deal of consternation. In a letter discussing Hayburn's original petition to Congress, Massachusetts' congressman Fisher Ames worried that the circuit court's refusal to hear pension claims gave aid and comfort to enemies of the Constitution. "At best," Ames said, "our business is all up hill, and with the aid of our law courts the authority of Congress is barely adequate to keep the machine moving; but when they condemn the law as invalid, they embolden the States and their courts to make many claims of power, which otherwise they would not have thought of." James Madison agreed, although he was more circumspect, merely noting that in refusing to enforce the act, "[t]he Judges have also called the attention of the Public to Legislative fallibility by pronouncing a law … unconstitutional and void—perhaps they may be wrong in the execution of their power—but such an evidence of its existence give inquietude to those who do not wish Congress to be controllable." *Hayburn's Case* may thus be seen as one of the earliest exercises of judicial review in defense of the Supreme Court's independence, and this is so even though the justices never issued a formal opinion (Presser, 62–3).

That the Supreme Court had the power to consider the constitutionality of acts of Congress seems to have been assumed by the middle part of the 1790s. In *Hylton v. United States* (1796), the court was presented with the question of whether a federal law imposing a tax on carriages violated the Constitution's prohibition on the imposition of "direct taxes." The case arose in 1794, when Congress passed a statute imposing a tax of sixteen dollars on each carriage owned by an individual or business. Daniel Hylton, a resident of Virginia, refused to pay the tax and the government commenced an action in the Virginia circuit court for nonpayment.

It appears from the record that the government had actually conspired with Hylton to obtain a judgment on the constitutionality of the carriage tax, for Hylton waived a jury trial in the action and the case proceeded to judgment on the basis of a "case stated," which is to say an agreed statement of facts. Yet, the facts so stated were comical in the extreme: The parties agreed that Hylton owned 125 carriages, which he kept for "his private use, and not let out to hire." The government contended, therefore, that he owed the sum of $2,000 in unpaid taxes, or $16 on each of 125 carriages. However, the parties also agreed that if the court were to give judgment for the government, Hylton was liable only to pay the sum of $16. It seems clear, therefore, that Hylton probably owned only a single carriage, but because the circuit courts were not given general federal question jurisdiction in the Judiciary Act of 1789, some means had to be found to bring the case within the courts' diversity jurisdiction. Thus, the government and Hylton essentially filed a false statement of facts to create a case that would exceed the circuit courts' jurisdictional limit of $500 and the Supreme Court's jurisdictional limit of $2,000. Obviously, the plan was to get the case before the Supreme Court to consider the constitutionality of the carriage tax, for when the case was tried before the circuit court, the judges were divided on the question. Normally, this would have meant that the government had lost. Hylton kept to the plan, however, and confessed judgment anyway so that the case could proceed to the Supreme Court.

Somewhat surprisingly, given the controversy following the justices' rather timid assertion of judicial supremacy in *Hayburn's Case*, the Supreme Court scarcely considered whether it had the power to determine the constitutionality of an Act of Congress. Instead, most of the justices simply assumed the power, and then went on to consider whether the carriage tax violated the Constitution's prohibition on Congress imposing "direct taxes" on the states. Only Justice Samuel Chase hesitated before pronouncing on the validity of the tax. According to Chase, the question before the court was whether the carriage tax was a "direct tax," which could only be levied on the states in proportion to their inhabitants, or whether it was comparable to an "indirect tax," such as a customs duty or excise tax, which could be levied on the articles involved without respect to population. Chase's concerns about the exercise of judicial review were evident in his handling of the question, for he began by expressing a willingness to defer to Congress. That body had obviously considered the distinction between direct and indirect taxes in configuring the carriage tax. As a result, Chase declared that "[t]he deliberate decision of the National Legislature ... would determine me if the case were doubtful, to receive the construction of the Legislature." In his view, however, the case was not "doubtful," and so he went on to consider the structure of the tax in light of several constitutional provisions.

Chase's hesitance about the legitimacy of judicial review was even more evident two years later in *Calder v. Bull* (1798). Here, Chase wondered aloud whether the Court could ever "have the power to decide that any law made by Congress, contrary to the Constitution of the United States, is void." As will be shown later, although Chase appeared certain that Congress did not have the power to pass an unconstitutional act, he was less convinced that the Supreme Court would have the right to declare such a statute void in the event Congress did so. Chase's views thus seemed to be somewhat unsettled on the question of whether the Supreme Court had the power to decide the constitutionality of acts of Congress. In *Hylton*, however, he apparently decided to consider the question because both parties had clearly constructed the case for the specific purpose of challenging the act. In the final analysis, Chase concluded that the tax was constitutional, and so held that he need not actually reach the question of whether the Supreme Court could declare an Act of Congress void. Instead,

Chase said, if the Court had such a power, "I am free to declare, that I will exercise it, but [only] in a very clear case." At best, therefore, *Hylton* seems to be another tentative example of the Supreme Court's willingness to exercise the power of judicial review over congressional action. A majority of justices assumed they had the authority to declare an Act of Congress void, although Justice Chase clearly expressed reservations, which he was to hold for some time.

The justices' adherence to the principle of judicial review was tempered by an equally strong adherence to the principle of the separation of powers. In a number of early cases, the justices were careful to defer to the legislative and executive branches when those branches acted within their proper constitutional sphere. Indeed, this deference extended to congressional legislation over the Court's own jurisdiction. An example of this can be seen in *West v. Barnes* (1791), discussed more fully later. After losing in a suit brought in the Rhode Island circuit court, West attempted to take an appeal to the Supreme Court. Unfortunately, the Judiciary Act required that a writ of error issue within ten days of the lower court's decision. Read literally, this would have required West to travel to Philadelphia and obtain a writ from the clerk of the Supreme Court in the specified time. The capriciousness of eighteenth century transport convinced West that such a journey would be impossible. Consequently, he obtained a writ of error from the clerk of the Rhode Island circuit court, along with a transcript of the proceedings, and forwarded these to the clerk of the Supreme Court, requesting that his appeal be docketed.

*West v. Barnes* thus became the first case ever appealed to the Supreme Court. It was also the first case to be dismissed. The Court rejected the appeal on the grounds that West had obtained the writ of error from the wrong court. The justices were of the opinion that a lower court could not issue a writ of error to itself, and thus the writ of error issued by the circuit court clerk was invalid. The Court noted the difficulty inherent in the ten-day requirement, but declared that it was helpless to remedy the situation. Because Congress had legislated the time limits, Congress alone would have to alter it. In so doing, the Court declined West's invitation to adopt an "equitable construction" of the statute, which is to say, interpret the statute so as to avoid an absurd result. Instead, Justice Iredell explained that construing the statute to remedy its obvious defect would, in effect, result in the Court usurping the authority of the legislature.

> [An] inconvenience does indeed exist. It is a very weighty one, and I heartily wish it was in the power of the Court, by a construction that could be justified, to remove it: but I think it is not.
>
> An argument grounded on inconveniences is, to be sure, in many instances, admissable, and in some even necessary. But I apprehend that it is to be used with great caution, lest a Court, under color of a construction of an act of the Legislature, should, in fact, encroach on the legislative authority, a thing of the utmost moment to be avoided.

Justice Wilson agreed, noting that if there was an inconsistency in the law, "it must be removed by *another* power" for the justices "act in the *judicial*, not in the *legislative* department." Justice Cushing echoed these sentiments, explaining that "[i]f inconveniences should arise, in carrying [the legislature's] laws into effect, with them lies the power of correcting the inconveniences, and not with us."

*West v. Barnes* is, therefore, an intriguing example of the way in which the early Supreme Court artfully balanced the Court's assertion of its prerogatives as a judicial body with a deference to the concerns of the political branches. While on circuit, members of the Supreme Court took the opportunity to assert the power of judicial review, invalidating state legislation that conflicted with the Constitution. On appeal, however, those same justices refused to adopt a liberal construction of an act of Congress where doing so would infringe on the legislature's prerogatives. The Court thus demonstrated an unflinching adherence to the role of the judiciary as a guardian of the constitutional order, while still maintaining a healthy respect for the principle of separation of powers.

## Judicial Review of State Legislation

The justices of the Supreme Court were particularly active in reviewing state legislation, although much of this activity occurred while they were presiding over the various circuit courts. The first of these cases arose during the November 1791 term of the Rhode Island Circuit Court, in *West v. Barnes*. This dispute arose after William West executed a mortgage on a farm he owned in favor of David Jenckes and his son, John. West hoped to pay off the mortgage from the proceeds of his crops, but a series of failures prevented him from doing so. West finally tendered payment of the mortgage to Jenckes in paper currency, but Jenckes refused to accept it, demanding payment in specie. Under a Rhode Island law then in force called the Emitting Act, the failure of a creditor to accept payment in paper money could result in the debt being declared satisfied. Relying on the provisions of this law, West deposited the money into the registry of the state superior court and sought to have the debt discharged. Hoping to avoid having the claim heard by an anti-creditor state court jury, Jenckes' heirs attempted an end run around the Rhode Island statute by suing West in the federal court.

West defended against this suit by claiming that his tender of payment in accordance with the terms of the Rhode Island statute made the claim moot. For their part, West's creditors contested the validity of the Emitting Act on the grounds that it violated the Constitution's "Contracts Clause," which prohibited the states from passing any law "impairing the obligation of contract." The circuit court, presided over by Chief Justice Jay, Justice Cushing, and District Judge Henry Marchant, rejected the

West's defense and upheld the creditors' claim. Although the judges did not explicitly hold that the Rhode Island statute was void, the rejection of West's defense of payment leads, rather inescapably, to the conclusion that they viewed the act as an unconstitutional interference with the obligation of contract. In any event, *West v. Barnes* was destined to be the first case appealed to the Supreme Court, although, as noted earlier, it was eventually dismissed on a technicality.

What the Rhode Island Circuit Court had done subtly in *West v. Barnes*, it soon did explicitly in *Champion v. Casey* (1792). Silas Casey was a Rhode Island merchant who suffered a series of financial setbacks during the latter part of the 1780s. He petitioned the Rhode Island general assembly for relief from his creditors, and the assembly responded by passing a resolution granting Casey a three-year period during which he would be free from arrest or attachment for debt. However, in June 1792, three British merchants brought suit for debt against Casey in the Rhode Island circuit court. Casey set up the assembly resolution as a defense, but the circuit court rejected the plea. Although the docket does not contain a full statement of the judges' reasoning, a local paper reported that the judges were "unanimously of the opinion, that, as by the Constitution of the United States, the individual States are prohibited from making laws which shall impair the obligation of contracts, and as the resolution in question, if operative, would impair the obligation of the contract in question, therefore, it could not be admitted to bar the action." *Champion v. Casey* thus appears to be the first case in which a federal court explicitly declared a state statute unconstitutional.

No doubt the most famous example of judicial review in the early republic occurred in *Van Horne's Lessee v. Dorrance* (1795), a case that is routinely (but mistakenly) cited as the first example of a federal court declaring a state law unconstitutional. It is important to note, however, that this case was almost exclusively concerned with a conflict between a state statute and a *state* constitution, and thus is a somewhat problematic exercise of judicial review.

*Van Horne* arose after the Pennsylvania legislature attempted to resolve a dispute between two groups of settlers claiming title to certain lands in the western part of the state. One group claimed ownership by virtue of grants given by the original proprietor of the colony, William Penn. A second group based its title on grants given by the Susquehanna Company, one of the many land speculation companies at work in the western reaches of the young nation. After a series of violent clashes between the two groups, the Pennsylvania general assembly sought to "quiet title" in the Connecticut settlers through the Conforming Act of 1787. This act essentially provided that those claiming ownership from the Susquehanna Company would take title to the land, while those whose titles were derived from Penn's grants would receive land elsewhere in the state.

One of those forced off the land in this fashion was Cornelius Van Horne. Unhappy with the legislative solution, Van Horne commenced an action for ejectment against John Dorrance, the man claiming title to Van Horne's land through the Susque-hanna Company. Dorrance immediately set up the Conforming Act as a defense to Van Horne's claim. Van Horne, of course, contended that the Conforming Act violated the provisions of the Pennsylvania state constitution prohibiting the state from depriving an owner of his property without compensation. After a fifteen-day trial, Justice Paterson charged the jury in what must be regarded as one of the most eloquent statements of the theory and scope of the power of judicial review.

Paterson began by making a very clear distinction between the unwritten English constitution and the written constitutions in the United States. Quoting Lord Coke, Paterson noted that the English constitutional scheme vests almost unlimited power in Parliament with the result that no court in the realm has the power to alter or control its acts:

> In England, from whence most of our legal principles and legislative notions are derived, the authority of the Parliament is transcendant and has no bounds." The power and jurisdiction of Parliament, says Sir Edward Coke, is so transcendant and absolute, that it cannot be confined, either for causes or persons, within any bounds.... It has sovereign and uncontroulable authority in the making, confirm-ing, enlarging, restraining, abrogating, repealing, reviving, and expounding of laws, concerning matters of all possible denominations, ecclesiastical or temporal, civil, military, maritime, or criminal: This being the place where that absolute despotic power, which must in all governments reside somewhere, is entrusted by the con-stitution of these kingdoms. All mischiefs and grievances, operations and reme-dies, that transcend the ordinary course of the laws, are within the reach of this extraordinary tribunal. It can regulate or new model the succession to the crown; as was done in the reign of Henry VIII. and William III. It can alter the established religion of the land; as was done in a variety of instances, in the reigns of king Henry VIII. and his three children. It can change and create afresh even the con-stitution of the kingdom and of Parliaments themselves; as was done by the act of union, and the several statutes for triennial and septennial elections. It can, in short, do every thing that is not naturally impossible; and therefore some have not scrupled to call its power, by a figure rather too bold, the omnipotence of Parlia-ment. True it is, that what the Parliament doth, no authority upon earth can undo."

Paterson noted that one reason Parliament could not be controlled was because Eng-land had no written constitution. This means, Paterson said, that "[i]t is difficult to say what the constitution of England is; because, not being reduced to written certainty and precision, it lies entirely at the mercy of the Parliament." The English constitution thus "bends to every governmental exigency; it varies and is blown about by every breeze of legislative humour or political caprice." Happily, Paterson noted, America stands on a different footing for every state has reduced its constitution to some written form. A written frame of government is superior to an unwritten one, Paterson said, because it embodies "the permanent will of the people, and is the supreme law of the land; it is paramount to the power of the Legislature, and can be revoked or altered only by the authority that made it." Having established the primacy of the written constitution, Paterson went on to declare that legislatures are mere "Creatures of the Constitution." They "owe their existence to the Constitution: they derive their powers from the Constitution," and, therefore, "all their acts must be conformable to it, or else they will be void."

> The Constitutiois the work or will of the People themselves, in their original, sovereign, and unlimited capacity. Law is the work or will of the Legislature in their derivative and subordinate capacity. The one is the work of the Creator, and the other of the Creature. The Constitution fixes limits to the exercise of legislative authority, and prescribes the orbit within which it must move. In short, gentlemen, the Constitution is the sun of the political system, around which all Legislative, Executive and Judicial bodies must revolve. Whatever may be the case in other countries, yet in this there can be no doubt, that every act of the Legislature, repugnant to the Constitution, as absolutely void."

Paterson went on explain the role of the judiciary in the constitutional scheme. For him, the power of judicial review was a function of the separation of powers: The people, in their constitutions, gave the legislatures power to make law; and they gave the courts the power to ensure that legislatures did not exceed their authority:

> I take it to be a clear position; that if a legislative act oppugns a constitutional principle, the former must give way, and be rejected on the score of repugnance. I hold it to be a position equally clear and found, that, in such case, it will be the duty of the Court to adhere to the Constitution, and to declare the act null and void. The Constitution is the basis of legislative authority; it lies at the foundation of all law, and is a rule and commission by which both Legislators and Judges are to proceed. It is an important principle, which, in the discussion of questions of the present kind, ought never to be lost sight of, that the Judiciary in this country is not a subordinate, but co-ordinate, branch of the government.

Paterson concluded that the Conforming Act violated the terms of the state constitution because it did not provide a proper means for assessing the compensation due the ousted landowners.

Paterson's opinion in *Van Horne* sounds very modern in its approach to the problem of judicial review. Indeed, many modern commentators point to this opinion as evidence of the Supreme Court's early embrace of the power to review the constitutionality of acts of the political branches. Yet, it is important to note that Paterson's view of judicial review may not have commanded a majority of the Supreme Court, at least in the early years. There are several reasons for this: First, Paterson's opinion was rendered in the form of a jury charge whilst on circuit. As the case was not appealed, the full Court did not have the opportunity to weigh in on Paterson's assertions. Secondly, there is evidence that other justices, most notably Samuel Chase, were more hesitant to assert the right to review the constitutionality of state legislation in every case. It bears remembering in this regard that *Van Horne* involved a challenge to a Pennsylvania statute on the grounds that it violated the Pennsylvania state constitution. It was not a claim that the statute violated the federal constitution. Thus, in *Van Horne*, Paterson was not construing federal law; he was instead assuming the power to interpret a state constitution. As will be seen, that is something that other justices might not have been completely comfortable doing.

Perhaps the Court's most extensive discussion of the power of judicial review of state legislation is found in *Calder v. Bull* (1798). Caleb Bull and his wife claimed ownership of certain land in Connecticut by virtue of a will executed in their favor by Normand Morrison, a grandson of another Normand Morrison, a prominent Connecticut physician. The Bulls' claim to the land was opposed by Calder and his wife, who claimed the land as heir of the elder Morrison. In March 1793, the probate court of Hartford County refused to record the grandson's will, thus setting aside the Bulls' claim to the land. However, the Bulls did not appeal this decision within the time required by statute, and there matters remained for almost two years. In the spring of 1795, however, the Bulls appealed directly to the Connecticut state legislature requesting that the decision of the probate court be vacated. The legislature responded with a statute setting aside the 1793 decree and ordering a new trial. After a rehearing in July 1795, the probate court reinstated the grandson's will, thus divesting the Calders of the land and giving title to the Bulls. This decision was eventually affirmed by the state Supreme Court in June 1796.

The Calders appealed to the U.S. Supreme Court arguing that the Connecticut statute setting aside the original probate court judgment and divesting them of title violated the federal Constitution's prohibition on the passage of *ex post facto* laws. Unlike *Van Horne*, which involved a challenge to a state law based on the state constitution, *Calder* was a challenge to a state law based on the federal constitution. The justices rejected Calder's appeal, but not before they had the chance to issue what was arguably the most detailed discussion of the power of federal courts to review the constitutionality of legislative enactments. Yet, while the members of the Court were unanimously of the opinion that the Supreme Court had the power of judicial review in some form, their opinions in *Calder* reflect a substantial amount of disagreement on the circumstances and manner in which the Court would be justified in its exercise. Of these opinions, Justice Chase's was the most extensive, and constituting an eloquent statement of the role of judicial review in a representative government.

Chase began his opinion by declaring "the self-evident proposition, that the several State Legislatures retain all the powers of legislation, delegated to them by the State Constitutions; which are not *expressly* taken away by the Constitution of the United States." Among these, he said, were the power to establish courts and the right to make regulations governing the conduct of trials in them. According to Chase, "all the powers that remain in the State Governments are indefinite" while those vested in the federal government are "are defined, and no constructive powers can be exercised by it." Having thus reaffirmed the doctrine of enumerated powers, Chase went on to consider whether there were any limits on the powers that might be exercised by state legislatures. In considering this subject, however, Justice Chase departed from what appeared to be a rather strict construction of the constitutional text to advance an expansive view of the power of judicial review. He began this portion of his opinion by declaring his opposition to the notion that a state legislature can be omnipotent, "or that it is absolute and without controul; although its authority should not be expressly restrained in the Constitution, or fundamental law, of the State." Instead, Chase believed that the social compact provided inherent limits on the legislature's power, and that these limits were to be found by examining the purposes for which the government was established:

> The people of the United States erected their Constitutions, or forms of government, to establish justice, to promote the general welfare, to secure the blessings of liberty; and to protect their persons and property from violence. The purposes for which men enter into society will determine the nature and terms of the social compact; and as they are the foundation of legislative power, they will decide what are the proper objects of it: The nature and ends of legislative power will limit the exercise of it.

According to Chase, therefore, acts of the legislature that are inconsistent with the ends for which the government was established are void, and an act of the legislature "contrary to the great principles of the social compact, cannot be considered a rightful exercise of legislative power." There are, he contended, "certain vital principles in our free Republican governments which will determine and over-rule an apparent and flagrant abuse of legislative power." As a result, "[t]he obligation of a law in governments established on express compact, and on republican principles, must be determined by the nature of the power, on which it is founded."

Chase's discussion to this point was largely dicta, for he himself admitted that it was unnecessary to the resolution of the case. After all, Calder's claim was founded on an explicit constitutional limitation and thus any discussion of natural law limitations on the exercise of legislative powers was largely superfluous. Consequently, Chase moved quickly to dispose of the issue at hand. He first noted that the Ex Post Facto

Clause applied to criminal, rather than civil statutes, and was inserted into the Constitution to prevent the abuses such laws had inspired in England. Bills of attainder, or bills of pains and penalties, often had the effect of making criminal that which had not been so before, or increasing the penalties for crimes after the fact. The federal Constitution's prohibition was, therefore, designed to be "an additional bulwark in favour of the personal security of the subject, to protect his person from punishment by legislative acts, having a retrospective operation." In short, Chase said, the Ex Post Facto Clause was not designed to address every statute having a retrospective effect. It was, rather, aimed at preventing Congress and the states from passing statutes criminalizing actions that were legal when taken.

According to Justice Chase, then, the Ex Post Facto Clause is largely confined to the realm of criminal law, and does not limit the state legislatures' ability to make laws altering property or contract rights. Instead, these rights were adequately protected by the Constitution's "Contracts Clause," which is a prohibition on laws impairing the obligation of contract, or the "Tender Clause," which prevents the states from making anything but gold or silver lawful currency. The distinction, Chase said, lay in the fact that the right of acquiring or alienating property is conferred by the civil society, and thus society itself may determine the circumstances under which pre-existing property rights might be altered. Chase noted that there were, in fact, situations in which it would be desirable to pass laws, which had the effect of altering existing property rights. For example, Chase recognized that government itself might pass laws taking property for public use. In such cases, however, the Fifth Amendment's Compensation Clause, rather than the Ex Post Facto Clause, would provide the appropriate remedy.

Having disposed of the federal constitutional question, the case might have ended here. However, the most interesting aspect of Chase's opinion comes after his discussion of retrospective laws. After declaring that natural law may provide the basis for judicial review, Chase went on to question whether federal courts might exercise the power of judicial review in this or any case. In Chase's opinion, the fact that a statute might violate a federal or state constitutional provision did not necessarily mean that courts were vested with power to prevent its operation. Thus, Chase refused to consider whether the Supreme Court had "jurisdiction to decide that any law made by Congress, contrary to the Constitution of the United States, is void." He then firmly declared his belief that the Supreme Court "has no jurisdiction to determine that any law of any state Legislature, contrary to the Constitution of such state, is void." Although it was his personal opinion that the law granting Bull a new trial was consistent with the powers given the legislature by the Connecticut constitution, Chase nonetheless said that the courts of Connecticut were "the proper tribunals" to decide that particular question.

This portion of Justice Chase's opinion is quite revealing. Modern lawyers and legal theorists take the notion of judicial review for granted. Indeed, John Marshall's assertion of the power of courts to review the constitutionality of legislation *Marbury v. Madison* (1803) often leaves readers with the impression that judicial review was a widely accepted practice at the turn of the nineteenth century. In *Calder*, however, Justice Chase expresses doubts that the Supreme Court could ever have the power to overturn the acts of a popularly elected assembly. Although he left open the question as to whether the Court might have power to review acts of Congress, he was certain that it could not have jurisdiction to review the acts of state legislature for conformity to a state constitution. This conclusion ran directly contrary to that of Justice Paterson, who, in *Van Horne's Lessee*, was clearly prepared to declare that Pennsylvania's Confirming Act violated that state's constitution.

For his part, Paterson seems not to have been terribly impressed by Chase's opinion in *Calder*. In own opinion, Paterson seems to have rejected Chase's assertion that the Supreme Court had no power to review the state legislation for conformity with a state constitution. On the contrary, Paterson clearly undertook to test the validity of the statute granting Bull a new trial against the provisions of the Connecticut constitution. He began by observing that the constitution of Connecticut is "made up of usages," rather than a written constitution. Paterson then considered whether the Connecticut legislature's grant of a new trial was consistent with both custom and use, and concluded that the Connecticut legislature had long exercised both judicial and legislative powers. If, therefore, the grant of a new trial in this particular case was considered as a judicial act, there would be "an end of the question" for the legislature had always retained the power to determine whether new trials ought to be granted. If, on the other hand, the statute was viewed as an exercise of legislative power, then the only question before the Court was whether the law violated the Ex Post Facto Clause. On this question, Paterson was in agreement with Chase, and concluded that the words, "ex post facto," when applied to a law, "refer to crimes, pains, and penalties" and not to retrospective laws in general.

It was left to Justice Iredell, therefore, to more fully articulate the justices' disagreement over the precise extent of the Supreme Court's power of judicial review. Although he ultimately concluded that the act of the Connecticut legislature was judicial, rather than legislative, and thus not within the power of the Supreme Court to review, he nonetheless took the opportunity to challenge Chase's assertion that natural law principles might serve as a check on legislative action. He did so by noting that in a case where a Constitution imposed no explicit limits on legislative action, there would be no power in any court to invalidate any action taken by such a legislature. Taking up Blackstone's famous theoretical example of a statute allowing a man to be a judge in his own cause, Iredell agreed that a statute that explicitly allowed a man to be both plaintiff and judge would be constitutional as long as the legislature expressly declared its intention to achieve that result. This would be the case, regardless of whether such a law would violate otherwise established norms of fairness. This view of the relationship between judicial and legislative power was the traditional one of parliamentary supremacy, which held that there was no power in England competent to invalidate an act of the king-in-parliament.

Iredell noted that Americans had wisely rejected this approach to legislative supremacy in favor of a more balanced distribution of powers. The state and federal constitutions all provided limits on legislative activity with the express purpose of "defin[ing] with precision the objects of legislative power, and [restraining] its exercise within marked and settled boundaries." As a result, Iredell said, if "any act of Congress, or the Legislature of a state, violates those constitutional provisions, it is unquestionably void; though, I admit, that as the authority to declare it void is of a delicate and awful nature, the Court will never resort to that authority, but in a clear and urgent case." If, on the other hand, a legislature passes an act that has not transgressed the explicit limits of its authority, courts are not empowered to strike such an act down, "merely because it is, in their judgement, contrary to the principles of natural justice." This is because the concepts of natural justice are "regulated by no fixed standard," and so the "ablest and purest men have differed upon the subject." In such a case, all a court could do is declare its opinion that the legislature—which Iredell admits is possessed of an "equal right of opinion"—has passed an act "inconsistent with the abstract principles of natural justice."

The decision in *Calder* is revealing in that it exposes some of the trepidations that still attended the use of judicial power in the early Supreme Court. Far from being a judiciary convinced of its power to "say what the law is," as John Marshall was later to declare, the opinions in *Calder* demonstrate a certain degree of hesitation on the part of the justices when confronted with the question of whether the courts should have the power to declare the acts of a duly constituted legislature invalid. Thus, Justice Chase clearly represented a populist line of thought which admitted the possibility that there might be some limitation on legislative power, but was more cautious about whether the courts were vested with the power to be the final arbiter of the constitutionality of legislative enactments. Moreover, while Justice Iredell appears to have been more willing to assert the power of judicial review, he did so somewhat cautiously, insisting that "the Court will never resort to that authority, but in a clear and urgent case." In the end, therefore, it seems clear that most of the members of the Supreme Court believed courts were possessed of the power of judicial review. However, the fragile nature of the federal edifice required that a great deal of discretion be exercised before the Court would exercise what Iredell called "a delicate and awful" power.

## Federal–State Relations

Throughout the years, one of the most troubling aspects of the Supreme Court's power to interpret the Constitution has been the potential for friction between proponents of states' rights and federal power. During the course of the ratification debates, antifederalists repeatedly argued that the new federal government would eventually overpower and destroy the governments of the several states. For their part, federalist writers repeatedly assured the public that the new Constitution would preserve the sovereignty of the states acting in their rightful sphere of action. According to James Madison, the Constitution established a government of "enumerated powers," in which the states retained "a very extensive portion of active sovereignty" (The Federalist No. 45). The problem for the early Supreme Court, however, was that the precise boundaries between state and federal power were never explicitly defined. As a result, in the early years of the Republic, the Court found itself involved in several important disputes over states' rights as well as its power to supervise state courts in their administration of federal law.

### Suits Against States

Article III of the Constitution gave the federal courts jurisdiction over "Controversies between two or more States [and] between a State and Citizens of another State." On its face, this provision had the effect of making the states subject to suit in the federal courts. At the same time, however, the traditional principle of "sovereign immunity" prohibited a sovereign from being sued without its consent. As a result, whether Article III was designed to abrogate the states' traditional sovereign immunity was a matter of tremendous significance, having important consequences for both foreign relations and interstate commerce. As one might expect, this question came before the Supreme Court very early in its history.

In fact, *Van Staphorst v. Maryland*, the very first case entered on the docket of the Supreme Court involved the question of state suability. Commenced in February 1791, the case involved a dispute between the state of Maryland and a group of Dutch bankers over the terms for repaying a loan the Dutch had extended at the end of the Revolution. After receiving a summons from the Supreme Court, the state entered an appearance without initially raising the question of sovereign immunity. In time, however, the state apparently thought better of its actions, and decided to try to settle the case rather than create a precedent, which in the words of a committee of the House of Delegates, "by which any individual foreigner may endanger the political and private rights of this state and her citizens."

Although the papers relating to the case have been lost, it appears that a settlement was agreed to sometime between December 1791 and February 1782, when the case was discontinued with the consent of both parties. Nonetheless, although Maryland never formally raised the issue of sovereign immunity, the case engendered a great deal of comment both inside and outside the state. In a pamphlet entitled *Observations upon the Government of the United States*, Massachusetts Attorney General James Sullivan rejected the idea that states could be brought before the bar of the Supreme Court. In his view, the Constitution did not abrogate the separate legal personality of states so as to create a "consolidated" government. On the contrary, Sullivan declared, there could be "nothing more absurd and ridiculous than to suppose the governments existing as separate governments, and yet to suppose them amenable before a civil tribunal of any kind, upon mean process." Moreover, Sullivan asserted, even if Maryland had consented to appear before the Supreme Court, its appearance could not "give a jurisdiction to the supreme court of the United States, which that court does not possess by the constitution of their power from the people of the states." Most importantly, Sullivan raised an argument that was to find its way into most of the cases concerning the suability of states: Article III's grant of jurisdiction over cases "between a state and a citizen of another state" was only meant to encompass suits in which the state itself was the plaintiff, not cases brought by private individuals against states.

Sullivan's argument was addressed in an anonymous pamphlet rather laboriously entitled, *An Enquiry into the Constitutional Authority of the Supreme Federal Court, over the Several States, in their Political Capacity*. This author, (who is now believed to be Timothy Ford), specifically confronted Sullivan's claim that Article III only authorises suits where the states themselves are plaintiffs. The author of the *Enquiry* rejects this assertion on the grounds that such a distinction is a violation of fundamental justice: "Rights and remedies," he says, "are always reciprocal." Thus, it is "an odious doctrine, that a state can compel justice from the citizens of a neighbouring state; but may withhold it from them during her pleasure." Such an "absurdity" could only spring from "a blindly devoted homage to the idol of state sovereignty" and "wages war with that divine principle, which lies at the foundation of the constitution, of establishing justice and ensuring domestic tranquillity." At bottom, however, the author of the *Enquiry* noted that the constitutional text is clear: The words of the clause "expressly declare" that the judicial power shall extend to "all *controversies between* two or more states, [and] a state and citizens of another state." The "import, spirit and necessary construction of which words are, that as on the one hand; every state may apply to this tribunal for justice against any state, individual, or any corporate body, in the nation; so they in their turns, possessing reciprocal rights, may appeal to this great and paramount source, and obtain *justice* when it is unconstitutionally withheld by any state."

The arguments raised by Sullivan's pamphlet and the *Enquiry* were to be repeated over and over again whenever the question of the suability of states arose. In fact, they were largely repeated in *Chisholm v. Georgia* (1793), a case that is likely one of the most well known of the Supreme Court's early cases. *Chisholm* arose as a result of a contract executed during the Revolution between the state of Georgia and a South Carolina merchant named Robert Farquhar. In late 1777, Georgia authorized two of its agents, Edward Davies and Thomas Stone, to purchase supplies from Farquhar for the war effort. Farquhar delivered the supplies, but Davies and Stone failed to pay even though they had received sufficient funds from the state to pay the debt. Farquhar made several attempts to obtain payment from the state, but he died in 1794. His executor, Alexander Chisholm took up Farquhar's claim, filing a petition with the Georgia general assembly in 1789. The assembly investigated Chisholm's claim, but ultimately concluded that the state was not liable because it had already paid Davies and Stone for the goods. The assembly answered that Chisholm ought to sue Davies and Stone in state court to recover the debt.

Apparently Davies and Stone were insolvent at the time, and so Chisholm filed suit against the state in the Georgia circuit court in February 1791, whereupon a summons was issued commanding Georgia to appear and answer at the next term of the court. The summons was served on Georgia Governor Edward Telfair in March of that year. Telfair promptly requested a legal opinion from the state's solicitor general, John Noel, who, along with attorney general Thomas Carnes, replied that "it never could be the intentions" of those who framed the Constitution "to subject the government of each or either of the States to be impleaded in the District, Circuit, or Supreme Foederal Courts without an express consent." Noel and Carnes noted Article III's grant of jurisdiction over suits "between a State and Citizens of other States or Aliens," but asserted that this clause "cannot be carried farther in its construction, than to Suppose the State or States in Such cases always plaintiffs or petitioners." They also argued that even if the state were subject to suit in federal court, Congress had not yet established any procedure by which such suits were to be tried. Without proper procedures, any proceedings taken in the case would be "nugatory." Noel and Carnes concluded by stating that it was their duty to "combat every attempt that may be made to infringe on the Sovereignty and Dignity of the State." They, therefore, cautioned the governor to refrain from taking any action that could "possibly be construed into a recognition of the jurisdiction of the Foederal Courts in Such Cases."

As a result, in October 1791, Georgia filed a plea to the jurisdiction to the circuit court, denying that any federal court could have jurisdiction over a claim against the state without its consent. For his part, Farquhar replied that Georgia's sovereignty was not a bar to consideration of the case because the Constitution specifically gave the federal courts jurisdiction over "Controversies between a State and Citizens of another State." The issue having been joined, the question of jurisdiction came squarely before the judges of the circuit court. As it happens, Justice Iredell was riding the southern circuit that term, and so presided over the Georgia circuit court with District Judge Nathaniel Pendleton.

After considering arguments on the question of jurisdiction, the judges decided that Farquhar's complaint should be dismissed. Iredell began his opinion by noting that "the Jurisdiction of the Courts of the U.S. is altogether *Special*" and thus, "[e]very

Plaintiff ought to show that he is entitled to come into them by the manner in which he states his case." For Iredell, therefore, it was incumbent on Farquhar to prove the existence of jurisdiction before the court could proceed. As to that question, Iredell noted the provision granting federal courts jurisdiction over suits against states; however, he pointed out that the Constitution seemed to provide that jurisdiction over such suits was in the Supreme Court alone. Iredell pointed out that Article III stated that the Supreme Court would have original jurisdiction over suits against states. He also noted that Article III did not provide for appellate jurisdiction over suits against states. If, therefore, the circuit courts had jurisdiction over such suits, there would be no appeal to the Supreme Court. That result was clearly illogical in light of the tremendous delicacy of suits against states. In his view, the Supreme Court was the only federal court with power to try such cases, although state courts might themselves still entertain such suits if authorized by the state itself.

Chisholm was not to be deterred, however. In February 1792, he commenced a new action against Georgia in the Supreme Court. A summons was issued ordering the state to appear at the August 1792 term of the court. When the case was called on August 11, Georgia failed to answer. This was in spite of the fact that the summons had been served on the governor some weeks before. As a result, U.S. Attorney General Edmund Randolph, who was representing Chisholm in a private capacity, moved the court for an order compelling the state to appear or suffer a default judgement to be entered against it. Alexander Dallas, who was representing Georgia before the Supreme Court in another case that term approached the justices and advised that although he had no instructions with respect to the *Chisholm* case, he suggested that the Court postpone consideration of Randolph's motion until the next term. The justices agreed and so put off a decision on Randolph's motion until the February 1793 term.

Governor Telfair made a report to the Georgia House of Representatives concerning the proceedings in the Supreme Court. In December 1792, the assembly passed a resolution declaring its opinion that Article III did not grant federal courts the power to "compel states to answer any process the said courts or either of them may sue out." On the contrary, the Georgia House was of the opinion that the Constitution only gave "a power to the said supreme court to hear and determine all causes commenced by a state as plaintiff against a citizen as defendant." Any contrary construction would, the assembly said, subject "the territory of the states and the treasuries thereof to the distresses or levies of a Foederal Marshal, which is totally repugnant to the smallest idea of sovereignty." Accordingly, the assembly declared that "the state of Georgia will not be bound by any decree or judgment of the said supreme court subjecting it to any process, judgement or execution it may issue" but would instead consider any such process "unconstitutional," "extrajudicial," and "*ipso facto* void."

As a result, Georgia again failed to appear when the Supreme Court met for its February 1793 term. When Attorney General Randolph's motion came on for argument the second day of the term, Jared Ingersoll and Alexander Dallas submitted the resolution of the Georgia House contesting the Supreme Court's assertion of jurisdiction, although they advised the court that they had no authority to represent the state in the matter. When no one rose to appear on Georgia's behalf, the court ordered Randolph to proceed with his argument.

Randolph began by noting Georgia's argument that Article III only envisioned states as plaintiffs and that no state could be compelled to be a defendant against its will. In reply, he argued that the Constitution envisioned a number of instances in which states could be made defendants. These included, of course, suits between states where one state would of necessity be a defendant. In addition, Randolph noted that the enforcement of numerous constitutional guarantees required that states become defendants. For example, he asked, how else could a person complain about the passage of an ex post facto law if he could not sue the state that enacted it? In the end, Randolph argued that subjecting states to suit was part of a delicate balance. In his view, any possible damage to their dignity must be weighed against the necessity of ensuring that states were subject to some control in the constitutional scheme. Randolph closed his argument by addressing the obvious political considerations of the case. He recognized that many people believed that some in the federal government were bent on a consolidation of national power, but he assured his listeners that "the prostration of State-rights is no object with me," and that the states "need not fear an assault from bold ambition" on the part of the federal government.

After Randolph concluded his argument, the justices enquired if any person present would offer an argument on behalf of the state. When no one stood up, the court enquired of A.J. Dallas, who had represented Georgia in another matter, if he would offer anything on behalf of the state. Dallas declined, stating that he had no instructions from the state. As a result, with Randolph's argument only, the court took the case under advisement and adjourned.

Two weeks later, the Supreme Court announced its decision. All the justices, except Iredell, who had rejected Chisholm's claim in the circuit court, agreed that the Constitution abrogated the states' sovereign immunity, making them subject to suit within the Supreme Court's original jurisdiction. Justices Cushing and Blair each undertook a rather straightforward textual analysis of the Constitution. Both justices noted that Article III provided that the "judicial Power" of the federal courts extended to controversies "between a State and Citizens of another state" and that the Supreme Court would have original jurisdiction in cases "in which a State shall be a Party." For Cushing and Blair, and to some extent Chief Justice Jay as well, Georgia's jurisdictional objections could be disposed of rather summarily.

Justice Blair began his opinion by noting that the Constitution expressly provided that federal courts would have jurisdiction over cases in which states were parties, and that in ratifying the Constitution, Georgia had expressly agreed to that jurisdiction. At the same time, Blair also noted that Georgia's objection to the Supreme Court's jurisdiction in this particular case was based on a hyper-technical reading of Article III. Georgia's supporters (for Georgia had, of course, not appeared in the case) claimed that the provision of Article III which gave the Supreme Court original jurisdiction over controversies "between a State and Citizens of another State" was meant to encompass only those cases in which a state was a plaintiff, and was not designed to allow a state to be made a defendant by a private citizen. Blair, however, rejected this view. He argued that order of parties in the clause had no real effect on the essence of the action. On the contrary, he said, putting the state first was merely a means of according some respect to the dignity of the states, but to read more into it would be useless.

> [I]s this [order of parties] alone a sufficient ground from which to conclude, that the jurisdiction of this Court reaches the case where a State is Plaintiff, but not where it is Defendant? In this latter case, should any man be asked, whether it was not a controversy between a State and citizen of another State, must not the answer be in the affirmative? A dispute between A. and B. is surely a dispute between B. and A. Both cases, I have no doubt, were intended; and probably the State was first named, in respect to the dignity of a State.

Blair also noted that the Constitution contemplates that states will be made defendants against their will in a variety of cases. These include controversies between a state and another state, as well as a suit by a foreign government against a state. With respect to the latter, Blair demonstrated that the order of parties had to be arbitrary; otherwise, the clause would make no sense. Thus, in providing that the judicial power would extend to cases between a state and a foreign government, the framers of the Constitution clearly envisioned that states would be made defendants by foreign governments. As Justice Blair noted, the idea that states could sue foreign governments, but not be a defendant in a case brought by a foreign government "seems to lose sight of the policy which, no doubt, suggested this provision, viz. That no State in the Union should, by withholding justice, have it in its power to embroil the whole confederacy in disputes of another nature." For Blair, then, the order in which parties were listed in Article III was of no account in determining the extent of the Supreme Court's jurisdiction, and thus, by the plain words of the constitutional text, states were amenable to suit by other states, by foreign governments, and by citizens of another state. "It seems to me," Blair concluded, "that if this Court should refuse to hold jurisdiction of a case where a State is Defendant, it would renounce part of the authority conferred, and, consequently, part of the duty imposed on it by the Constitution; because it would be a refusal to take cognizance of a case where a State is a party."

Justice Cushing made some of the very same points as Justice Blair, although he took up the question of whether a strict textual reading would do damage to the dignity of the states. Cushing noted that Georgia's supporters argued that subjecting states to suit by average citizens would "reduce States to mere corporations, and take away all sovereignty." Cushing did not think this objection had much force, however. Instead, he noted that the Constitution made numerous exceptions to the sovereignty of states in its division of powers between the states and the federal government. These included restrictions on the states' ability to coin money, to declare war, raise armies, or impair the obligation of contract. Such restrictions had not yet been thought to destroy state sovereignty, although they imposed limits on the states' freedom of action. Subjecting states to suit was just one more of these restrictions. In Cushing's words, restrictions on both the states and the national government were "thought necessary to maintain the Union; and to establish some fundamental uniform principles of public justice, throughout the whole Union." As a result, "no argument of force can be taken from the sovereignty of States" for "[w]here it has been abridged, it was thought necessary for the greater indispensable good of the whole." Nonetheless, Cushing noted, if, in the end, subjecting states to suit is found to be "inconvenient in practice" the Constitution provides a means by which its terms can be amended; but, until the clause in question is amended, the Court is bound to uphold it.

Chief Justice Jay continued this theme. He noted that in forming the Constitution, the people of the United States, "acting as sovereigns of the whole country," abolishing a Constitution by which it was their will, that the State Governments should be bound, and to which the State Constitutions should be made to conform." One aspect of this Constitution was that many prerogatives formerly possessed by the states were transferred to the national government. Jay noted that Georgia did not necessarily object to being sued in the Supreme Court, for the state seemed to concede that it was liable to be sued by another state. Rather, he said, Georgia's main objection was that it did not believe a single citizen should have the right to make it a defendant against its will. In Jay's view, this was simply a numbers game: Why, he asked, would is it more objectionable to be sued by a single person but not by a hundred thousand? A suit by a single person would have the same process and effect as being sued by another state. The complaint, Jay noted, seemed simply to be that the state's dignity was impugned if it was forced to deal with a single person. Jay contended that there was a certain incoherence in Georgia's position, however. After all, he said, Georgia has already attempted to intervene in a suit between private citizens in *Brailsford v. Spalding*, and thus was at that moment attempting to sue two citizens of South Carolina. "That rule is said to be a bad one, which does not work both ways; the citizens of Georgia are content with a right of suing citizens of other States; but are not content that citizens of other States should have a right to sue them."

Justice Wilson eschewed a straightforward textual analysis and took a rather more elaborate approach. Accordingly, he authored a lengthy and detailed opinion containing a long discussion of natural law, legal history, and jurisprudential theory. Much of this discussion has often been thought to be extraneous, and one contemporary commentator rather dryly noted that Wilson's opinion read "more like an epic poem than a Judge's argument." This opinion was grounded in Wilson's view of natural law. Man, he said, was "the workmanship of his all perfect CREATOR," while a state was merely "the *inferior* contrivance of man." Wilson then noted that the federal Constitution incorporated this very principle when it recognized that the ultimate sovereignty of government resided in the people, not the states. Consequently, the "inference which necessarily results, is, that the Constitution[,] ordained and established by [the] people; and, ... in particular by the people of *Georgia, could* vest jurisdiction or judicial power over those States and over the State of *Georgia* in particular." In giving the Supreme Court jurisdiction over suits between a State and citizens of another state, therefore, the Constitution merely reflected the people's desire to subject one of their creations to the authority of another.

For his part, Justice Iredell repeated his opinion first expressed in the circuit court that the Supreme Court lacked jurisdiction over Chisholm's case. He began by noting that while Article III appeared to confer jurisdiction on the Supreme Court to hear suits against states, that jurisdiction required something more. Article III, he said, "can only be carried into effect by acts of the Legislature appointing Courts, and prescribing their methods of proceeding." This meant that before the Supreme Court could proceed in any case, Congress had to prescribe the way in which the Court was organized and the rules of procedure. Congress had clearly done part of that work in the Judiciary Act when it set forth the number of justices and established certain rules for the conduct of cases. However, more was required before the Supreme Court could have jurisdiction over a suit against a state. This is because in Section 14 of the Judiciary Act, Congress decreed that federal courts would have the power to issue those writs "not specifically provided for by statute," which were "agreeable to the principles and usages of the common law." As a result, Iredell said, Congress did not leave the justices free to fashion any remedy they chose to meet the situation. Instead, in order for the Supreme Court to entertain a suit against a state, it must be shown that a writ could be issued against a state that was "agreeable" to traditional common law usage. In the absence of such proof, the Court was powerless to create its own and must refrain from taking any action until such time as Congress had seen fit to prescribe an appropriate writ. In this particular case, that meant that Chisholm had to demonstrate that either the particular law of Georgia or the principles of law common to all the states collectively allowed for writs of execution to be issued to the state.

Iredell then went on to demonstrate that the traditional common law modes of proceeding did not encompass such a procedure. On the contrary, he said, an action for assumpsit could never lie against the king. Instead, the only means by which a subject might obtain redress on a contract was through a petition to the king or Parliament.

Iredell noted that during the course of oral argument, Attorney General Randolph suggested that the Supreme Court did not need to await any instructions from Congress on the manner of proceeding in suits against states. According to Iredell, however, Randolph's argument came down to this: "[T]he moment a Supreme Court is formed, it is to exercise all the judicial power vested in it by the Constitution, by its own authority, whether the Legislature has prescribed the methods of doing so, or not." Iredell objected to this assertion on the grounds that the Court is "an organ of the Constitution and the law, not of the Constitution only, in respect to the manner of its proceeding," and in the absence of instructions from Congress, the Court has "no right to constitute ourselves an *ossinica brevium* or take any other short method of doing what the Constitution has chosen … should be done in another manner." Moreover, as Iredell notedCongress had done something. It had decreed that the Court should issue writs according to the "usages of the common law." Thus, any argument that the justices could make new ones would violate the plain text of Section 14. For Iredell, therefore, the case was very simple: Because Congress had decreed that the Supreme Court could issue only those writs "agreeable" to the common law, it was incumbent upon the plaintiff to show that the type of writ he asked, a writ which sought execution against a state, was agreeable to past practise. Having failed to carry that burden, Chisholm's suit had to be dismissed.

Justice Iredell was unable to convince the other justices of the correctness of his position with the result that the Court ultimately held that the state of Georgia be ordered to appear at the next term of the Court or face the prospect of a default judgement. The decision in *Chisholm* thus opened the door to all manner of suits against states. Chisholm himself was less than satisfied with the result, however. At the Supreme Court's next term in August 1793, Georgia appeared to "shew cause" why the judgment should not be entered against the state. With the consent of counsel for both parties, the court postponed argument on Chisholm's motion for default until the February 1794 term. When the court met again, it entered judgment for Chisholm and ordered that a jury be empanelled to assess damages. No jury trial was ever held, however. Instead, the matter was postponed over and over again. It was eventually dropped from the Supreme Court docket in 1798, when the court ordered all suits against states dismissed following ratification of the Eleventh Amendment.

At first glance, Chisholm's failure to take any further action in the case is puzzling. Having received a judgment in default, he had the right to have the damages assessed by a jury and obtain writs of execution for payment of the sums due. On closer examination, however, it appears that Chisholm's inaction was simply prudence, for he had apparently decided that Georgia was unlikely to pay any judgment that might be rendered against it, regardless of what the Supreme Court said. As executor of the Robert Farquhar's estate, Chisholm no doubt concluded that spending further effort on lawyers and legal proceedings would be a waste of time and money. Meanwhile, Peter Trezevant, Farquhar's son-in-law, petitioned the Georgia legislature directly for a settlement of the claim. In December 1794, the legislature awarded Trezevant a number of certificates in an amount substantially less than the value of the original claim. Farquhar's heirs then spent the better part of fifty years trying to get the state to redeem the certificates. They were finally paid in 1847.

Meanwhile, although Iredell's legal reasoning was controversial, his political instincts were acute. The day after the Court announced its decision in *Chisholm*, Massachusetts Congressman Theodore Sedgewick introduced a proposal in the House for an amendment to the Constitution designed to overturn the Supreme Court's opinion. The following day, another Massachusetts Federalist, Caleb Strong, introduced a similar amendment in the Senate. Although neither body took up these proposals immediately, it was not long before the clamor for a legislative reversal of *Chisholm* was too much for Congress to resist. State legislatures throughout the country expressed their outrage at the Court's attempt to abrogate the principle of sovereign immunity. For its part, the lower house of the Georgia legislature passed a bill providing that any federal marshal who attempted to execute any writ resulting from the *Chisholm* case would be declared a felon and suffer death by hanging without benefit of clergy. The upper house refused to go along with this rather drastic proposal, however.

The furor was so great that in the end that the Senate overwhelmingly agreed to propose the following amendment to the Constitution for ratification by the several states:

The Judicial Power of the United States shall not be construed to extend to any Suit in Law or Equity, commenced or prosecuted against one of the United States by Citizens of another State or by Citizens or Subjects of any foreign State.

The House concurred, and the proposed amendment went to the states in March 1794. Strangely enough, it received the requisite number of ratifications within a year of its being proposed. Unfortunately, not all of the states that had approved the amendment had notified Congress of ratification. As a result, it was not until January 8, 1798, that President Adams formally notified Congress that proof of the required ratifications had been received and that, consequently, the Eleventh Amendment was in effect.

Ratification of the amendment resulted in a complete reversal of the Supreme Court's decision in *Chisholm v. Georgia*. However, the years between *Chisholm* and formal notification of the ratification saw a number of other cases wend their way through the Supreme Court docket. One such case was *Oswald v. Allen* (1795), which involved a suit on a simple employment contract filed against the State of New York, and which became the only case against a state by a private individual ever tried in the Supreme Court. It ended with the state being found liable for damages for failure to honor a contract entered into during the Revolution.

The case arose as a result of New York's appointment of John Holt to be the state's public printer at a rate of £200 per year. Holt served in that capacity for several years, but was apparently never paid in full for his services. After his death in 1784, Holt's executors brought several petitions to the New York assembly requesting payment, but these were all denied. Eleazer Oswald, Holt's son-in-law and a resident of Pennsylvania, finally brought suit in the Supreme Court in 1791, seeking damages in excess of $31,000.

The summons was served upon New York's governor and attorney general in August 1791, although it did not provoke any immediate outcry. Within the year, however, rumblings of discontent were heard throughout the state. New York was, after all, commonly regarded as strongly anti-federalist in many respects. Moreover, then-governor George Clinton and Supreme Court Chief Justice John Jay were longstanding political rivals. Indeed, by the spring of 1792, New York's Federalists had nominated Jay as a candidate for governor of New York in the coming election. A confrontation between Clinton and the man nominated to unseat him could not, therefore, have been unexpected. Consequently, New York ignored the summons issuing out of the Supreme Court and refused to enter a plea to Oswald's suit.

When New York failed to answer, Oswald's attorneys moved for a writ compelling the state's appearance in the Supreme Court. This motion presented the Court with a dilemma, as issuing the requested writ would obviously be quite provocative. In notes that were never actually published in the case, Justice Iredell considered the problem of whether a state could be made a defendant in a suit brought by a citizen of another state. Anticipating the opinion he would later deliver in *Chisholm v. Georgia*, Iredell questioned whether the Court had any jurisdiction in any proceeding brought by a private individual. Although he noted Article III's grant of power to hear controversies between states and citizens of other states and foreign countries, Iredell believed it was incumbent upon Congress to provide rules for the trial of such cases. In the absence of any new rules, Iredell argued that the Supreme Court should not set them up. As a result, the traditional modes of determining such cases must prevail, which meant that Oswald should petition the New York legislature for relief.

In the event, the Court was able to avoid the immediate problem, because the original summons appeared to be defective in that it failed to specify Oswald's citizenship. As Justice Iredell also pointed out, the Supreme Court only had jurisdiction over suits between a state and citizens of another state. It did not have any power to hear cases involving New York and its own citizens. In addition, the original summons did not appear to have been served in the time allotted by the rules. As a result, Iredell suggested that the original summons be dismissed and the plaintiff commence a new action.

After several attempts to obtain proper service, a new summons ordering the state to enter an appearance in the Supreme Court at the February 1793 term was finally served on Governor Clinton in January of that year. New York again ignored this writ when the Supreme Court convened for its February term. This time, however, the ground had shifted. The question of state suability had been fully considered by the Court in *Chisholm v. Georgia*. The decision affirming the Court's power to hear suits against states made New York's refusal to appear a more risky proposition. Relying on its decision in *Chisholm*, the Supreme Court issued an order declaring that a default judgement would be entered in Oswald's favor unless the state appeared at the next term. In effect, this order meant that unless New York appeared in August 1793, judgement would be entered for Oswald, and a jury of Pennsylvanians would decide what damages the state would pay. In an effort to forestall that possibility, Jared Ingersoll was retained by the state to enter a plea to the Court's jurisdiction. On August 5, 1793, Ingersoll filed a plea in which he asserted that the New York was a "free, sovereign, and independent State" and could not be compelled to answer any claim brought in the Supreme Court or any other court without its consent.

At this point, *Oswald v. New York* took a strikingly different turn from other cases involving state sovereignty. Whereas other states had strongly resisted the Supreme Court's attempts to assert jurisdiction over them, New York's legislature eventually authorized the state's attorney general to appear and defend Oswald's action on the merits. This change of strategy was largely the result of a dramatic change in New York's political climate. The elections for the state assembly held in 1793 produced a radical overhaul of that body so that when the assembly convened in early 1794, Federalists dominated both houses. Intent on resisting Republican Governor George Clinton at every turn, the assembly eventually rejected Clinton's recommendation that it pass a resolution condemning the Supreme Court's decision in *Chisholm*. It then authorized attorney general Nathaniel Lawrence to defend the state against Oswald's claim.

A year passed while both sides took depositions, one of which was actually the deposition of John Jay, the chief justice. Jay had been a member of the New York convention when Holt was hired. (The fact that a sitting chief justice was called to be a witness in the case did not appear to trouble any of the parties as Jay left on his mission to England shortly thereafter and never returned to the bench.) Finally, on February 5, 1795, a jury was empanelled and a trial held before Justices Wilson, Blair, Iredell, and Paterson. The bulk of the trial, which lasted a single day, consisted of reading the various depositions taken during the previous year. Those submitted on behalf of Oswald tended to show that his father-in-law, Holt, had been retained as the public printer by the state at an agreed rate of £200 per year and that he had served for approximately seven years in that capacity. For its part, New York contended that Holt was hired for only a single year and that he had been paid for his services.

The jury eventually returned a verdict in Oswald's favour in the amount of $5,315 in damages and $.06 in costs. A short time later, Oswald wrote a letter to New York Governor Clinton demanding payment of that sum. Clinton forwarded Oswald's letter to the assembly which authorized payment on condition that Oswald sign a release of all claims. Six months later, Oswald died of yellow fever in Philadelphia.

As noted earlier, land claims were also a source of great concern to the states during the ratification process. Over the years, title to lands in the west had been heavily disputed by various grantees. These disputes often involved titles received from various land companies, which were formed to profit from speculation in land. As a result, claimants to land frequently found themselves in court either suing to defend their title from other claimants or suing to eject those who had claims from other sources. The fact that state governments were the source of many of these titles created the possibility that the states themselves would be drawn into these very complicated disputes. One of these cases, *Hollingsworth v. Virginia*, found its way to the Supreme Court within a short time after the Court opened for business.

*Hollingsworth* was the culmination of a long-standing dispute over the ownership of lands in what is now West Virginia. The case had its origins in an event occurring in Pontiac's War (1763). During the course of the war, Indians had taken or destroyed property belonging to merchants and traders in the Ohio Valley, the value of which was estimated at the time to be approximately £85,916, in New York currency. The injured parties formed the Indiana Company to obtain compensation from the Indians in the form of a land grant. The company had 85,916 shares, which were distributed to the merchants in an amount proportional to their various losses. At the Council of Fort Stanwix, in 1768, the chiefs of the Six Nations granted a total of 1.8 million acres to the holders of the company as compensation for their losses (Lewis, 33–65).

The Indiana Company encountered opposition to its grant almost immediately. Virginia regarded the grant as a violation of its charter of 1609, which gave the colony title to lands within its charter boarders extending from "sea-to-sea." In addition, prominent Virginians, such as George Washington and George Mason, represented competing claimants to the same land. When the Indiana Company took steps to offer portions of the land for sale to the public in 1776, the Virginia Convention, which was then acting as a provincial legislature, passed several resolutions denying the validity of the grant and warning all persons that Virginia would not recognize any title to the lands in question that were not approved by the state's general assembly. Numerous attempts to get the Virginia assembly to approve the grant were rejected, with the result that the Virginia assembly passed a resolution declaring the Indiana Company's grant to be "utterly void, and of no effect." Finally, in 1779, Virginia announced its intention to divide the disputed land into counties and open a land office to sell grants for its own profit (Lewis, 216–217; 221–222).

The dispute eventually found its way before the Continental Congress. Representatives for the Indiana Company filed a number of petitions, which ultimately resulted in Congress passing a resolution in 1779 asking that Virginia cease selling the land in question, at least until the end of the war. Virginia's assembly responded to this request with a resolution of its own, affirming her own sovereignty and denying Congress' power to interfere in matters within her own territory. Congress tried again to resolve the dispute in 1781 by inviting Virginia to send delegates to a conference with representatives of the Indiana Company and others claiming western lands, but the state refused, asserting that it would "derogate[] from the sovereignty of a State to be drawn into a contest by an individual or company of individuals." Powerless to force Virginia to address the company's claims, the Continental Congress took no further action.

There matters stood until the new Constitution was drafted in Philadelphia in 1787. The potential for conflict over the Indiana Company's grant was evident almost immediately upon completion of the document. In April 1788, shortly before the Virginia ratifying convention was to convene, Virginia governor Edmund Randolph wrote a letter to James Madison expressing his concern that controversy over the company's claim would soon rear its head. Randolph believed that Article III's grant of jurisdiction over suits between states and citizens of other states would revive the dispute. Such a suit would no doubt cause confusion among settlers who were currently living on the land and whose titles would now be called into question. Moreover, Virginia's taxpayers stood to lose a great deal of money if the Indiana Company was ultimately successful in a suit in federal court.

Randolph's predictions were correct. The Indiana Company's claim was discussed several times during the course of the convention's debates. George Mason warned that if the Constitution were ratified, the Indiana Company would use the federal courts to take the land out of the hands of those who had received their grants from Virginia. Mason predicted that "20,000 families" would be "reduced to ruin and misery, driven from their farms, and obliged to leave their country." (Kaminski & Saladino, 1200) James Madison attempted to rebut Mason's dire warnings by arguing that Mason had misinterpreted Article III's provision giving federal courts jurisdiction over suits involving states. According to Madison, it was "not within the power of individuals to call any State into Court. The only operation it can have, is, that if a State should wish to bring suit against a citizen, it must be brought before a Federal Court" (Kaminski & Saladino, 1414). Patrick Henry, an ardent opponent of the Constitution, rejected Madison's interpretation as "perfectly incomprehensible." In Henry's view, the plain words of Article III gave the federal courts power to hear suits involving states "without discriminating between plaintiff and defendant." (Kaminski & Saladino, 1422–23)

However, John Marshall, the future chief justice, agreed with Madison. No one, Marshall said, should "think that a State will be called to the bar of the Federal court" (Kaminski & Saladino, 1433).

As might have been expected, it was not long before the Indiana Company decided to take advantage of Article III's grant of jurisdiction over suits against states. In October 1789, only one month after the federal courts were established by the Judiciary Act, representatives of the shareholders announced their intention to bring suit against Virginia. Before filing the action, however, the company made several attempts to petition the Virginia assembly to settle its claims. When these efforts failed, a suit was filed by the heirs of William Grayson, a shareholder in the Indiana Company, against the state of Virginia seeking $233,124.66 in damages. On August 11, 1792, the Supreme Court issued a subpoena ordering the state to appear at the February 1793 term. Virginia's governor Henry Lee forwarded the subpoena to the Virginia assembly for its consideration. The House of Delegates eventually passed a resolution declaring that the claims of the Indiana Company had already been decided by the legislature and thus "cannot be again called into question, before any Tribunal than the General Assembly … without a dangerous and unconstitutional Assumption of power." The assembly also resolved "that the Jurisdiction of the supreme Court of the united States, does not and cannot extend to this case" and that "the State cannot be made a defendant in the said Court at the suit of any individual or individuals."

Unfortunately, for Governor Lee, the assembly did not provide any specific instructions as to how to handle the suit. For his part, the state's attorney general, James Innis, worried that the Court would enter judgement if the state failed to appear. However, Innis was equally convinced that an appearance would be construed as an acceptance of the court's jurisdiction. Innis, therefore, suggested that the governor himself travel to Philadelphia for the Supreme Court's February 1793 term so as to be on hand to make decisions as to how to approach the litigation. Innis' advise seems to have been motivated by the fact that the Supreme Court was set to decide the case of *Chisholm v. Georgia*. A decision in that case would obviously have important repercussions for similar suits then pending.

The court's decision in *Chisholm* affirming the suability of states provided new urgency to the proceedings. A few days after the decision in *Chisholm*, a new subpoena was issued removing William Grayson and substituting Levi Hollingsworth, a wealthy Philadelphia merchant, as plaintiff. This substitution was necessary to remedy a defect in the pleadings, because Grayson was a citizen of Virginia and diversity of citizenship was required in order for the Supreme Court to have jurisdiction. This subpoena was served on the state with the result that the assembly passed a resolution decrying the decision in *Chisholm*. This decision, the assembly said, was "incompatible with, and dangerous to the sovereignty and independence of the individual states, as the same tends to a general consolidation of these confederated republics." The assembly also passed a resolution urging its senators and representatives in Congress to "unite their utmost and earliest exertions" toward the passage of a constitutional amendment reversing the decision in *Chisholm*.

The case remained on the docket for several more years, during which attorneys for the company sought to compel the state's appearance. The Court eventually issued another subpoena to the state ordering it to appear at the February 1797 term. The state failed to appear as ordered and so the Court permitted the company to proceed *ex parte*. The justices granted the company's motion to appoint commissioners to begin to take evidence in preparation for trial. For its part, Virginia was counting on the ratification of what was to be the Eleventh Amendment to prevent the suit from being completed. By late 1797, Virginia officials expected that ratification would come at any time thus putting an end to *Hollingsworth* and all other cases then pending against states.

Finally, on January 8, 1798, President Adams informed Congress that the Eleventh Amendment had received the required number of ratifications. The amendment provided that "the judicial power of the United States shall not be construed to extend to any suit in law or equity, commenced or prosecuted against one of the United States, by citizens of another state, or by citizens or subjects of any foreign state." At the Supreme Court's next term, held in February 1798, Attorney General Charles Lee moved the court to consider whether it could still have jurisdiction over suits against states. Although counsel in several cases then pending argued that the amendment was prospective in nature, on February 14, 1798, the justices unanimously held that "the amendment being constitutionally adopted," the court could not have "any jurisdiction, in any case, past or future, in which a state was sued by the citizens of another state, or by citizens or subjects of any foreign state." *Hollingsworth v. Virginia*, along with several other cases then pending, was dismissed the very same day, the court having "no Jurisdiction of this Cause."

Revolutionary-era legislation punishing suspected Tories gave rise to other claims against states as well. One of these, *Vassall v. Massachusetts* (1793), was commenced against the Bay State to obtain compensation for property taken by the commonwealth during the war. It began when William Vassall, a wealthy Boston merchant, left the state for England in the summer of 1777. Originally Vassall claimed that he left because he was an old man who was desirous of avoiding the tumult of war. Later on, however, he claimed that he had left because he could not supervise his Jamaica plantation from Massachusetts while the colony was at war with England. Whatever the true motives behind Vassall's departure, Massachusetts decided to treat him as a Tory. In 1780, the state government took control of Vassall's property, although it did not actually confiscate it. Instead, the state mortgaged his Boston mansion for $50,000 and auctioned off the furniture in order to raise funds for the war.

Upon the signing of the treaty of peace, Vassall assumed that he would have no difficulty obtaining possession of his property. Because the state had not formally confiscated his property, he believed that he was entitled to repossession under the terms of the treaty requiring restoration of all property confiscated from loyalists. Unfortunately, the state refused to comply with the terms of the treaty. Instead, it allowed Vassall to take possession of his mansion, but only if he agreed to assume the £50,000 mortgage taken out by the state. It also refused to make any restitution for the furniture and other personal property sold at auction.

After unsuccessfully petitioning the Massachusetts General Court for relief, Vassall commenced an action against the state in the Supreme Court in February 1793, a few days prior to the Supreme Court's decision in *Chisholm*. A subpoena was issued commanding the state to appear at the August 1793 term, but no one appeared on the state's behalf. Indeed, the case appears to have simply languished on the docket. It was continued from term to term for the next several years until it was ultimately dismissed "with costs" in February 1797. None of the papers in the case exist today, so it is difficult to say exactly why it was ultimately dismissed. It may be that Vassall failed to prosecute the case and some have theorized that the impending passage of the Eleventh Amendment might have convinced him that his claim would ultimately fail (Marcus, 369, n. 80). Nevertheless, although the Supreme Court appears not to have rendered any opinion in the matter, *Vassall* is interesting for the surprisingly thoughtful debate it provoked in the Massachusetts General Court as well as the state's newspapers on the question of whether states could be subject to suit by private individuals.

This debate began when, upon receiving the summons in *Vassall*, Governor John Hancock issued a proclamation calling for a special session of the legislature to convene in September 1793. Hancock's proclamation was greeted with almost universal approbation.

For their part, those who had opposed the ratification of the Constitution used the debate to proclaim, "I told you so." Writing in the Massachusetts Mercury, *Marcus* reminded his readers that supporters of the Constitution had repeatedly asserted that no state would be subjected to suit in the federal courts if the Constitution was ratified. According to *Marcus*, Massachusetts would not have ratified the Constitution if it were clear that states would be subject to suit at the instance of private individuals:

The power which the Federal Government has, to call into their Courts, a Commonwealth or State, to answer the demand of a foreigner (perhaps a tory) was powerfully opposed in the Convention of this and other Commonwealths and States in the Union. It was debated in our Convention with great strength and propriety, that the power once given, would not only endanger the sovereignty of the Commonwealth, but would open a door for the tories and refugies to sue for estates which were forfeited to, and justly confiscated by, their country from which they had deserted in an hour of distress…. It was idle in the extreme, for the States to alienate a power, and retain only the hope of its never being exercised; a power the more dangerous when alienated, as we now see, that it leads to a direct consolidation of the governments of the Union into one.…

For *Marcus* and others, the Supreme Court's decision in *Chisholm* confirmed their worst nightmare. Opening the door to suits by aliens, in particular, had the potential to expose the states to substantial financial liabilities. The amount of confiscations and damage done to the property of Tories and other British subjects during and after the war was likely astronomical. Thus, allowing states to be sued for damages in such cases would likely drain the treasuries of quite a few. In short, if Tories could sue states for damages in federal courts, Massachusetts' taxpayers had better get ready to pay dearly.

When the General Court finally convened, Governor Hancock presented an address in which he set forth the basic problem. Governments, he said, should always be prepared to do justice; but he noted "there are certain inherent principles in the Constitution of each, which can never be surrendered without essentially changing the nature, or destroying the existence of the Government." Thus, Hancock "could not conceive that the People of this Commonwealth, when they, by their Representatives in Convention, adopted the Constitution of a General Government, expected that each State should be held liable to answer on compulsory civil process, to every individual resident in another State, or in a foreign kingdom." He then suggested two ways of dealing with the decision in *Chisholm*. On the one hand, the state could oppose the exercise of jurisdiction asserted by the Supreme Court. In the alternative, the state might also take a more conciliatory path and agree that the Court's decision was correct as a matter of pure textual interpretation, but that an amendment clarifying the provisions of Article III and reaffirming state sovereignty was, therefore, necessary.

The General Court appointed a joint committee to draft a response to Hancock's report. The committee quickly reported its conclusion that it was "not expedient" that a state should be subject to suit in the federal courts and that Massachusetts' representatives in Congress should work toward the immediate adoption of an amendment to the Constitution. The State Senate approved the report without much debate, but the report was more controversial in the House. While almost no one thought that states should be subject to suit, many members of the House were dissatisfied with the tone of the committee's report. They believed that the state ought to make a more determined objection to the *Chisholm* decision. Thus, William Martin argued that the General Court ought to clearly condemn the justices' decision. Contrary to the assertions of others, Martin did not think that there was anything improper in the legislature "declaring their opinion against a measure, which a majority of the Judges had decided to be a law." Indeed, he noted that the English Parliament had "often reprimanded their Judges" and that "he should always consider Judges as not infallible."

Representative John Davis expressed something of the opposite view. While he was opposed to the suability of states, he expressed himself equally opposed to pretending that the constitutional text did not say what it in fact did:

> The articles in the Constitution, on which the decision was grounded, it was said, would admit of a different construction. The opinions of some respectable members of the Federal Convention had been quoted, who declared it not to be the sense of that body to convey the power now claimed by the Supreme Court. It had been affirmed by many, that the Convention of this State did not understand such a power to be conveyed. It had been observed that it was not expressly declared that, that an individual might sue a State, and in case of doubt the construction should be in favour of the State: And it was also affirmed that such a surrender of Sovereignty was without precedent in history.... [B]ut when we had a solemn instrument before us, which we could all read, and ought to understand, and which was composed and considered with so much care and caution, [one ought] not consent to resort to the opinions of any man, however reputable, to support a construction, variant from the plain language of the instrument.

Davis also pointed out that the Constitution was ratified by the whole people themselves, and that any attempt to call into question the people's understanding of the document would only give aid to those who said popular government was bound to fail. As a result, Davis asked, "[w]ould we strengthen and confirm the doctrines of despots, as well as the enemies of the Constitution, by declaring to our sister States and to the world, that the people of this Commonwealth did not comprehend the Constitution which they had adopted, or that they had suffered themselves to be duped and deceived?"

In the end, General Court passed a more simple resolution declaring the assembly's belief that giving the federal courts jurisdiction over suits against states was "unnecessary and inexpedient" and "dangerous to the peace, safety and independence of the several States, and repugnant to the first principles of a Federal Government." Ultimately, however, the entire debate was eventually rendered moot by the ratification of the Eleventh Amendment. In overturning the Supreme Court's decision in *Chisholm*, the amendment prevented the Supreme Court from having any further jurisdiction over suits against states, effectively leaving the states free from the fear that they would, as John Hancock put it, be "held liable to answer on compulsory civil process, to every individual resident in another State, or in a foreign kingdom."

## Review of State Court Decisions

The fact that states might no longer be able to be sued in federal courts did not mean that the potential for friction between the state and federal governments was eliminated.

For while states might no longer be sued directly, the Supreme Court's power to hear appeals from the decisions of state courts in matters involving the constitutionality of state or federal statutes granted by Section 25 of the Judiciary Act, created the possibility of conflict in a number of cases. The Court itself seemed cognizant of the pitfalls, however, and in several early cases exercised its power of review rather sparingly.

The first such case arose in 1792, when Stephen Hooper of Massachusetts sued Thomas Pagan and his brothers in the Massachusetts state courts to recover the proceeds of the sale of the brigantine *Thomas* and her cargo. The dispute began when a privateer owned by the Pagans captured the *Thomas*, which was owned by Hooper, in the waning days of the Revolution. The Pagans sought to have the captured ship declared a prize by the British vice-admiralty court in Halifax, Nova Scotia, but the court rejected the claim on the grounds that the vessel was taken after the cessation of hostilities. On receiving the admiralty court's decree, the Pagans sought to appeal the decision to the decision to the High Court of Appeals in Prize Causes in London. At the same time, Hooper and the Pagans agreed to sell the ship and its cargo pending the outcome of the appeal. After the sale, however, the Pagans took no further action to prosecute their appeal, although they kept the money.

There matters stood until Thomas Pagan, the youngest of the Pagan brothers went to Massachusetts on family business in 1788. Upon his arrival in the state, Hooper commenced a suit against the Pagans in the Massachusetts courts asking that the proceeds of the sale of the *Thomas* paid over to him. The Pagans sought to have the suit dismissed on the grounds that the common law courts could not have jurisdiction over prize cases, but the Massachusetts Supreme Judicial Court rejected this defense. The court admitted that it could never have jurisdiction over the question of prize, but noted that the basis of the suit was simply the Pagan brothers' agreement to pay over the money from the sale of the ship if their appeal were denied. Since the Pagans had done nothing to prosecute the appeal in over five years, they were not entitled to hold the money.

Hooper's Massachusetts law suit inspired the Pagans to obtain an appeal of the original vice-admiralty court decision. After several months, they obtained a decree in London affirming their right to the proceeds of the sale. This decree was based on the fact that Hooper had failed to appear in the High Court of Admiralty in England, rather than on the merits of the original question of prize. Nonetheless, the Pagans refused to pay the Massachusetts judgment, and Thomas Pagan was eventually arrested and imprisoned on a writ of execution. Almost immediately, the case became the subject of a flurry of diplomatic correspondence, as various British ministers demanded that the Washington administration obtain Pagan's release from jail. For his part, Pagan sought review of the Massachusetts decision in the United States Supreme Court.

Pagan's request for review ran into one very significant obstacle. Section 25 of the Judiciary Act allowed Supreme Court review of a state Supreme Court decree only where it was alleged that the state court had committed an error in the interpretation of *federal law* apparent "on the face of the Record." Thus, the Supreme Court could only take jurisdiction of cases in which state courts had declared a federal law unconstitutional or upheld a state law against a claim that it conflicted with the federal Constitution. The problem for Pagan, therefore, was that the Massachusetts court did not base its decision on a question of federal law and so no error would be apparent "on the face of the Record." Nonetheless, after some hesitation, Justice Wilson was eventually prevailed upon to sign a writ of error instructing Massachusetts' highest court to return a record of the proceedings of the case for review. Unfortunately, the writ was directed to the Massachusetts "Supreme Court," rather than to the "Supreme Judicial Court." The Massachusetts judges refused to take notice of the writ when served upon them on the grounds that no such court existed.

Massachusetts Chief Justice Francis Dana subsequently wrote to Chief Justice Jay advising that the state court judges would entertain a proper writ in "due form," whereupon Pagan's attorneys sought a new writ. This time, however, the full court insisted on having a hearing before it decided whether to reissue the original writ. Although he argued strenuously for Supreme Court jurisdiction, Pagan's attorney was ultimately forced to admit that the Massachusetts decision was not based on federal law, and thus no error would be apparent on the record. Attorney General Edmund Randolph then rose to urge the Court to accept jurisdiction in light of the important diplomatic consequences of the case. The justices declined this invitation, however, and unanimously voted to refuse reissuance of the writ without some proof that the Massachusetts court had committed an error of law that would be apparent on the face of the record.

The Court's refusal to intervene in Pagan's case reveals the early justices' tendency to be strict constructionists in their interpretation of the first Judiciary Act. The justices were clearly aware of the possibility of conflict that attended the federal courts' power to review the decisions of state courts, and so they tread very cautiously, only undertaking to review state court actions when the jurisdiction was evident. At the same time, however, the justices appeared to be quite willing to review the decisions of the state courts when those courts undertook to interpret federal law.

One such example is found in *Penhallow v. Doane's Administrators* (1795). This case began in 1777, when the privateer *McClary*, owned by John Penhallow of New Hampshire, captured the brigantine *Lusanna*, owned by Elisha Doane of Massachusetts. At the time of her seizure, the *Lusanna* was carrying papers indicating she was a British vessel. When the ship was libeled in the New Hampshire state admiralty court, Doane attempted to argue that the vessel's British registry was a ruse designed to allow the *Lusanna* to avoid seizure by the English navy and return to America. Unfortunately for Doane, however, the case was tried in Portsmouth, the *McClary*'s home port, with the result that the jury returned a verdict for the captors. The judge then ordered that the *Lusanna* and her cargo be sold and the proceeds be distributed to the *McClary*'s crew and owners.

Doane immediately asked leave to appeal the verdict to the Committee on Appeals, a body composed of members of the Continental Congress that heard appeals from prize cases in the various state admiralty courts. However, the New Hampshire admiralty judge denied the appeal, on the grounds that New Hampshire law did not permit an appeal to Congress. Doane, therefore, sought review in the New Hampshire Superior Court, which held a second trial in March 1778. This trial ended in a hung jury, and so a third trial was held in September of the same year. This third jury also returned a verdict in favor of the *McClary*, whereupon Doane again requested an opportunity to appeal to Congress. The New Hampshire Superior Court denied this request as well, and the *Lusanna* and her cargo were subsequently sold. Unwilling to leave matters there, Doane petitioned Congress to intervene and order the proceeds of the sale to be turned over to him. This petition was eventually referred to the Court of Appeals in Cases of Capture, the successor to the Committee on Appeals. The Court of Appeals took up Doane's petition and in September 1783, decreed that the decision of the New Hampshire courts should be overturned and the proceeds of the *Lusanna*'s sale returned to Doane.

New Hampshire refused to recognize the Court of Appeals' ruling, however. Moreover, Doane himself died, leaving the administrators of his estate to carry on. After several fruitless efforts to obtain enforcement of the congressional decree in various state courts, Doane's administrators exhibited a libel in 1792 in the newly created federal District Court for the District of New Hampshire against Penhallow and the agent for the *McClary*'s crew. The case was immediately transferred to the docket of the New Hampshire circuit court because John Sullivan, the New Hampshire district judge, had represented the *McClary*'s owners when Doane's appeal was pending before Congress. After some delay, the case came before the circuit court in October 1793. Justices Blair and Wilson were assigned to the New Hampshire court that term, but Wilson recused himself because he represented the *Lusanna*'s owners in the congressional Court of Appeals. Justice Blair was thus left alone to render a decision.

The primary question before the circuit court remained the jurisdiction of the former congressional Court of Appeals. As they had on several occasions before, the *McClary*'s owners contended that the congressional court did not have the power to review the decisions of the New Hampshire Superior Court. In a rather sweeping opinion, Justice Blair rejected this position, holding that Congress' power to review the decisions of state admiralty court was not dependent on any specific grant of jurisdiction. According to Blair, Congress' power to review prize cases was inherent in its power to wage war on behalf of the several states. In delegating to Congress the power to conduct military operations, New Hampshire and the other colonies had implicitly given Congress the power to review prize cases. Consequently, Blair did not review the merits of the claims to the *Lusanna*. Instead, he viewed the case merely as a question of jurisdiction. Having found that the case was properly before the congressional Court of Appeals, Blair had no trouble in declaring that its decrees must be given effect. He, therefore, ordered that Penhallow pay Doane's administrators damages for the wrongful detention of the *Lusanna*, and appointed commissioners to determine the exact amount due. The commissioners reported back during the fall 1794 term of the New Hampshire circuit court recommending that Doane's executors be awarded the sum of $38,000 in damages and $154 in costs. Justice Cushing, who presided over that term of the circuit court, accepted the commissioners' report and entered judgment for Doane's executors accordingly.

Penhallow appealed the circuit court decision to the Supreme Court, which heard arguments in the case during the February 1795 term. Only four justices were on hand to hear argument in the case. Chief Justice Jay was in England attempting to negotiate a treaty of commerce and Justice Wilson recused himself because of his earlier representation of the *Lusanna*'s owners. As they had done in the circuit court, Penhallow's lawyers argued that the circuit court could not enforce the decree of the congressional Court of Appeals because the congressional court did not have jurisdiction over Doane's claim. It took eight days for counsel on both sides to lay out the arguments on the jurisdictional question, but in the end, the justices unanimously upheld the congressional court's jurisdiction.

The majority agreed with Justice Blair that the Confederation Congress possessed inherent power to determine prize cases because Congress was the body authorized to wage war on behalf of the United States. The Court began by considering whether the confederation Congress had the power to institute courts to try prize cases. This was necessary, as Justice Paterson noted, because if Congress prior to the Articles of Confederation lacked power over prize, its decisions as to the distribution of the proceeds of the *Lusanna* must be set aside.

Paterson made short work of this argument. Eschewing a theoretical exposition, Paterson took a more practical view of the problem. "The powers of Congress were revolutionary in their nature," he wrote, "arising out of events, adequate to every national emergency, and co-extensive with the object to be attained." Congress was "the general, supreme, and controuling council of the nation, the centre of the union, the centre of force, and the sun of the political system." Because Congress itself came into force of necessity, the only way to determine the true scope of its powers was to determine what powers it actually exercised. Congress conducted the war because all the states agreed that Congress was the body best able to do it. Because the power to regulate prize is inherent in the power to conduct war, the several states impliedly consented to Congress' scheme for regulating prize cases.

Justice Iredell largely agreed with this formulation. "The powers of Congress at first were little more than advisory," he said, "but, in proportion as the danger increased, [Congress'] powers were gradually enlarged, either by express grant, or by implication arising from a kind of indefinite authority, suited to the unknown exigencies that might arise." Among these powers, Iredell said, was the power of "external sovereignty," which was the power to represent the various states before in other nations as well as the power to conduct war. In his view, Congress had the final say in prize cases because the question of prize is to be determined by the law of nations. Indeed, Iredell said, a prize court is, in reality, "a court of all the nations in the world, because all persons in every part of the world, are concluded by its sentences." Thus, the power over prize "ought to belong to the national sovereignty" alone. Although Iredell was troubled by the idea that the congressional committee on appeals might have the power to overrule the decisions of a New Hampshire state court prior to the ratification of the Articles of Confederation in 1781, he put aside these concerns because the original decree had been affirmed by the congressional Court of Appeals created by the Articles of Confederation.

The Court had "little difficulty" with the question of whether Congress had power over prize after the ratification of the Articles of Confederation in 1781. The Ninth Article of that document specifically gave Congress "sole and exclusive power" to establish rules for prize cases. In pursuance of that article, Congress created the Court of Appeals in Prize Cases, which heard and rejected Penhallow's claim to the *Lusanna*. The decree of the Court of Appeals was, therefore, "conclusive and final."

The only remaining question was whether the newly created federal district court for the District of New Hampshire had the power to enforce the decrees of the old Court of Appeals. For Paterson, the question admitted of little doubt. In his view, because both the congressional Court of Appeals and the New Hampshire admiralty court ceased to exist after the ratification of the Constitution in 1789, the federal district court was the only court that could possibly have jurisdiction. Article III of the Constitution gave federal district courts sitting in admiralty exclusive jurisdiction over cases *in rem*, which is the very definition of a prize case. Neither party could have appealed to any other court. Justice Iredell agreed, noting that the Judiciary Act of 1789, gave the federal district courts "the whole original jurisdiction" in admiralty cases, thus, if the district court did not possess jurisdiction over prize, "no court can be instituted adequate to that purpose."

Having concluded that the Court of Appeals did have jurisdiction over the claim, the Supreme Court refused to re-examine the merits of the case. The Court ordered that the circuit court decree be given effect, although it modified some of Justice Blair's conclusions as to the amount of damages ultimately payable by the captors. In commenting on Doane's sixteen-year wait for relief, Justice Paterson offered something of an apology for the law's tardiness, finally concluding that "[j]udges may die, and courts be at an end; but justice still lives, and, though she may sleep for a while, will eventually awake, and must be satisfied."

The decision in *Penhallow v. Doane* is significant in several respects. First, in upholding the jurisdiction of the congressional Court of Appeals, the justices struck a further blow for the supremacy of the national government in matters of war and foreign affairs. Second, in holding that federal courts created under the Constitution had prize jurisdiction, the Court recognized an admiralty jurisdiction that was technically broader than that of the English courts of admiralty. *Penhallow* is perhaps most important, however, as an example of the Supreme Court's readiness to supervise the actions of the state courts in matters touching upon federal power. Convinced that the case was really one about the power of the national government to wage war, the justices did not hesitate to declare that federal courts would have the final word on controversies that arose in the context of that war.

## Revenue and Commerce

One of the primary aims of those who met at the Constitutional Convention was the creation of a stronger national government with the power to regulate both interstate and international commerce. This is because throughout the 1780s, the several states imposed onerous and sometimes conflicting regulations on trade. Merchants and commercial interests repeatedly complained that the patchwork scheme of regulation impeded commerce, stunted the growth of manufactures, and hindered the development of an extensive commercial republic. In drafting the Constitution, therefore, the delegates to the Philadelphia Convention gave Congress the power to regulate all aspects of interstate and international commerce.

The framers of the Constitution were also well aware of the difficulties the Confederation Congress faced in managing the nation's financial affairs. Under the old Articles of Confederation, Congress lacked the power to raise revenue on its own. As a result, in order to meet its needs, Congress was forced to request funds or supplies from the states, and then hope that the state governments would deliver. As one might expect in such a system, however, it was not long before the states began to ignore Congress' requests. Indeed, even at the height of the fighting during the Revolutionary War, states repeatedly failed to provide their fair share to support the military effort. Within a very short time, therefore, Congress was reduced to becoming a supplicant, pleading with the states to send money to pay soldiers or buy food and equipment. Lacking any means to force the states to comply with its requests, Congress ultimately authorized military leaders to confiscate supplies from the populace to make up for the states' unwillingness to provide the funds or materiel necessary to continue the battle (Harrington, *Regulatory Takings*). Determined not to repeat the same mistake, the Philadelphia Convention provided that Congress would have the power to raise revenue through the imposition of tariffs and excise taxes, as well as through "indirect" taxes levied on the states.

At first glance, most of the cases involving the exercise of the power to regulate trade granted under the Commerce Clause would seem to make their way to the federal courts via the so-called "federal question" jurisdiction. Yet, when drafting the first Judiciary Act, the Senate judiciary committee feared a backlash from advocates of states' rights if the federal courts were given too broad a jurisdiction. Consequently, the lower federal courts were not given any federal question jurisdiction in the Judiciary Act of 1789. As a result, most cases concerning federal questions originally came before the state courts, with appeals going to the U.S. Supreme Court from the decisions of state supreme courts. Congress was not so hesitant when it came to allocating jurisdiction over revenue cases; however, most members understood that the power to impose taxes would be meaningless if the federal government was forced to rely on state courts to prosecute violators of federal revenue laws. The federal courts were, therefore, given power to try all cases arising from breaches of these laws exclusive of the courts of the states. Throughout the 1790s, then, the Supreme Court found itself at the center of several important controversies concerning revenue and commerce.

## Protecting the Revenue: Whiskey Rebels and Fries' Rebellion

The justices of the early Supreme Court recognized that the new nation's finances were in a precarious position. Indeed, in his very first charge to a grand jury while on circuit, Justice Wilson encouraged the Pennsylvania grand jury to pay particular attention to violations of the customs laws because it was clear that federal revenues "will long arise chiefly from duties, and from imposts on articles of consumption." Chief Justice Jay made a similar point a few weeks later when charging the New York grand jury. "The right ordering and management" of the revenue was essential to the maintenance of the government, Jay declared, and, therefore, every citizen who "fraudulently withdraws his Shoulder from the common Burthen, necessarily leaves his Portion of the weight to be borne by others."

Congress' decision, in 1790, to fully fund the national debt and assume the debts of the states made the collection of the revenue even more important to the nation's fortunes. The following year, Congress passed an excise law imposing taxes on domestically produced whiskey to make up the shortfall in revenue received from import duties. This new tax proved to be the source of a great deal of discontentment. Those on the frontier bitterly complained about the unfairness of taxing a product so essential to the rural and western states, while the manufactures of New England and the coast went untouched. The complaint wasn't that the duty was too high, however. Rather, the crux of the problem lay in the fact that in the absence of specie, whiskey served as a form of currency in many parts of the interior. Lacking either banks or hard currency, many westerners used "wet goods" to bargain for "dry goods." The excise tax was, therefore, a tax on currency. Moreover, in many parts of the country, distilling grain into whiskey was the only feasible way of moving a crop to market. The absence of good roads or canals meant that western farmers did not plant grain for the purpose of selling cereal goods. Instead, they distilled grain into whiskey as a means of moving a commodity. It was, after all, far easier to transport barrels of whiskey in wagons than it was to ship dry grain in bulk.

The justices of the Supreme Court attempted to quell some of this unhappiness in a series of grand jury charges designed to educate the public about the importance of the excise law. For example, in charging the Massachusetts circuit court grand jury, Chief Justice Jay reminded his listeners that the whiskey tax was necessary in order to raise the sums "required by the government to discharge those debts which were the price of our liberties." Yet, opposition to the excise law continued to build in spite of these efforts. By the late summer of 1792, residents of western Pennsylvania began to openly resist any action to collect the tax. They harassed officials sent to collect the tax and forced many to abandon their offices. Alarmed by these developments, Treasury Secretary Hamilton urged President Washington to take strong action against the resistance. Chief Justice Jay cautioned patience, however. He advised the president that "no strong Declarations should be made unless there be ability & Disposition to follow them up with strong Measures." President Washington issued a proclamation urging compliance with the law and warning of harsh punishment for those who interfered with collection of the tax, nothing was done to suppress the opposition until the spring of 1794, when David Lennox, the United States Marshal in Pennsylvania, was ordered to serve summonses charging sixty-four individuals with violating the revenue laws. Most of the papers were served without incident; but Lennox encountered heavy opposition in Allegheny County. Within weeks, armed resistance had broken out and what has since become known as the "Whiskey Rebellion" began. The breakdown in order became so widespread that President Washington called upon the states to send troops to quell the disturbance. Almost twelve thousand troops marched through western Pennsylvania driving the rebels into the hills, although only twenty prisoners were brought back to Philadelphia to stand trial for treason in the circuit court.

Justice William Paterson presided over the Pennsylvania circuit court that year, and his conduct has often been characterized as overly partisan. In charging the grand jury, he declared that treason was "the highest crime of a civil nature," and that all who take arms against the government or who "prevent the regular administration of justice" are chargeable with it. Of particular concern, Paterson said, are those "who make insurrections under pretense of redressing national or public grievance." Observance and obedience to the law are the "great bulwark of public liberty," Paterson declared, while licentiousness is the "bane of republics" and "more to be dreaded than hosts of external foes." As a result, it was "incumbent on those who love the law to be vigilant in protecting it against assaults from within."

Paterson's charge had its intended effect, for the grand jury returned indictments against twenty-four defendants. Only ten of these were actually brought to trial, however, and then only two of the ten were finally convicted. Nonetheless, it was in the trial of these last two that Justice Paterson appeared to succumb to the temptation to mold events in such as way as to secure a guilty verdict. For example, in charging the trial jury in the prosecution of Philip Vigol, Paterson asserted, "with respect to the evidence, the current runs one way." There was not, he said, "the slightest possibility of doubt" that Vigol clearly intended to commit treason. Paterson practically dared the jury to acquit the defendant by concluding his summation with the assertion that "the crime is proved." Still, Paterson advised the jury that if it had any doubt about the case, it could find a special verdict stating the facts and he would declare the proper result. They returned a verdict of guilty the following day. Two days later, Paterson instructed the jury in the trial of John Mitchell that "the prisoner must be found guilty" for there was "no doubt" that the object of the insurrection was to overawe the government and prevent the operation of its laws. After this jury, too, rendered a verdict of guilty, the court sentenced both defendants to be hanged, although President Washington pardoned the men after entreaties from several prominent citizens.

The Whiskey Rebellion had far-reaching effects on the course of American law and politics. On the one hand, the manner in which the rebellion was put down gave further legitimacy and strength to the national government. This was in marked contrast to Congress' impotence in the face of Shays' Rebellion in 1787. That conflict simmered for quite some time, with Congress being unable to mount any effective action in response until Shays' followers were eventually routed by militia from Massachusetts and other New England states. Nonetheless, while the Whiskey Rebellion provided an opportunity for Washington's administration to demonstrate a certain firmness of resolve, it also had the effect of solidifying a growing opposition to Federalist policies in the trans-Appalachia region. Since the earliest days of the old Confederation, westerners had long complained that the national government too often favored the interests of the commercial classes residing on the seaboard. Many on the frontier saw the imposition of the tax on whiskey as a burden imposed on the west primarily to benefit wealthy speculators in the large cities. As a result, while the national government's defeat of the Whiskey Rebels effectively ended the threat of anarchy, Republicans would soon tap the widespread unhappiness with government policy on the frontier in their effort to wrest the reins of government from the Federalists.

Resistance to the imposition of federal taxes was an ever-present problem even after the Whiskey Rebellion. As tensions with France increased in 1797–1798, the United States began to make preparations for war. In an effort to pay for rising defense costs, the federal government imposed a tax on houses, akin to a modern property tax.

The tax was assessed by calculating the value of a house on the basis of the number of windows it had. This method of valuation not only provided a rough estimate of the owner's wealth, but also allowed the property to be valued without the need to enter upon it or secure cooperation from the occupants. The tax was immediately controversial, and in the spring of 1798, a group of Pennsylvania farmers banded together to prevent the tax assessors from making the necessary property valuations. When several of the protesters were arrested, John Fries led a group of armed men to the local jail and freed the prisoners from the marshal's custody. Fries was subsequently arrested for treason and tried in the Pennsylvania circuit court. After the jury returned a guilty verdict, however, Justice Iredell ordered a new trial when it was determined that one of the jurors had expressed a bias toward Fries before the trial. Fries remained in jail until the spring of 1800, when Justice Samuel Chase presided over the circuit court. Chase was concerned that the Fries' first trial had lasted almost ten days, causing a backlog in the civil docket. As a result, he was determined to move matters along more speedily in order to "get through all the business which had accumulated on the civil side."

One reason the first trial had taken so long was that Fries' lawyers insisted on arguing the definition of treason to the jury. During the trial of the Whiskey Rebels in 1794, Justice Paterson asserted that treason consisted in forcibly preventing a federal officer from executing his office. At his first trial, however, Fries' lawyers argued that this was too broad a definition, and so spent a great deal of time attempting to convince the jury that such an expansive definition of treason would be liable to abuse by partisan judges and prosecutors. For his part, Justice Chase was determined not to have a repeat of this debate. As a result, before the second trial began, Chase prepared a statement of the law of treason, which he proceeded to hand to the jury once they had taken their seats. Fries' lawyers were outraged at what they thought was a blatant attempt to prejudice the jury before the evidence was heard, and they announced their decision to withdraw from the case. Chase urged the lawyers to remain, but they refused. Instead, Fries' lawyers convinced him that Justice Chase's statement of the law all but guaranteed a conviction. Consequently, they advised Fries that his best hope under the circumstances was to seek a presidential pardon. The lawyers thus recommended that Fries serve as his own counsel so as to present a more sympathetic figure when he was convicted. Fries was, in fact, convicted and sentenced to death. As his lawyers predicted, however, President Adams pardoned Fries a few months later.

The trial of John Fries became something of a cause celebre. While Justice Chase's conduct in the case might appear to be unobjectionable to most modern legal practitioners, his refusal to allow Fries' lawyers to argue both law and fact to the jury was quite controversial. This was because for most of the eighteenth century, American lawyers and judges repeatedly asserted that juries were finders of both fact and law. Chief Justice Jay summed up the prevailing view in his opinion in *Georgia v. Brailsford*:

> [O]n questions of fact it is the province of the jury, on questions of law, it is the province of the court to decide. But it must be observed that by the same law which recognizes this reasonable distinction of the jurisdiction, [the jury have] nevertheless a right to take upon [itself] to judge both, and to determine the law as well as the fact in controversy.

Thus, in precluding Fries' lawyers from making arguments on the law, Justice Chase challenged long-standing expectations about the allocation of authority between the judge and jury. In fact, Chase's decision was so controversial that his actions in the Fries trial formed the basis of several of the articles of impeachment brought against him in 1805.

## The American Law of Admiralty

Closely related to the revenue and commerce powers was the Constitution's grant of jurisdiction to the federal courts to hear cases of "admiralty and maritime Jurisdiction." The English admiralty court had long been one of the most controversial aspects of the legal system. Originally established to handle piracy and prize cases, the jurisdiction of the admiralty court eventually included a wide variety of civil and criminal matters. The civil, or "instance," jurisdiction included actions for maritime contract and tort, such as suits for cargo damage, seaman's wage claims, and salvage. The criminal jurisdiction encompassed crimes such as piracy and mutiny. Throughout its history, however, the admiralty court was under constant attack because of its reliance on what were regarded as foreign legal procedures. This was because the admiralty, unlike common law courts, did not use juries in most cases, and often did not require witnesses to give testimony in court at trial. Instead, in many cases, admiralty courts allowed witnesses to give their statements in writing in advance of the trial and the statements were simply entered into evidence.

Admiralty courts were particularly controversial in the colonies. On the one hand, they performed a valuable service to the shipping and merchant communities because they provided a forum for the efficient and speedy resolution of traditional maritime contract claims. Unlike English courts, however, the American "vice-admiralty" courts also had jurisdiction over breaches of the revenue and trade laws. The Crown's practice of trying violators of the customs laws without juries in vice-admiralty courts became one of the most often cited examples of British oppression in the years leading to the outbreak of the Revolution.

Notwithstanding this history, the framers of the Constitution insisted on giving the federal courts jurisdiction over admiralty cases. The primary reason for this was the widespread understanding that admiralty cases often had an international component. Prize cases, for example, routinely involved claims by some foreign national that the property seized by a privateer belonged to a neutral. Similarly, many commercial cases of contract, salvage or cargo damage usually involved merchants or ship owners located in one or more foreign countries. Giving federal courts admiralty jurisdiction was thus one more way of ensuring that matters affecting foreign relations would be heard in the federal courts.

The fact that admiralty courts had long proven themselves useful in the collection of the revenue was also a factor militating in favor of their being continued in the new frame of government. Indeed, one of the most important aspects of admiralty courts was their ability to proceed *in rem* against a vessel or cargo seized for violating the customs laws. An *in rem* proceeding is one in which the seized property is itself made the defendant. Consequently, on discovering smuggled or "uncustomed" goods, a customs agent need not actually find the person who illegally landed them. Rather, he could simply seize the goods and proceed against them in the admiralty court. An owner whose goods were wrongfully seized might appear to contest the validity of the charge of failing to pay customs duties, but a smuggler would not. If the owner were unsuccessful in rebutting the government's charge, or if no one appeared to claim the goods, the court would enter a decree against the property and order its sale. The proceeds of the sale would then be deposited into the treasury.

The drafters of the first Judiciary Act also recognized the value of admiralty procedure, especially to the collection of the revenue. Most members of Congress expected that the bulk of federal revenues would come from duties on imported foreign goods, at least in the early years of the new government. As a result, the first Judiciary Act gave the federal district courts jurisdiction over "seizures and forfeitures under the laws of impost, navigation, or trade." In effect, this meant that federal courts were given a jurisdiction over admiralty and trade cases that was at least as broad as that of the much maligned colonial vice-admiralty courts. Of course, the drafters of the Judiciary Act were cognizant of the controversial history of admiralty courts in America, and so, in an effort to reduce the possibility of complaint, Congress made a distinction between seizures made on land and those made on water. Seizures made on the high seas or the navigable waters of the United States were to be tried on the "admiralty side" of the district court without juries. "Inland seizures," or seizures made on land, although properly within the admiralty jurisdiction of the district court, were to be tried by juries. While there was some irony in vesting federal courts with the power to try revenue cases without juries, most of the drafters apparently assumed that nonjury trials would be less controversial because federal judges, rather than crown appointees, would conduct them. No longer were admiralty courts mere tools of royal authority; they were, instead, instruments of a representative government.

The propriety of the distinction between seizures on land and those on water eventually came before the Supreme Court in a prosecution for violating the Neutrality Act. This statute was designed to help preserve American neutrality in the war between England and France by outlawing the exportation of arms and ammunition to either of the warring powers. It also prohibited the arming or "fitting out" of a privateer in American ports. In 1796, the French privateer, *La Vengeance,* was seized by the marshal of the New York district for attempting to export a cargo of canon and muskets. After a nonjury trial, the district court decreed the ship forfeit, but the circuit court reversed the decree on appeal.

In the Supreme Court, Attorney General Charles Lee decided to mount a novel attack on the circuit court decision, arguing that the trial in the district court should have been before a jury, which would not have been reviewable on appeal. The basis of the objection was Section 9 of the Judiciary Act, which provided that "the trial of issues of fact, in the district courts, in all causes except civil causes of admiralty and maritime jurisdiction, shall be by jury." Lee noted that the traditional rule dividing admiralty from common law depended on whether the facts giving rise to the complaint occurred on land or water. In addition, the English "tidewater" limit on jurisdiction held that all aspects of a transaction had to occur exclusively on water for a case to be within the admiralty. Lee argued that because the act of illegally exporting arms is "done part on land, and part on sea" the crime couldn't be tried in an admiralty court.

Just before argument on this point began, Chief Justice Ellsworth advised counsel in the case that the Court was already of opinion that the case was within the jurisdiction of the admiralty. Nonetheless, the Court proceeded to allow Lee to make his argument, and the following day Ellsworth announced that the Court "did not feel any reason to change the opinion, which they had formed upon the opening of the case." The report of the case does not indicate whether the Court gave any reasons for its decision, other than to note that "exportation is entirely a water transaction." What seems clear, however, is that in rejecting the English tidewater rule being advocated by Attorney General Lee, the Supreme Court was concerned that allowing juries to try seizures in admiralty would endanger the safety of the revenue. After all, the main reason royal officials began to prosecute revenue cases in the vice-admiralty before the Revolution was the inability to obtain convictions from juries.

The decision *La Vengeance* was significant in that it demonstrated the early federal courts' pragmatic approach to the problem of precedent. In cases where the English rules did not pose any great hardship or particular national security concern, they were followed. But, where they were thought to be inconvenient or an obstacle to the development of American commerce—and especially to the protection of the revenue—English rules were jettisoned in favor of the development of an admiralty jurisprudence that more accurately reflected the new nation's particular geographic and commercial situation.

## *Foreign Relations*

One commentator has characterized the early Supreme Court as "a national security court," one which spent most of its first decade "grappling with important issues affecting the nation's security." Indeed, those years were marked by the justices' "ongoing efforts to assist the Washington and Adams administrations in evolving a stable relationship with the European powers—especially France and Great Britain" (Casto 1995, 71).

### *The Great British Causes*

Trade relationships between England and her former colonies had always been close. As might be expected with any colonial enterprise, the mother country had long been the source of most of the capital used to exploit the resources of her various plantations. This was especially true in the case of Virginia and the southern colonies. Because hard currency was scarce in the colonial economy, colonial planters often financed their crops on credit. British merchants provided the sums necessary for seed and other supplies with the expectation that the loans thus extended would be repaid after the harvest. By the time of the American revolution, therefore, American indebtedness to British merchants was in excess of four million pounds, with the five southern colonies accounting for 83 percent of that total.

The outbreak of war between England and the colonies was a disaster for British merchants. Colonial debtors naturally refused to repay debts due British subjects, and there was little chance that any American court would be hospitable to the claims of enemy citizens. The various state legislatures added to creditors' difficulties by passing a series of statutes limiting British citizens' right to collect on debts owed them. Some of these statutes prevented courts from hearing debt cases, while still others prohibited the issuance of the writs necessary to execute on judgments. However, the most serious obstacle to a British creditor's recovery was the various confiscation or sequestration acts. These laws either confiscated or froze property owned by British subjects, often including debts. Virginia's Sequestration Act of 1777 was typical of these laws. It provided that Virginia citizens owing money to any British subject could discharge the debt by paying the sums due into the Virginia treasury. Once paid into the treasury, the debtor had no further obligation to the creditor. Measures such as these became one of the primary points of contention between Britain and the United States throughout the two decades following the end of the revolution.

During the course of the peace negotiations, the British repeatedly insisted that Americans make good on debts owing to British subjects. Although the American commissioners doubted whether the states would comply with British demands, they eventually agreed to language in Article 4 of the treaty, which decreed "Creditors on either Side Shall meet with no lawful Impediment to the Recovery of the full value in Sterling Money of all bona fide debts heretofore contracted." For their part, the British agreed in Article 7 to evacuate their troops from the United States without "carrying away any Negroes or other Property of the American inhabitants." As expected, the treaty's debt provisions proved difficult to enforce. Under the old Articles of Confederation, Congress did not have the power to force states to comply with its decrees. Consequently, the states freely ignored Article 4 throughout the 1780s, consistently preventing the recovery of British debts in American courts.

In drafting the Judiciary Act, therefore, Oliver Ellsworth and the other members of the Senate judiciary committee sought to ensure that some provision would be made for the adjudication of debt claims. Resolving the debt problem was not merely a matter of national honor. On the contrary, the refusal of states to enforce the peace treaty damaged the new nation's ability to negotiate future international agreements. Even more importantly, the inability of creditors to obtain a remedy in American courts greatly impeded the nation's ability to attract badly needed capital for future economic development. The Judiciary Act's diversity and alienage provisions were thus designed, in part at least, to settle the debt problem.

Almost immediately after opening for business, therefore, the circuit courts were flooded with claims by British creditors. One of the earliest of these was that of Samuel Brailsford and partners against James Spalding, a resident of Georgia, and two of his partners. In April 1791, Brailsford, a British merchant, sued Spalding in the Georgia circuit court for a debt arising before the start of the American Revolution. Spalding did not deny the existence of the debt. Instead, he contended that Georgia's sequestration act precluded recovery of debts contracted before the war. In essence, Spalding argued that state law prohibited him from paying his British creditor.

Shortly after the suit began, the State of Georgia attempted to intervene in the action, claiming that it had a right to any monies that may have been due on the debt. Georgia was reluctant to have its rights to the money determined in a suit between private parties and in which it had no representation. Although Justice Iredell and District Judge Nathaniel Pendleton expressed a great deal of sympathy for Georgia's position, they reluctantly concluded that the circuit court could not take cognizance of the state's claim. They noted that, under Article III of the Constitution, the Supreme Court had original and exclusive jurisdiction over suits involving states. Accordingly, the judges determined that the circuit court suit would have to proceed without Georgia being made a party.

The circuit court eventually concluded that Georgia's sequestration act did not extinguish Spalding's debt and that there was no bar to Brailsford's recovery. Fearing that Brailsford might be paid before it had a chance to be heard, the state filed a bill in equity in the Supreme Court asking that any monies owed by Spalding be deposited with the circuit court until Georgia's claim to the money could be determined by the

Supreme Court. Two justices, Thomas Johnson and William Cushing, were of the opinion that Georgia's request for an injunction should be denied. They concluded that the state's right to the money could be adequately protected in a suit at law, and thus did not require extraordinary relief. The remaining four justices, Blair, Iredell, Wilson, and Jay, voted to grant the injunction. Although they differed in their reasoning, the majority was convinced that the wise thing to do was, as Chief Justice Jay wrote, to "stay the money in the hands of the marshal, 'till the right to it is fairly decided; and so avoid the risque of putting the true owner to a suit, for the purpose of recovering it back." Subpoenas then issued commanding that Brailsford and Spalding appear and answer Georgia's claim to the debt.

Brailsford and Spalding moved to dismiss Georgia's claim when the Supreme Court convened in February 1793. The primary basis for their motion was Section 16 of the Judiciary Act, which prevented the Supreme Court from exercising equity jurisdiction where "a plain, adequate and complete" remedy might be had at common law. In essence, the defendants asserted that Georgia's attempt to prevent Brailsford from being paid was premature. They argued that the proper course was for Spalding to pay the debt as directed by the lower court, and then let Georgia make its claim against Brailsford in the Supreme Court. In this way, a jury would have the opportunity to determine whether Georgia's claim was valid.

After four days of argument on the question, the justices refused to lift the injunction. Justices Iredell and Blair held that the case could proceed in equity, although for different reasons. Iredell admitted that Georgia might have a remedy at law, but contended that such a remedy did not appear to be "plain, adequate or complete." Blair, on the other hand, believed that there was an adequate remedy at law, but worried that if the money were paid to Brailsford Georgia might ultimately be defeated in pursuing that remedy because Brailsford, a British subject, might leave the country with the money before the state's claim could be decided. Leaving the money in the marshal's hands was, in Blair's view, the most effective means of ensuring that all claims to the money could be joined together in a single proceeding. Writing for the majority, however, Chief Justice Jay opined that there was a complete remedy at law and ordered the case to be tried on the law side of the court's docket. The majority ordered the injunction to be lifted if the state did not bring an action at law by the start of the next term.

Georgia did eventually file suit against Brailsford on the law side of the Supreme Court, with the result that the February 1794 term saw *Georgia v. Brailsford* become the first jury trial ever held in the Supreme Court. Once the trial began, the lawyers for the parties presented over four days of argument to the jury. The state contended that, as a sovereign at war, it had the power to confiscate debts owed to British subjects and that its sequestration act had done precisely that. As for the treaty of peace between the United States and Great Britain, Georgia asserted that no provision of the treaty specifically nullified the state's act. For their part, the defendants argued that whether or not the debt had been sequestered or confiscated, the peace treaty "totally" repealed the sequestration act, thus reviving Brailsford's claim to the debt.

Notwithstanding the significance of the legal question, Chief Justice Jay delivered a remarkably brief charge. No doubt Jay sensed that the jury's endurance was at an end after four days of lawyers' arguments, for he wryly remarked that the jury "are now, if ever you can be, completely possessed of the merits of the cause." As a result, Jay merely informed the jury that the justices were themselves unanimous in their opinion that the Georgia sequestration act did not confiscate the debt and that the treaty of peace had the effect of reviving Brailsford's claim. The jury eventually returned a verdict for Brailsford, whereupon the Court dissolved the injunction. Brailsford was now free to seek payment of the debt from Spalding in accordance with the verdict in the circuit court. Unfortunately, he spent the remaining years of the decade attempting to obtain the sale of Spalding's property to satisfy the judgment without much success.

*Georgia v. Brailsford* was significant in two respects. First, it gave the early Supreme Court the opportunity to consider the nature of its equitable powers, the Constitution's grant of which was always a bit controversial. Second, and perhaps more important, the case provided the occasion for the Court to consider the extent to which treaties were in fact the "law of the land," thus laying the groundwork for the resolution of cases with even more significance for foreign affairs in the future, the most notable of which was *Ware v. Hylton.*

The fact that British creditors were now offered a forum for the resolution of their disputes did not necessarily mean that they would ultimately be successful. For, once suit was filed, American debtors used a variety of tactics to deprive creditors of a recovery. Indeed, the most striking feature of British debt litigation in the federal courts was the fact that it gave rise to a whole new series of legal maneuvers designed to frustrate the creditor's right to payment. In Virginia, in particular, the use of what were called "special pleas" succeeded in delaying the adjudication of debt cases for many years. The special pleas were a set of legal defenses grounded on the fact that the plaintiff in the suit was a British subject. The first special plea was based on the Virginia Sequestration Act of 1777, and argued that Virginia citizens who paid their debts into the Virginia treasury were excused from payment. The second special plea interposed Virginia's Forfeitures Act of 1779, which had declared all British property forfeit to the commonwealth. The third special plea asserted that the peace treaty between Britain and the United States was void because a state of war still existed between the two nations. Evidence for this defense was found in the fact that the British had not yet abandoned the forts on the western frontier. Finally, the fourth special plea argued that the defendant's obligation on the debt was "totally annulled" by the dissolution of the British colonial government in 1776.

One of the most interesting aspects of the special pleas was that they were primarily the work of John Marshall, the future chief justice, whose law practice at the time was largely devoted to representing wealthy Virginia planters and merchants. In crafting the special pleas as he did, Marshall sought to draw the circuit courts away from the interpretation of traditional common law rules, and into the realm of deciding public policy. This was largely because the common law was not on the debtors' side. Thus, in setting up the Treaty of Paris as a defense, Marshall and other debtors' counsel, demanded that the federal courts decide whether a treaty was in effect. In addition, in setting up the state statutes as defenses, the defendants also sought to have the courts determine the precise circumstances under which treaties entered into by the United States would abrogate a state statute. Faced with momentous questions as these, then, it is not surprising that the judges of the circuit court repeatedly delayed in giving their opinion.

The first hearings on debt cases did not begin until November 1791, almost eighteen months after the earliest suits were filed. By this time, there were over two hundred cases pending on the Virginia docket alone. As a result, rather than decide each one, Justices Blair and Johnson, joined by District Judge Cyrus Griffin, decided to take up a test case, *Jones v. Walker*, in hopes that a decision on the special pleas would resolve a great many of the cases then pending. Needless to say, the *Jones* case attracted a great deal of attention and was watched by all sides to see just how the court would dispose of the special pleas.

The case was brought by the surviving partner of the English firm of Farrel & Jones against Dr. Thomas Walker. Walker had made a payment into the Virginia state loan office of £2,150 on May 25, 1779, which he now claimed constituted a complete defense to the merchants' claim under the Sequestration Act. John Marshall and Patrick Henry led Walker's defense. Arguments on the special pleas lasted over a week, but in the end, the case had to be adjourned after Justice Blair was forced to leave the bench due to the death of his son. The case was not set for rehearing until eighteen months later, when Chief Justice Jay, Justice Iredell and Judge Griffin presided over the May 1793 circuit court. By this time, the plaintiff in the original case had died, and so another case, *Ware v. Hylton*, was substituted as the test case.

After hearing arguments a second time, the circuit court judges proceeded to rule on the four special pleas. They made quick work of the fourth, which claimed that all debts were extinguished by the change in government caused by the Revolution, noting that the new Virginia state government consistently acted as though prewar debts continued to exist. The court also rejected the second plea, which contended that the Virginia forfeiture law divested British subjects of their property. The court noted that this law "must have been inadvertently pleaded" because the forfeiture law contained a provision specifically exempting British debts from forfeiture. This left only the third special plea, which argued that the peace treaty was no longer in force because of British violations, and the first special plea, which asserted that the Virginia Sequestration Act relieved the debtor of the obligation to pay if he deposited the debt with the state loan office.

The third special plea presented the most difficult problem for the court. After all, it demanded that the circuit court consider a political question, that of whether or not a treaty of the United States was in force. The essence of the plea was that American debtors were relieved of the obligation to make good on their debts because Britain had not honored its obligations under the treaty. The question was an explosive one. In effect, the defendants were demanding that the court determine whether British violations of the treaty had risen to the point that the treaty itself might no longer be in force. Moreover, if in fact, the treaty was abrogated, did that mean that a state of war still existed between the United States and Great Britain? Nonetheless, even assuming such a question existed, the case presented a far more difficult problem: Was the federal court the proper entity to make such a determination? In the end, the judges declined the defendant's invitation to rule on this point. Chief Justice Jay held that the federal courts had the power to determine whether a treaty was valid, but this determination was limited to ascertaining whether the treaty was properly made and ratified. Whether a treaty had been broken, and thus no longer in force, was a matter for the political branches to decide. Justice Iredell agreed, asserting that federal judges must regard a treaty as "valid and obligatory" until such time as Congress declared it void.

Having refused to invalidate the peace treaty, the only question before the court was whether the Virginia Sequestration Act was consistent with the treaty's provisions. As noted earlier, the debtor argued that the Sequestration Act invalidated that part of the debt paid into the loan office, a point on which Justices Iredell and Blair were both agreed. They held that the mere ratification of the peace treaty did not annul the Virginia law. Instead, they said, Congress had to take some affirmative act to nullify state laws inconsistent with treaty obligations before the Virginia statute would be invalid. Iredell recognized that Congress might surrender the rights of private parties in making treaties, but, he contended, "such a sacrifice is not to be presumed." Rather, Iredell said, some sort of "special words" ought to be used to make the case clear. Having failed to do so, it should not be assumed that Congress intended to alter the status of state laws affecting the payment of private debts. Jay, of course, disagreed, contending that the provisions of the peace treaty were self-executing and that any statute contrary to its terms was void upon ratification by the Senate. "The necessity of making a peace," Jay said, "authorizes the sovereign to dispose of things even belonging to private persons." It "necessarily follows," therefore, "that the discharge and substitution [provided for by the Sequestration Act] were within the reach of a treaty [and] were liable to be modified, impaired or totally annulled by it."

The circuit court's decision in *Ware* was a prime example of the early federal judges' desire to "split the baby" to avoid direct confrontation between the states and the national government. In refusing to render a decision on the validity of the treaty, the judges upheld the federal government's power to conduct foreign relations free from the interference of state laws. In so doing, they struck a blow for the Supremacy Clause, affirming Congress' power to declare war and ratify treaties. At the same time, the majority's decision to uphold the Virginia Sequestration Act in the face of the treaty was an attempt to avoid drawing the federal courts into a direct confrontation with the proponents of states' rights. Striking down a state statute at this stage in the young nation's development would clearly have explosive consequences. In addition, the judges also hoped that deciding the case in this fashion would eliminate the possibility that hundreds of Virginia debtors would have their estates confiscated for repayment of prewar debts. Yet, this compromise was inherently unstable. As Jay pointed out in his dissent, Virginia's statute made Article 4 of the peace treaty a nullity, and if left in force it would effectively render the federal government's power to conduct foreign relations a mere illusion.

Ware, of course, was not to be so easily put off. He appealed to the Supreme Court, which eventually reversed the circuit court. In taking up the case, the Court was conscious of the delicate nature of the problem. Upholding the validity of the treaty would expose American debtors to substantial liabilities for past debts. Indeed, the amounts involved were such as to put in doubt the solvency of a large portion of the Virginia gentry. Added to this was the fact that British actions in the years since the circuit court had rendered its decision had inflamed public opinion. American ships and cargoes had been seized and American seamen impressed to serve aboard British men-of-war. In the spring of 1794, a bill in Congress to suspend commercial intercourse with Britain had lost by a single vote, while bills to sequester prewar debts had been introduced in both the House and Senate. Moreover, by the time *Ware* came before the Supreme Court, the terms of the Jay Treaty had been made public, with the result that there was rioting in the streets over what many believed were too liberal concessions for little return. Article 6 of Jay's Treaty complicated the debt problem even further by providing that the United States government would make "full and complete compensation" to British creditors who could not receive payment of their debts "in the ordinary course of justice." As a result, the Supreme Court's decision in *Ware* would have enormous consequences for the federal government, which might now be called upon to make good on hundreds of thousands of dollars to Britain's frustrated creditors.

As in the circuit court, the primary question before the Supreme Court was whether the Virginia Sequestration Act remained as a bar to recovery of debts falling within its terms notwithstanding the terms of the treaty of peace. Justice Chase delivered the first opinion on this question and his opinion is commonly regarded as a well-reasoned discussion of the relationship between treaties and state statutes under the constitutional scheme. Chase began by asserting the supremacy of the Virginia legislature during the Revolution. In his view, the people of Virginia established a constitution providing for a free, sovereign and independent state in 1776. Under the terms of this constitution, the legislature of Virginia was "for ever thereafter invested with the supreme and sovereign power of the state." Chase added that as a sovereign state, Virginia possessed the full power to wage war except in so far as she delegated any of that power to the general government. With respect to confiscation of debts, Chase concluded that no such delegation occurred. As a result, Chase said, "[t]here is no question but the act of the Virginia Legislature … was within the authority granted them by the people of that country; and this being admitted, it is a necessary result, that the law is obligatory on the courts of Virginia, and, in my opinion, on the courts of the United States." The statute in question was validly within the powers of the legislature and thereby operated as a bar to any recovery on the part of the creditor.

Debtors listening to Chase's opinion up to this point could not but be cheered by what they had heard. Long regarded as an advocate of states' rights, Chase seemed on course to deliver a resounding victory to the forces of state sovereignty. Unfortunately for those inclined to support debtor interests, however, Chase made a stunning turn when confronted with the question of whether Article IV of the peace treaty nullified the Virginia law. In a passage that is remarkable given his oft-stated reservations about the power of judicial review, Justice Chase declared that state statutes must fall prostrate before the terms of a treaty duly ratified by the federal government. Chase went even further on this point than necessary, for he considered both the status of treaties under the old Articles of Confederation as well as under the Constitution of 1787.

With respect to the former, Chase noted that Article 9 of the Articles of Confederation provided that "the United States in Congress assembled, shall have the sole and exclusive right and power of determining on peace, or war, … and of entering into treaties and alliances." According to Chase, this grant "has no restriction, nor is there any limitation on the power in any part of the confederation. A right to make peace, necessarily includes the power of determining on what terms peace shall be made. A power to make treaties must of necessity imply a power, to decide the terms on which they shall be made." Consequently, sacrificing public or private property to obtain peace would seem to be a valid exercise of the treaty power. More to the point, Chase noted, "treaties made by Congress, according to the Confederation, were superior to the laws of the states; because the Confederation made them obligatory on all the states."

Yet even assuming he was wrong on this point, Chase asserted that the Constitution resolved any ambiguity on this point:

> If doubts could exist before the establishment of the present national govern-
> ment, they must be entirely removed by the 6th article of the Constitution, which

provides "That all treaties made, or which shall be made, under the authority of the United States, shall be the Supreme law of the land; and the Judges in every State shall be bound thereby, any thing in the Constitution, or laws, of any State to the contrary notwithstanding." There can be no limitation on the power of the people of the United States. By their authority the State Constitutions were made, and by their authority the Constitution of the United States was established; and they had the power to change or abolish the State Constitutions, or to make them yield to the general government, and to treaties made by their authority. A treaty cannot be the Supreme law of the land, that is of all the United States, if any act of a State Legislature can stand in its way. If the Constitution of a State (which is the fundamental law of the State, and paramount to its Legislature) must give way to a treaty, and fall before it; can it be questioned, whether the less power, an act of the State Legislature, must not be prostrate? It is the declared will of the people of the United States that every treaty made, by the authority of the United States, shall be superior to the Constitution and laws of any individual State; and their will alone is to decide. If a law of a State, contrary to a treaty, is not void, but voidable only by a repeal, or nullification by a State Legislature, this certain consequence follows, that the will of a small part of the United States may controul or defeat the will of the whole. The people of America have been pleased to declare, that all treaties made before the establishment of the National Constitution, or laws of any of the States, contrary to a treaty, shall be disregarded.

It is hard to imagine a more definitive statement of supremacy than this, and it is made all the more startling given Justice Chase's repeated caution in his other discussions of judicial review. Nonetheless, it is clear that by this time, at least, Chase had become concerned enough to recognized the dangers unbridled state power posed to the Republic at large and to its conduct of foreign affairs.

Justice Iredell delivered the original judgement rejecting Ware's claims in the circuit court, but took the opportunity to restate his earlier reasoning when the case was decided in the Supreme Court. He began by affirming Virginia's right to confiscate the debt under the law of nations. For Iredell, the real question was whether the Treaty of Paris made the state statute invalid, and here, Iredell was a bit more inventive. While frequently regarded as a proponent of the power of judicial review, Iredell advanced an important limitation in *Ware*. While it is clear that he believed that acts of a state legislature, which were contrary to the express provisions of the federal Constitution or statute were void, Iredell introduced a substantial qualification with respect to treaties. In effect, he appeared to believe that a treaty alone did not necessarily serve as the basis for declaring state statutes void. That is to say, notwithstanding the plain language of Supremacy Clause—which declared that treaties should be the "supreme Law of the land"—Iredell seems to have believed that unless a treaty specifically repealed or annulled an act, it could not be used to strike down state laws.

Iredell's conclusion was based on his conception of treaties. For him, a treaty was "a solemn promise by the whole nation, that such and such things shall be done, or that such and such rights shall be enjoyed." Moreover, treaties generally contain two types of articles. The first are articles that are to be considered "executed" or complete in themselves. These are articles that require no further action on anyone's part. Thus, the article in the Treaty of Paris declaring that the United States was free and independent was of immediate effect. Such an article was a statement of a fact or condition. Similarly, the article giving Americans the unfettered right to fish on the Grand Banks was also complete upon the execution of the treaty. The second type of article is those provisions that are "executory" and that require some further action on the part of the signatories. These articles are, in effect, promises by the nation that a particular thing will be done, but they are not effective until they are "carried into execution in the manner which the Constitution of [the] nation prescribes." Thus, Iredell said, although the peace treaty contained a provision declaring that all prisoners of war would be freed, no gaoler or military officer would have been justified in simply releasing those in his charge without receiving further orders from the commander-in-chief. Similarly, the article declaring that creditors "meet no lawful impediment" required some act of Congress repealing state laws creating such impediments in order for them to be considered void.

Iredell noted that this was the traditional view of treaties in England—which was, after all, the other signatory to the treaty at issue in *Ware*. He argued that when the King makes any stipulation of a legislative nature in a treaty it must be carried into effect by an act of Parliament. The Parliament, Iredell said, "is considered as bound, upon a principle of moral obligation, to preserve the public faith, pledged by the treaty, by passing such laws as its obligation requires; but until such laws are passed, the system of law, entitled to actual obedience, remains de facto, as before." As regards Article IV, therefore, state laws limiting creditors' rights remained in force until they were repealed by some subsequent legislative act, whether that act was of the state or Congress. In support of this position, Iredell noted that Congress itself seems to have understood this requirement. Even after passage of the treaty, Congress did not take upon itself to declare any state statute creating impediments void—and this was for good reason: the confederation Congress did not, after all, have the power to pass any act binding on the states. Instead, Congress was limited to "recommending" the repeal of all acts inconsistent with the execution of the treaty, but at no time did it presume to take upon itself the power to actually effect a repeal on its own. This, noted Iredell, seems to be proof that the treaty was not itself sufficient to be used as a basis for striking down a state statute.

Iredell believed that the ratification of the Constitution did not alter this result. In fact, Iredell believed that one of the main purposes of the Supremacy Clause was to prevent precisely the sort of problems that had arisen with respect to enforcement of the Treaty of Paris. The treaty, he said, was "binding in moral obligation, but could not be constitutionally carried into effect" under the Articles of Confederation. The Supremacy Clause provided the remedy for these difficulties. However, even if the treaty were self-executing, it did not, in Iredell's view, provide for any remedy against the current defendants. On the contrary, Iredell believed that the most the treaty could have accomplished was to remove impediments existing at the time the treaty was ratified. In his view, if a debt had been extinguished by law prior to the ratification of the treaty, that debt could not be revived. In support of this theory, Iredell posed the following hypothetical:

> If a statute requires a will of lands to be executed in the presence of two witnesses; and a will is actually executed in that manner, and the statute is afterwards repealed, and three witnesses are made necessary, the will executed in the presence of two others, when the former statute was in being, would be undoubtedly good....

Consequently, Iredell said, a statute that absolved a debtor of liability for a debt, as the Virginia statute did, should be considered valid as nothing in the treaty or any subsequent statute specifically nullified the provisions of the original statute. In his view, the creditor was still entitled to payment, just not from this particular debtor.

In the end, however, Justice Iredell's reservations about the self-executing nature of treaties failed to convince the remaining justices. As a result, while they differed on the precise legal effect of Virginia's sequestration law, a majority of the justices had no trouble in concluding that Article 4 of the peace treaty "remov[ed] all lawful impediments, repeal[ed] the legislative act of Virginia ... and with regard to the creditor annull[ed] everything done under it." The treaty "reinstat[ed] the parties; the creditor and debtor before the war, are creditor and debtor since; as they stood then, they stand now."

The Supreme Court's decision in *Ware* was a ringing endorsement of the federal government's power to make and enforce treaties with foreign nations. Yet, the immediate effect of the decision was less apparent (Casto 1995, 101). After the Supreme Court's decision, the way was now clear to the resolution of British debt cases, but that did not mean that creditors had an easy time obtaining payment. Many debtors still refused to pay, and forced the creditor to bring suit before juries in the debtor's home state. The result was that many juries repeatedly refused to award a creditor interest on the debt in spite of repeated instructions by federal judges that interest was due. Even when the creditor was successful in obtaining a judgment, he often found that the debtor had very little assets from which to secure payment. In time, the political branches recognized that the debt problem was not to be solved through judicial means. Instead, on January 8, 1802, Britain and the United States signed a convention in which the United States government agreed to pay the sum of £600,000 in full and final settlement of all British claims.

## The Neutrality Controversy

Without doubt, the central problem facing the new nation in its conduct of foreign affairs in the 1790s was developing a stable relationship with the two great European powers. The ongoing series of wars between France and Great Britain during the latter part of the eighteenth century was a constant source of friction between Europe and the new nation. America's primary aim was to prevent itself from being drawn into the conflict, and thus both the Washington and Adams administrations sought to maintain a position of neutrality with respect to the warring parties. Yet this policy was destined to be complicated by the fact that Americans were ambivalent about their relationship with both France and England. On the one hand, the United States was an English-speaking nation, with deep cultural and economic ties to Great Britain (Casto 1995, 72). Not only did many Americans trace their family roots to England, America's political outlook was colored by three hundred years of English constitutional history. Buttressing these cultural ties was an extensive network of commercial relations. At the time of the ratification of the Constitution, almost 75 percent of American exports went to Great Britain, while 90 percent of the country's imports came from England (Elkins & McKitrick, 68–74). Notwithstanding these close ties, however, there remained a great deal of friction in America's relationship with the mother country. As noted earlier, the United States was in violation of Article 4 of the peace treaty, which required that there be "no impediment" to the recovery of British debts. For their part, the English were in violation of Article 7, which required them to evacuate the forts on the western frontier. In addition, British troops ignored the provision in the peace treaty forbidding them from carrying off slaves belonging to American planters (Casto 1995, 73).

Relations with France during this same period were little better. In the early part of the 1790s, many Americans felt a deep sense of gratitude for French help during the course of the revolution. During the war, the French government offered significant financial assistance to Congress allowing the new nation to purchase supplies for the military. French troops fought with American soldiers in the latter phase of the conflict and it was a French fleet that prevented Cornwallis' retreat at Yorktown (Casto 1995, 73). At the outset, the French Revolution gratified many Americans' sense of political kinship with the French people. The French had, after all, deposed a tyrannical king and replaced him with a government ostensibly established on republican principles. As a result, in the years immediately following the French Revolution in 1789, it appeared to many Americans that France and the United States were destined to march together in the vanguard of a worldwide movement toward liberty and equality. Things changed, however, once the French Revolution turned more violent and oppressive. The start of the Reign of Terror, which was followed by the execution of the French king, horrified many Americans, especially those of a conservative bent. For staunch Federalists in particular, the corruption of the French Revolution represented the worst excesses of mob rule and provided a warning to those in the United Sates who sought to rise to prominence by exciting public passions.

The outbreak of war between France and Britain in 1793 placed the United States in a difficult position, and a significant rift in public opinion was soon apparent. On the one side, a sizeable portion of the American people still held a deep affection for France and urged the American government to support her in the war against England. Others, however, were reluctant to do anything that would damage relations with Britain, which remained America's largest trading partner. This division was made even more complicated by the fact that the 1778 Treaty of Alliance between France and the United States contained provisions granting French naval vessels and privateers the right to use American ports for military operations. The French treaty was to prove embarrassing to the United States because it had been negotiated at a time when the United States herself was at war with Great Britain. Now that Britain and the United States were at peace, the terms of the treaty severely constrained American efforts to remain above the fray.

President Washington was determined to find some way to avoid having the new nation drawn into the war between the great powers, and so he sought the advice of his cabinet on crafting the proper means for protecting American neutrality. Unfortunately, the cabinet was divided on this point. Although neither Alexander Hamilton nor Thomas Jefferson, the two most important members of the cabinet, wanted to enter the war on either side, they disagreed on the precise form in which American neutrality should be expressed. Hamilton argued for a strict neutrality, which would essentially ignore America's treaty obligations to France. Jefferson, on the other hand, sought to find some means by which the United States might proclaim its neutrality while still allowing some measure of support for a nation he believed was the United States' natural ideological ally.

Washington consulted his cabinet about the proper scope of American neutrality. As noted above, these consultations soon engaged Chief Justice John Jay, who took an active role in advising Treasury Secretary Hamilton on the legal issues raised by the treaty with France. Finally, on April 22, 1793, President Washington issued a proclamation declaring America's intention to "pursue a conduct friendly and impartial towards the belligerent powers" and warning Americans to avoid "committing, aiding, or abetting hostilities" against any of the belligerent powers. The proclamation also authorized federal officials to initiate prosecutions against American citizens who attempted to aid either side.

Unfortunately, while the cabinet was engaged in discussions about the neutrality proclamation, France's minister to the United States, Edmund Genet, was busy taking steps to use the United States as a base for conducting naval operations against British interests. Almost immediately after his arrival in Charleston, South Carolina, Genet began issuing commissions to American citizens to act as privateers authorized to prey on British shipping. He also took steps to outfit several American merchant ships as armed raiders, recruited American seamen to serve in them, and purchased supplies and armament for French warships. Genet's activities were a source of great concern to the Washington administration. After all, having proclaimed its neutrality between the warring parties, the American government could not now sit idly by while one of them turned American ports into bases for military activity. The Washington administration lodged a formal protest with the French government concerning Genet's activities, but to no effect. For his part, Genet contended that the treaty of alliance between the United States and France authorized his activities, and that the United States could not prevent his efforts to defend French interests without violating the treaty.

At issue was the wording of Article 22 of the treaty, which provided that "[i]t shall not be lawful for any foreign privateers not belonging to [French or American citizens] who have Commissions from any other Prince or State in enmity with either Nation to fit their Ships in the Ports of either the one or the other of the aforesaid Parties." Genet argued that the phrase, "not belonging to," created the implication that French and American privateers might be fitted out in the ports of the respective countries, but that those of other countries could not (Casto 1995, 76). Genet also made a number of technical legal arguments in an attempt to show that even if the treaty prohibited the outfitting of privateers, his activities did not fall within the scope of the prohibition. For example, he argued that cutting holes into the side of a merchantman for use as cannon ports was permissible as long as the cannon themselves were not mounted.

While the legal debate raged, Genet's privateers caused considerable difficulties for Anglo-American relations. Within weeks of his arrival in early April 1793, privateers bearing commissions issued by Genet began capturing British vessels at an alarming rate. By May 1793, George Hammond, the British ambassador, complained vehemently about Genet's activities, as well as the American government's inability to put a stop to them. Hammond even went so far as to warn that Britain would regard America's failure to end French military activities on its soil as a breach of her own professed neutrality, leaving open the possibility of war between Britain and the United States.

Genet further complicated matters by creating "consular courts" to adjudicate the status of prizes taken by French and American privateers. Under the traditional law of prize, the captor of a vessel belonging to a belligerent power was entitled to share in the proceeds of the sale of the vessel and its cargo. To do so, however, the captor was required to obtain a decree of condemnation from a prize court declaring that the vessel was a lawful prize, and not the property of a citizen of a neutral country. Once the vessel was condemned by a prize court, the captor was free to sell the vessel and cargo, and distribute the proceeds as required by his commission. Without a decree of condemnation, however, the captor would have a difficult time selling the prize because potential purchasers could not be certain they would obtain good title to the vessel.

Genet's privateers might have solved this problem by sailing their prizes to a port in France or the French West Indies, and obtain a decree of condemnation from a prize court there. This solution was impractical, however, because the distances involved would not only delay the time between capture and sale, but also increase the likelihood that the British might recapture the vessel. This was especially true for Americans holding French commissions. After all, it was one thing for a French vessel to take its prizes back home, but quite another for an American to sail his prizes to a foreign port and rely on the justice of a foreign court system. Genet's consular courts eliminated those difficulties. By issuing commissions to French "consuls" to hear prize cases in various American ports, Genet allowed both American and French privateers to bring captured British vessels into the nearest American port, thereby reducing the possibility of recapture and creating greater incentives for American citizens to join in his naval adventures.

Matters came to a head in May 1793, when a British merchant ship, *The William*, was captured by a French privateer off the coast of Maryland. Gideon Henfield, an American seaman serving aboard the French vessel, was put in charge of *The William*, and brought the captured vessel into Philadelphia where it was immediately condemned by the French consul. Henfield was then arrested for violating the terms of the neutrality proclamation, and the British owners of *The William* commenced suit in the federal court in Philadelphia demanding the return of their ship and its cargo.

The owners' suit placed the legitimacy of the French consular courts squarely before district judge Richard Peters. Their basic contention was that the capture took place within the territorial waters of the United States and was, therefore, a violation of the law of nations. The privateer, on the other hand, contended that the question of whether a vessel was a lawful prize was left to the courts of the belligerent nations alone. In the event, Peters agreed with the captors' lawyer and dismissed the case. While he agreed that the seizure probably occurred in American waters, Peters adhered to the traditional admiralty rule, which stated that the courts of a neutral nation couldn't have prize jurisdiction. As a result, without some special legislative authorization, which Peters did not find in any federal statute, the federal court could not review the decisions of another nation's prize courts because the United States herself was not at war with any nation. Judge Peters' decision in *The William* was followed by other district court judges as well. In fact, within a very short time, the district courts of New York and South Carolina dismissed cases brought by English owners to recover vessels taken by French privateers.

The federal judges' refusal to take jurisdiction over the prize cases was a matter of embarrassment for the administration, especially for Secretary of State Thomas Jefferson who had been assuring the British ambassador for several months that federal courts would vindicate the rights of British citizens. As a result, President Washington made a formal request to Congress to enact legislation giving federal courts jurisdiction over prize cases, notwithstanding the fact that the United States was itself not at war (Casto 1995, 83–84). Before Congress could act on Washington's request, however, the Supreme Court took up the case of *Glass v. The Sloop Betsy.*

In late 1793, a French privateer, called the *Citizen Genet,* (the vessel on which Gideon Henfield served), captured the sloop *Betsey* along with her cargo off the American coast. The *Betsey* was brought into Baltimore where she was libeled as prize before one of the French consular courts. While in Baltimore, the *Betsey*'s owners filed a libel in the federal district court demanding restitution of the sloop on the grounds that ship and her cargo were owned by citizens of Sweden and the United States, both of which were neutral countries in the war between France and England. The captors contested the jurisdiction of the court, contending that the district court did not have any power to hear prize cases. After a brief hearing on the case, the district judge, William Paca, agreed with the captors that American courts could not take jurisdiction over prize cases and denied the request for restitution. The circuit court affirmed that decree and the *Betsey*'s owners appealed to the Supreme Court.

While it might seem somewhat strange today, the captors' claim that no federal court could have jurisdiction over the case was well grounded, at least as a matter of legal precedent. They contended that the heart of the case was a question of prize. That is to say, the claim for restitution was integral to the determination of whether a vessel belonging to a belligerent had been lawfully taken on the high seas. If that question was answered in the affirmative, there could be no claim for restitution. The captors claimed that neither the Constitution, the Judiciary Act, nor the law of nations gave the federal district court sitting in admiralty jurisdiction over prize cases, and thus the claim for restitution had to be dismissed.

The captors based their argument on a long line of judicial precedent both in England and other countries, which held that admiralty courts did not generally have prize jurisdiction, because prize was a power that could only be exercised by a sovereign at war. In the normal course, therefore, admiralty judges only had power over prize cases when issued with special commissions pursuant to an act of Parliament, often referred to a "prize acts." These acts were generally passed at the start of hostilities with a foreign nation and set forth both the rules for taking prizes and the manner in which prize cases were to be adjudicated. "Prize courts" thus came into existence at the outbreak of hostilities; and when the war ended, the courts would go out of business. As a matter of convenience, commissions to hear prize cases were usually issued to the judges of the various admiralty and vice-admiralty courts, although they need not have been. Consequently, there was no such thing as a "prize court" in the absence of war. Given this background, the captors of the *Betsey* claimed that the federal district courts could not have prize jurisdiction both because Congress had not passed any "prize act" and because the United States was not then at war with any party. As a result, they argued, "if the district court is now a court of prize, it is a court without rules, to determine what is or what is not, lawful prize."

For their part, the owners of the *Betsey* and her cargo pointed out that both the Constitution and the Judiciary Act gave the district courts jurisdiction over "civil causes of admiralty and maritime jurisdiction." They contended that the term "civil" was used "in contra distinction" to the word "criminal," and was meant to give the federal district courts all the jurisdiction that might have been possessed by admiralty courts. In other words, in using the words, "all civil causes of admiralty and maritime jurisdiction," the Constitution intended to give federal courts power over all non-criminal admiralty cases, including both normal commercial maritime claims, (the so-called "instance" cases), as well as cases of prize.

The captors responded to this argument by noting that the term "civil" when used to describe admiralty jurisdiction is not meant to distinguish between criminal and noncriminal cases. Rather, they pointed out that the term "civil" is almost exclusively used to refer to the manner in which "instance" cases are decided: "Civil causes cannot possibly include captures, or the legality of prize which can only be made in time of war. The words are used to denote that the causes are not to be foreign causes, or arising from, and determinable by, the *jus belli*, but are such as relate to the community, arising in the time of peace, and are determinable by the civil or municipal law." In the view of the captors, therefore, no federal court could have jurisdiction over the question of prize absent a prize act and some declaration of war by Congress. This does not mean that the owners of the vessel and her cargo were without remedy, however. On the contrary, under the traditional law of nations, if a vessel had been taken unlawfully, it was left to the executive power to vindicate the rights of the injured party. Accordingly, in this particular case, the owners of the vessel and cargo should have addressed their petition to the King of Sweden and the President of the United States, who would then be charged with vindicating the rights of their citizens.

Six days after hearing arguments in the case, the Supreme Court unanimously ruled that federal courts did have the power to review prize cases, including cases of prize adjudged by the so-called "consular courts." In so doing, the justices rejected the traditional view of the limits of admiralty jurisdiction, and claimed for the federal courts an expanded power to adjudicate prize cases. Yet, while the justices were clear on the result, they provided almost no legal support for their conclusion. This was no doubt because the opinion in *Glass* was simply contrary to well-established judicial precedent and the principles of the law of nations. In short, the justices simply seem to have determined that the old way of doing things did not suit America's particular legal and political situation, and so decided to abandon old rules and create new law.

Nevertheless, having decided that federal courts could determine prize cases did not necessarily resolve the issues raised by *Glass*, for standing in the way of the British owners' recovery was the principle of comity. This principle requires courts of one nation to give deference to the decisions of the duly constituted courts of another, especially in cases of prize. Theoretically, then, federal courts ought to have deferred to the decisions of the French consular courts on the question of whether a particular vessel was a prize, regardless of whether American courts had prize jurisdiction or not. The law of nations simply did not permit admiralty courts in one country to re-visit prize determinations made in another admiralty court. Recognizing the difficulties posed by this problem, the justices asked counsel for the parties to present argument on the validity of the French consular courts. In a rather strange twist, the lawyers for the French government advised the Court that they were not prepared to argue the point. The Supreme Court then declared that "no foreign power can of right institute, or erect any court of judicature of any kind" on American soil. This conclusion left American courts free to disregard the decisions of the consular courts because they were not validly constituted under American or international law.

The decision in *Glass* is significant because it resolved several vexing problems, not all of which were legal ones. First and foremost, *Glass* put an end to the operation of the so-called consular courts, ensuring that only federal courts would have the power to adjudicate the legality of prize cases on American soil. At the same time, it authorized the lower federal courts to order the restoration of vessels and cargoes taken in violation of American neutrality. Perhaps more importantly, in expanding the reach of the district courts' admiralty jurisdiction, the Supreme Court demonstrated a willingness to discard traditional legal rules where those rules were ill suited to America's particular geographic, economic, or political situation. Moreover, in denying the lawfulness of the French consular courts, the justices struck a further blow for American independence and the power of the American government to conduct its foreign relations without interference from nations who sought to make it a client state. Yet, while *Glass* clearly gave the lower federal courts the power to order restitution of ships taken in violation of American neutrality, the Court did not provide clear guidance as to how the remedy was to be applied. As a result, French warships and privateers continued to prey on British shipping, and continued to bring their prizes into American ports. Almost a year after the opinion in *Glass*, therefore, the British consul in Charleston was heard to complain that "notwithstanding [the fact that] the laws of the United States are so grounded against any breach of neutrality, the French here evade them, and arm as many privateers as ever." Nonetheless, while *Glass* succeeded in ending the use of consular courts to try prize cases, it failed to provide any avenue by which a captor might obtain a decree of condemnation. This was no omission, however. As Judge Peters noted in his district court opinion in *The William*, the idea that the courts of a neutral nation would set themselves up as prize courts would be but a "solecism in jurisprudence." As a result, after *Glass*, it was clear that while no court was available on American soil to decide the question of "prize or no," the lower federal courts would not hesitate to take upon themselves the power to order the restoration of property taken as a result of the violation of American law.

The problem of when restitution was to be ordered left open in *Glass* was addressed in a series of cases that made their way to the Supreme Court in 1796. In these cases, the Court attempted to provide some guidance for lower courts in administering the remedy of restitution. The most significant of these cases was *Talbot v. Jansen* (1796), which involved a French privateer's seizure of a Dutch merchant vessel on the high seas. At the time of the capture, The Netherlands was at war with France thus, the capture appeared to be legitimate under the law of nations. However, the Dutch owners of the vessel sought restitution in the federal court because the French privateer was owned and manned by Americans. The privateer had also been built and armed in the United States in violation of American law. The district court in Charleston, South Carolina, ordered restitution of the merchant ship to its Dutch owners, and the Supreme Court, ignoring certain ambiguities in the federal Neutrality Act as well as the Treaty of Alliance with France, affirmed. For the Supreme Court, the mere fact that the privateer had been armed and manned in the United States invalidated any seizures by it.

Not every prize carried into American ports was liable to be restored, however. This was because the treaty with France clearly permitted French vessels to sail their prizes into American ports without interference by American courts. As a result, in the absence of any proof that the prize had been taken in violation of American neutrality, federal courts refused to order restitution of vessels captured on the high seas. Throughout 1796, therefore, the Supreme Court considered the claims of several British owners for restitution and rejected most of them. For example, in *Moodie v. The Alfred*, the Court rejected a claim for restitution where the privateer was built in the United States, but armed and manned in a French port. Similarly, in *Moodie v. The Phoebe Anne*, the Supreme Court denied restoration where a French privateer, armed and manned in France, had undergone extensive repairs in Charleston. Benjamin Moodie, the British consul in South Carolina who acted as the nominal plaintiff in most restoration suits, complained about the Supreme Court's restrictive approach by noting that "nothing but the ownership [of a privateer] being in American citizens will cause a restoration of prizes." While accurate to some extent, Moodie's complaint was overstated, at least in so far as it ignored the fact that the Supreme Court would seem to have allowed restitution whenever a privateer was originally outfitted in the United States or was owned by American citizens. This distinction, while perhaps somewhat technical, was perfectly consistent with American obligations under the treaty with France.

In the end, the Supreme Court's approach to the neutrality question reflected the rather difficult position in which the United States was placed in any war between the two great European powers. Allowing the French free use of American ports to conduct a maritime war against England would clearly have been a breach of America's professed neutrality and would have justified Britain in considering the United States an ally of France. At the same time, however, American obligations to France under the 1778 Treaty of Alliance dictated that American ports be open to French, as well as English, vessels. The fact that the French legitimately took advantage of this openness to repair or resupply French warships and privateers was certainly a sore point for British officials. Yet, the United States could not have closed its ports to the French without violating its treaty obligations and appearing to side with the British. Thus, in closing the consular courts and preventing the arming of privateers in American ports, the Supreme Court obviated Britain's biggest grievance. At the same time, however, in refusing to order restitution of captures legitimately made on the high seas, the Court upheld America's treaty obligations to its former ally. While neither side was completely satisfied with the Supreme Court's attempt to occupy this middle ground, the Court's solution was simply the best that could have been crafted under the circumstances.

## Jay's Treaty and the Quasi-War

The American government's attempt to pursue a course of neutrality in the years between 1793 and 1796 was soon eclipsed by conflict with England. Over the years, tensions with Great Britain over trade and maritime matters steadily increased to the point where many observers believed that war between the United States and her former enemy was unavoidable.

On the American side, a major cause of resentment was Great Britain's failure to evacuate the forts on the western frontier in violation of the 1783 Treaty of Peace. Many Americans suspected that British military officials were using the western forts to incite the Indians to attack American settlements on the frontier. British occupation of the forts also prevented Americans from consolidating gains in the lucrative fur trade. As a result, beginning in 1793, members of the Republican party in the House of Representatives, led by James Madison and with support from Thomas Jefferson, sought to impose economic sanctions against England. These sanctions would not only punish England for her recalcitrance, but also had the added advantage of aligning American interests with those of France.

Meanwhile, British officials complicated matters by drafting a plan for the English conquest of the French West Indies. In 1793, an Order in Council was issued authorizing the seizure of any neutral vessel carrying goods to or from one of the

French islands. With the closure of British ports in the West Indies to American vessels after the Revolution, American merchants had developed a thriving trade with a number of French colonies in the Caribbean. Because the Order in Council was kept secret, American merchantmen had no idea what trouble lay in store. As a result, over two hundred and fifty American vessels were captured when a large fleet of British cruisers swept into the area. More than one-half of these were quickly condemned by British vice-admiralty courts resulting in a substantial loss of both ships and cargoes to American commerce (Ritcheson, 299–305).

Americans reacted angrily to what they regarded as British perfidy. Even those members of Congress inclined to favor stronger relations between England and the United States now believed that the United States had no choice but to prepare for war. Nonetheless, President Washington determined to make one last effort at avoiding conflict. With the advice of his cabinet, Washington nominated Chief Justice John Jay to lead a mission to Great Britain for the purpose of negotiating a resolution of American grievances as well as the regularization of commercial relations between the two countries.

Jay's service as secretary of foreign affairs during the Confederation period made him eminently qualified to serve as "minister plenipotentiary" to Great Britain, although his nomination did not meet with universal enthusiasm. On the contrary, French sympathizers in the Senate believed that Jay was too pro-British, and feared that any treaty he negotiated would result in American being drawn more firmly into the English imperial orbit. Others opposed Jay's nomination on constitutional grounds, arguing that service as an officer of the executive branch was inconsistent with Jay's obligations as a member of the judiciary. As a result, during the course of the Senate debate, New York's Aaron Burr moved the Senate to declare that permitting "judges of the Supreme Court to hold at the same time any other office or employment emanating from and holden at the pleasure of the Executive is contrary to the spirit of the Constitution, and, as tending to expose them to the influence of the Executive, is mischievous and impolitic." Burr's motion was defeated, however, and Jay's nomination approved by a large majority.

Jay set sail for England in the spring of 1794. Once there, he hoped to obtain some compensation for vessels seized in the West Indies, the evacuation of the forts on the western frontier, and payment for slaves carried away during the Revolution. He also hoped to negotiate a commercial treaty that would provide expanded markets for American merchants and traders. In spite of the many grievances on both sides, Jay found that the British government was generally receptive to idea of negotiating an end to the disputes that had arisen between the two countries. As a result, by the spring of 1795, Jay succeeded in obtaining an agreement with the British government, although he did not succeed in getting as many concessions as he had hoped. Under the terms of what was soon to become known as "Jay's Treaty," Britain agreed to surrender the forts on the western frontier by June 1796. Britain also agreed to enter into a commercial alliance by which American ships were granted the privilege of trading with India and the West Indies. These concessions came at a rather high price, however, for in exchange for these relatively modest gains, Jay was forced to abandon America's previous commitment to the principle of freedom of the seas. Put simply, the principle permitted neutrals to trade with belligerents so long as they did not carry war materiel or supplies. As a maritime nation without a large navy, the United States was a strong and early proponent of the idea that "free ships make free goods." Moreover, in addition to agreeing abandon the freedom of the seas, Jay was also forced to agree that the United States would no longer allow the French to outfit privateers in its ports and to ban the sale of seized British vessels by the French consular officials.

Jay's treaty was controversial when its terms were finally released to the public. Jay himself was vehemently attacked in the Republican press. Meetings were held throughout the country at which Jay and his treaty were roundly condemned. Most of the treaty's opponents believed that Jay had given up too much in order to gain too little. Abandoning the freedom of the seas was certainly the main point of contention, although many opponents argued that the British promise to evacuate the western forts was no concession at all, since the 1783 Treaty of Peace already obligated them to do that. They also noted that Jay's Treaty required the United States to agree that pre-war debts owed to British subjects were not amenable to confiscation; but no provision was made concerning payment for slaves carried off by the British army in 1783 (Bemis, 232–251, 258–261).

Although the Senate eventually ratified Jay's treaty, the struggle for ratification took its toll and resulted in a number of changes in the political landscape. On finding that he had been elected governor of New York while in France, Jay stepped down as chief justice and returned home. In his place, President Washington nominated South Carolina's John Rutledge, who himself had resigned his commission as an associate justice of the Supreme Court a few years earlier. Unfortunately, the Senate rejected Rutledge's nomination after Rutledge had attacked Jay's Treaty in the most virulent terms. As a result, in March 1796, President Washington nominated Connecticut Senator Oliver Ellsworth, the architect of the first Judiciary Act, to serve as chief justice, and the Senate confirmed the nomination a few days later.

While controversial, Jay's Treaty had the effect of reducing tensions between the United States and Great Britain. As a result, in the latter part of the 1790s the major foreign affairs problem became the deterioration of relations with France. For the French, the ratification of Jay's Treaty was a slap in the face. After all, many Frenchmen believed that the United States owed its very existence to French help. As if that were not enough, the French government contended that the United States owed a sister republic at war with the forces of monarchy both sustenance and support. In French eyes, therefore, Jay's Treaty amounted to a rejection of the Treaty of Alliance and put the United States firmly on England's side in the war in Europe.

Consequently, France determined to bring the United States into line. It began by involving itself in the 1796 presidential election. In a series of manifestoes published in American newspapers, France's ambassador to the United States, Pierre Adet made a direct appeal to the American people to elect Thomas Jefferson. Adet announced the suspension of diplomatic relations between the United States and France, as well as the inauguration of a tough new maritime policy. His aim was to bully Americans into rejecting John Adams, and replacing Washington with Thomas Jefferson, who was at this time quite supportive of French aims. In the end, however, Adet's actions did little to sway public opinion; and there is some evidence that his ham-handed attempts to manipulate public opinion actually backfired.

France reacted angrily to John Adams' election. Within a few months, the Directory ordered Charles Cotesworth Pinckney, the American ambassador in Paris, to leave the country, and French seizures of American shipping increased. In the spring of 1797, the United States prepared for war, as Congress considered bills increasing the size of the army and calling for the construction of three new frigates for the navy. In spite of these actions, President Adams continued to hope that war could be avoided. As a result, in a move that was to provoke vehement opposition from members of his own Federalist party, President Adams suddenly decided to send a peace mission to France in an effort to forestall the outbreak of hostilities. The mission consisted of three distinguished public servants, South Carolina's Charles Cotesworth Pinckney, Virginia's John Marshall, and Massachusetts' Elbridge Gerry. The delegation was instructed to negotiate compensation for American property confiscated by French cruisers and secure a release of America's obligation to defend the French West Indies imposed by the 1778 Treaty of Alliance. In exchange for these concessions from France, the United States would agree to put France on an equal footing with Great Britain in commerce and trade.

The mission to France was doomed to failure, however. Upon their arrival in Paris, the American commissioners were forced to wait for weeks without being formally received by the Directory. Then, just when the Americans decided to return home, they were approached by a mysterious group of intermediaries, known only as "X," "Y," and "Z," who promised to obtain an audience with the Directory if the Americans paid a bribe of $250,000 to the Directors, promised to make a loan to France of $12 million, and offer an apology for remarks President Adams made to Congress in the spring of 1797. It has long been supposed that these emissaries acted on behalf of Talleyrand, the French minister of foreign affairs. Nonetheless, the American commissioners refused this advance, and asked for their passports. Pinckney and Marshall returned home immediately, although Gerry remained in France for a few months longer.

Before leaving for home, the American delegation prepared a report to President Adams detailing the treatment they received at the hands of Tallyerand and his minions. The president attempted to keep the correspondence secret, but Republicans in Congress, who were generally sympathetic to the French cause, suspected that the communications from the American mission indicated that the French government was in favor of a negotiated settlement of differences between the two nations. They surmised that President Adams was determined to push the United States into war, and so was deliberately trying to suppress information about France's peaceful intentions. In an ironic twist, Republicans loudly demanded that the president publish the correspondence from the commissioners in Paris. Adams did so.

It was immediately apparent that the Republicans had miscalculated badly. Publication of the dispatches in April 1798 revealed that the French had treated America's ambassadors with disdain. Public opinion was aroused, and many both in and out of Congress, now demanded war with France. Unfortunately, the United States was poorly prepared for such an endeavor. At this point in its history, the United States Navy consisted of three frigates, while the army had a total of 3,500 men, most of which were engaged in garrisoning forts along the western frontier. As a result, France took advantage of America's military weakness to launch an undeclared naval war. By mid-summer 1798, French privateers swarmed along the American coast, and within a few months, unarmed American merchantmen were being captured in alarming numbers. Congress responded by ordering the construction of forty new ships for the navy and tripling the size of the army. Trade with France was ended and the 1778 Treaty of Alliance was suspended. In spite of French provocations, President Adams refrained from asking Congress to formally declare war. Nonetheless, for all intents and purposes, a state of war did exist between the two nations, and by the end of 1798, the U.S. Navy, led by the famous frigates, *Constitution, Constellation,* and *United States,* was actively engaged in armed conflict with French vessels. In addition, Congress provided for the commissioning of hundreds of privateers to prey on armed French merchantmen and cruisers. The "Quasi-War" had begun.

The fact this was an undeclared war had important legal implications. Congress never authorized an all-out assault on French shipping. Instead, it limited American vessels to attacking only armed French merchantmen, privateers, or ships of the line. Unarmed French shipping was immune from American assault. These limitations meant that the total number of French ships actually taken was rather small, and most captures were made by U.S. Navy warships. Nonetheless, the Supreme Court was called upon to examine a number of interesting legal questions as a result of several of these captures, the most important of which was raised in *Bas v. Tingy* (1800).

In 1799, an American merchantman named *Eliza,* was captured by a French privateer on the high seas. While en route to a French port to be condemned, the *Eliza* was recaptured by the *Ganges,* an American naval vessel. The *Ganges* brought the merchantman into a safe port, whereupon the master of the *Ganges*, Captain Tingy, filed a claim for salvage on behalf of himself and his crew. There was little doubt that Tingy and the crew of the *Ganges* had rendered a valuable service in saving the vessel and thus were entitled to some salvage award, but it was ultimately left to the Supreme Court to determine the amount of the compensation. The Court's task was complicated by the fact that federal statutes provided two different measures of compensation. A statute of June 1798, provided for a salvage award of one-eighth the value of a vessel recaptured and delivered to its owners, while a statute passed in March 1799, provided for a larger amount. This later statute gave those who recaptured a vessel one-half the ship's value where the vessel had been "re-taken from the enemy."

On one level, the Court was called upon to undertake some rather basic statutory analysis and resolve an apparent conflict between two different federal laws. On another level, however, the Court's resolution of the case had potentially explosive political consequences. This is because in order to decide which statute applied, the Court had to determine whether France could be considered an enemy of the United States. Lawyers for the *Eliza*'s owners argued that France could not be considered an enemy of the United States because Congress had not formally declared war on the French republic. For their part, however, Tingy's lawyers argued that a formal declaration of war was unnecessary, and that the fact that the two nations were engaged in open hostilities was sufficient to make France an enemy of the United States.

The justices unanimously concluded that France was, in fact, an enemy at the time the *Eliza* was retaken by the *Ganges*. As Justice Chase put it, "Congress is empowered to declare a general war, or congress may wage a limited war; limited in place, in objects, and in time." In the case of France, it was clear that the United States was engaged in a "limited, partial, war. Congress has not declared war in general terms; but congress has authorized hostilities on the high seas by certain persons in certain cases." Accordingly, the recaptors were entitled to salvage in the amount of one-half the ship's value.

The significance of the decision in *Bas* was not lost on the political classes. In determining that the United States was at war, the Supreme Court recognized, for the first time, the controversial principle that national government might wage war without a formal declaration by Congress. Some feared that in so doing, the Court overlooked the provision in the Constitution, which arguably envisioned a formal declaration of war by Congress before the commencement of hostilities. Yet, unlike the modern debate about the extent to which the president can conduct military operations without specific congressional authorization, it is important to note that the Supreme Court in *Bas* appeared to have assumed that even in the case of an undeclared war, the precise nature and conduct of hostilities was a matter to be determined by Congress, and not the president. As Justice Paterson noted in his opinion in *Bas*, the war with France was limited to the extent permitted by Congress, noting that only "[a]s far as congress tolerated and authorized the war on our part, so far may we proceed in hostile operations." Justice Chase was more explicit:

> [With regard to the undeclared war with France there] is no authority given to commit hostilities on land; to capture unarmed *French* vessels, nor even to capture *French* armed vessels lying in a French port; and the authority is not given, indiscriminately, to every citizen of *America*, against every citizen of *France*; but only to citizens appointed by commissions, or exposed to immediate outrage and violence.]

In essence, the Court in *Bas* implied that the Constitution's provision giving Congress alone the power to declare war was designed to preserve the legislature's right to determine whether hostilities ought to be commenced against a foreign government, thus limiting the ability of the executive to bring the United States into war without the people's consent. At the same time, however, the Court clearly recognized that Congress might direct the war in any fashion it saw fit, including the conduct of limited attacks or even a gradual escalation of hostilities.

The decision in *Bas v. Tingy* came at the height of tensions between France and the United States. Indeed, by the early part of 1799, President Adams was under considerable pressure to seek a formal declaration of war from Congress. At the same time, however, through a series of intermediaries, the French Directory made it known that a new American ambassador would be welcome in France, if the United States should decide to send one. President Adams concluded that this overture was, in fact, an invitation to commence peace negotiations. Consequently, on February 18, 1799, Adams nominated William Vans Murray, then minister at The Hague, to be minister plenipotentiary to the Republic of France. High Federalists, who generally sought war with France, greeted the nomination with disgust. A delegation of Federalist senators met with the president and advised him that the Senate would not approve the sending of a new ambassador to France. Adams was undeterred. He promptly informed the delegation that if the Senate rejected his plan to reopen negotiations, he would resign the presidency and allow vice president Jefferson to become the next president. Convinced that Jefferson as president was an evil to be avoided at all costs, the senators backed down. A compromise was reached whereby the Senate agreed to approve opening negotiations, provided they were conducted by a delegation of three. Adams quickly agreed, although he promised the senators that he would not allow the delegation to depart until he had received assurances that it would be properly received by the French government. No one, after all, wanted a repeat of the XYZ affair.

In any event, President Adams decided to nominate William Vans Murray, Patrick Henry, and Chief Justice Oliver Ellsworth to serve on the peace delegation. Patrick Henry declined the proffered post on the grounds of advanced age, leaving Adams to select North Carolina's Governor William R. Davie in Henry's place. As with Jay's nomination to be minister to Great Britain in 1794, Ellsworth's nomination implicated concerns about dual office holding. This time, however, most senators put aside their reservations and voted to appoint the chief justice notwithstanding the fact that he would continue to hold two federal offices at the same time. One observer commented on this phenomenon by noting that Ellsworth's staunch Federalist views ensured that "many Senators will make a sacrifice of their most settled opinions." In the end, the nomination was approved by a vote of twenty-three to six, and the peace delegation sailed for France in November 1799. Seven months of negotiations resulted in the Treaty of Mortefontaine, which effectively brought an end to the Quasi-War.

## Criminal Law

The Constitution did not grant federal courts any specific jurisdiction over crimes, although it clearly anticipated the criminal cases would come before them. Although, the Judiciary Act set forth procedures for trying criminal cases and disposing of appeals, it did not clearly specify the precise nature of the federal courts' criminal jurisdiction. No doubt, most members of both the Constitutional Convention and the first Senate Judiciary Committee assumed that Congress would enact a series of criminal statutes, and that violations of these laws would be prosecuted in the federal courts; and, as it happened, a separate Senate committee was, in fact, drafting a crimes code at precisely the same time the Judiciary Committee was considering the judiciary bill.

When completed, the first Judiciary Act did not give the Supreme Court any jurisdiction at all in criminal cases. Instead, the district courts were given power to try minor crimes and offences, which the Judiciary Act defined as crimes for which the penalty did not exceed a fine of one hundred dollars or six months' imprisonment. More serious offenses were to be tried in the circuit courts. In accordance with traditional 18th-century English practice, neither the Constitution nor the Judiciary Act provided for appeals in criminal cases. As a result, the Supreme Court itself did not dispose of any criminal appeals, although the requirement that the justices ride circuit ensured that members of the nation's highest court participated in the adjudication of criminal matters. As might be expected, however, the prosecution of crimes and offences quickly became an important part of the justices' work. Throughout the 1790s controversy over the adjudication of criminal cases made the federal courts one of the primary sources of discontent with the national government and an important battleground in the growing strife between the Federalist and Republican parties.

### The Common Law of Crimes

It seems likely the drafters of the first Judiciary Act expected that most criminal cases would arise in the context of the revenue and admiralty jurisdiction. After all, at this point in the nation's history, the most important source of income for the new government was duties on imported goods and excise taxes imposed on manufactures. While most revenue cases were tried as civil matters, it was clear that criminal penalties for violating the customs or tax laws were necessary if the nation's revenue was to be secured. Other crimes were also contemplated; however, the first Congress did not actually get around to enacting any criminal legislation until almost a year after the new government opened for business. Indeed, it was not until April 30, 1790, that Congress passed a crimes code. This statute provided penalties for a variety of offences, including treason, piracy, perjury, bribery of public officials, interfering with the mails and counterfeiting the public securities of the United States. Fortunately, the lack of a statutory basis for federal jurisdiction did not pose any great difficulty in the first few sessions of the federal courts because most of the cases which came before them involved crimes occurring on the high seas and so were tried pursuant to the courts' admiralty jurisdiction. In time, however, the increasingly complicated nature of American relations with England and France opened the door to greater difficulties.

The first test came after the publication of President Washington's Neutrality Proclamation in April 1793. As noted above, the proclamation was designed to keep the United States from being drawn into the war between France and Great Britain by forbidding American citizens from taking any steps to aid one of the belligerent powers. Yet, despite Washington's resolve, not every American was inclined to remain a mere bystander. In May 1793, Gideon Henfield, an American citizen serving aboard the French privateer, *Citizen Genet,* was arrested after he brought a prize into the port of Philadelphia. Within weeks, he was indicted for violating the terms of the Neutrality Proclamation and forced to stand trial at a special session of the Pennsylvania circuit court.

*Henfield's Case* (1793) was problematic for both the administration and the courts. On a political level, it presented again the question of what role the new nation ought to play in the conflict in Europe. Prosecuting Henfield invited Americans to consider whether their country ought to remain neutral in a war between a sister republic and a monarchy. Of greater importance to the federal courts, however, was the question of jurisdiction. After all, the Neutrality Proclamation was an act of the executive in pursuit of the administration's foreign policy. No federal statute made it a crime to aid the French cause. On what basis, it was asked, could Henfield's prosecution be commenced?

Members of President Washington's cabinet were unanimous in arguing that Henfield was guilty of violating the law of nations. Thus, Attorney General Edmund Randolph asserted that Henfield was "punishable because treaties are the supreme law of the land," and Henfield violated the provisions of the treaty between the United States and Great Britain which provided that the citizens of the two countries were at peace. In addition, Randolph argued, Henfield was "indictable at the common law, because his conduct [came] within the description of disturbing the peace of the United States."

Most of the members of the Supreme Court appeared to agree with Randolph. In charging the Pennsylvania grand jury, Justice James Wilson argued that Henfield could be prosecuted in federal courts. Although he did not explicitly adopt Randolph's view that Henfield was guilty of disturbing the peace, Wilson instructed the grand jury that Henfield's conduct violated the law of nations. Moreover, Wilson said, because the law of nations was incorporated into the common law of the United States, Henfield might be prosecuted in accordance with the common law without regard to whether a specific federal statute outlawed his activities. In the face of such argument, the grand jury had no choice but to indict Henfield, and the case was set for trial in July 1793 (Presser, 71).

Justices Wilson and Iredell presided over Henfield's trial in the circuit court. During the course of the trial, William Rawle, the U.S. attorney for the district, argued that individuals gave up the right to wage war on their own the moment they entered into a civil society. Otherwise, Rawle said, "a few individuals, for avaricious purposes, might involve the nation in a war." Henfield's offense was against the law of nations, and thus the common law, because it threatened to bring the United States into war against its will. As was to be expected, Henfield's lawyers vigorously argued that the case should be dismissed because the indictment did not state an offence at common law. In addition, since no federal statute outlawed giving aid to the French, the circuit court could not have jurisdiction over the crime charged. Justice Wilson was not deterred, however. Relying on a 1764 opinion by Lord Mansfield in a case called *Triquet v. Bath*, Wilson instructed the jury that Henfield's conduct violated the law of nations, which was itself incorporated in the common law:

> It has been asked by [Henfield's] counsel ... against what law has he offended? The answer is, against many and binding laws. As a citizen of the United States, he was bound to ... keep the peace in regard to all nations with whom we are at peace. This is the law of nations; not an *ex post facto* law, but a law in existence long before Gideon Henfield existed.

Whatever the justices' views on the subject, however, the Pennsylvania jury was unimpressed. It quickly returned a verdict of not guilty, setting off celebrations throughout the city, including a lavish dinner in Henfield's honor. Congress reacted to the decision by enacting a statute the following year enforcing the provisions of Neutrality Proclamation by making it a crime for any American to outfit a privateer or give aid to one of the belligerent powers.

*Henfield's Case* raised a fundamental problem of constitutional law: Even assuming that the law of nations was incorporated into the common law, there remained the question of whether federal courts had the power to try common law crimes at all. Some argued that, as a government of enumerated powers, the national government had only those powers expressly given it in the Constitution itself. With respect to the federal courts, this meant that federal judicial power extended only to those subjects contained in Article III. Thus, while Article III clearly envisioned the prosecution of criminal offences, the text of the Article does not specifically give federal courts the power to try common law crimes. Consequently, those who supported federal court jurisdiction over common law crimes were forced to interpret the text of Article III rather broadly. At least two of the justices, Iredell and Paterson, were quite willing to do so. Both found a solution to the problem of common law prosecutions in Article III's grant of jurisdiction over cases "arising under" the Constitution or laws of the United States. On its face, the clause clearly envisioned jurisdiction over offences punishable under a statute passed by Congress. However, both Iredell and Paterson took the position that the clause also served as a grant of power over common law crimes because the common law was part of the law of the United States. In charging the spring 1794 South Carolina circuit court grand jury, therefore, Justice Iredell repeated the arguments made by Justice Wilson in *Henfield's Case*. Like Wilson, Iredell asserted that the common law of both England and the colonies had long encompassed violations of the law of nations so that an "offense against the Law of Nations might have equally been injurious to the public welfare and to individuals, if committed by an inhabitant of this country as if committed in England." Neither the Revolution nor the federal Constitution altered this fundamental rule. "The change in government could not do away with the Common Law in this particular … except in cases where its operation was absolutely inconsistent with the change in our situation." Iredell noted that Congress had the power to define criminal offenses by statute, but he also declared that where the statutes are silent, "the common law which existed before (so far as it is applicable to our present situation) must still operate."

For his part, Justice Paterson asserted that the common law was an inherent part of the American legal system. "The common law," he said, "attached to the people, whether they met partially as of a state, or generally as of the United States" and every part of the Union was "entitled to the common law as a common right." As a result, upon ratification of the federal Constitution, that part of the common law relevant to the national government and its enumerated powers became a part of federal law. Common law prosecutions were within the federal courts' jurisdiction because they were cases "arising under" the Constitution.

Undoubtedly, Chief Justice Ellsworth delivered the most forceful—and controversial—exposition of the validity of the federal common law of crimes in a charge to a South Carolina grand jury in 1799. Ellsworth began by noting that offences against the United States are "*chiefly* defined in the statutes," but he also asserted that federal courts have the power to prosecute common law crimes in two other instances. The first of these involved "acts contravening the law of nations." Although he did not elaborate on this theme, Ellsworth clearly had in mind prosecutions like that brought against Gideon Henfield for violating the Neutrality Proclamation or perhaps attacks on an ambassador. The second category included "acts manifestly subversive of the national government, or some of its powers specified in the constitution." Ellsworth placed offenses against the security or safety of the government, such as bribery of public officials, interfering with federal officers in the conduct of their duties, or even sedition, into this second category. Such a power was necessary, Ellsworth asserted, because every government must have the ability to defend itself from attack regardless of whether any legislative body had ever explicitly proscribed these acts. At the same time, Ellsworth cautioned his listeners that he claimed only a limited power for the federal courts, one that encompassed a doctrine of "misdemeanors." He did not, in other words, envision a broad power in the federal courts to criminalize all wrongful conduct under the guise of the common law of crimes. Instead, he believed that federal courts had the power to try crimes only where the offences were "manifestly subversive of the national government."

Whatever the precise theoretical basis for common law prosecutions, it was clear that the majority of the justices of the Supreme Court believed that the federal courts had jurisdiction over common law crimes. The one significant exception was Justice Samuel Chase, who in 1798 had the opportunity to weigh in on the subject in a case brought in the Pennsylvania circuit court, entitled, *United States v. Worrall* (1798). Worrall was indicted for trying to bribe Tench Coxe, the federal Commissioner of Revenue, in an effort to obtain a federal contract to build a lighthouse. At the time, the federal criminal statutes outlawed only bribery of federal judges, and did not cover the Commissioner of Revenue. A prosecution was possible, therefore, only if it had some common law basis.

At trial, Worrall's counsel, A.J. Dallas, argued against federal court jurisdiction of the offense. He contended that the federal courts' power was limited to the specific grants of authority contained in Article III of the Constitution. Although the Constitution gave federal courts jurisdiction over cases "arising under" federal laws, Dallas asserted that the phrase encompassed only positive, written laws duly passed by Congress. When Dallas had concluded his argument, the attorney for the district, William Rawle began to address the court. During the course of this presentation, Justice Chase, who presided with District Judge Richard Peters, stopped Rawle and enquired if the prosecution was one solely based on the common law. When Rawle responded that it was, Chase immediately halted the proceedings and delivered himself of a lengthy opinion in which he argued that the Constitution's implicit grant of power to Congress to pass criminal statutes necessarily precluded federal courts from having the power to entertain prosecutions at common law. In Chase's view, federal courts could not entertain a prosecution under the common law of crimes because "the

United States, as a Federal government, have no common law." On the contrary, he said, there was a common law of England and of the individual states, but neither the Constitution nor any federal statute adopted the provisions of the common law. Consequently, Worrall's prosecution was invalid.

Chase's argument, while elegant, did not convince Judge Peters, who believed that Worrall's offence struck at the heart of government. According to Peters, federal courts must have the power to prosecute crimes that interfere with the proper structure and operation of the federal government if only as a matter of self-preservation. Peters argued that "[w]henever an offense aims at the subversion of any Federal institution, or at the corruption of its public officers, it is an offense against the well-being of the United States; [and] from its very nature, it is cognizable under their authority." Peters' differences with Chase on this point presented an important procedural problem. Because the court was divided on the law, the judges suggested that Worrall appeal his case directly to the Supreme Court. To their surprise, however, Worrall refused. Apparently, he decided that such an appeal was hopeless, since most of the justices had already expressed approval of common law prosecutions (Presser, 95). After "a short consultation," during which one contemporary observer suggested that other members of the Supreme Court were consulted, Justice Chase acquiesced in sentencing Worrall to three months imprisonment and a $200 fine.

Among the members of the Supreme Court, Justice Chase was largely alone in his opposition to the prosecution of common law crimes in federal courts. In charging grand juries in the years following *Worrall*, almost every justice expressed the opinion that the prosecution of common law crimes was proper. The justices' agreement on this point became a source of great concern to opponents of the Federalist administration. Republicans complained that the use of the doctrine of common law crimes would be extended to eventually deprive the citizenry of their rights. They argued that the doctrine of common law crimes was vague and would allow aggressive federal prosecutors to harass and intimidate opponents of the government. Federalists, on the other hand, contended that the prosecution of common law crimes was a necessary means of self-preservation. They asserted that the prosecution of common law crimes was essential for reaching those acts that might not explicitly be described in a federal statute. This debate continued to rage throughout the 1790s and was only finally put to rest in *United States v. Hudson & Goodwin* (1812), in which the Supreme Court held—without any apparent explanation—that federal courts lacked the power to try common law crimes.

## The Alien and Sedition Acts

Justice Chase's opinion in *Worrall* proved quite disturbing to the administration and its supporters. The case was decided in 1798, at the height of tensions between the United

States and France, when most political observers believed that war with France was imminent. Congress and the executive branch were making preparations for increasing the size of the army, building more ships for the navy, and constructing fortifications along the coast. In the midst of these preparations, concerns grew about the size of the "French faction" in the United States. Federalists in Congress worried that French sympathizers would attempt to disrupt the war effort by weakening the government through the publication of scandalous material about its officers and policies. As a result, led by Congressman Robert Goodloe Harper, the House of Representatives took up consideration of a bill to punish seditious speech.

The crime of sedition had long been recognized as common law, and sedition prosecutions had frequently been commenced against those who published material designed to bring the government into disrepute. During the seventeenth century, officials in England often used sedition trials to silence those who opposed the Crown; while in the colonies, crown appointees relied on sedition laws to punish critics of royal government. Arguably, the most famous American sedition trial was that of John Peter Zenger, publisher of the *New York World*, who was accused of libeling the royal governor of New York in 1734. A jury acquitted Zenger in spite of efforts by the judge to badger them into producing a guilty verdict. The *Zenger* trial, and others like it, helped give sedition prosecutions a bad name. Many Americans looked askance at sedition laws because of their use as instruments of repressive government.

Fears that the federal government would use sedition prosecutions to limit criticism of its actions were increased in the summer of 1798, when Benjamin Franklin Bache, publisher of the vehemently antifederalist newspaper, *Aurora*, was arrested and charged with libeling President Adams. The case was brought at common law, and so resurrected the earlier debate about the legitimacy of common law prosecutions in federal courts. This aspect of the case, combined with the fact that the prosecution appeared to be an attempt to suppress political dissent, led many to accuse the Federalist administration of being as arbitrary as any of King George's colonial governors. In the event, however, Bache's prosecution had to be abandoned after he died during the yellow fever epidemic that swept Philadelphia during the fall of 1798. John Daly Burk, editor of the New York newspaper, the *Time Piece*, faced a similar prosecution that same summer. He was arrested and charged with common law sedition in July 1798, after accusing the Federalist administration of embarking upon a scheme to reverse the gains of the American Revolution and transform the nation into an aristocratic state. Burk was not an American citizen, and so his prosecution, too, was abandoned after he promised to leave the country. He never did. Instead, he fled to Virginia where he became something of a playwright.

Republicans reacted with disdain when the House of Representatives took up consideration of a sedition bill in the spring of 1798. Even some Federalists were uneasy, but most defenders of the administration had long since come to the conclusion that the widespread hostility to the prosecution of common law crimes meant that Congress had to provide specific statutory authorization for sedition trials. Nonetheless, in an effort to allay concerns about the harshness of sedition prosecutions, the drafters of the bill included a provision allowing truth to be a defense to a sedition prosecution. This was a change from the rigor of the common law, which made the mere publication of scandalous material a crime regardless of whether the information was true or not. With this important amendment, the Sedition Act became law on July 14, 1798.

As fate (or politics) would have it, one of the first prosecutions under the Sedition Act was commenced against Congressman Matthew Lyon of Vermont. Lyon had long been a target of Federalist ire. During the highly charged partisan atmosphere prevailing in the House during the latter part of 1797, Lyon became embroiled in controversy with Federalist members at every turn. When insulted by Connecticut Congressman, Roger Griswold, Lyon spat in Griswold's face. Griswold returned to the floor a few days later and beat Lyon about the head with a cane. Lyon was able to grab a pair of tongs from the fireplace and the two men wrestled across the floor of the House until they were parted by others. Federalists immediately decried the behavior of the "Spitting Lyon" and sought his expulsion from the House. Republicans rallied to Lyon's defense, however, and the effort to expel him failed for want of a two-thirds vote.

The Sedition Act opened the door to new possibilities for Lyon's opponents. Shortly after its passage, Federalists in Vermont instigated a prosecution against Lyon for publishing an attack on President Adams in a Vermont newspaper. Justice William Paterson presided over Lyon's trial, which was held in Rutland in the fall of 1798. At the trial, Lyon attempted to defend against the charge by arguing that the Sedition Act violated the First Amendment, and was, therefore, unconstitutional. Paterson refused to permit this line of argument, however, and Lyon was quickly convicted. He was sentenced to four months' imprisonment and a fine of $1,000. Federalists hailed Lyon's prosecution and imprisonment as a triumph over "the unbridled spirit of opposition to government," but their elation was short lived. Lyon became a martyr to the Republican cause and an example of the heavy-handedness of the Federalist-dominated judiciary. He ran for reelection to Congress from his jail cell and was victorious. When Congress reconvened in February 1799, Lyon proudly took his seat, causing one Federalist newspaper to wryly remark that he "looked remarkably well for a gentleman just out of jail."

Although most of the justices of the Supreme Court appear to have been in support of the Sedition Act, none was more vigorous in upholding its aims than Justice Chase. A firm supporter of President Adams, especially during the presidential election campaign of 1800, Chase believed that "a licentious press is the bane of freedom, and the Peril of Society." He, therefore, set out to ensure that the press was kept within its proper limits, and looked to the Sedition Act to assist him in his work. Chase's first opportunity occurred during the trial of Thomas Cooper in the Pennsylvania circuit court in spring of 1800. Cooper was a transplanted English radical who became a Republican newspaper editor. The previous year, he published an article in which he accused President Adams of having damaged the nation's credit so severely that it was forced to borrow money at usurious interest rates during peacetime. Cooper defended himself at trial and tried to prove the truth of his assertions. He claimed that the absence of a declared war between the United States and France meant that the two nations were at peace. Paying high interest rates on the national debt was, therefore, unwarranted. While Cooper's claims might have been technically true, they were certainly matters of opinion. Unfortunately for him, however, Justice Chase decided that Cooper's aims were malicious. Chase, therefore, instructed that jury that Cooper had the burden of proving the truth of his charges against the president "beyond a marrow." In so doing, Chase ensured Cooper's conviction since it was difficult, if not impossible, for anyone to prove the truth of matters of judgment or opinion "beyond a marrow." (Presser, 123)

Justice Chase took an even more aggressive line during the trial of the Virginia printer, James Thompson Callender. While en route to Richmond to preside over the Virginia circuit court, a friend gave Chase a copy of Callender's most recent book, *The Prospect Before Us*. Callender was a rather unsympathetic character. He was both scandalmonger and a rabid Republican, often using his press to launch the most vicious attacks on his Federalist opponents. In *The Prospect Before Us*, Callender accused President Adams of being a "professed aristocrat" who had "proven faithful and serviceable to British interests." He also claimed that Adams had devoted his "utmost efforts" toward "provoking a French war."

That Callender was a lightning rod for every point of contention between Federalists and Republicans was evident during the course of his trial. Although a man of limited means, a team of the Old Dominion's most distinguished lawyers represented Callender, and many suspected that Thomas Jefferson himself was paying Callender's legal fees. Unfortunately for their client, at least one member of this distinguished group later admitted that the lawyers' purpose in taking Callender's case was to "render a service, not to the man, but to the cause." Consequently, they put forth an aggressive defense, confronting Chase at every turn, and ultimately provoking the volatile justice into making several important tactical, albeit political, errors.

The first controversy arose after the government concluded its case. When it came time for the defense to open, Callender's lawyers attempted to call Colonel John Taylor whose testimony was designed to prove the truth of Callender's claim that Adams was "a professed aristocrat." Justice Chase refused to permit the witness to be called, however. While noting the plain words of the statute guaranteeing the right of the defendant to prove truth as a defense, Chase ruled that a witness could only testify if he were going to prove the truth of the entire libel not just a part. Chase reasoned that because Taylor could not offer evidence as to the truth of the other eighteen counts, he was disqualified from being a witness at all.

Unable to produce a witness who could testify to the truth of every element of the libel, Callender's lawyers gave up on arguing the facts. Instead, they turned their attention to the jury and sought to argue that the Sedition Act was unconstitutional. Modern courts do not permit lawyers to make legal arguments to juries, but such a practice was well established in the latter part of the eighteenth century. Chase, however, would have nothing to do with it. Instead, he insisted that the power to decide whether acts of Congress violated the Constitution was vested in the judges alone, and that juries were not competent to make such a determination. The problem for Chase was one of uniformity in law. Juries, he said, could not be trusted to decide whether an act of Congress is constitutional because "the opinions of petit juries will very probably be different in different states." The same could not be said about judges, for while judges might make mistakes, an appeals court can review their decisions. Yet, "if juries made mistakes, there can be no revision or control over their verdicts, and therefore, there can be no mode to obtain uniformity in the decisions."

While Chase's arguments about the wisdom of allowing juries to render verdicts on the constitutionality of federal statutes might have made some sense, Callender's lawyers knew that juries had always had the right to determine legal questions in Virginia. What's more, they knew that everyone in the courtroom knew it as well. Consequently, they engaged in a bit of political theatre. Having been precluded from arguing the law to the jury, a right long claimed by Virginia defendants, Callender's lawyers folded up their papers and walked out of the courtroom. Chase was undeterred, however. He quickly summed up the evidence for the jury, which then convicted Callender two hours later.

Although Justice Chase can rightfully be regarded as the most openly partisan of the members of the first Supreme Court, other justices shared his beliefs. Throughout the first decade of its existence, the members of the court often seem to consciously administer the criminal law in an effort to support administration policy (Casto 1995, 126). They were well aware that the new government had not yet gained a degree of stability and so seized upon the criminal prosecutions that came before them as a means of providing a measure of stability and security to the administration and its policies. That they seemed to use the common law of crimes to broaden the jurisdiction of the federal courts, and seized upon the Sedition Act as a particularly useful tool in that effort, had the unfortunate effect of making the justices appear unduly partisan in their administration of the law and ultimately aided Republicans in their characterization of Federalists as monarchists bent on subverting the rights of the people.

## *References and Further Reading*

Bemis, Samuel Flagg, *Jay's Treaty: A Study in Commerce and Diplomacy* (New York: Macmillan 1923).

Casto, William. *The Supreme Court in the Early Republic* (Columbia, SC: University of South Carolina Press, 1995).

DeConde, *The Quasi-War: The Politics and Diplomacy of the Undeclared War with France, 1797–1801* (New York: Charles Scribner's Sons, 1966).

Elkins, Stanley, and Eric McKitrick, *The Age of Federalism* (New York: Oxford University Press, 1993).

Farrand, Max, ed., *Records of the Federal Convention of 1787*, 4 vols. (New Haven, CT: Yale University Press, 1966).

Holt, Wythe. "'To Establish Justice': Politics, the Judiciary Act of 1789, and the Invention of the Federal Courts," *Duke Law Journal* (1990): 1421.

Marcus, Maeva, ed., *Documentary History of the Supreme Court of the United States, 1789–1800*, 6 vols. (New York: Columbia University Press, 1985–2000).

_____, *Origins of the Federal Judiciary: Essays on the Judiciary Act of 1789* (New York: Oxford University Press, 1992).

Presser, Stephen B. *The Original Misunderstanding: The English, the Americans, and the Dialectic of Federalist Jurisprudence* (Durham, NC: Carolina Academic Press, 1991).

Ritcheson, Charles R. *Aftermath of Revolution: British Policy Toward the United States, 1783–1795* (Dallas: Southern Methodist University Press, 1969).

Ritz, Wilfred J. *Rewriting the History of the Judiciary Act of 1789: Exposing Myths, Challenging Premises, and Using New Evidence* (Wythe Holt and L. H. LaRue, eds., Norman, Oklahoma: University of Oklahoma Press, 1990).

Slaughter, Thomas P. *The Whiskey Rebellion* (New York: Oxford University Press, 1986).

Smith, James Morton. *Freedom's Fetters: The Alien and Sedition Laws and American Civil Liberties* (Ithaca, NY: Cornell University Press, 1956).

Goebel, Julius, Jr., *History of the Supreme Court of the United States: Antecedents and Beginnings to 1801* (New York: Macmillan, 1971).

# 4

# *Legacy and Impact*

## *The Supreme Court's Role in the New Frame of Government*

### *Advisory Opinions*

The early Supreme Court was played a role in government that is unique, and which is unlikely ever to be repeated. During the course of the two centuries following Chief Justice Marshall's opinion in *Marbury v. Madison* (1803), the Supreme Court has often adopted something of an adversarial posture with respect to the other branches of government. Wielding the power of judicial review, the Supreme Court in the post-*Marbury* era is often regarded as a check against overreaching by the executive or legislative branches, protecting individual rights and serving as the means by which the powers of government are constrained in accordance with constitutional principles. Over the years, therefore, the Court has found it necessary to oppose the political branches, striking down legislation or executive action where it believed Congress or the president had overstepped their bounds.

The justices of the Jay and Ellsworth Courts saw their role quite differently, however. Rather than viewing the Court as a check on the powers of government, it appears that most of the early justices believed that their role was to uphold and support the national government against efforts to weaken its powers. This is seen most clearly in the justices' willingness to render advisory opinions to the administration. Chief Justices Jay and Ellsworth, in particular, did not hesitate to offer advice or suggestions to members of the executive branch. No doubt the frequency with which the two chief justices were consulted was a function of their singular expertise. After all, prior to becoming chief justice, Jay had served as secretary of foreign affairs in the confederation government, as well as minister to Spain, and, finally, as one of the commissioners appointed to negotiate the peace treaty with Great Britain. It probably seemed natural, therefore, that President Washington and his cabinet would call upon Jay to render an opinion in the Nootka Sound crisis or in the drafting of the Neutrality Proclamation. Similarly, Chief Justice Ellsworth had a long and distinguished career in national affairs, first in the Constitutional Convention and then as one of the original members of the United States Senate. While in the Senate, Ellsworth was the chief architect of the Judiciary Act, a role that undoubtedly gave him special insights into the functioning of the judicial system. As a result, when members of the Cabinet later sought advice about the constitutionality of the Sedition Act or other criminal matters, Ellsworth would have been a likely choice to provide it.

Yet, even after the full court's refusal to render a formal advisory opinion during the neutrality controversy, the justices continued to provide advice to members of the executive branch throughout the 1790s. The range of opinions on which the justices' opinion was sought was quite broad, encompassing matters as diverse as the drafting of a sedition law and the repurchase of securities by the Sinking Fund. That members of the cabinet would seek the opinion of the justices on such a broad range of matters seems somewhat strange to modern observers. That the justices would be content to provide the requested advice is even more startling. After all, it could not have escaped the justices' attention that many of the matters on which they were called to express an opinion would eventually find their way before the courts. For example, in 1798, Tench Coxe, the Commissioner of Revenue, asked Justice Paterson to give an opinion on the subject of whether an attempt to bribe a federal official could be prosecuted in the absence of a statute specifically covering the offense. Paterson thought that such an offense might be prosecuted at common law. A few months later, therefore, John Worrall was indicted at common law for offering a bribe to Commissioner Coxe to influence the award of a contract to build a lighthouse. An even more troubling example of the same practice (at least to modern eyes) can be found in Chief Justice Ellsworth's opinion on the constitutionality of the Sedition Act. As debate over passage of the Sedition Act continued in Congress, Secretary of State Timothy Pickering wrote the chief justice requesting his opinion as to whether the Sedition Act was constitutional. Ellsworth wrote back a few weeks later and expressed the view that nothing in the original Constitution or the First Amendment necessarily precluded enforcement of the act. Pickering subsequently ordered the prosecution of a number of Republican newspaper editors.

It is important to note that in the two examples just cited, neither of the issues on which the justices gave their opinions would likely find their way to the Supreme Court itself. This is because the Supreme Court had no appellate jurisdiction in criminal cases at the time. On the other hand, it is clear that both Justice Paterson and Chief Justice Ellsworth would have expected questions concerning the common law of crimes or the constitutionality of the Sedition Act to come before them while they were presiding over criminal trials in the circuit courts. Indeed, modern observers can be excused for assuming that the mere fact that there would be no possibility of Supreme Court review of decisions rendered while on circuit would have made the justices especially sensitive to the impropriety of rendering advisory opinions in criminal cases. This is especially the case where, as here, the justices' advice was probably instrumental in initiating the prosecutions in the first place.

On other matters, the impact of advisory opinions is less clear. This, too, is a function of jurisdiction, especially on more abstract questions. For example, the federal courts were not given so-called "federal question" jurisdiction until 1896. As a result, giving advice on matters such as the House of Representatives' demand for papers relating to the Jay Treaty (Chief Justice Ellsworth), the constitutionality of a proposal to repurchase portions of the public debt (Chief Justice Jay), or the extent of the president's power to appoint a public printer (Justice Chase), was unlikely to involve the Court directly in disputes between the executive and legislative branches. The justices could, therefore, render advice to members of the other branches without fear of later having to rule on the controversy.

Still, the justices' willingness to give advisory opinions remains puzzling to modern observers. Although giving formal advisory opinions remains a well-established practice in many state supreme courts, individual state or federal judges uniformly decline to provide written advisory opinions on request. One reason for this is the concern that judges not be seen to prejudge the merits of controversies that might someday come before them. Another reason is the belief that the adversarial system is best designed to ensure that the merits of a case are fully briefed and aired before judges come to a conclusion. Thus, many state courts that do provide advisory opinions *en banc* often invite, or even require, interested parties to appear and argue the merits before an opinion is issued. Rendering advice solely on the basis of a government official's submission not only limits the range of opinion and information that might be brought to bear to inform the judges' opinion, but leaves the opinion open to being challenged as being biased in favor of the government.

Given these concerns, one is left to wonder why the early justices would have been willing to play such a role. The answer, it seems, can be found in the fact that the justices were generally prone to think of themselves as full participants in the experiment that was the new national government. Unlike members of the modern Supreme Court, who often like to appear as impartial referees or watchdogs over the activities of the political branches, the justices of the Jay and Ellsworth courts tended to view the judiciary as the third leg of a three-legged stool. In their view, the courts were simply one part of an integrated whole. Their job was to support the national government by providing an independent forum where the central government's concerns would receive a fair and respectful hearing. To the extent the justices were referees at all, they were more likely to be mediators between the national government and the states, for in the absence of federal question jurisdiction, the early Supreme Court was unlikely to become involved in disputes between the national legislature and the executive. In addition, the justices' varying opinions on the extent of the Court's power to declare acts of Congress void, combined with a more limited view of the role of the

Bill of Rights in protecting individual liberty, meant that the time was not yet ripe for the Court to become the primary defender of individual rights.

In light of all this activity, the early Supreme Court's refusal to provide a formal advisory opinion during the neutrality controversy seems odd when set against the willingness of individual justices to provide advice to various members of the cabinet. It appears that the justices were willing to make such a distinction in order to preserve the Court's institutional independence. Almost every American jurist knew the history of the Crown's attempt restrain and coerce royal judges, and none was inclined to repeat the experience. In insisting that the powers of government remain distinct and separate, therefore, the justices were doing no more than helping to ensure that the principles of republican government would be preserved. While it is certainly true that the judges saw themselves as partners in the struggle to establish a new government, they were equally cognizant of the need to remain formally and functionally independent of the political branches. They understood that establishing a precedent whereby the members of the Supreme Court would be expected to provide extrajudicial advice would open the door to future expectations. They feared that perhaps, in time, the Court would be pressured to provide cover for an executive bent on pursuing unpopular policy.

In fact, the neutrality controversy provided a perfect example of that very danger. The cabinet's request for an advisory opinion came at a time of great political turmoil. Americans were deeply divided over the question of American support for France in her war against England. Many Americans believed that the Washington administration ought to provide more support for its old ally, and some even urged that the new nation enter the war on France's side. Others, however, believed that America's best hope lay in re-establishing her traditional cultural and trade relationships with England, and thus staunchly opposed any measure that would provoke a confrontation with the mother country. This divergence in public opinion placed the administration in an unwinnable position, for a large segment of the public would be unhappy no matter what policy it adopted. One way of blunting this effect, therefore, was to seek an opinion from the Supreme Court. It seems likely that Washington and his cabinet hoped that the expected negative public relations impact of the proposed neutrality policy could be minimized if the Court could be convinced to offer an interpretation of the Treaty of Alliance with France that supported the government's position.

If this were, in fact, the administration's strategy, it is clear that the members of the Court were also aware of the public relations problem. No doubt the justices knew that any opinion they expressed on the subject of neutrality would be bound to upset a large segment of the public. More importantly, at this point in time, the justices were about to approach Congress with a petition to obtain relief from the rigors of circuit riding. It is doubtful, therefore, that the Court would have wanted to antagonize those on either side of the aisle by injecting themselves into what was certainly the most contentious political problem of the day. In short, the justices simply saw no profit in formally rendering advice on so public and difficult a controversy, and, thus, politely declined to be drawn into the debate.

As a result, whether it did so intentionally or not, in refusing to render an advisory opinion on neutrality, the Court achieved two very important objectives:

First, by grounding its refusal on the principle of separation of powers, the justices struck a modest blow for judicial independence. After all, this was the first time in which the Supreme Court formally refused to comply with a request from either of the political branches. While it is true that all of the justices had earlier provided advisory opinions, they did so in the guise of individual letters to members of the cabinet. This time, however, the Court was definitive in its rejection, thus demonstrating that it would not always be ready to fulfill the wishes of the other two branches.

Second, the refusal to provide an advisory opinion went a long way toward ensuring that the Court would retain some measure of esteem. At this point in its history, opinions of the Supreme Court had not yet achieved the level of respect or deference that often (though not always) accompany its pronouncements today. The justices knew that involving the Court in what were essentially political decisions would have the tendency of making it appear to be a political as well as judicial body. By refusing to be drawn into the controversy, therefore, the justices took the first step in establishing the Supreme Court's impartiality in the eyes of the public.

## The Grand Jury and the Political Charge

While it is clear that the justices sought to retain their independence, they never lost sight of the fact that they were part of a new experiment in government, whose success was not yet fully guaranteed. Consequently, the members of the early Supreme Court took almost every opportunity to encourage support for the federal government. One of the most interesting ways in which they tried to mold public opinion was in the delivery of what were obviously and consciously "political charges" to the grand juries of the various circuit courts.

As noted in Chapter 2, during the first decade of the Court's life, the justices were each required to "ride circuit." This duty took them around the country presiding over criminal and civil trials at stated intervals during the year. Shortly after the opening of the circuit court in a particular place, the members of the grand jury would be summoned and sworn. The presiding justice then gave the grand jury a short speech, or "charge," in which he explained the nature of their duty and encouraged them to identify and bring forward wrongdoers. Throughout the 1790s, the justices often used these charges as opportunities to educate the populace in the basics of citizenship.

These speeches were no off-the-cuff presentation, however. Because grand jury charges were often printed in local newspapers and then reprinted in papers throughout the country, the justices took special care to prepare their remarks, cognizant that they were addressing a much wider audience than those actually present in the courtroom. Knowing they were addressing the population at large, the justices often tailored their remarks to generate support for the national government and its policies. Thus, as one scholar has noted, in its early years, the justices of the Supreme Court often acted as "Republican schoolmasters," self-consciously using almost any opportunity to inculcate their audience with an appreciation of civic virtue, and the importance of the federal government in securing the liberty and prosperity of the wider public (Lerner, 127–29).

In general, one sees several themes running through the various charges. Foremost among these is the close connection between self-restraint and liberty (Lerner, 137). The justices recognized that the people's ability to choose their governors meant that no government could long survive if it lost the confidence of the people. As a result, expecting blind adherence to Solomonic pronouncements about what "the law is" would be unlikely to achieve popular support. It was necessary, therefore, that the justices should convince the public to adopt their pronouncements and opinions without the need for coercion or constraint.

In many cases, the first step in obtaining this assent was to link the success of the new government to the individual's self-interest. Consequently, in his first grand jury charge in the spring of 1790, Chief Justice Jay asserted that it "cannot be too strongly impressed on the minds of all of us how greatly our individual prosperity depends on our national prosperity, and how greatly our national prosperity depends on a well organised, vigorous government." According to Jay, material prosperity was a direct consequence of a community's respect for law. He, therefore, cautioned his listeners to be wary of the dangers posed by the "unlimited sway of a majority" or the "[u]nlicensed indulgence to all the passions of men." Each man should consider, Jay said, "that his liberty and his prosperity cannot be secured without forming a common interest with all the other members of the society to which he belongs."

This appeal to material interest was accompanied with exhortations to support the new federal constitution. Having shown that liberty needed order to survive, the justices often expressed the view that the federal constitution was quite nigh perfect in helping provide the essential balance between protecting the rights of the people and promoting prosperity. Thus, in his spring 1790 charge, Chief Justice Jay gave an extensive oration extolling the virtues of the new government, a government in which Americans now had "more perfect opportunities for choosing, and more effectual means of establishing their own government, than any other nation has hitherto enjoyed." In a similar vein, Justice Iredell opined that in ratifying the federal Constitution, the people of the United States have demonstrated that a "higher degree of freedom consistent with any government at all, is not exercisable by human nature." For his part, Chief Justice Ellsworth would later declare that the national government was the "palladium of American liberty" and the "ground of national hope."

In making this connection between material prosperity and order, the justices often hinted the federal constitution was culmination of a divine plan. Thus, in a charge delivered in Virginia in 1793, Chief Justice Jay declared that to oppose the Constitution was tantamount to sedition:

> The People of the United States being by the Grace and favour of Heaven free, sovereign and independent, had a Right to choose the form of national Government which they should judge most conducive to their Happiness and Safety. They have done so, and have ordained and established the one which is specified in their great and General Compact or Constitution.... To this great Compact every Citizen is a Party, and consequently every Citizen is bound by it. To oppose the operation of this Constitution and of the Government established by it, would be to violate the Sovereignty of the People, and would justly merit Reprehension and Punishment.

Nonetheless, while "Heaven" might have bestowed a near-perfect government on the people of the United States, it was up to them to ensure its continued stability. This meant that some form of popular restraint was essential to the preservation of the national enterprise. Thus, the justices noted that in a republican government there are numerous opportunities for individual disappointment. Having been invited to express his opinion on the issues of the day, the citizen was obliged to "cheerfully submit" to the will of the majority. This meant avoiding faction and partisanship, as well as being wary of the wiles of men "impelled by avarice or ambition, or both." As Chief Justice Ellsworth once noted, the success of the national enterprise depended on a citizenry thoroughly committed to "vigilance, constant diligence, and an fidelity for the execution of laws." Chief Justice Jay later made the connection even more explicit:

> Let it be remembered that civil Liberty consists not in a Right to every Man to do just what he pleases, but it consists in an equal Right to all the Citizens to have, enjoy, and to do, in peace, Security and without Molestation, whatever the equal and constitutional Laws of the Country admit to be consistent with the public Good. It is the Duty and the Interest therefore of all good Citizens, in their several Stations, to support the Laws and Government which thus protect their Rights and Liberties.

This is not to say that the justices' grand jury charges were always grand pronouncements of political theory. On the contrary, throughout the first decade, most of the justices used their charges to comment on important political events or controversies, even when those events did not require any specific action on the part of the grand jury or the courts. The earliest, and most obvious, examples of this truly political charge are the series of charges delivered by the various justices during the neutrality controversy of 1793.

As noted earlier, the neutrality controversy was one situation in which the sentiment of a large segment—perhaps even a majority—of the public was in favor of open and active support of France in its war with Great Britain. Indeed, it appears that the Washington administration's policy of neutrality was directly contrary to the national mood and temperament. Under these circumstances, therefore, the justices had no little difficulty in convincing the public to support Washington's Neutrality Proclamation. As a result, little more than a month after the proclamation was issued, Chief Justice Jay found himself in front of the Virginia circuit court grand jury urging support for the policy of neutrality.

Jay urged his listeners to remember the traditional rule that one had an obligation in civil society to use his property or liberty in such a way as not to injure others. With that in mind, he asserted that the purpose of any free government is to constrain men so as to act in accordance with that principle. In the case of the war between France and England, therefore, the Neutrality Proclamation did nothing more than prevent individual citizens from using their liberty to bring the United States into war against its will. Viewed in that light, the proclamation merely restrained the conduct of individuals where it had the potential to injure the rights of the wider community. Restraining those who would take sides in the war without the consent of the nation would work an injury to the material prosperity of the whole:

> He is not a good citizen who violates his contract with society, and when society execute their laws, they do no more than what is necessary to constrain individuals to perform that contract, on due operation and observance of which the common good and welfare of the community depend; for the object of it is to secure to every man what belongs to him, as a member of the nation; and by increasing the common stock of property, to augment the value of his share in it.

Jay also cautioned that if the United States was to assume her rightful place among the nations of the world, she must conduct herself in accordance with the law of nations. One aspect of this law was the principle that neutral nations cannot act to aid or abet the military objectives of a belligerent during war without sacrificing the rights and protections that accompany neutrality. More to the point, Jay noted that the law of nations required neutral powers to prevent their citizens from taking any act that was inconsistent with the nation's professed neutrality. Viewed in this light, Jay said, the Neutrality Proclamation was "exactly consistent with and declaratory of the conduct enjoined by the law of nations." The proclamation's prohibition on individuals assisting the French war effort was not only consistent with, but required by, the principles of the law of nations. As a result, the grand jurors were now duty-bound to support the neutrality policy and were themselves charged with rooting out violations of the proclamation wherever they might find them.

The justices continued their policy of commenting on international affairs throughout the remainder of the decade. As the Quasi-War with France raged in 1798–1799, Justice Iredell used his charge to the Pennsylvania grand jury to justify the John Adams' defensive measures. France's deprivations and insults, Iredell claimed, had forced America into a position of "holding the rejected Olive Branch in one hand, [and] a sword in the other." The nation, he said, was "in a sort of middle path between peace and war, where one false step ma lead to the most ruinous consequences."

In the first decade, the justices used their charges to focus on a wide variety of domestic concerns as well. These included commentary on the Whiskey Rebellion, the validity of prosecutions under the common law of crime, and the Alien and Sedition Acts. In dealing with each, the justices strove to exhort the public to patience, and to inculcate in the citizenry the importance of putting aside their individual opinions in favor of the policies developed by their lawfully elected leaders.

To some extent, while the political charge was a relatively common occurrence, most of the justices recognized that they trod on very thin ice when delivering one. That is to say, while most justices did not shy from giving a political charge, they knew that the effectiveness of the charge depended on tone and context. If the political charge was designed to convince, it needed to be phrased in terms that would command assent, rather than appear as a pronouncement *ex cathedra*. Nonetheless, most justices understood this concept; Samuel Chase seemed to be something of an exception. Like other justices, Chase seemed to understand that the political charge was fraught with difficulty; yet, when he took the bench he often seemed heedless of the controversy he was about to provoke. Thus, in charging the spring 1800 Delaware grand jury, Chase is said to have told the jurors that "a highly seditious temper had manifested itself in Delaware" and that their duty was to root it out. Chase did not name the printer, but he ordered the district attorney to search the local papers until he discovered the identity of the man to whom Chase referred. Chase was even more intemperate in charging the 1803 Maryland grand jury. There, he expressed outrage at an amendment to the Maryland constitution guaranteeing universal suffrage. Expanding the vote, Chase declared, would "certainly and rapidly destroy all protection to property, and all security to personal liberty; and our republican constitution will sink into a mobocracy, the worst of all possible governments." This charge was later to form the basis of one of the articles of impeachment against him. What made Chase's charges different is not so much his point of view. On the contrary, Chase's opinions on most matters were largely consistent with those of the other justices. Instead, what distinguished Chase's charges from those of his colleagues was the way in which he delivered them. As one scholar has noted, Chase often started "not from where his audience was, but from where (in his judgment) they ought to be" (Lerner, 153). Still, in delivering charges on sedition or republican values, Justice Chase followed the well-established practice of other Supreme Court justices in the first decade.

Although there was great danger inherent in commenting on political questions, the justices seemed to have weighed the political calculus and decided that their role was to use almost every public occasion as an opportunity to build support for the fledgling national government. In short the justices understood not only the tenuous nature of their own position, but that of the republic as a whole. They knew that, in the early days at least, almost every significant political confrontation had the potential to tear the nation apart. Thus, they "took it upon themselves to mould public sentiment inasmuch as it lay in their power to do so" (Lerner, 178). They knew that popular opinion was everything, and so they used the grand jury charge to educate the people on the virtues of federalism and respect for the rule of law. In so doing, they not only made their own positions secure; they made the republic safe for republicanism (Lerner, 178).

## Judicial Review

The question of whether any court had the power to overturn the acts of a democratically elected legislature was one that generated controversy throughout the latter part of the eighteenth century. While most political and legal thinkers would have agreed with Justice Paterson's assertion in *Van Horne's Lessee* that "every act of the Legislature, repugnant to the Constitution, is absolutely void," it was not at all clear what would happen if the legislature insisted on passing an unconstitutional act. After all, it is one thing to say that the legislature may not violate the constitution. It is quite another to say what should be done when it has.

It is this problem of remedy lay that at the heart of the controversy over judicial review in the new American republic. While no one thought that legislatures could disregard the constitution, there was some doubt as to whether judges could refuse to enforce even an obviously unconstitutional act. This concern was based on a rather simple premise: While the theory of the constitution as a social compact rejected the principle of legislative omnipotence, it did not necessarily abolish the principle of legislative supremacy. Under this view, the constitution was "a rule to the legislature only," and courts could not use the terms of the constitution as an excuse for failing to give effect to a properly enacted piece of legislation. To do so would be to compound the wrong done by the legislature and vest the judiciary with powers beyond those given it in the constitution. "How," it was asked, "could the judiciary undertake to declare an act of the assembly void without taking upon itself the right to make legislation?" For opponents of judicial review, therefore, the only remedy for legislative violations of fundamental law remained popular action. The people could petition the assembly to alter the law or oust the offenders in the next election. If these methods of political persuasion failed to convince the legislature to change course, revolution was the only option left (Harrington, Judicial Review, 71–72). The outlines of this debate are seen most clearly in a lively exchange of correspondence during the course of the Constitutional Convention between the future Justice James Iredell and Richard Spaight, who was then one of North Carolina's delegates to the Philadelphia Convention. Iredell initiated the discussion with his publication of a defence of judicial review in a North Carolina newspaper entitled, *To the Public*. This article is arguably the most eloquent contemporary defense of the power of judicial review, and some believe that it inspired the writing of both James Wilson and Alexander Hamilton on the same subject.

Iredell began his defense by rejecting the doctrine of legislative supremacy. He noted that in forming their various constitutions Americans "were not ignorant of the theory *of the necessity of the legislature being absolute in all cases*, because it was the great ground of the British pretensions." Yet, when they had the chance to form governments of their own, Iredell asserted, Americans "decisively gave our sentiments against it." As a result, Iredell had "no doubt, but that the power of the Assembly is limited and defined by the constitution." After all, he said, the Assembly is but "a *creature* of the constitution," and thus had "no more right to obedience on other terms, than any different power on earth has a right to govern us."

Iredell's rejection of the principle of legislative supremacy was hardly controversial. Indeed, even the most vigorous opponents of the power of judicial review would have agreed that an act passed in violation of the constitution was void. The question Iredell was forced to confront, therefore, was what remedy was available in a case where the legislature insisted on passing an unconstitutional act. He noted the opposition's assertion that the only remedy available to overturn an unconstitutional act was popular action, either in the form of petition or revolution; but Iredell rejected this position on the grounds that the two alternatives were largely illusory as remedies. Limiting the people's redress to a petition, he argued, "implies a supposition, that the electors hold their right by the *favour of their representatives*." As to the remedy of revolution, Iredell argued that such was a "dreadful expedient indeed." After all, leaving the people to resort to revolution would be to encourage only the most "calamitous" consequences. More importantly, Iredell noted, revolution is hardly a reasonable alternative because it offers no remedy by which the unconstitutional abuse of minority rights can be redressed. "Nothing can be powerful enough to effect [a revolution] in a government like ours, but *universal oppression*," Iredell argued. As a result, a "thousand injuries may be suffered, and many hundreds ruined, before [revolution] can be brought about." If the people are limited to revolution as the only means of redressing legislative over reaching, then they will be forced to bear the imposition of numerous small breaches of the constitution until such time as there is "universal oppression."

Having rejected the adequacy of petition and revolution as remedies, Iredell asserted that the judiciary must have the power to refuse to enforce unconstitutional acts. However, in making this argument, Iredell was not arguing for the type of judicial review advanced by John Marshall in *Marbury*. He was not, in other words, arguing that the judiciary was possessed of some superior power "to say what the law is." Instead, Iredell advocated a much more limited place for judicial review, one which was based on the judiciary's traditional role in resolving conflicts of law:

> The duty of [the judiciary] … is to decide according to the *laws of the State*. It will not be denied … that the constitution is a *law of the state*, as well as an act of Assembly, with this difference only, that it is the fundamental law, and unalterable by the legislature, which derives all its power from it. One act of Assembly may repeal another act of Assembly. For this reason, the latter act is to be obeyed, and not the former. An act of Assembly cannot repeal the constitution, or any part of it. For that reason, an act of Assembly, inconsistent with the constitution, is void, and cannot be obeyed, without disobeying the superior law to which we were previously and irrevocably bound.

In essence, Iredell argued that the power of judicial review is little more than the power to determine which of two conflicting laws should be given effect. The fact that the constitution is "fundamental law" means that statutes that are not in accordance with its terms are to be considered invalid. For Iredell, therefore, judicial review is simply an exercise in statutory construction, a function that common law judges had already performed for many years. Furthermore, the judiciary's power to reject unconstitutional statutes is a function of the judges' office, as servants of the people with delegated powers, albeit of a different order than those given the legislature.

Over the years, Iredell's defense has been extended to support a much more expansive reading of judicial review than he actually expressed in 1787. In fact, it is important to note that Iredell did not believe that courts had any special competence to determine constitutional questions. Indeed, according to Iredell, judges should not have the power to decide constitutional questions in the abstract or even to resolve doubtful constructions. In his view, judges are not "appointed arbiters, and to determine as it were upon any application, whether the Assembly have or have not violated the Constitution; but when an act is necessarily brought in judgement before them, they must, unavoidably, determine on way or another." Iredell thus advanced a very limited concept of judicial review, one centered on the judges' traditional role in deciding conflicts of law. Moreover, the exercise of this power was limited to situations where the judges were confronted with a concededly unconstitutional act, which is to say an act that violated some obvious, long-held fundamental right, such as a statute violating the right to trial by jury or one depriving a citizen of property without just compensation. Nothing in *To the Public* supports the argument that judges had the power "to say what the law is" in cases where the constitutionality of an act was subject to doubt.

Still, Iredell's rather limited argument for judicial review was not universally accepted. While serving as a delegate to the Constitutional Convention in Philadelphia, North Carolina's Richard Spaight wrote Iredell expressing concern about the idea that judges would have the power to overturn acts of the assembly. Spaight admitted that state legislatures had passed unjust laws during the 1780s, but he flatly denied that the judiciary had the power to refuse to enforce them:

> "[I]t would have been absurd, and contrary to the practice of all the world had the [North Carolina] Constitution vested such powers in them, as they would have operated as an absolute negative on the proceedings of the Legislature, which no judiciary ought ever to possess: and the State, instead of being governed by the representatives in general Assembly, would be subject to the will of three individuals, who united in their own persons the legislative and judiciary powers, which no monarch in Europe enjoys."

Spaight assumed that some means of keeping the legislature in check was needed, but he believed that such a mechanism must be specified in the Constitution itself. In the absence of a clear grant of judicial review, Spaight argued, the only remedy for the passage of an unconstitutional act was to be found in "the annual election" of the legislature.

The disagreements represented in this exchange were reflected in the early Supreme Court's approach to the problem of judicial review. While some of the justices clearly believed that the Court possessed an almost unfettered power to review statutes for unconstitutionality, others, most notably Justice Chase, were more hesitant. This divergence in opinion can be seen in the writings of various justices over the course of the 1790s. For example, Justice Paterson in *Van Horne's Lessee* left no doubt that he believed that courts had the power to overturn acts of legislative bodies, while Justice Chase's opinion in *Calder v. Bull* reveals that he had some qualms about that very power. The disagreement was not about whether legislatures could violate the terms of the written constitution. No one thought that. On the contrary, the debate was simply about remedy: What was the Court's function when a legislative body passed a decidedly unconstitutional act? The justices' answers seemed to depend—first, on whether the legislature in question was Congress or a state assembly—and, second, on whether the federal or state Constitution was at issue. Moreover, even when the justices seemed to agree on the right of the Court to overturn legislation, as in the Pension Act cases, they often tread carefully so as not to provoke unnecessary political confrontations. The justices' opinions reveal their differing answers to these problems.

## *Judicial Review of State Legislation*

When it came to reviewing the actions of state legislatures, most of the justices concluded that the federal courts had the power to strike down legislation that conflicted with the federal Constitution. The two cases rendered on circuit in Rhode Island, *West v. Barnes* (1791) and *Champion v. Casey* (1792), provide clear evidence that the justices understood the Supremacy Clause to give the circuit courts the power to review the constitutionality of state legislation. In both these cases, the justices were confronted with a statute passed by a state legislature that conflicted with the federal Constitution. *West* involved a legislative attempt to alter the terms of a pre-existing contract by permitting payment of the debt in paper, rather than in specie. Chief Justice Jay and Justice Cushing apparently had little difficulty holding that the statute conflicted with the federal Constitution's Tender Clause. Similarly, in *Champion*, Jay and Cushing rejected the Rhode Island legislature's attempt to protect a debtor from his creditors on the grounds that the statute violated the federal Constitution's Contracts Clause.

Yet, while the decisions in *West* and *Champion* laid the groundwork for later exertions of the power of judicial review of state legislation, the justices remained at odds over the precise circumstances under which such review would be appropriate. Thus, in *Van Horne's Lessee* (1795), Justice Paterson, perhaps the most aggressive advocate of judicial power, had no difficulty declaring that Pennsylvania's Conforming Act violated the compensation clause of the Pennsylvania constitution. In so doing, Paterson delivered an eloquent defence of judicial review, asserting, "the Constitution is the Sun of the political system, around which all Legislative, Executive, and Judicial bodies must revolve." Consequently, "if a legislative act oppugns a constitutional principle" it is "the duty of the Court to adhere to the Constitution, and to declare the act null and void."

Yet, while Paterson's assertions might be considered a reasonable statement of the theory of judicial review in the abstract, his application of the theory in this particular case was problematic in the extreme. This is because, unlike *West* and *Champion*, *Van Horne* did not involve a claim that a state statute conflicted with the federal constitution. Instead, the claim in *Van Horne* was that a *state* statute violated the terms of the *state* constitution. Paterson, a member of the federal judiciary, was thus being asked to determine a fundamental question of state law. This point is often overlooked by scholars considering *Van Horne*, mainly because Paterson's rather lofty discussion of the theory of judicial review seems so much in accord with the modern view of the subject. However, Paterson's approach would likely be controversial today, as the modern Supreme Court has generally eschewed any power to review state legislation for conformity with state constitutions. On the contrary, established principles of federalism require that the Court leave such questions to the highest courts of the states, on the theory that state courts should be the final arbiters of state law. It is unclear, therefore, how much one can read into Paterson's opinion in *Van Horne*. One reason this is so is that the circuit court decision was never appealed to the full Supreme Court. As a result, we are left to guess how far other justices would be willing to go in reviewing the constitutionality of state legislation, and, indeed, opinions of other justices in later indicate that the full Court might not have been willing to embrace Paterson's rather aggressive approach to judicial review.

*Calder v. Bull* (1798) presents one such instance. In *Calder*, the Supreme Court was presented with the question of whether a Connecticut statute violated the terms of the federal Constitution. Although, the Court ultimately upheld the statute in question, the opinions in the case are revealing. For his part, Justice Chase expressed some reservations about the Supreme Court's power of judicial review. While he clearly believed that both written and unwritten constitutions imposed limits on legislative authority, he was concerned about whether the judiciary ever had the power to overturn a legislative act for lack of conformity with the constitution, although the degree of Chase's discomfort seems to have depended on the source of the enactment and the constitution in question. Thus, with respect to acts of Congress, Chase refused to say whether the Supreme Court had the power to decide "any law made by *Congress*, contrary to the Constitution of the *United States* is void." At the same time, however, Chase was unequivocal in his belief that the Supreme Court had no "*jurisdiction* to determine that any law of any state *Legislature* contrary to the Constitution of such *state* is void." Instead, Chase believed that the Supreme Court's power of judicial review was clearly limited to only those cases in which a state statute was alleged to violate the *federal* constitution. Thus, he was content to test the Connecticut state against the federal Constitution's Ex Post Facto clause, but not against the terms of the Connecticut constitution itself. The latter claim, Chase said, must be brought in the courts of Connecticut.

On the surface, then, it appears that Chase believed that the only basis for the exercise of judicial review by federal courts was to be found in the plain words of the Supremacy Clause. That is to say, for Justice Chase, the power of judicial review was limited to determining whether a state statute conflicted with the *federal* constitution. In rejecting the power to determine whether the Connecticut law conflicted with Connecticut's constitution, therefore, Chase seemed to clearly reject the approach to judicial review taken by Justice Paterson in *Van Horne*. On the contrary, it would appear from his comments in *Calder* that Justice Chase would have rejected any power in the federal courts to determine whether a state statute conflicted with a state constitution.

Without doubt, however, the most obvious example of judicial review of state legislation occurred in *Ware v. Hylton* (1796). In this case, the Court was confronted with an act of the Virginia legislature that appeared to conflict with the terms of a treaty, and thus violated that part of the Constitution's Supremacy Clause, which provides that "all treaties made, or which shall be made, under the authority of the United States, shall be the supreme law of the land."

On appeal to the Supreme Court, by a vote of four to one, the justices rejected the special pleas. The majority held that Article IV of the treaty superceded state laws that prevented the recovery of debts owed to British subjects. In so doing, the Court eliminated a very significant irritant in Anglo-American diplomatic relations. However, the case is also interesting for the way in which Justice Iredell appears to advance an important qualification to his earlier-stated theory of judicial review. As noted earlier, Iredell was an early proponent of the federal courts' power to review the constitutionality of both state and federal statutes. And, while he obviously had no difficulty with the concept of striking down laws that conflicted with the text of the Constitution, he clearly had reservations about the Supreme Court's ability to strike down legislation for nonconformity with a treaty.

Justice Iredell upheld the validity of the treaty, but declared that Article IV was not self-executing. In his view, in order for state acts to be annulled, Congress had to take specific action to put Article IV into effect. Its failure to do so meant that state actions to confiscate or sequester debts remained valid. In support of this argument, Iredell likened the problem to that faced by those holding British prisoners of war. The treaty provided that such prisoners ought to be released: but, he noted, no gaoler would be authorized to simply free all his prisoners unless he received more specific instructions from Congress or the President. So, it was with the debt question: Article IV provided that creditors "should meet with no lawful impediment" in recovering their debts, but it was up to Congress to determine precisely what sort of "impediments" were affected by this clause before a state law could be annulled. In taking this position, Iredell tried to strike a balance between the limits of state and federal power. He upheld the power of the national government to enter into treaties that would be the "supreme law of the land," while at the same time, avoiding the need to declare a state statute unconstitutional.

There are two different explanations for Iredell taking this position. The first, and more cynical, possibility is that Iredell's hesitance in *Ware* might simply have been a function of the fact that he was a southerner who was well acquainted with the difficulties for southern farmers posed by the debt cases. At the time of the Revolution, farmers in his home state of North Carolina were second only to Virginia's in the amount of debt owed to British creditors. Iredell surely knew, therefore, that a decision upholding the claims of British creditors would mean ruin for countless farmers throughout the South. On the one hand, therefore, adopting a strict reading of the treaty would prevent widespread economic dislocation. Iredell might also have believed that upholding the British claims would have been catastrophic for the Republic itself. Given the tremendous hostility toward British merchants and the British government after the Revolution, Iredell might simply have feared that serious political repercussions in the South might have resulted in widespread unrest or even calls for withdrawal from the Union. North Carolina, after all, had rejected the federal Constitution when it was first proposed, and there remained a strong current of antifederalism in the South. In taking a hard line in *Ware*, Iredell might simply have been trying to exercise a bit of restraint to prevent political and social unrest.

A second, and more likely, possibility is that Iredell meant what he said. That is to say, Iredell generally approached the problem of judicial review as one akin to the type of statutory interpretation well known to common law judges throughout the ages. In considering the constitutionality of a statute, Iredell took the position that the role of the judge was simply to resolve conflicts between the provisions of two conflicting "statutes," one that was created by the people themselves and the other by a legislative body subject to their authority. In effect, Iredell believed that the role of the courts in exercising the power of judicial review was simply to weigh laws passed by the legislature against the "supreme" law of the Constitution. Where the text of the former conflicted with the Constitution, then the Constitution must prevail. For Iredell, therefore, the problem posed by *Ware* was primarily one of textual ambiguity, which could not clearly be resolved in favor of the treaty. Although, he had no doubt that the Supremacy Clause made treaties the "supreme Law of the Land," he was unconvinced that the treaty's provisions clearly contradicted state laws sequestering or confiscating British debts; hence, his insistence on some further act on the part of Congress to clarify the extent to which former laws were affected or annulled by the treaty. In short, Iredell was not convinced that the vague wording of Article IV operated as an immediate repealer of all state laws concerning debt, thereby undoing acts that the law had long considered to have been effective. Far from being a rejection of the power of judicial review, Iredell's decision in *Ware* can be seen as an interesting example of the limits of judicial power that was entirely consistent with his oft-stated understanding of the role of the judiciary in the constitutional scheme.

## *Judicial Review of Acts of Congress*

Whether the Supreme Court had the power to overturn acts of Congress for nonconformity with the federal Constitution was a matter of great importance to the early Supreme Court. As noted earlier, many of the justices considered the Court as one part of a larger experiment in government. They, therefore, were frequently concerned about the way in which their actions affected both public perception and the actual workings of government. As a result, when confronted with the question of whether Congress had passed an act that violated the terms of the Constitution, the justices knew they had to tread very carefully. After all, at this point in its history, the federal Constitution was still very much a work in progress, and there were many who still harbored reservations about the wisdom of the entire enterprise. Any decision of the Supreme Court declaring that Congress had overstepped its authority would certainly have given opponents of the Constitution grounds to resurrect all the old fears of an oppressive and tyrannical national government. At the same time, however, the justices were well aware of the need to protect the integrity of the Constitution itself. Consequently, their treatment of the problem of judicial review of congressional legislation reflected an attempt to strike a delicate balance between support for the infant Republic and adherence to legal principle.

*Hayburn's Case* (1792) presented the first real test of this balancing act. The Pension Act's requirement that the circuit court prepare a list of pensioners for review by the Secretary of War was rejected by all the justices in some way or another. Their objections were based on the fact that an executive branch official would have the power to review decisions of the circuit courts, a procedure that essentially made the courts' decrees merely provisional. Under these circumstances, the circuit court judges would not then be acting in a judicial capacity, for only a higher judicial body can set aside the judgements of those below. Instead, in giving the Secretary of War power to intervene where there was evidence of "imposition or mistake," the Pension Act gave the appearance that, in pension cases at least, the judiciary was subordinate to the executive. As a result, the members of the Supreme Court could not accept the Pension Act's allocation of responsibility without doing violence to their belief in the principle of separation of powers, and more particularly, to their belief that the judiciary was co-equal with the political branches in the constitutional scheme.

This conclusion presented the members of the Supreme Court with an obvious dilemma, however. The new government was little more than three years old, and the Court itself was even younger. For the justices to publicly declare the Pension Act unconstitutional would not only create dissension between the branches of the federal government, it would also provide support to those who were not yet reconciled to the new frame of government. As a result, although the justices were confident that the Pension Act violated the separation of powers, they chose to avoid a direct confrontation with Congress. Thus, Chief Justice Jay and Justice Cushing refused to hear pension claims while sitting as members of the New York circuit court, although they were willing to prepare a pension list while acting as "commissioners" appointed by "official rather than personal designation." In so doing, they clearly indicated their belief that the Pension Act was unconstitutional while still ensuring that the act's charitable purposes were given effect. The remaining justices were less cooperative, however, and refused to hear any pension claims while sitting as members of the various circuit courts.

The fact that the Supreme Court never issued a formal opinion on the Pension Act controversy was merely a function of the way in which the case presented itself. The Pension Act did not create litigants in the traditional sense because proceedings under the act were in the nature of an administrative, rather than adversarial, process. Instead, those desiring to be added to the pension list were simply required to present themselves before the circuit court to be examined by the judges. If the judges determined that the petitioner was entitled to a pension, his name was to be added to the list. Those whose petitions were denied by the circuit court could then appeal to the Secretary of War to have their names appended at a later date.

The justices' refusal to hear pension claims was, therefore, a refusal to undertake a duty imposed on them by statute. As a result, the only way the constitutionality of the Pension Act could come before the Supreme Court was through the writ of mandamus, which was essentially a petition to compel a government official to perform the duties of his office. This was precisely the route Attorney General Edmund Randolph attempted to take in *Hayburn's Case*. In petitioning the full Court for a writ compelling the Pennsylvania circuit court to prepare the pension list, Randolph sought to force the Supreme Court to make a formal determination as to the constitutionality of the Pension Act. It is not clear why the attorney general would have wanted to provoke this confrontation, since all the justices had already expressed the opinion that the act was unconstitutional. That they had done so while on circuit would not have made Randolph's case any stronger. Perhaps he simply thought the matter needed some clarity, and thus hoped to settle things once and for all; or, he may have thought that a formal decision declaring the Pension Act unconstitutional would convince Congress to amend it.

It may be, however, that Randolph was actually attempting to resolve a much more fundamental question: Did the Supreme Court have the power to invalidate an Act of Congress? To modern observers, long steeped in the tradition of judicial review, the question seems an idle one. They often point to Alexander Hamilton's description of judicial review in to *Federalist* No. 78, in which he asserted, "the courts of justice are to be considered as the bulwarks of a limited Constitution against legislative encroachments." Moreover, at least since *Marbury*, and certainly after Dred Scott (18 –) and *Lochner* (1905), the Supreme Court has not hesitated to strike down statutes that conflict with the federal Constitution.

In the early 1790s, however, the question may not have seemed that obvious. There is, after all, no explicit textual provision in the federal Constitution giving the Supreme Court the power of judicial review. The only provision directly relevant to that power is contained in Article VI, the so-called "Supremacy Clause," which provides that the Constitution and federal laws are to be considered the "supreme law of the land" notwithstanding "any Thing in the Constitution or Laws of any State to the Contrary." In effect, therefore, the Constitution seems to provide a basis for judicial review of *state* legislation that is contrary to the *federal* Constitution; but the Supremacy Clause does not specifically provide for the power of judicial review of *congressional or presidential* action. Indeed, the clause says nothing about the relationship between the Supreme Court and the political branches of the federal government. Thus, if the Supreme Court has the power to review the actions of the political branches, that power must be implied from the text of Article III or from the broader structure of the Constitution as a whole.

As a result, while it is clear that the justices believed that the Pension Act was unconstitutional, it also appears that the Court labored mightily to avoid having to render a formal opinion on the subject. No doubt this reluctance was motivated by a desire to avoid public controversy where possible; however, it also seems that some of the justices were not yet willing to conclude that the Supreme Court should be the final arbiter in constitutional controversies. Indeed, perhaps the most that can be said with certainty is that the members of the early Supreme Court made a clear distinction between judicial review of state and federal legislation. Thus, the Supremacy Clause gave the justices more confidence in considering whether state legislation conformed to the federal constitution. The Supreme Court's ability to strike down acts of Congress was another matter altogether, implicating both political and legal considerations. As the matter was not clearly capable of being resolved by direct reference to the constitutional text, the Supreme Court, in *Hayburn's Case*, determined to tread lightly, attempting to assert its independence while avoiding, as much as possible, a direct confrontation with the political branches. As noted in Chapter 3, however, the justices were saved from having to render a conclusive opinion on the subject of judicial review in *Hayburn's Case*. Perhaps fearing the worst, Congress eventually revised the statute and removed the circuit courts from the pension process. This amendment made the case moot and permitted both the Court and Congress to put aside the question until a later day.

Four years passed before the Supreme Court was again confronted with the question of whether it had the power to review acts of Congress for conformity with the constitution. In *Hylton v. United States* (1794), the Court was forced to determine whether a federal tax imposed on carriages violated the constitution's prohibition on "direct taxes." Although only a few years had passed since *Hayburn's Case*, the Supreme Court in 1796 seemed less concerned about its power to test the constitutionality of acts of Congress. Perhaps this is because *Hylton* did not really require an extensive exposition of the theory of judicial review. The case, after all, turned on a simple question: whether a tax on carriages was in the nature of a duty, and thus an "indirect tax" permitted by the constitution, or whether it was a "direct" tax requiring apportionment between the states according to the census.

In rendering their opinions, most of the justices confined themselves to attempting to define "direct" and "indirect" taxes, and did not address the problem of judicial review at all. Instead, the justices simply assumed the power to consider whether the act was constitutional or not. The exception was Samuel Chase. While he, too, devoted the bulk of his opinion to the question of direct and indirect taxes, Chase expressed some reservations about the extent of the Supreme Court's power of judicial review. Chase ultimately concluded that the tax was in the nature of a duty, and thus within Congress' power; however, he noted that this conclusion absolved him from having to undertake a thorough analysis of the Court's power of judicial review. Instead, he hinted that the Supreme Court's power to strike down acts of Congress would extend only to cases where the legislature had clearly violated the plain terms of the Constitution. If the Court had the power of judicial review, Chase asserted, it should be exercised only "in a very clear case." On the other hand, if there were any ambiguities with respect to the constitutionality of a congressional enactment, Chase believed that the Supreme Court ought to defer to Congress's opinion and uphold the statute.

Chase was not alone in his hesitance, however. Other justices seemed to agree that the Court ought to tread carefully when considering the constitutionality of congressional action. For example, in his opinion in *Calder*, Justice Iredell, who on other occasions advocated for an extensive power of judicial review, expressed sentiments similar to those of Chase, asserting that "[i]f any act of Congress ... violates those constitutional provisions, it is unquestionably void; though, I admit, that as the authority to declare it void is of a delicate and awful nature, the Court will never resort to that authority, but in a clear and urgent case."

In the final analysis, it would appear that the early Supreme Court justices had little doubt that the Supreme Court must have the power to review and strike down acts of both Congress and the state legislatures when such acts conflicted with the federal constitution. With respect to state legislation, the justices seemed to have little difficulty testing the constitutionality of state statutes. This seems to be largely a function of both text and politics. On the one hand, the constitution's Supremacy Clause appeared to give specific warrant for review of state legislation. In terms of politics, of course, the justices were also well aware of the complications for both national and international policy caused by the states during the Confederation period. They, therefore, clearly understood that the young Republic could not long survive if state legislatures were free to violate the terms of the constitution with impunity.

Exercising judicial review of congressional action was a rather more delicate proposition. As members of a co-equal branch of government, the justices were somewhat more restrained in their willingness to directly confront the political branches. There were two reasons for this. The first was political: The new frame of government was closely watched by opponents both at home and abroad. The justices knew, therefore, that a decision declaring an act of Congress or the president invalid would have a tendency to cast doubt on the legitimacy of the federal enterprise. The second reason was more substantive, and was based on considerations about the proper role of the judiciary in a republic. While modern judges and scholars are by and large content with the idea that the Supreme Court should be the final arbiter in questions of constitutional interpretation, the early justices were less sure of their role in that regard. On the contrary, they appeared to believe that some deference to Congress was appropriate. Thus, in *Hylton*, Justice Chase asserted that he would defer to the "receive the construction of the Legislature" in "doubtful" cases, while Justice Iredell would later assert in *Calder* that the Court would declare an act of Congress void only in "clear and urgent" cases.

Somewhat surprisingly, however, Justice Chase in *Calder* also espoused a controversial test for measuring the constitutionality of a statute. In discussing legislative power in *Calder*, Chase asserted that the legislature must be controlled even if specific limits are not set forth in a written constitution. Thus, he declared, "I cannot subscribe to the omnipotence of a State Legislature, or that it is absolute and without controul; although its authority should not be expressly restrained by the Constitution, or fundamental law, of the State." The limits of legislative power must be found in the "purposes for which men enter into society." In the case of the United States, these limits are to be found in the various constitutions, which were created by the people to "establish justice, to promote the general welfare, to secure the blessings of liberty; and to protect their persons and property from violence." Legislative power is, therefore, confined to these ends, and any act contrary to them must be void:

> There are acts which the Federal, or State, Legislature cannot do, without exceeding their authority. There are certain vital principles in our free Republican governments, which will determine and over-rule and apparent and flagrant abuse of legislative power; as to authorize manifest injustice by positive law; or to take away that security for personal liberty, or private property, for the protection whereof the government was established. An act of the Legislature (for I cannot call it a *law*) contrary to the great first principles of the social compact, cannot be considered a rightful exercise of legislative authority.... To maintain that our Federal, or State, Legislatures possess such powers, if they had not been expressly restrained, would, in my opinion be a political heresy, altogether inadmissable in our free republican governments.

For Justice Chase, therefore, the legislature's power is limited by unspoken as well as written constraints. The only question is whether any court has the power to ultimately declare that the legislature has violated the social compact. Like Richard Spaight and other traditional advocates of legislative supremacy, Chase hesitated when confronted with the idea that unelected judges would restrain the acts of a democratically elected assembly. Thus, while natural law might furnish the basis for declaring a legislative act void; the right to declare it lay with the people alone, to be exercised in their capacity as electors—or, if necessary, revolutionaries.

Justice Chase's concept of natural law restraints on legislative power has often been misunderstood. Indeed, Justice Iredell himself seems to have mistaken Chase's meaning. In his own opinion in *Calder*, Iredell chided Chase and other "speculative jurists" who have held that "a legislative act against natural justice must, in itself, be void." Iredell contended that such a power could never be vested in any court, for to do so would make the judiciary something of a super-legislature:

> If … the Legislature of the Union, or the Legislature of any member of the Union, shall pass a law, within the general scope of their constitutional power, the Court cannot pronounce it to be void, merely because it is, in their judgment, contrary to the principles of natural justice. The ideas of natural justice are regulated by no fixed standard: the ablest and the purest men have differed upon the subject; and all that the Court could properly say, in such an event, would be, that the Legislature (possessed of an equal right of opinion) had passed an act which, in the opinion of the judges, was inconsistent with the abstract principles of natural justice. There are then but two lights, in which the subject can be viewed: 1st. If the Legislature pursue the authority delegated to them, their acts are valid. 2d. If they transgress the boundaries of that authority, their acts are invalid. In the former case, they exercise the discretion vested in them by the people, to whom alone they are responsible for the faithful discharge of their trust; but in the latter case, they violate a fundamental law, which must be our guide, whenever we are called upon as judges to determine the validity of a legislative act.

Yet, while Iredell was certainly correct in his assertions about the difficulty of ascertaining the bounds of natural law, one cannot escape the feeling that he misunderstood the subtlety of Chase's position: Chase was content to allow natural law to set the limits of legislative authority because he did not believe that the courts necessarily had the power to overturn acts of the legislature. Chase asserted that natural law provided a basis for the people to declare a legislative act void, but he did not imply that courts would have the same power, at least with respect to acts of Congress. In this regard, Chase was firmly in the camp of those who believed that the real problem with judicial review was one of remedy: For Chase, it was one thing to assert that the legislature cannot pass an unconstitutional act, but it was quite another to say what must be done when the legislature has, in fact, done so.

The justices' treatment of the problem of judicial review in the context of state legislation evidences a rather nuanced approach. In the post-*Marbury* era, many commentators have read too much into Chief Justice Marshall's assertion that the judiciary is vested with the power "to say what the law is." Indeed, the modern Supreme Court itself assumes the role of final arbiter in a wide range of constitutional disputes. The justices of the Jay and Ellsworth courts appear to have tread more carefully. When it came to interpreting the validity of state legislative enactments, the justices quickly made several important distinctions. While they were clearly convinced that the Supremacy Clause gave them the power to test the validity of state legislation for conformity with the federal constitution, it appears that most justices, with the exception of Justice Paterson, had reservations about the power of the Court to test state statutes for conformity with the constitutions of the states. Moreover, although it is also clear that most of the justices believed that the Court had the power to review the constitutionality of congressional enactments, most had concerns about the impact of the Courts' doing so. Thus, both Justice Chase, the Court's most reluctant supporter of judicial review, and Justice Iredell, a clear proponent of judicial power, expressed the view that the Court should defer to the political branches whenever possible and only strike down congressional legislation in "clear and urgent" cases. In sum, the most that can be said about the early Supreme Court's view of judicial review is that it was in progress. When it came to review of state legislation, the justices were confident that both the constitutional text and the necessities of federalism gave them the authority to declare state acts invalid. When it came to congressional action, however, it seems that the justices were somewhat slower in finding their way. In the earliest years, they tended to tread somewhat lightly. While they certainly understood the theoretical basis for judicial review in the context of the separation of powers, they refrained from any full-throated assertion of judicial supremacy in matters of constitutional interpretation. That assertion would be left for John Marshall to make.

## Federalism and State Sovereignty

Defining the proper boundaries between state and national authority was perhaps the most difficult challenge facing the early Supreme Court. This is because, in the very early years at least, the real center of power resided in state governments, which had a more intimate connection with the public than the newly created federal government sitting in a distant national capital. After all, the creation of a large federal bureaucracy was at least a century in the future, and thus the average person could go through the bulk of his life never having any contact at all with a federal officer or agency. Moreover, unlike today, when the federal income tax absorbs so much attention and wealth, most people paid taxes to state or local governments. If they found themselves in legal difficulty, they likely encountered local sheriffs and/or they sued each other in state courts. And, if they voted at all, they cast their ballots for local and state officers. Indeed, in the first decade of the American republic, the average citizen cast his vote for only one federal officer, a member of the House of Representatives. U.S. Senators and presidential electors were still chosen by state legislatures, while the President appointed federal judges.

As a result, most strong federalists sought to wean important segments of the community away from reliance on state governments and increase the bonds of attachment between them and the new national government. This was, in fact, one of the primary purposes behind Hamilton's plan to assume state revolutionary war debts in the Assumption Bill. Hamilton thought that having the federal government assume the states' debts would create a commonality of interest between the national government and the commercial elite. During the confederation, the states had made varying attempts to pay off the debt, leaving holders of the notes very much in doubt as to whether they would ever be paid. This lack of confidence gave rise to speculation on a grand scale, often resulting in the holders of the original debt selling the notes for far less than face value. That many of these sellers were soldiers who had received the certificates in lieu of pay in specie gave the problem a moral dimension that was to complicate efforts to enact the plan. Nonetheless, Hamilton believed that having the federal government take over the state debt would provide stability and increase confidence in the new national government. He correctly reasoned that holders of the notes would be very supportive of any government that took it upon itself to pay the debt. In having the federal government assume the debts of the states, Hamilton made holders of state obligations cheerleaders for the national enterprise.

Hamilton also knew that with the obligation to pay debt would come the need to raise revenue. Once the federal government assumed the whole of the revolutionary war debt, he argued, it must raise sufficient revenue to meet the obligation. The passage of the Funding Bill and other revenue measures fulfilled this need. These acts then gave rise to an extensive apparatus for the enforcement that stretched into every state. Once in place, the machinery for taxation might be used to support other ventures as well. Assumption and Funding quickly gave the national government both force and purpose beyond the expectations of those who believed that the states would remain the primary locus of power in the federal enterprise. Indeed, it appears that some supporters of Hamilton's economic plan dreamed that the state governments would eventually whither away for lack of anything important to do.

The most obvious threat to the aspirations of national power came from supporters of states' rights who were generally suspicious of the "centralizing tendencies" of the newly formed federal union. While the ratification of the Constitution and the Bill of Rights went a long way toward dampening antifederalist fervor, a significant segment of the population, especially in the southern and western regions, continued to harbor fears that the national government would eventually supplant and destroy those of the states. The federal courts were looked upon with particular suspicion, as many erstwhile antifederalists expressed the view that the federal courts would become the instruments by which state authority was suppressed and supplanted. Chief Justice Jay himself remarked on this hostility in a letter to New York Senator Rufus King, in December 1793, remarking that "[t]he foederal courts have Enemies in all who fear [their] Influence on State objects." Proposals to curtail the jurisdiction and powers of the federal courts were, therefore, in almost constant circulation. At the same time, most federalists believed that national interests would not be adequately protected in state courts. As a result, the justices of the Supreme Court often took pains to ensure that the powers of the federal government were given the highest consideration when disposing of the cases that came before them.

Perhaps the most difficult task facing the federal government in the early years was attempting to ensure that the states would yield to its authority. Most federalists were cognisant of the fact that centralized government under the Articles of Confederation had been an utter failure in that regard. Because the Articles specifically provided that each state would retain its sovereignty, the confederation Congress had no real power to compel any action on the part of the states. Instead, Congress was limited to passing "resolves" recommending that state governments implement a particular policy or making "requisitions" for supplies. The states, of course, were free to ignore both these kinds of resolves, and they often did. The system held together while the war raged, but once the danger had passed, the states increasingly pursued their own interests with little regard for congressional directives. Nowhere was this individualism more apparent than in the conduct of commercial and economic policy. With the end of the war, states crafted economic regimes that resulted in a complicated system of tariffs and other barriers to trade. Goods imported from one state to another were subject to duties, landing fees, or transit fees (Denning, 59–68). State policies not only impeded domestic commerce; the multiplicity of state laws as well as the seeming arbitrariness of state judiciaries often embarrassed the United States in the conduct of foreign relations.

Supporters of a stronger national government learned the lessons of confederation quite well. In drafting the Constitution, federalists ensured that the scope of federal power was rather carefully articulated, although they did not specify precisely how disputes between the state and national governments would be resolved. While the Supremacy Clause clearly made federal laws superior to those of the states, it did not set forth any means by which state and federal conflicts of law would be determined. Although it might be contended that the Supremacy Clause contains an implicit grant to the federal courts of the power of judicial review to strike down offending state laws, one ought to keep in mind that the gulf between making and enforcing a judicial decree can be wide indeed.

The early Supreme Court was well aware of this problem. On the one hand, the justices were convinced that federal courts must have the power to invalidate state laws that interfered with the constitutional exercise of federal power. On the other hand, the justices were equally cognizant of the uncertainties involved in attempting to enforce their decrees. They knew that heavy-handed attempts to decree compliance on the part of the states would be met with indifference, if not outright resistance. More importantly, the Court itself was respectful of state sovereignty. While all of the justices were firm supporters of the new Constitution, none was interested in attempting to make the states mere political subdivisions of the national government. As a result, the Supreme Court's early jurisprudence on state–federal relations evidences a desire to balance the need to safeguard the national government's right to exercise its powers without interference from the states with an appropriate level of deference to the prerogatives of the states.

As it began its first decade of existence, therefore, the Supreme Court was faced with a number of challenges in defining the proper relationship between state and federal authority. Indeed, almost immediately after convening for its first session, the Court was forced to deal with the delicate matter of defining the precise extent of state sovereignty. In *Chisholm v. Georgia* (1793), the Court confronted the problem of whether states would be amenable to suit by private individuals. As might be expected, the Court's answer to that question provoked a great deal of controversy, the implications of which are still felt today. In addition, the Court was also required to provide the general outlines of federal power. Although the Constitution established a national government of enumerated powers, it was left to the Supreme Court to define the extent to which the federal government might compel or inhibit action by the states. In particular, in *Penhallow v. Doane* (1795) and *Ware v. Hylton* (1796), the Court had to define the nature of congressional power in the new constitutional scheme.

## Suits Against States

The idea that states might be sued in federal courts was immediately controversial in the new Republic. It is often asserted that having assumed the incidents of sovereignty during the Revolution, states were immune to suit to the same extent as the Crown had been. In fact, however, there appears to have been a great deal of misinformation as to just how firmly entrenched the doctrine of sovereign immunity was in the English legal system. The popular conception was embodied in the assertion that "the king can do no wrong" and thus could not be sued in his own courts. The reality was quite different, however. In fact, by the time of the Revolution, a number of legal devices existed to allow a subject injured by some act of the king's ministers to obtain redress. These included the *monstrans de droit*, or a petition of right, which was essentially a plea to the Crown. The idea was that the king's justices would not suffer a wrong to remain unremedied. In addition, an injured party might also maintain a suit for damages at common law against the king's officers in their individual capacity (Gibbons, 1895–1896; Jacobs, 5–6; Massey, 87–88).

Colonial practice was riddled with even more exceptions. Almost every colony provided some means by which a party injured by government action could obtain redress. In many colonies, the assembly entertained petitions seeking compensation for injury. In the corporate colonies, such as Connecticut, Rhode Island, and Massachusetts, the colonial charter contained provisions permitting suits against the government under certain circumstances, while in others, the practice of bringing suit against government officials in their individual capacities remained an important avenue of redress. After independence, several states drafted constitutions that specifically authorized suits against the state, and it appears that even where no specific authorization existed, most states continued to provide some means by which compensation for injuries caused by government officials might be obtained in state courts or legislatures (Gibbons, 1896–1899; Massey, 89–90).

It appears, therefore, that in spite of later protestations to the contrary, suits against states were a well-established practice at the time of the framing of the Constitution. Nonetheless, by the latter part of the 1780s a number of factors had arisen that would have made such suits particularly troublesome, especially if brought in the newly created federal courts (Marcus, 2). In the first place, the states were heavily in debt as a result of the Revolution, and many of them had made little progress in paying those debts on time or in accordance with the terms of the original contracts. Many states thus feared that creditors would flood the courts seeking to force the states to pay up. In addition, thousands of Tories had seen their property confiscated or sequestered after the end of hostilities in violation of the peace treaty, and many states worried that they would be held liable to provide compensation to them. On top of all this were numerous conflicts involving land grants set the stage for a flood of litigation that had the potential to bankrupt more than a few of the states' treasuries (Marshall, 1365–66).

Without doubt, however, the most obvious source of potential claims stemmed from the various efforts on the part of the states to confiscate or sequester pre-war British debts (Marcus, 2; Gibbons, 1900–01). This was especially true in cases where the states had merely sequestered, rather than confiscated, British debts. In those cases, the state did not actually confiscate the debt, which would have resulted in its being extinguished. Instead, most sequestration acts recognized the validity of the debt but allowed the debtor to pay it off in depreciated paper currency. As a result, if the federal courts were to hold that the original debtors were discharged by virtue of a sequestration act, it might be argued that the state had been substituted as debtor to the original British creditor. Indeed, this was precisely the position later taken by Justice Iredell in *Ware v. Hylton*. At the time of the drafting of the Constitution, therefore, the idea that the states might be liable to the full value of sequestered British debts "in sterling money" had to be a frightening prospect.

Given these facts, it might seem strange that the subject of state sovereign immunity was not raised when the Constitutional Convention debated the substance of the judiciary article. However, if one considers that most of the members of the Philadelphia convention were ardent supporters of a stronger centralized government, and that the convention itself had been called in response to the widespread perception that the states' refusal to honor their obligations was detrimental to the development of the new nation, it might be assumed that the framers of the Constitution welcomed the possibility that states would be subject to suit in the federal courts. Hence, the drafters included a provision in Article III, which provided that the "judicial Power shall extend to … Controversies … between a State and Citizens of another State; … and between a State, or the Citizens thereof, and foreign States, Citizens or Subjects." The only concession the framers appeared to offer to the dignity of the states was a provision declaring that the Supreme Court would have "original jurisdiction" over all cases "in which a State shall be a Party."

This provision did not escape notice entirely, however. During the ratification debates, several antifederalist writers criticized the proposed constitution on the grounds that it abrogated the states' sovereign immunity. For example, during the course of the New York ratification debate, Brutus asserted that subjecting a state "to answer in a court of law to the suit of an individual" would be "humiliating and degrading to a government, and, what I believe, the supreme authority of no state ever submitted to." In attempting to rebut this criticism, Alexander Hamilton ignored the plain words of Article III, and blithely asserting in *The Federalist* No. 81 that it was "inherent in the nature of sovereignty" of a state that it "not be amendable to the suit of an individual *without its consent*." Not to be put off, antifederalists continued to raise the subject in the various state ratifying conventions. For example, Virginia's George Mason theorized that land claims would find their way before the federal courts. "Is this not disgraceful?" he asked. "Is this State to be brought before the bar of justice like a delinquent individual? Is the sovereignty of the State to be arraigned like a culprit, or private offender? Will the States undergo this mortification?" (Kaminski & Saladino, 1406). Others at the Virginia convention attempted to blunt Mason's criticisms by asserting that Article III only contemplated suits in which the states themselves were plaintiffs and not a suit brought by a private individual against a state (Kaminski & Saladino, 1414, 1433). Patrick Henry dismissed this explanation, stating that if "Gentlemen pervert the most clear expressions, and the usual meaning of the language of the people, there is an end of all argument" (Kaminski & Saladino, 1423). Meanwhile, Edmund Randolph, himself a supporter of the Constitution, agreed with Mason's interpretation, although he thought the provision a useful one. No doubt referring to the possibility that the states might use the principle of sovereign immunity to avoid their obligations, Randolph challenged the delegates, asking, "if there can be honesty in rejecting a Government, because justice is to be done by it? … Are we to say, that we shall discard this Government, because it would make us all honest?" (Kaminski & Saladino, 1427, 1454–55).

Although several state ratifying conventions proposed amendments eliminating the provision giving federal courts the power to entertain suits against states, these provisions were never adopted. Instead, in the first Judiciary Act in 1789, Congress gave the Supreme Court original, although not exclusive, jurisdiction over controversies "between a state and citizens of other states, or aliens." This provision set the stage for the first great confrontation between the states and the national government in *Chisholm v. Georgia* (1793).

In many ways, the *Chisholm* case was the culmination of a decade-long struggle to secure compliance with the 1783 treaty of peace with Britain. The problem of debts owed to British merchants complicated relations between England and the United States for more than ten years. The British, of course, used the inability to obtain payment on the debt as an excuse to refuse to evacuate forts on the western frontier. Meanwhile, Americans insisted that the failure to pay compensation for the slaves carried away by the British army at the close of the war absolved them from having to pay debts due British merchants. Indeed, by 1793, relations between the two nations were at a low ebb, and war again seemed imminent. For many months, Secretary of State Jefferson had been assuring Britain's ambassador that the British merchants would be able to obtain redress in the federal courts. Meanwhile, states continued to worry about the impact of British debt cases on their treasuries. After all, many debtors had paid sums into state treasuries or loan offices in accordance with state statutes that absolved them of liability for doing so. As a result, the idea that states would be subject to suit by individuals from around the nation and abroad on these "sequestered" debts was hardly a welcome prospect.

The justices who finally took up *Chisholm* in February 1793, were faced with a rather elementary problem of constitutional interpretation. They had in hand a text, Article III, which provided that the Supreme Court would have jurisdiction over controversies "between a State and Citizens of another State." On its face, therefore, the Constitution seemed to provide for precisely the kind of action at issue in *Chisholm*. At the same time, however, the justices were clearly aware that a strong strain of antifederalism lingered in the body politic. They also knew that the question of state sovereign immunity had been controversial during the course of the ratification debates. For example, the justices were well aware that when the subject of state suability came up, supporters of the Constitution often denied that Article III made states liable to suit by private individuals. They knew, in other words, that James Madison, Rufus King, and Alexander Hamilton had repeatedly assured antifederalists that states could not be made defendants in private civil actions. At the same time, however, they also knew that many other federalists freely admitted that states should be made subject to suit in order to ensure that the states would be subject to the "law of the land." Thus, for every Madison who urged that Article III only contemplated suits wherein a state was a party, there was a Randolph who argued in favor of state suability as one means of "mak[ing] us all honest." In short, the justices knew that the "original understanding" was difficult to ascertain and that those who were involved in the ratification debates were clearly divided on the question of the states' immunity from suit.

Thus, while there were certainly some who boldly declared that the aim of Article III was to make states amenable to suit as a means of ensuring accountability, there were others, perhaps even more vocal, who believed that any attempt to abrogate the states' sovereign immunity was unacceptable. Although it is obviously difficult from this distance in time to determine who had the better of the argument, it does seem likely that some consensus against state suability was reached, if only to put the matter aside to another day. After all, objections to Article III's apparent abrogation of sovereign immunity had been raised in several state ratifying conventions and federalists repeatedly asserted that the proposed constitution would not subject the states to suit by private individuals. As a result, when it came to arguing the merits of *Chisholm*, it might be argued that supporters of states' rights were simply guilty of taking federalists at their word.

On the other hand, the idea that states would be subject to suit could not have been a surprise to those who read it. As Massachusetts' John Davis noted, it could not be a good thing to declare to the world that the American people "did not comprehend the Constitution which they had adopted." In effect, then, the best that could be said for the supporters of states' rights was that they had changed their minds in the years since the Constitution was ratified. In other words, hostility toward the national government's economic and diplomatic policies, much of which was dependent on assuring the British government that the peace treaty would be enforced, convinced many lukewarm supporters of the Constitution that ratification of Article III had been a mistake.

All of this is conjecture, of course, yet, it seems that whatever opinions the justices had about the original understanding of Article III's abrogation of sovereign immunity, they were clearly concerned about the impact the decision would have on the current political situation. Justice Iredell, in particular, knew the depth of southern hostility toward the idea that British creditors might recover their debts with interest and land titles might be disturbed, while American slave owners would not receive any compensation for the slaves carried off by the British at the end of the war. He no doubt feared that a decision opening the federal courts to suits against states would provoke a potentially violent reaction on the part of the southern states. Iredell, therefore, sought to avoid the problem with a relatively narrow reading of Section 14 of the Judiciary Act. That section provided that federal courts would have the power to issue only those writs "agreeable to the principles and usages of law." For Iredell, therefore, in order for the Supreme Court to have jurisdiction over a state, it had to be shown that the common law had traditionally recognized such writs. Since no such writ had ever specifically been known to the common law, the Court was powerless to act. The only way to solve the problem was for Congress to pass a statute providing specific authorization for such writs. In the absence of such legislation, the Court could not take upon itself to make up new writs.

Iredell's strategy appears to have been to force the issue into Congress and let the various sides debate the very sensitive issue of state suability in the political realm, allowing the Court to avoid the controversy entirely. Iredell clearly believed that the depth of southern hostility was such that the Union itself might be imperiled. During the course of arguments in the case, Attorney General Randolph urged the justices to create the writ themselves, asserting that the Constitution and the Judiciary Act gave the Supreme Court the power to create writs necessary for carrying into effect its jurisdiction. Iredell, however, rejected this suggestion noting that the "Attorney General's doctrine" was "pregnant" with the possibility of great evil. Few could have mistaken Iredell's warning. "The southern states might leave the Union before they would pay for the security of the northern frontier by complying with the terms of a treaty that had been ignored for at least a decade" (Gibbons, 1924). As an alternative, Iredell supposed that a decision in favor of Chisholm would result in increased calls for a second constitutional convention with no telling where that would lead.

Iredell's warnings failed to persuade the other justices, however, most of whom believed that enforcing the peace treaty was essential to the peace and security of the new nation. Thus, Chief Justice Jay, who had extensive experience negotiating with the British during the course of his tenure as Secretary of Foreign Affairs in the old confederation, insisted that national honor required that the states be held accountable. In his view, a nation that could not compel its constituent parts to conform to the law was no nation at all. Foreign nations would have no incentive to deal with the United States as a nation on an equal footing unless the national government had the power to "not only cause justice to be done to each [state] ... but also to cause justice to be done by each." For his part, Justice Wilson was already on record as rejecting the idea that states could not be sued in federal courts. During the Pennsylvania ratifying convention, Wilson asserted that inability to force the states to honor their treaty obligations was a primary consideration in adopting the new Constitution in the first place. As he said then, the clause giving federal courts jurisdiction over suits against states "will show the world that we make the faith of treaties a constitutional part of the character of the United States; that we secure [the] performance [of the Treaty of Paris] no longer nominally, for the judges of the United States will be enabled to carry it into effect, let the legislatures of the different states do what they may."

Iredell was thus alone in his fears. Most of the other justices appeared to believe that enforcing the peace treaty was essential and that Iredell's fears were probably overstated. Most justices seemed to have been convinced that asserting jurisdiction over the states was essential to securing the nation's diplomatic and economic future. In crafting their opinions, therefore, the fact that the original understanding was somewhat cloudy was an advantage. The justices adopted a textual approach to the problem, reading Article III in accordance with its terms. That this textual approach produced results at odds with the increasingly republican tenor of American politics and resulted in calls for an amendment to the Constitution re-establishing what proponents of states' rights claimed was the original understanding on sovereign immunity.

*Chisholm* is significant not only because it resolved one of the most important problems of federalism confronting the early nation, but it was also the first case in which the Supreme Court consciously interpreted a specific provision of the Constitution. The problem, of course, was that the Article III's grant of jurisdiction over suits involving states was itself a product of constructive ambiguity. No doubt many of those who drafted and ratified the Constitution believed that states should be subject to federal jurisdiction, but there was another, equally vocal group of opponents who believed that any attempt to subject the states to suits by individuals would constitute a violation of sovereign immunity. Indeed, the fact that many antifederalists believed that proponents of the Constitution were intent on establishing a "consolidated" government would have made any frontal assault on the principle of state sovereign immunity untenable.

As a result, *Chisholm* remains controversial even today. Scholars continue to debate the whether the case was a correct reading of the framers' intent on the question of state sovereign immunity. Indeed, for many years, the prevailing view of the case was the Court's opinion "fell upon the country with a profound shock," causing the states to rise up in righteous indignation and demand the passage of an amendment reinstating the original intentions of the founders (1 Warren, 96). These scholars contend that *Chisholm*, while a correct reading of the literal text of Article III, misconstrued the intentions of the framers of the Constitution, who had never assumed that the states would be called before the bar of any federal court. This is, in fact, the view taken by the Supreme Court itself somewhat later in *Hans v. Louisiana* (1890), when it declared that the decision in *Chisholm* sent a "shock of surprise throughout the country" by departing from the original understanding of the framers that states could not be sued without their consent. According to the *Hans* Court, the Eleventh Amendment was necessary to re-establish that original understanding in federal jurisprudence. That amendment provides that the "Judicial Power of the United States shall not be construed to extend to any suit in law or equity, commenced or prosecuted against one of the United States by Citizens of another State, or by Citizens or Subjects of any Foreign State." In *Hans*, the Court appears to have accepted the view advanced by Hamilton and Madison that Article III only applied to cases in which the states themselves were plaintiffs. That these statements were contradicted by others who also attended the Philadelphia Convention seems not to have made much of an impression on the Court.

As a result, the belief that the Eleventh Amendment was designed to re-establish a principle of general sovereign immunity allowed the Court in *Hans* to hold that states were immune to suit from any private party, regardless of the basis of jurisdiction. Some years later, in *Principality of Monaco v. Mississippi* (1934), the Court went even further and held that states were immune to suits brought by foreign governments, even though these suits were not specifically mentioned in the amendment. After *Hans* and *Principality of Monaco*, therefore, the states have been afforded a measure of sovereign immunity that might not have been entirely warranted by the terms of the original constitutional text or by the Eleventh Amendment. Over the years, this question has given rise to a cottage industry in the academic world, in which various commentators attempt to explain the original understanding of Article III and the Eleventh Amendment.

In fact, three schools of thought seem to dominate the discussion. Both reject the view taken by the Supreme Court in *Hans* and *Principality of Monaco*, and attempt to show that the drafters of the Eleventh Amendment were not necessarily intent on precluding all suits against states. On one side are the "diversity theorists" who hold that the Eleventh Amendment does not prevent a suit against a state if the suit were brought under federal question jurisdiction. In other words, this view holds that the Eleventh Amendment was designed merely to eliminate suits by individuals when brought under the Court's diversity jurisdiction. Thus, suits brought under federal question jurisdiction would be allowed (Amar, 1473–92). On the other side of the debate are those who advance a "congressional abrogation theory." These theorists hold that the Eleventh Amendment only restricts the Supreme Court's authority to abrogate the states' immunity, but does not prevent Congress from creating causes of action specifically subjecting the states to suit (Nowak, 1413–69). Finally, a third school argues that the Eleventh Amendment should be read literally. That is to say, after passage of the amendment, states are immune from suit brought by out-of-state residents and aliens, but are still amenable to suit by their own citizens (Marshall, 1342–71). In the end, however, the problem with scholarly attempts to discern the original understanding of both Article III and the Eleventh Amendment is that the historical record on the problem of sovereign immunity is rather mixed. In fact, the problem facing modern scholarly commentators is precisely that which faced the Supreme Court in *Chisholm* itself.

## Conclusion

Perhaps the most important characteristic of the Supreme Court in its early years was the justices' desire to play a role in the formation and continuance of the federal enterprise. At almost every turn, the justices appeared to the conscious of the Court's importance in helping to support the independence of the national government against encroachments from the states and foreign governments. Having witnessed firsthand the impotence of the national government under the old Articles of Confederation, the justices of the early Supreme Court were all firm supporters of the new Constitution. They believed that the government created under it was the best hope for the security and prosperity of the new nation. Consequently, the justices of the Jay and Ellsworth Courts often appeared to use their office to support the power of the national government whenever possible.

This tendency can be most readily seen in the way in which the justices used their position to engender support for the new Constitution among the citizenry. The grand jury charges rendered while on circuit often read like political speeches, encouraging the populace, and reminding them, in the word of Chief Justice Jay, that it was the "the Duty and the Interest … of all good Citizens, in their several Stations, to support the Laws and Government." In addition, the justices willingness to render advisory opinions on an individual basis is also evidence of their willingness to assist in supporting the national government whenever necessary. It would be inconceivable today that any member of the Supreme Court would willingly offer legal or political advice to members of the executive branch. Doing so would be regarded as a gross violation of the principle of judicial independence and might possibly place a justice in an unresolvable conflict of interest should any matter arising from rendering such an opinion every find its way to the Court. Yet, the early Supreme Court justices seem not to have labored under the same type of reservations. On the contrary, while they resisted the President's request for a formal advisory opinion in the neutrality controversy, most of the justices appeared to harbor no reservations about assisting the administration on an informal basis. Their willingness to provide advise on law, politics, and diplomacy is rather astonishing evidence of the justices' belief that, as federal officials, they had a duty to support the government so long as their assistance did not directly interfere with their judicial office. While modern observers might counter that offering advice, even on an informal basis, to the executive branch would be a clear violation of the principle of separation of powers, it is clear that late 18th century concepts of judicial independence did not go so far.

The justices' formal activities reveal a similar approach. Unlike the modern Supreme Court, which often seems to function today primarily as a check on the activities of the political branches, the early justices appear to have considered themselves as a partners in the federal enterprise. This is not to say that the early justices were mere pawns of Congress or the President. On the contrary, in both the neutrality controversy and *Hayburn's Case*, they demonstrated quite clearly their willingness to chart an independent course, resisting pressure from both the administration and Congress. Thus, while it is true that they understood that one aspect of the Court's role was to keep the other branches of the federal government within their appointed spheres, it does appear that the justices believed that the greatest danger to the early Republic was most likely to come from overreaching by the states. This tendency is demonstrated by the Court's approach to the problem of judicial review. Thus, when it came to overturning statutes of Congress, the justices repeatedly expressed reluctance about doing so. For example, in *Hayburn's Case* (1792), when confronted with a statute they believed clearly violated the principle of the separation of powers, the justices all avoided making any public declaration of unconstitutionality. While they were unanimous in their opinion that the Pension Act could not withstand constitutional scrutiny, they attempted to avoid a public confrontation by expressing that opinion in letters to the President. In so doing, they clearly hoped to avoid having to invalidate an act of Congress passed within a short time of the government's founding. The justices knew, after all, that many people harbored doubts about the powers given to Congress under the Constitution, and they feared that such a declaration would only provide fodder to those who continued to assert that giving so much power to Congress was a mistake. When it came to acts of the state legislatures, however, the Court seemed to harbor very few reservations about its power to declare such acts unconstitutional. Thus, in *Ware v. Hylton* (1796), the Court had little difficulty striking down a Virginia law that conflicted with a treaty; and in *Calder v. Bull* (1978), the Court harbored no reservations about its power to review the acts of state legislatures for conformity with the federal constitution. Although the justices ultimately upheld the statute at issue in *Calder*, it is clear that they had no doubts about their power to invalidate unconstitutional state laws. In sum, the justices' approach to the problem of judicial review evidenced their belief that the states were more likely than the political branches of the federal government to destabilize the delicate balance created by the Constitution.

In the final analysis, the first ten years of the Supreme Court's history was marked by a certain conservatism, which is evidenced in both the content of their decisions and their manner of judging. It is clear that the justices' desire to support the national government coloured their approach to legal disputes. In laying the foundations for judicial review, authorizing suits against states, interpreting treaties, protecting the revenue, and adjudicating various criminal cases, more often than not, the justices tended to craft opinions that strengthened or preserved the power of the national government in the constitutional scheme. This is not to say that they overrode or ignored legal doctrines that limited federal power. On the contrary, the justices routinely recognised that the Constitution created a federal government of enumerated powers. When necessary, they were confident in their ability to set limits on the political branches of the national government. In many others, however, the justices were equally confident that the Constitution intended to establish a central government that would have the vigor and energy to assert its prerogatives over those of the states. This should not really be surprising, however. After all, the nature of the cases which came before them in the early years were bound to present questions about the scope of federal power. Being first in line, the justices of the Jay and Ellsworth Courts were fated to hear the first challenges to the assertion of federal power and to provide the earliest interpretation of many of the most important constitutional provisions. In doing so, however, the justices often seemed to adopt an instrumentalist interpretation. More importantly, it must be remembered that the Constitution itself was rather conservative in its approach. Many of the justices had played a role in its drafting and ratification, and it seems that in their view, at least, the Constitution was established to provide for a strong national government. In fulfilling their role as the first interpreters of that document, therefore, the justices were obviously attempting to strengthen that which they themselves had laboured so hard to create.

# References and Further Reading

Akhil Reed Amar, "Of Sovereignty And Federalism," 96 *Yale Law Journal* (1987): 1425.

Denning, Brandon P, "Confederation-Era Discrimination Against Interstate Commerce and the Legitimacy of the Dormant Commerce Clause Doctrine," 94 *Kentucky Law Review*(2005): 37.

Gibbons, John J. "The Eleventh Amendment and State Sovereign Immunity: A Reinterpretation," *83 Columbia Law Review* (1983): 1895.

Harrington, Matthew P. "Judicial Review Before John Marshall," 72 *George Washington Law Review* (2003): 51.

Jacobs, Clyde E. *The Eleventh Amendment and Sovereign Immunity* (Westport, CT: Greenwood Press, 1972).

Kaminski, John P. and Gaspare J. Saladino, *The Documentary History Of The Ratification Of The Constitution* (Madison: State Historical Society Of Wisconsin, 1976–1993), Volume 10.

Lerner, Ralph, "The Supreme Court As Republican Schoolmaster," *1967 Supreme Court Review* (1967): 127.

Lewis, George E. *The Indiana Company, 1763–1798: A Study In Eighteenth Century Frontier Land Speculation And Business Venture* (Glendale, CA: Arthur H. Clark, 1941).

Marcus, Maeva. *The Documentary History of the Supreme Court of the United States* (New York: Columbia University Press, 1994), Volume 5.

Marshall, Lawrence C. "Fighting The Words Of The Eleventh Amendment," 102 *Harvard Law Review* (1989): 1365.

Massey, Calvin R. "State Sovereign Immunity and the Tenth And Eleventh Amendments," 56 *University Of Chicago Law Review* (1989): 87.

Nowak, John E. "The Scope of Congressional Power to Create Causes of Action Against State Governments and the History of the Eleventh and Fourteenth Amendments," 75 *Columbia Law Review* (1975): 1413.

Warren, Charles. *The Supreme Court In United States History* (Boston, Little Brown & Co., 1923).

# The Definitive Treaty of Peace Between Great Britain and the United States (1783)

In the name of the most holy and undivided Trinity.

It having pleased the Divine Providence to dispose the hearts of the most serene and most potent Prince George the Third, by the grace of God, king of Great Britain, France, and Ireland, defender of the faith, duke of Brunswick and Lunebourg, arch-treasurer and prince elector of the Holy Roman Empire etc., and of the United States of America, to forget all past misunderstandings and differences that have unhappily interrupted the good correspondence and friendship which they mutually wish to restore, and to establish such a beneficial and satisfactory intercourse, between the two countries upon the ground of reciprocal advantages and mutual convenience as may promote and secure to both perpetual peace and harmony; and having for this desirable end already laid the foundation of peace and reconciliation by the Provisional Articles signed at Paris on the 30th of November 1782, by the commissioners empowered on each part, which articles were agreed to be inserted in and constitute the Treaty of Peace proposed to be concluded between the Crown of Great Britain and the said United States, but which treaty was not to be concluded until terms of peace should be agreed upon between Great Britain and France and his Britannic Majesty should be ready to conclude such treaty accordingly; and the treaty between Great Britain and France having since been concluded, his Britannic Majesty and the United States of America, in order to carry into full effect the Provisional Articles above mentioned, according to the tenor thereof, have constituted and appointed, that is to say his Britannic Majesty on his part, David Hartley, Esqr., member of the Parliament of Great Britain, and the said United States on their part, John Adams, Esqr., late a commissioner of the United States of America at the court of Versailles, late delegate in Congress from the state of Massachusetts, and chief justice of the said state, and minister plenipotentiary of the said United States to their high mightinesses the States General of the United Netherlands; Benjamin Franklin, Esqr., late delegate in Congress from the state of Pennsylvania, president of the convention of the said state, and minister plenipotentiary from the United States of America at the court of Versailles; John Jay, Esqr., late president of Congress and chief justice of the state of New York, and minister plenipotentiary from the said United States at the court of Madrid; to be plenipotentiaries for the concluding and signing the present definitive treaty; who after having reciprocally communicated their respective full powers have agreed upon and confirmed the following articles.

Article 1: His Brittanic Majesty acknowledges the said United States, viz., New Hampshire, Massachusetts Bay, Rhode Island and Providence Plantations, Connecticut, New York, New Jersey, Pennsylvania, Maryland, Virginia, North Carolina, South Carolina and Georgia, to be free sovereign and independent states, that he treats with them as such, and for himself, his heirs, and successors, relinquishes all claims to the government, propriety, and territorial rights of the same and every part thereof.

Article 2: And that all disputes which might arise in future on the subject of the boundaries of the said United States may be prevented, it is hereby agreed and declared, that the following are and shall be their boundaries, viz.; from the northwest angle of Nova Scotia, viz., that angle which is formed by a line drawn due north from the source of St. Croix River to the highlands; along the said highlands which divide those rivers that empty themselves into the river St. Lawrence, from those which fall into the Atlantic Ocean, to the northwesternmost head of Connecticut River; thence down along the middle of that river to the forty-fifth degree of north latitude; from thence by a line due west on said latitude until it strikes the river Iroquois or Cataraquy; thence along the middle of said river into Lake Ontario; through the middle of said lake until it strikes the communication by water between that lake and Lake Erie; thence along the middle of said communication into Lake Erie, through the middle of said lake until it arrives at the water communication between that lake and Lake Huron; thence along the middle of said water communication into Lake Huron, thence through the middle of said lake to the water communication between that lake and Lake Superior; thence through Lake Superior northward of the Isles Royal and Phelipeaux to the Long Lake; thence through the middle of said Long Lake and the water communication between it and the Lake of the Woods, to the said Lake of the Woods; thence through the said lake to the most northwesternmost point thereof, and from thence on a due west course to the river Mississippi; thence by a line to be drawn along the middle of the said river Mississippi until it shall intersect the northernmost part of the thirty-first degree of north latitude, South, by a line to be drawn due east from the determination of the line last mentioned in the latitude of thirty-one degrees of the equator, to the middle of the river Apalachicola or Catahouche; thence along the middle thereof to its junction with the Flint River, thence straight to the head of Saint Mary's River; and thence down along the middle of Saint Mary's River to the Atlantic Ocean; east, by a line to be drawn along the middle of the river Saint Croix, from its mouth in the Bay of Fundy to its source, and from its source directly north to the aforesaid highlands which divide the rivers that fall into the Atlantic Ocean from those which fall into the river Saint Lawrence; comprehending all islands within twenty leagues of any part of the shores of the United States, and lying between lines to be drawn due east from the points where the aforesaid boundaries between Nova Scotia on the one part and East Florida on the other shall, respectively, touch the Bay of Fundy and the Atlantic Ocean, excepting such islands as now are or heretofore have been within the limits of the said province of Nova Scotia.

Article 3: It is agreed that the people of the United States shall continue to enjoy unmolested the right to take fish of every kind on the Grand Bank and on all the other banks of Newfoundland, also in the Gulf of Saint Lawrence and at all other places in the sea, where the inhabitants of both countries used at any time heretofore to fish. And also that the inhabitants of the United States shall have liberty to take fish of every kind on such part of the coast of Newfoundland as British fishermen shall use, (but not to dry or cure the same on that island) and also on the coasts, bays and creeks of all other of his Brittanic Majesty's dominions in America; and that the American fishermen shall have liberty to dry and cure fish in any of the unsettled bays, harbors, and creeks of Nova Scotia, Magdalen Islands, and Labrador, so long as the same shall remain unsettled, but so soon as the same or either of them shall be settled, it shall not be lawful for the said fishermen to dry or cure fish at such settlement without a previous agreement for that purpose with the inhabitants, proprietors, or possessors of the ground.

Article 4: It is agreed that creditors on either side shall meet with no lawful impediment to the recovery of the full value in sterling money of all bona fide debts heretofore contracted.

Article 5: It is agreed that Congress shall earnestly recommend it to the legislatures of the respective states to provide for the restitution of all estates, rights, and properties, which have been confiscated belonging to real British subjects; and also of the estates, rights, and properties of persons resident in districts in the possession on his Majesty's arms and who have not borne arms against the said United States. And that persons of any other decription shall have free liberty to go to any part or parts of any of the thirteen United States and therein to remain twelve months unmolested in their endeavors to obtain the restitution of such of their estates, rights, and properties as may have been confiscated; and that Congress shall also earnestly recommend to the several states a reconsideration and revision of all acts or laws regarding the premises, so as to render the said laws or acts perfectly consistent not only with justice and equity but with that spirit of conciliation which on the return of the blessings of peace should universally prevail. And that Congress shall also earnestly recommend to the several states that the estates, rights, and properties, of such last mentioned persons shall be restored to them, they refunding to any persons who may be now in possession the bona fide price (where any has been given) which such persons may have paid on purchasing any of the said lands, rights, or properties since the confiscation.

And it is agreed that all persons who have any interest in confiscated lands, either by debts, marriage settlements, or otherwise, shall meet with no lawful impediment in the prosecution of their just rights.

Article 6: That there shall be no future confiscations made nor any prosecutions commenced against any person or persons for, or by reason of, the part which he or they may have taken in the present war, and that no person shall on that account suffer any future loss or damage, either in his person, liberty, or property; and that those who may be in confinement on such charges at the time of the ratification of the treaty in America shall be immediately set at liberty, and the prosecutions so commenced be discontinued.

Article 7: There shall be a firm and perpetual peace between his Brittanic Majesty and the said states, and between the subjects of the one and the citizens of the other, wherefore all hostilities both by sea and land shall from henceforth cease. All prisoners on both sides shall be set at liberty, and his Brittanic Majesty shall with all convenient speed, and without causing any destruction, or carrying away any Negroes or other property of the American inhabitants, withdraw all his armies, garrisons, and fleets from the said United States, and from every post, place, and harbor within the same; leaving in all fortifications, the American artilery that may be therein; and shall also order and cause all archives, records, deeds, and papers belonging to any of the said states, or their citizens, which in the course of the war may have fallen into the hands of his officers, to be forthwith restored and delivered to the proper states and persons to whom they belong.

Article 8: The navigation of the river Mississippi, from its source to the ocean, shall forever remain free and open to the subjects of Great Britain and the citizens of the United States.

Article 9: In case it should so happen that any place or territory belonging to Great Britain or to the United States should have been conquered by the arms of either from the other before the arrival of the said Provisional Articles in America, it is agreed that the same shall be restored without difficulty and without requiring any compensation.

Article 10: The solemn ratifications of the present treaty expedited in good and due form shall be exchanged between the contracting parties in the space of six months or sooner, if possible, to be computed from the day of the signatures of the present treaty. In witness whereof we the undersigned, their ministers plenipotentiary, have in their name and in virtue of our full powers, signed with our hands the present definitive treaty and caused the seals of our arms to be affixed thereto.

Done at Paris, this third day of September in the year of our Lord, one thousand seven hundred and eighty-three.

# The Constitution of the United States (1787)

## Article III

Section. 1. The judicial Power of the United States shall be vested in one supreme Court, and in such inferior Courts as the Congress may from time to time ordain and establish. The Judges, both of the supreme and inferior Courts, shall hold their Offices during good Behaviour, and shall, at stated Times, receive for their Services a Compensation, which shall not be diminished during their Continuance in Office.

Section. 2. The judicial Power shall extend to all Cases, in Law and Equity, arising under this Constitution, the Laws of the United States, and Treaties made, or which shall be made, under their Authority;—to all Cases affecting Ambassadors, other public Ministers and Consuls;—to all Cases of admiralty and maritime Jurisdiction;—to Controversies to which the United States shall be a Party;—to Controversies between two or more States;— between a State and Citizens of another State;—between Citizens of different States;—between Citizens of the same State claiming Lands under Grants of different States, and between a State, or the Citizens thereof, and foreign States, Citizens or Subjects.

In all Cases affecting Ambassadors, other public Ministers and Consuls, and those in which a State shall be Party, the supreme Court shall have original Jurisdiction. In all the other Cases before mentioned, the supreme Court shall have appellate Jurisdiction, both as to Law and Fact, with such Exceptions, and under such Regulations as the Congress shall make.

The Trial of all Crimes, except in Cases of Impeachment, shall be by Jury; and such Trial shall be held in the State where the said Crimes shall have been committed; but when not committed within any State, the Trial shall be at such Place or Places as the Congress may by Law have directed.

Section. 3. Treason against the United States, shall consist only in levying War against them, or in adhering to their Enemies, giving them Aid and Comfort. No Person shall be convicted of Treason unless on the Testimony of two Witnesses to the same overt Act, or on Confession in open Court. The Congress shall have Power to declare the Punishment of Treason, but no Attainder of Treason shall work Corruption of Blood, or Forfeiture except during the Life of the Person attainted.

## *Article VI*

Section 1. All debts contracted and engagements entered into, before the adoption of this constitution, shall be as valid against the United States under this constitution, as under the confederation.

Section 2. This constitution, and the laws of the United States which shall be made in pursuance thereof; and all treaties made, or which shall be made, under the authority of the United States shall be the supreme law of the land; and the judges in every state shall be bound thereby, any thing in the constitution or laws of any state to the contrary notwithstanding.

Section 3. The senators and representatives before-mentioned, and the members of the several state legislatures, and all executive and judicial officers, both of the United States and of the several states, shall be bound by oath or affirmation, to support this constitution; but no religious test shall ever be required as a qualification to any office or public trust under the United States.

# The Judiciary Act of 1789

An Act to establish the Judicial Courts of the United States

Sec. 1. Be it enacted, That the supreme court of the United States shall consist of a chief justice and five associate justices, any four of whom shall be a quorum, and shall hold annually at the seat of government two sessions, the one commencing the first Monday of February, and the other the first Monday of August. That the associate justices shall have precedence according to the date of their commissions, or when the commissions of two or more of them bear the same date on the same day, according to their respective ages.

Sec. 2. That the United States shall be, and they hereby are, divided into thirteen districts, to be limited and called as follows, ...

Sec. 3. That there be a court called a District Court in each of the aforementioned districts, to consist of one judge, who shall reside in the district for which he is appointed, and shall be called a District Judge, and shall hold annually four sessions, ...

Sec. 4. That the beforementioned districts, except those of Maine and Kentucky, shall be divided into three circuits, and be called the eastern, the middle, and the southern circuit.... [T]hat there shall be held annually in each district of said circuits two courts which shall be called Circuit Courts, and shall consist of any two justices of the Supreme Court and the district judge of such districts, any two of whom shall constitute a quorum. Provided, That no district judge shall give a vote in any case of appeal or error from his own decision; but may assign the reasons of such his decision....

Sec. 9. That the district courts shall have, exclusively of the courts of the several States, cognizance of all crimes and offenses that shall be cognizable under the authority of the United States, committed within their respective districts, or upon the high seas; where no other punishment than whipping, not exceeding thirty stripes, a fine not exceeding one hundred dollars, or a term of imprisonment not exceeding six months, is to be inflicted; and shall also have exclusive original cognizance of all civil cases of admiralty and maritime jurisdiction, including all seizures under laws of impost, navigation, or trade of the United States.... And shall also have cognizance, concurrent with the courts of the several States, or the circuit courts, as the case may be, of all causes where an alien sues for a tort only in violation of the law of nations or a treaty of the United States. And shall also have cognizance, concurrent as last mentioned, of all suits at common law where the United States sue, and the matter in dispute amounts, exclusive of costs, to the sum or value of one hundred dollars. And shall also have jurisdiction exclusively of the courts of the several States, of all suits against consuls or vice-consuls, except for offenses above the description aforesaid. And the trial of issues in fact, in the district courts, in all cases except civil causes of admiralty and maritime jurisdiction, shall be by jury....

Sec 11. That the circuit courts shall have original cognizance, concurrent with the courts of the several States, of all suits of a civil nature at common law or in equity, where the matter in dispute exceeds, exclusive of costs, the sum or value of five hundred dollars, and the United States are plaintiffs or petitioners; or an alien is a party, or the suit is between a citizen of the State where the suit is brought and a citizen of another State. And shall have exclusive cognizance of all crimes and offenses cognizable under the authority of the United States, except where this act otherwise provides, or the laws of the United States shall otherwise direct, and concurrent jurisdiction with the district courts of the crimes and offenses cognizable therein.... And the circuit courts shall also have appellate jurisdiction from the district courts under the regulations and restrictions herinafter provided....

Sec. 13. That the Supreme Court shall have exclusive jurisdiction of all controversies of a civil nature, where a state is a party, except between a state and its citizens; and except also between a state and citizens of other states, or aliens, in which latter case it shall have original but not exclusive jurisdiction. And shall have exclusively all such jurisdiction of suits or proceedings against ambassadors or other public ministers, or their domestics, or domestic servants, as a court of law can have or exercise consistently with the law of nations; and original, but not exclusive jurisdiction of all suits brought by ambassadors or other public ministers, or in which a consul or vice-consul shall be a party. And the trial of issues in fact in the Supreme Court in all actions at law against citizens of the United States shall be by jury. The Supreme Court shall also have appellate jurisdiction from the circuit courts and courts of the several states in the cases hereinafter specially provided for and shall have power to issue writs of prohibition to the district courts, when proceeding as courts of admiralty and maritime jurisdiction, and writs of mandamus, in cases warranted by the principle and usages of law, to any courts appointed, or persons holding office under the authority of the United States....

Sec. 25. That a final judgment or decree in any suit, in the highest court of law or equity of a State in which a decision in the suit could be had, where is drawn in question the validity of a treaty or statute of, or an authority exercised under, the United States, and the decision is against their validity; or where is drawn in question the validity of a statute of, or an authority exercised under, any State, on the ground of their being repugnant to the constitution, treaties, or laws of the United States, and the decision is in favour of such their validity, or where is drawn in question the construction of any clause of the constitution, or of a treaty, or statute of, or commission held under, the United States, and the decision is against the title, right, privilege, or exemption, specially set up or claimed by either party, under such clause of the said Constitution, treaty, statute, or commission, may be re-examined, and reversed or affirmed in the Supreme Court of the United States upon a writ of error, the citation being signed by the chief justice, or judge or chancellor of the court rendering or passing the judgment or decree complained of, or by a justice of the Supreme Court of the United States, in the same manner and under the same regulations, and the writ shall have the same effect as if the judgment or decree complained of had been rendered or passed in a circuit court, and the proceedings upon the reversal shall also be the same, except that the Supreme Court, instead of remanding the cause for a final decision as before provided, may, at their discretion, if the cause shall have been once remanded before, proceed to a final decision of the same, and award execution. But no other error shall be assigned or regarded as a ground of reversal in any such case as aforesaid, than such as appears on the face of the record, and immediately respects the before-mentioned questions of validity or construction of the said constitution, treaties, statutes, commissions, or authorities in dispute.

# Washington's Neutrality Proclamation (1793)

By THE PRESIDENT of the UNITED STATES of America,

A PROCLAMATION.

Whereas it appears that a state of war exists between Austria, Prussia, Sardinia, Great Britain, and the United Netherlands, of the one part, and France on the other; and the duty and interest of the United States require, that they should with sincerity and good faith adopt and pursue a conduct friendly and impartial toward the belligerant Powers;

I have therefore thought fit by these presents to declare the disposition of the United States to observe the conduct aforesaid towards those Powers respectfully; and to exhort and warn the citizens of the United States carefully to avoid all acts and proceedings whatsoever, which may in any manner tend to contravene such disposition.

And I do hereby also make known, that whatsoever of the citizens of the United States shall render himself liable to punishment or forfeiture under the law of nations, by committing, aiding, or abetting hostilities against any of the said Powers, or by carrying to any of them those articles which are deemed contraband by the modern usage of nations, will not receive the protection of the United States, against such punishment or forfeiture; and further, that I have given instructions to those officers, to whom it belongs, to cause prosecutions to be instituted against all persons, who shall, within the cognizance of the courts of the United States, violate the law of nations, with respect to the Powers at war, or any of them.

In testimony whereof, I have caused the seal of the United States of America to be affixed to these presents, and signed the same with my hand. Done at the city of Philadelphia, the twenty-second day of April, one thousand seven hundred and ninety-three, and of the Independence of the United States of America the seventeenth.

GEORGE WASHINGTON

April 22, 1793

# The Whiskey Rebellion (1794)
## Washington's Proclamation

By the president of the United States of America

A PROCLAMATION

Whereas, combinations to defeat the execution of the laws laying duties upon spirits distilled within the United States and upon stills have from the time of the commencement of those laws existed in some of the western parts of Pennsylvania.

And whereas, the said combinations, proceeding in a manner subversive equally of the just authority of government and of the rights of individuals, have hitherto effected their dangerous and criminal purpose by the influence of certain irregular meetings whose proceedings have tended to encourage and uphold the spirit of opposition by misrepresentations of the laws calculated to render them odious; by endeavors to deter those who might be so disposed from accepting offices under them through fear of public resentment and of injury to person and property, and to compel those who had accepted such offices by actual violence to surrender or forbear the execution of them; by circulation vindictive menaces against all those who should otherwise, directly or indirectly, aid in the execution of the said laws, or who, yielding to the dictates of conscience and to a sense of obligation, should themselves comply therewith; by actually injuring and destroying the property of persons who were understood to have so complied; by inflicting cruel and humiliating punishments upon private citizens for no other cause than that of appearing to be the friends of the laws; by intercepting the public officers on the highways, abusing, assaulting, and otherwise ill treating them; by going into their houses in the night, gaining admittance by force, taking away their papers, and committing other outrages, employing for these unwarrantable purposes the agency of armed banditti disguised in such manner as for the most part to escape discovery;

And whereas, the endeavors of the legislature to obviate objections to the said laws by lowering the duties and by other alterations conducive to the convenience of those whom they immediately affect (though they have given satisfaction in other quarters), and the endeavors of the executive officers to conciliate a compliance with the laws by explanations, by forbearance, and even by particular accommodations founded on the suggestion of local considerations, have been disappointed of their effect by the machinations of persons whose industry to excite resistance has increased with every appearance of a disposition among the people to relax in their opposition and to acquiesce in the laws, insomuch that many persons in the said western parts of Pennsylvania have at length been hardy enough to perpetrate acts, which I am advised amount to treason, being overt acts of levying war against the United States, the said persons having on the 16th and 17th of July last past proceeded in arms (on the second day amounting to several hundreds) to the house of John Neville, inspector of the revenue for the fourth survey of the district of Pennsylvania; having repeatedly attacked the said house with the persons therein, wounding some of them; having seized David Lenox, marshal of the district of Pennsylvania, who previous thereto had been fired upon while in the execution of his duty by a party of armed men, detaining him for some time prisoner, till, for the preservation of his life and the obtaining of his liberty, he found it necessary to enter into stipulations to forbear the execution of certain official duties touching processes issuing out of a court of the United States; and having finally obliged the said inspector of the revenue and the said marshal from considerations of personal safety to fly from that part of the country, in order, by a circuitous route, to proceed to the seat of government, avowing as the motives of these outrageous proceedings an intention to prevent by force of arms the execution of the said laws, to oblige the said inspector of the revenue to renounce his said office, to withstand by open violence the lawful authority of the government of the United States, and to compel thereby an alteration in the measures of the legislature and a repeal of the laws aforesaid;

And whereas, by a law of the United States entitled "An act to provide for calling forth the militia to execute the laws of the Union, suppress insurrections, and repel invasions," it is enacted that whenever the laws of the United States shall be opposed or the execution thereof obstructed in any state by combinations too powerful to be suppressed by the ordinary course of judicial proceedings or by the powers vested in the marshals by that act, the same being notified by an associate justice or the district judge, it shall be lawful for the President of the United States to call forth the militia of such state to suppress such combinations and to cause the laws to be duly executed. And if the militia of a state, when such combinations may happen, shall refuse or be insufficient to suppress the same, it shall be lawful for the President, if the legislature of the United States shall not be in session, to call forth and employ such numbers of the militia of any other state or states most convenient thereto as may be necessary; and the use of the militia so to be called forth may be continued, if necessary, until the expiration of thirty days after the commencement of the of the ensuing session; Provided always, that, whenever it may be necessary in the judgment of the President to use the military force hereby directed to be called forth, the President shall forthwith, and previous thereto, by proclamation, command such insurgents to disperse and retire peaceably to their respective abodes within a limited time;

And whereas, James Wilson, an associate justice, on the 4th instant, by writing under his hand, did from evidence which had been laid before him notify to me that "in the counties of Washington and Allegany, in Pennsylvania, laws of the United States are opposed and the execution thereof obstructed by combinations too powerful to be suppressed by the ordinary course of judicial proceedings or by the powers vested in the marshal of that district";

And whereas, it is in my judgment necessary under the circumstances of the case to take measures for calling forth the militia in order to suppress the combinations aforesaid, and to cause the laws to be duly executed; and I have accordingly determined so to do, feeling the deepest regret for the occasion, but withal the most solemn conviction that the essential interests of the Union demand it, that the very existence of government and the fundamental principles of social order are materially involved in the issue, and that the patriotism and firmness of all good citizens are seriously called upon, as occasions may require, to aid in the effectual suppression of so fatal a spirit;

Therefore, and in pursuance of the proviso above recited, I. George Washington, President of the United States, do hereby command all persons, being insurgents, as aforesaid, and all others whom it may concern, on or before the 1st day of September next to disperse and retire peaceably to their respective abodes. And I do moreover warn all persons whomsoever against aiding, abetting, or comforting the perpetrators of the aforesaid treasonable acts; and do require all officers and other citizens, according to their respective duties and the laws of the land, to exert their utmost endeavors to prevent and suppress such dangerous proceedings.

In testimony whereof I have caused the seal of the United States of America to be affixed to these presents, and signed the same with my hand. Done at the city of Philadelphia the seventh day of August, one thousand seven hundred and ninety-four, and of the independence of the United States of America the nineteenth.

G. WASHINGTON

# An Act in addition to an "Act for the Punishment of Certain Crimes Against the United States" (The Sedition Act of 1798)

SECTION 1. Be it enacted by the Senate and House of Representatives of the United States of America, in Congress assembled, That if any persons shall unlawfully combine or conspire together, with intent to oppose any measure or measures of the government of the United States, which are or shall be directed by proper authority, or to impede the operation of any law of the United States, or to intimidate or prevent any person holding a place or office in or under the government of the United States, from undertaking, performing or executing his trust or duty, and if any person or persons, with intent as aforesaid, shall counsel, advise or attempt to procure any insurrection, riot, unlawful assembly, or combination, whether such conspiracy, threatening, counsel, advice, or attempt shall have the proposed effect or not, he or they shall be deemed guilty of a high misdemeanor, and on conviction, before any court of the United States having jurisdiction thereof, shall be punished by a fine not exceeding five thousand dollars, and by imprisonment during a term not less than six months nor exceeding five years; and further, at the discretion of the court may be ho]den to find sureties for his good behaviour in such sum, and for such time, as the said court may direct.

SECTION 2. And be it farther enacted, That if any person shall write, print, utter or publish, or shall cause or procure to be written, printed, uttered or published, or shall knowingly and willingly assist or aid in writing, printing, uttering or publishing any false, scandalous and malicious writing or writings against the government of the United States, or either house of the Congress of the United States, or the President of the United States, with intent to defame the said government, or either house of the said Congress, or the said President, or to bring them, or either of them, into contempt or disrepute; or to excite against them, or either or any of them, the hatred of the good people of the United States, or to stir up sedition within the United States, or to excite any unlawful combinations therein, for opposing or resisting any law of the United States, or any act of the President of the United States, done in pursuance of any such law, or of the powers in him vested by the constitution of the United States, or to resist, oppose, or defeat any such law or act, or to aid, encourage or abet any hostile designs of any foreign nation against United States, their people or government, then such person, being thereof convicted before any court of the United States having jurisdiction thereof, shall be punished by a fine not exceeding two thousand dollars, and by imprisonment not exceeding two years.

SECTION 3. And be it further enacted and declared, That if any person shall be prosecuted under this act, for the writing or publishing any libel aforesaid, it shall be lawful for the defendant, upon the trial of the cause, to give in evidence in his defence, the truth of the matter contained in Republication charged as a libel. And the jury who shall try the cause, shall have a right to determine the law and the fact, under the direction of the court, as in other cases.

SECTION 4. And be it further enacted, That this act shall continue and be in force until the third day of March, one thousand eight hundred and one, and no longer: Provided, that the expiration of the act shall not prevent or defeat a prosecution and punishment of any offence against the law, during the time it shall be in force.

APPROVED, July 14, 1798.

# Key People, Laws, and Events

## Adams, John

Born in Braintree, Massachusetts, in 1735, John Adams originally wanted to be a farmer, but his father wanted him to train for the ministry. Educated at Harvard College, Adams spent the years immediately after graduation as a schoolmaster in Worcester, during which time he decided to study for a career in the law. He was admitted to the bar in 1758, although he was not immediately successful, laboring in the shadow of his more famous cousin, Samuel.

Adams was an early convert to the revolutionary cause, being inspired in part by James Otis's arguments in the Writs of Assistance case in 1760. In 1770, Adams agreed to defend the British soldiers accused of murder in the Boston Massacre. His eloquent defence of the soldiers provided him with a degree of notoriety, and he was soon elected to the Massachusetts legislature. In 1774, John Adams was elected one of Massachusetts' delegates to the First Continental Congress.

While in Congress, Adams served as chairman of the Board of War and was a member of the committee that drafted the Declaration of Independence. In 1778, Congress appointed Adams as one of the commissioners to negotiate a treaty of alliance with France. The following year, he returned to Massachusetts where he was elected a delegate to that state's constitutional convention. The resulting constitution was almost entirely Adams' handiwork.

Adams returned to Europe in 1780, where he served as minister plenipotentiary to the Dutch republic and successfully negotiated desperately needed loans with Dutch bankers. Shortly thereafter, he was named as one of the American commissioners charged with negotiating a treaty of peace with England and was later appointed the United State's first ambassador to the Court of St. James.

Adams was not a delegate to the Constitutional Convention in 1787, although he strongly supported the proposed Constitution. He was elected the nation's first vice president in 1788. In 1796, Adams was the standard bearer for the Federalist party and was ultimately successful in defeating Thomas Jefferson in a very close contest for president. Divisions in the party, combined with public unhappiness with Federalist policies during Adams' administration, ultimately resulted in his being defeated for re-election in 1800.

## Alien and Sedition Acts

Rising tensions with France in the spring of 1798 became the impetus for a series of statutes designed to prepare the United States for war. In May and June 1798, Congress approved an increase in the size of the army and appropriated funds for the building of new ships. Fearful of "Jacobins" in their midst, many in Congress urged the passage of legislation designed to punish those who would give aid and comfort to the French. The result was a series of statutes designed to restrain public dissent.

The Naturalization Act (June 18, 1798) imposed restrictions on American citizenship, increasing the time an alien had to wait before he could become a citizen. The Alien Act (June 25) authorized the president to expel any alien whom he deemed "dangerous to the peace and safety of the United States," regardless of the nationality of the alien. The Alien Enemies Act (July 6, 1798) was to come into force during wartime and authorized the president to detain or deport citizens of any country engaged in hostilities with the United States. The Sedition Act (July 14, 1798) made it a crime to publish "false, scandalous and malicious writing or writings against the government of the United States."

Prosecutions under the Sedition Act commenced in the summer of 1798 and were roundly criticized by observers in both parties. Ultimately, these prosecutions went a long way toward stirring up hostility toward the Federalist party and may have contributed to its defeat in the election of 1800.

## Antifederalism

There are two movements in the latter part of the 18th century that might justifiably be called "antifederalist."

The first of these was the movement to prevent ratification of the federal Constitution as drafted by the Philadelphia Convention in the summer of 1787. This movement was rather diverse in its aims and arguments, although a few general points might be made about it. Some "anti-federalists" opposed the new constitution because they believed it created too a strong a central government. They worried that the central government under the proposed Constitution was so strong that it would eventually overpower, and ultimately destroy, the governments of the states. Theirs was an argument grounded in state sovereignty. Others opposed the Constitution because of a fear that it had too many "monarchical" tendencies. They feared the powers of the president and the Senate, in particular, and argued that the new Constitution would eventually result in the creation of a new monarchy and aristocracy. Still others believed that the Constitution did not provide adequate protection for individual rights and insisted that some sort of bill of rights was required before the Constitution could be ratified. Finally, it is also clear that some antifederalists opposed the new Constitution simply because it threatened their own personal political or economic interest.

This first antifederalist movement found its highest expression in the works of numerous writers during the course of the ratification debates. Almost as soon as the Philadelphia Convention finished its work in September 1787, both supporters and opponents of the Constitution began a flurry of essays and articles in newspapers around the country setting forth the arguments in support of their respective positions. Thus, Alexander Hamilton, John Jay, and James Madison crafted a series of essays for New York newspapers under the pseudonym *Publius* urging ratification of the Constitution. These essays were eventually collected and published in a volume called *The Federalist*. Meanwhile, antifederalists wrote equally well-reasoned arguments against ratification under pseudonyms such as *Cato*, *Brutus*, *Centinel*, and the *Federal Farmer*.

Although the antifederalists did not succeed in preventing ratification of the Constitution, they did prevent two states, North Carolina and Rhode Island, from ratifying immediately. In addition, their objection to the omission of a bill of rights was powerful enough to force supporters of the Constitution to ultimately promise that a bill of rights would be submitted to Congress and the states almost immediately upon ratification. James Madison made good on this promise when he introduced a proposed bill of rights to Congress on June 4, 1789.

The second antifederalist movement was of a different character. It arose in the early part of the 1790s and was largely a movement in opposition to the centralizing policies of the administration George Washington, as represented by fiscal and economic program put forth by Treasury Secretary Alexander Hamilton. In general, these later antifederalists opposed Hamilton's broad construction of the constitutional text, which he used to support the establishment of a national bank and the assumption of state and continental debts. They also opposed Hamilton's desire to use federal fiscal and economic policy to support commercial interests, strengthen trade relations with Great Britain, and increase the public debt. In time, the objections of this antifederalist movement provided the impetus for the creation of a new political party under the leadership of Thomas Jefferson, called the "Republican" party, in opposition to Hamilton's "Federalists."

## Bank of The United States

In his *Report on the Public Credit* of December 14, 1791, Treasury Secretary Alexander Hamilton proposed a number of measures designed to stabilize the national government's fiscal affairs. One aspect of this program was the creation of a national bank. This bank would serve as the national government's chief fiscal agent as well as assisting in the collection of taxes. In addition, notes issued by the bank would serve as a convenient currency, an economic measure that was particularly desirable in an economy woefully short of specie. Perhaps most important, however, was the idea that the bank would provide a number of services to the mercantile community including the provision of loans for economic development projects.

Legislation creating the bank was introduced in Congress on January 3, 1791. The bill passed the Senate on January 20, but soon became bogged down in the House. Many members harbored doubts about the wisdom of creating a large government bank that would have the power to greatly influence the economy. Others raised constitutional objections. Led by James Madison, opponents of the bank argued that Congress lacked the power to charter a bank because the federal government was one of limited powers. Supporters of the bill argued, however, that the Constitution's "necessary and proper clause" authorized Congress to take any act that would assist in implementing one of the powers specifically assigned to the federal government.

The federalist-dominated House eventually passed the bank bill and forwarded it to President Washington for signature. Before signing, however, Washington asked members of the cabinet to provide advise on the constitutionality of the bank bill. This request generated a series of very remarkable letters containing a fascinating debate about the powers of the national government. Attorney General Edmund Randolph and Thomas Jefferson urged Washington to veto the bill on the grounds that the word "necessary" as used in the constitutional text should be interpreted to mean "absolutely" or "indispensably" necessary, which would mean that a bank could not be chartered unless it was "required" in order to implement one of Congress' other powers. Treasury Secretary Hamilton rejected this interpretation, arguing instead that the term should be construed to mean "needful, requisite, incidental, useful, [or] conducive to" the exercise of federal powers.

In the end, Washington signed the bank bill on February 25, 1791. However, the debate over the constitutionality of the bank may be seen as the origin of what was later to become known the doctrine of "strict construction."

## Battle of Fallen Timbers (1794)

The Battle of Fallen Timbers has been called the "last battle of the American Revolution." It was fought on August 20, 1794, between an Army led by General "Mad" Anthony Wayne and a confederacy of Indian tribes who opposed American expansion into the territory of the Ohio River valley.

The battle's name is taken from the fact that it was fought amidst a pile of trees toppled by a tornado just north of the Maumee River in present-day Maumee, Ohio. The American army had been dispatched to the territory by President Washington to build a series of forts between the Ohio and Maumee Rivers. While en route, Wayne's army was met by 1,000 warriors led by a Miami war chief, named Little Turtle, and accompanied by the Shawnee chief Blue Jacket and the Delaware chief Buckongahelas.

It is estimated that fewer than 100 men died on either side, but at the end of the day it was clear that the Americans had been victorious. This victory resulted in the signing of the Treaty of Greenville in 1795, which established a boundary line (later called the "Greenville Treaty Line") between Indian lands and territory open for white settlement. This line was soon breached by white settlers, however, but after Fallen Timbers, the Indians' ability to prevent these incursions was limited.

## Bill of Rights

In drafting their own constitutions, most states enumerated a list of rights that were regarded as fundamental. Among these were guaranteeing the right to free speech and the free exercise of religion, as well as restrictions on the power of government. The original version of the Constitution produced by the Philadelphia Convention in 1787 did not contain a bill of rights, an omission that caused immediate controversy. Antifederalists seized on this omission and urged rejection of the Constitution until a bill of rights was included in the text. For their part, federalists asserted that a bill of rights was unnecessary because the proposed national government had only very limited powers and could not infringe upon the rights of the people.

Ratification of the Constitution was largely achieved after federalists in several state ratifying conventions promised to introduce a bill of rights once the new Congress convened. Virginia's James Madison made good on that promise in April 1789 when he introduced a list of amendments to the Constitution shortly after the first Congress convened. Based on Virginia's 1776 Bill of Rights, Madison's amendments contained protections for speech and religion, as well as providing protections to an accused in criminal actions. After making certain revisions, Congress submitted a proposed list of twelve amendments to the states in September 1791. Of these, only ten received the required ratification of three-fourths of the states by 1791.

## Continental/Confederation Congress

The First Continental Congress convened in Philadelphia's Carpenters Hall on September 5, 1774. The idea for a meeting of delegates from all the colonies was advanced a year earlier by Benjamin Franklin in response to British actions taken after the Boston Tea Party. Only twelve of the then-existing thirteen colonies sent delegates. Georgia, which was then suffering from repeated Indian attacks on the western frontier, declined to participate because it feared that the royal government might withdraw the troops on whom the colony relied for its defense. Among the delegates in attendance at this first session were some of the most prominent men in the colonies, including Samuel Adams, Patrick Henry, Richard Henry Lee, George Washington, John Jay, and John Dickinson.

This first session of Congress did not advocate independence from Britain. Instead, it focused its energies on attempting to secure a fair hearing for American grievances in London. As a result, during this session, Congress considered a number of measures designed to reconfigure the United States's relationship with the Mother Country. These included the "Galloway Plan" of union, which would have created an American parliament to govern the colonies in conjunction with the Parliament at Westminster. Congress could not agree on this plan because delegates were sharply divided on whether continued union with England was desirable. In the end, the delegates took two concrete steps: First, they composed a petition to the King setting forth the colonists' views of their rights as Englishmen and their grievances. Second, in an effort to put pressure on the ministry in London, Congress adopted the "Continental Association," which called for a boycott of British goods. The First Continental Congress adjourned in late October 1774, agreeing to reconvene in the spring 1775, if colonial grievances had not been adequately addressed.

The outbreak of hostilities at Lexington and Concord in April 1775 resulted in a new Congress reconvening in Philadelphia in May of that year. This "Second Continental Congress" was presided over by Massachusetts' John Hancock, and was forced to confront the fact that the United States was now in open revolt. Congress's first task was to take control of the rough and tumble American army now forming outside of Boston, and thus on June 23, it appointed George Washington as commander-in-chief. Congress also urged the various states to begin to form governments in those places where the royal government now ceased to function.

As in the First Congress, many of the delegates did not necessarily believe that a complete break with England was desirable. Instead, led by Pennsylvania's John Dickinson, these delegates argued that Congress should continue to find some way of reconciling with England. During the summer of 1775, Congress sought to justify the United States's action, again dispatching an address to the king, which has come to be known as the "Olive Branch Petition." When this petition failed to receive a response, Congress drafted a second remonstrance entitled "Declaration of the Causes and Necessity of Taking up Arms" in which it openly raised the possibility of independence for the colonies.

The Crown's refusal to consider the colonists' grievances ultimately resulted in Congress declaring American independence in July 1776. Thereafter, its efforts were directed toward winning the war with England and securing international recognition for the new government. Yet, while the various states were able to band together for the purpose of waging war, they were largely unable to agree on much beyond that necessity, as Congress remained largely a collection of ambassadors from sovereign states. In these early years, therefore, the Congress lacked the power to pass legislation that was binding on the states. Instead, it had to content itself with passing nonbinding resolutions requesting that the states take, or refrain from taking, a particular action. In addition, lacking the power to tax, Congress was limited to making requests for funding or supplies from the states, but the states were free to disregard or alter these requests as they saw fit.

The impotence resulted in various calls for strengthening Congress' powers. As a result, in July 1776, the delegates appointed John Dickinson to head a committee to draft a plan of union. The result was the Articles of Confederation and Perpetual Union, adopted by Congress in 1777, but not ratified by the various states until 1781— after hostilities had almost come to an end. While the Articles put Congress on a more regular footing, they failed to remedy the most serious defects in the government. Congress remained unable to regulate trade, impose taxes, or adequately enforce its resolutions.

With the formal end of war with England in 1783, Congress proved ineffective in dealing with the severe economic problems that followed. Over time, many delegates simply failed to appear, and Congress was occasionally forced to adjourn for lack of a quorum. The defects of the "Confederation Congress" convinced many that a stronger national government was necessary. As a result, the Confederation Congress put in motion its own demise by calling for a convention to meet at Philadelphia in the spring of 1787 for the purpose of "revising" the Articles of Confederation. This convention, which met from May through September 1787, produced the document that would ultimately become the United States, which on ratification put the Confederation Congress out of business.

## Convention of Mortefontaine

The years 1798–1799 were marked by ongoing conflict between the United States and France. One feature of this conflict was the "Quasi-War" in which vessels of both countries attacked each other on the high seas. In an effort to bring an end to the conflict, President Adams dispatched a delegation composed of Chief Justice Oliver Ellsworth, William R. Davie, and William Vans Murray to France to negotiate a peace. Aware that the conflict was detrimental to the interests of both countries, France agreed to discuss an end to hostilities, which culminated in the Convention of 1800, which was signed at Mortefontaine.

Historians have been rather ambivalent about the actual terms of the treaty, generally concluding that the United States sacrificed much in exchange for minor concessions on the part of France. For example, the United States agreed to relinquish approximately $12 million in claims by U.S. citizens against France for destruction caused to American ships and cargo in exchange for little more than a promise to end hostilities. In the end, however, while most observes believed that the nation might have held out for a better deal, Americans were relieved to see the end of hostilities and the need for taxes to support the ongoing war effort.

Bank of the United States

## Court of Appeals in Cases of Capture

It was not long after the outbreak of hostilities between England and her colonies in April 1775 that the Continental Congress recognized the need to create courts that would be competent to adjudicate matters of prize taken on the high seas. In fact, General Washington wrote Congress in 1775 recommending that some court be established to handle cases of ships taken as prize on the high seas. Congress agreed with Washington that the law of war dictated the need for some court to determine the fate of "such vessels and cargoes belonging to the enemy, as shall fall into the hands of, or be taken by inhabitants of the United Colonies." Congress eventually passed a resolution recommending that each of the states establish a prize court and providing that appeals from the state courts would be reviewed by Congress.

From 1776 to 1780, appeals were handled by various committees of Congress. However, as the volume of appeals grew, the committee was eventually replaced by a court called the Court of Appeals in Cases of Capture. The court was composed of three permanent judges who received salaries from the continental Congress. By the end, the court had disposed of all the cases that had come before it, with the result that Congress suspended salary payments to the judges in 1785. The court was briefly reconvened in 1786, and its last session was held on May 16, 1787.

Problems with the prize court system were apparent almost from the start. Most states provided that prize cases would be heard by juries, which meant that captors often brought their claims of prize before juries in their home states. As a result, state court juries frequently rendered verdicts that favored local captains and shipowners and violated the rights of neutrals.

Congress's reservation of authority to hear appeals proved to be an illusory protection. In the first place, states retained the right to determine how appeals might be taken to Congress, and many states severely limited the circumstances under which cases might be taken up on appeal. Even when an appeal was allowed, Congress had difficulty enforcing its decrees in those cases where it reversed the state court verdict. Throughout the war years, states frequently defied Congress and simply refused to comply with congressional decisions, which conflicted with verdicts rendered by state court juries. Many of these cases involved the capture of foreign vessels, with the result that Congress was repeatedly besieged by complaints from foreign governments that the rights of their citizens were being trampled upon.

By the end of the war, many both inside and out of government were concerned about the problems posed by allowing state courts to hear admiralty cases. As a result, when the subject of courts and their jurisdiction came up in the constitutional convention, the experience with the state prize courts was no doubt in many members' minds when the constitutional convention took up the question of admiralty jurisdiction.

## Excise Act (1791)

A key part of Alexander Hamilton's economic program called for the assumption of state debts by the federal government. Having taken on this debt, it was now necessary for the federal government to devise some means by which the debt could be retired. The result was the Excise Act of 1790. This act provided for a tax on domestically distilled spirits and established an elaborate system of collection. Its enforcement engendered protests in the back country, eventually leading to the Whiskey Rebellion of 1794.

## Farewell Address (1796)

George Washington was the nearly unanimous choice to be the first president of the United States. In fact, it is believed that many potential opponents of the federal Constitution only supported ratification on the assumption that Washington would be the new nation's first leader. In his first term, Washington seemed to justify the faith placed in him by so many of his contemporaries. He skillfully guided the nation through several early crises, most importantly keeping the new nation from being dragged into the continuing series of wars plaguing Europe.

Washington's cabinet was a fractious group, however. Treasury Secretary Alexander Hamilton's economic program provoked opposition from Secretary of State Jefferson. Hamilton and Jefferson also had differing views on the proper role the United States should adopt in the war between England and France. Hamilton urged greater support for England, the United States's historic trading partner, while Jefferson believed that the United States should support a sister republic in its battle with monarchy. Neither Jefferson nor Hamilton believed that the United States should abandon its policy of neutrality, however.

In time, the differences between Hamilton and Jefferson began to take on a partisan cast. Hamilton came to lead what was soon referred to as the Federalist party, while Jefferson's followers took to calling themselves "Republicans." Although President Washington attempted to steer clear of direct association with either party, it seems that he was generally inclined to adopt the Federalist position on many matters.

After eight years in office, Washington was determined to retire to Mount Vernon. As he prepared to leave office, he decided to draft an address to the nation in which he would attempt to provide some guidance for the nation in both domestic and international affairs. Of particular concern to Washington was the increasing partisanship that was taking hold in the government. Washington believed that the rise of political parties was unhealthy for a democracy. He, therefore, urged his contemporaries to put aside their differences and unite for the common good. In addition, Washington implored his readers to steer clear of foreign attachments. The country, he said, the United States should have free and open commerce with all, and must avoid being drawn into "entangling alliances" with foreign nations.

Contrary to popular belief, however, Washington did not recommend a policy of isolationism. Instead, he noted that the United States's treaty of alliance with France had provided some benefits, but he also reminded his readers of the difficulties that the treaty had posed during the early years of his administration. Washington thus cautioned the United States's leaders to "act for ourselves and not for others."

The "Farewell Address" was instantly regarded as a classic of American political thought. It was read annually in Congress for many years and was printed in schoolbooks for generations. For almost 150 years, the address provided the justification for the United States's traditional isolationism. As a result, it was not until 1949 that the United States would sign a treaty of alliance with a foreign government.

## Federalism

Federalism is commonly regarded as system of government organization in which a group of states or political entities are bound together in a compact in which sovereign power is constitutionally divided between a central government and the constituent political units. This distribution of powers is the essence of federalism and ensures that sovereign power is divided in such a way as to prevent any political unit from exercising complete authority over all subjects.

Prior to the ratification of the Constitution in 1788, each American state was largely sovereign, except to the extent it has surrendered some of its powers to the government created by the Articles of Confederation. The Constitution established a more definite form of federalism based on the doctrine of "enumerated powers." This doctrine holds that the formerly sovereign states have collectively delegated certain powers to the national government (such as the power to wage war or coin money), and the national government is sovereign when it acts pursuant to those delegated powers. For their part, the states retain their sovereignty in all areas not specifically ceded to the national government. Both the states and the national government thus share sovereignty, with each being free to exercise power in its respective realm, although there are areas where the two sovereignties share power.

## Federalist, The

*The Federalist* is the name given to a collection of 85 articles written for newspapers in New York arguing for ratification of the Constitution. The articles were written by Alexander Hamilton, James Madison, and John Jay, under the pseudonym *Publius*, between October 1787 and April 1788. The first thirty-six articles were published in book form in March 1788, with the remainder printed in a second volume in May of the same year.

After the Philadelphia Convention finished its work in September 1787, a number of antifederalist critics took to the newspapers to urge rejection of the proposed Constitution. Among the most important of these were essays published by *Cato* and *Brutus*, both of whom argued that the Constitution was subversive to the powers of the states and dangerous to the liberties of the citizenry. At the time, New York was essential to the ratification process, not only because of its size and economic strength, but also because it was located at the very centre of the new nation. If New York failed to ratify, the nation would be split into two geographic sections.

Fearful of the strength of the anti-federalist opposition, Alexander Hamilton began the series in October 1787. His goal was to both explain the text and structure of the proposed Constitution as well as demonstrate its superiority over the Articles of Confederation. At bottom, however, he sought to "give a satisfactory answer to all the objections" what had thus far been raised by the Constitution's opponents. In keeping with the contemporary conceit, Hamilton chose a Roman pseudonym to disguise his authorship. The name, *Publius*, was taken from Publius Valerius, one of the founders of the Roman republic. Hamilton wrote the bulk of the essays, although the exact number has been a subject of some dispute. It is generally believed that Hamilton wrote 52, Madison 28, and Jay 5.

## French Revolution

The French Revolution is generally regarded as a turning point in the political history of Europe. Beginning in 1789 and lasting until Napolean's coup d'etat brought an end to the First Republic in 1799, the revolution resulted in a drastic restructuring in almost all aspects of French society.

A number of causes are said to have inspired the revolution. There was, of course, a generalized desire for liberty and personal freedom, and a long-standing resentment of nobility and privilege, and a deep-seated hostility to the powers of the church. Economic factors also loomed large, however. The movement to revolution was accelerated by an increasingly poor economic situation caused by a very heavy national debt requiring ever-larger tax increases on the populace. In addition, there was widespread famine and food scarcity in the months just preceding the outbreak of revolution.

The French Revolution had its immediate origins in the meeting of the Estates General called for May 1789. The Estates was a body traditionally composed of the clergy (the First Estate), the Second Estate (the nobility), and the Third Estate (the bourgeoisie). King Louis XVI summoned the Estates General in order to obtain their consent to a new tax structure necessary to alleviate a severe economic dislocation caused by France's burdensome national debt. Shortly after convening in the spring of 1789, the Third Estate voted to constitute itself as the "National Assembly," and declared that this new body would now conduct France's political affairs with or without the other Estates. In time, the clergy and a large portion of the nobility decided to join in this body, ultimately allowing this new body to reconstitute itself as the National Constituent Assembly.

On July 11, 1789, the king dismissed those ministers in the government who supported reform. This action convinced many that a royal coup was in the works. Consequently, the people of Paris attacked the Bastille. Although the prison held only seven prisoners at the time (four forgers, two lunatics, and a rapist), its fall was a power symbol of the coming of the end of the *ancien regime*. Revolutionary spirit spread through the countryside, and an agrarian insurrection commenced in earnest.

Over the next few years, the National Constituent Assembly abolished feudalism, disestablished the church, and proclaimed a Declaration of the Rights of Man. The Assembly also drafted a constitution providing for a government akin to a constitutional monarchy. This new constitution created a new Legislative Assembly, which would have primary law-making authority, although the king would have the power to appoint ministers and would retain a limited veto power.

War with Prussia and Austria in 1792 created havoc in French politics, with royalists and radical republicans attempting to channel the chaos of war to their own ends. In August 1792, a group of insurgents took the king and queen prisoner. A short time later, the National Assembly was declared dissolved, and a new government called the Convention took power. The Convention eventually created a new system of government with legislative power resting in a National Convention and executive power given to a Committee of Public Safety.

Meanwhile, the Prussian and Austrian monarchies threatened war on the people of France should they fail to re-install Louis XVI on the throne of France. This "Brunswick Manifesto" merely hastened the king's death as many in the government believed that Louis would conspire with foreign monarchs to subvert the rights of the people of France. Louis XVI and his queen, Marie Antoinette, were subsequently condemned to death and executed (1793).

In time, the Committee of Public Safety came under the control of Maximilien Robespierre, who led the Jacobins (radical revolutionaries) in the Reign of Terror (1793–1794). Over 1,200 people went to their deaths on the guillotine for "counter-revolutionary activity." Eventually, however, the people of France rejected the extremism of the Reign of Terror. Robespierre was eventually overthrown and a new government, the Directory, took control. The Directory governed France for four years, although it became increasingly unpopular. In time, Napoleon Bonaparte, commanding the French army in Paris, successfully suppressed opposition to the Directory, while gaining a great deal of power for himself. Finally, on November 9, 1799, Bonaparte staged a coup himself, taking power and bringing an end to France's First Republic.

## Fries's Rebellion

In 1798, the United States appeared to be heading toward war with France. Congress voted to authorize the construction of several new armed ships for the Navy, the building of fortifications along the coast, and an increase in the size of the Army. In order to finance part of these measures, Congress imposed a direct tax of $2 million dollars on the states. The tax was to be levied on houses, land, and slaves. Pennsylvania's portion of the tax was roughly $237,000, but because there were relatively few slaves in the state, the tax was largely assessed against houses. The value of a dwelling was based upon the number of windows it had.

The tax was controversial, particularly among Pennsylvania's German population. Almost immediately after its provisions became known, Pennsylvanians began to resist. Led by John Fries (1764–1825), an itinerant auctioneer, a group of farmers organized themselves to oppose attempts by assessors to determine the value of properties in the southeastern part of the state. In March 1799, the governor of Pennsylvania called out the militia to put down the revolt, and Fries and several others were arrested and brought to trial in Philadelphia. They were eventually convicted and sentenced to death for treason, but President Adams pardoned them in April 1800. Fries's Rebellion is also occasionally called the "hot water rebellion" in recognition of the practice of pouring hot water on the heads of those sent to determine the value of houses.

## Genet, Edmond Charles (1763–1834)

Edmund Charles Genet was born in Versailles to Edme' Jacques Genet, a specialist in Anglo-American affairs in the French foreign ministry. The Genet family was relatively well connected, moving in *philosphe* circles and being acquainted with Benjamin Franklin during his time in Paris.

Genet inherited his father's office in the foreign ministry in 1781 and was subsequently appointed secretary to the French mission in St. Petersburg. After the outbreak of the French Revolution in 1789, Genet was appointed charge' d'affaires, but his republican leanings so offended the Empress Catherine II (the Great) that Genet was recalled in 1792. He returned to Paris where he was welcomed by the Girondinist government, which had taken power after the arrest of Louis XVI.

The French government dispatched Genet to the United States in early 1793, and he arrived in South Carolina as minister plenipotentiary. Genet and his government assumed that the United States and France should form a republican alliance against monarchist tyranny. While they did not expect that the United States would join the war in Europe, they did expect that the American government would offer France the same kind of financial and logistical support it has received from Versailles during the American Revolution. Genet's instructions included securing a renegotiation of the 1778 Treaty of Alliance, repayment of the United States's war debt to France, and the outfitting of privateers to harass British shipping. He was also instructed to explore the possibility of enlisting American aid for an expedition against Spanish interests in Louisiana and Florida.

For its part, the American government had been deliberating the appropriate posture toward France long before Genet's arrival in the United States. Treasury Secretary Alexander Hamilton was opposed to any action that would disrupt trade relations between the United States and Great Britain and so warned against providing any assistance to France. Hamilton argued that the 1778 Treaty of Alliance was made with the French king and that upon his death, the treaty was void. Secretary of State Thomas Jefferson, who generally supported France's revolutionary aims, argued that treaties were made between countries, not heads of state, and, therefore, the treaty remained in force. Genet's arrival in the United States forced President Washington to confront the problem head on. Washington ultimately decided to receive Genet as French minister, thereby recognizing the revolutionary government, and implicitly the validity of the 1778 treaty. At the same time, however, Washington issued his now-famous Neutrality Proclamation in which he declared the United States's intention to remain neutral in the war between France and the other European powers.

Citizen Genet had other ideas, however, and was determined to pursue his aims regardless of the American government's proclaimed neutrality. Almost as soon as he arrived on American soil, Genet began issuing commissions to privateers and assisted in outfitting them to prey on British shipping. He also began planning for an attack on Spanish possessions. During his six-week trip from Charleston to the national capital in Philadelphia, Genet was greeted by enthusiastic crowds professing support for the French republic. Genet took this reception as proof that the American public did not agree with the administration's policy of neutrality, and so took steps to make direct appeals to the people.

His continued defiance of the rules against outfitting privateers and his interference in domestic politics caused even Jefferson to abandon the French minister. In July 1793, President Washington asked for Genet's recall. France's new Jacobin government was only too happy to accede to Washington's request, and dispatched a new minister, Joseph Fauchet, who arrived in the United States in February 1794 with a warrant for Genet's arrest. Realizing that Genet's return to France would result in his execution, Washington refused to assist in having the former minister deported. Genet was permitted to remain in the United States and eventually married Cornelia Clinton, daughter of New York's governor George Clinton. He eventually became an American citizen and spent the rest of his life avoiding politics and working on various scientific projects. He died in Schodack, New York.

## Gerry, Elbridge (1744–1814)

Elbridge Gerry was born in Marblehead, Massachusetts, to the son of a prominent local merchant. Gerry was educated at Harvard College, and upon graduation, he entered the family business. Appalled by the Boston Massacre, Gerry entered local politics in 1770, and was elected a member of the Massachusetts General Court in 1772. It was there that he met his guide and mentor, Samuel Adams. With Adams's support, Gerry became a member of the Massachusetts Committee of Correspondence in 1773, and was the author of the famous Circular Letter.

In 1774, Gerry was elected a member of the Massachusetts Provincial Congress, where he served on the committee of supply as well as the committee of safety. Gerry was responsible for preparing supplies for the groups of minutemen then forming in the colony. Some of these stores were assembled in Lexington and Concord and became the object of the British raid on those towns in April 1775.

Gerry was elected a member of the Second Continental Congress in 1776, where he emerged as one of the earliest and most vociferous advocates of independence. He remained in Congress until 1785, when he retired from public life. The following year, he married and settled in Cambridge, Massachusetts. The outbreak of Shays' Rebellion later that year convinced Gerry that a stronger national government was required if the new nation was to survive. He was thus elected as one of Massachusetts' representatives to the Constitutional Convention in Philadelphia.

In the convention, Gerry was regarded as something of a moderate. He was deeply suspicious of the more democratic schemes of government, but he also feared that a powerful central government posed a danger to the people's liberties. While Gerry contributed in significant ways to what became the final draft of the Constitution, he ultimately refused to sign it when completed by the Convention in September 1787. He believed that the document had three central flaws: In his view, the lacking a bill of rights meant that personal liberties were insecure. He also believed that the document should have provided for a more balanced sharing of power between the states and the central government. In addition, he thought that the national government had been given too much military power. Gerry strongly supported ratification in spite of his refusal to sign, however. He was elected a member of Congress and ultimately helped shape the Bill of Rights.

In 1787, President Adams made Gerry one of the commissioners charged with negotiating a peaceful solution to the ongoing conflict with France. Along with John Marshall and Charles Coatesworth Pinckney, Gerry spent several long months in France attempting to negotiate with the French. The demand by Talleyrand and his agents for bribes, in what has become known as the "X,Y,Z Affair" caused Marshall and Pinckney to leave France and return to the United States. Gerry, however, remained in Paris much to the disgust of his colleagues. In the end, however, Gerry's refusal to leave paid dividends as he was later able to provide assurances that France had changed its position and was willing to negotiate an end to the Quasi-War.

Gerry was elected governor of Massachusetts from 1810 to 1812. It was during his second term as governor that Gerry helped enact a bill providing for the redrawing Massachusetts senatorial district lines in a bizarre fashion. One of these districts was said to look like a salamander, and one wag declared that it was a "Gerrymander." As a result, the practice of drawing the boundaries of electoral districts for political advantage has long since been dubbed "gerrymandering."

In 1812, Gerry was elected Vice President of the United States on the same ticket with James Madison. He served only two years of his term and died in office in 1814.

## Hamilton, Alexander (1757–1804)

Alexander Hamilton was born on the island of Nevis, in the British West Indies. His father deserted the family when Alexander was eight, and his mother died three years later. Hamilton was apprenticed to a commercial firm and proved to be so gifted in business that he eventually took charge of the company's operations. When he was fifteen, Hamilton departed for the mainland and eventually enrolled at King's College (now Columbia University).

While in New York, Hamilton found himself drawn to the centre of revolutionary activity. He spoke at several public rallies and wrote several political tracts during the winter of 1774–1775. With the outbreak of war, he helped organize an artillery company and was eventually commissioned a captain in the Continental Army. Hamilton's organizational skills brought him to General Washington's notice, and he was later appointed as one of Washington's aides-de-camp. He served in this capacity until being granted a field command in 1781.

Hamilton's service in the military convinced him that the current form of government was untenable, and he believed that Congress's inability to adequately provision or direct the army put the republic itself in danger. After the war, he returned to New York to engage in the practice of law. In July 1782, Hamilton was appointed a member of the confederation Congress, where he repeatedly urged that the Articles of Confederation be amended to provide Congress with an independent source of revenue.

Hamilton's law practice flourished, and he quickly became a leading member of the bar. He was elected a delegate to the Constitutional Convention in Philadelphia, but attended its sessions only rather intermittently and had a negligible effect on its proceedings. During the course of the proceedings, however, Hamilton made a remarkable speech in which he proposed a president and senate elected for life and a house of representatives elected for three-year terms. While he did not advocate a monarchy, as many critics later charged, Hamilton did urge that the United States "ought to go as far [as monarchy as possible] in order to attain stability and permancy, as republican principles would admit."

Although Hamilton's views had little impact on the final form of the constitution, his efforts during the ratification debate were indispensable. It is said that he recruited John Jay and James Madison to author a series of essays under the collective pseudonym, *Publius*, urging ratification of the proposed Constitution. These essays were printed in newspapers in New York and reprinted throughout the states. They were extremely influential in amassing support for the Constitution in New York, a state that was crucial to ratification and that boasted substantial antifederalist sentiment. These essays were eventually collected under the title *The Federalist*, and remain an important reference for interpretation of the Constitution today.

President Washington appointed Hamilton as the first Secretary of the Treasury in 1789, and it is in this position that Hamilton made what might be his greatest contribution to American government. Hamilton had an acute mind, full of numerous schemes and devices for encouraging commerce and industry. In 1790, Hamilton put forth a plan to pay off the debts incurred by both the Continental Congress and the various states during the course of the Revolution. His goal in doing so was twofold: First, Hamilton believed that paying off that part of the debt owed to foreigners was essential to establishing the United States's credit overseas. He was concerned that defaulting of debts due to foreigners would impede the new nation's ability to obtain future credit, which would be essential to the development of the country's economy and infrastructure. Second, Hamilton believed that having the federal government "assume" the debts of the states would engender support for the new Constitution among the commercial segment of society. If those owed state debts were able to receive a return from the federal government, they would surely become supporters of the new federal system.

Hamilton's "assumption plan" was controversial required some method of funding. He proposed paying off the federal government's new debt through increased excise taxes, especially on whiskey, and duties on imported goods. The tax on whiskey was especially controversial and ultimately resulted in what has since become known as the Whiskey Rebellion.

The apex of Hamilton's financial plan was his proposal for the creation of a national bank. Hamilton believed that a bank would help the nation's economy by issuing notes that would serve as a convenient form of currency, an economic measure that was particularly desirable in an economy woefully short of specie. In addition, Hamilton expected that the bank would provide a number of services to the mercantile community including the provision of loans for economic development projects.

Hamilton's economic plans were opposed by many both in and out of Congress. Among the most vocal opponents were Thomas Jefferson, then Secretary of State, and James Madison, who was then a member of the House of Representatives. Opponents argued that the assumption plan penalized states that had already paid off large portions of their revolutionary debt. They argued that these states would wind up not only paying off their debt but that of states which had done little or nothing to pay off their own debt.

Jefferson and Madison also argued that the assumption plan was unfair in that it favored the interests of commercial speculators over the original holders of the debt. Of particular concern in this regard were Revolutionary War soldiers and others who had received certificates from the states or Congress for providing services or supplies to the Continental Army. Many of these had long ago given up hope that they would receive money in exchange for the certificates and thus had sold them to speculators at pennies on the dollar. Jefferson and Madison argued for discrimination between original holders of the certificates and speculators. They demanded that those who had borne the brunt of supporting the revolutionary cause ought to receive full value and that speculators should only receive some discounted amount. Hamilton opposed discrimination both because he believed it impractical and because he believed the paying the full face value of the nation's securities was essential to restoring public confidence in the national government.

In the end, the basic elements of Hamilton's economic plan were enacted into law. The controversy over his plans became the genesis of a growing party conflict. Those who opposed Hamilton's economic program also found themselves allied in opposition to other elements of the administration's policy. In time, these opponents came to be known as "Republicans" while those who supported Hamilton and the Washington administration's program came to be called "Federalists."

Hamilton resigned as Secretary of the Treasury in January 1795. Thereafter, he returned to the private practice of law in New York City. Hamilton clashed with President Adams who believed that Hamilton exercised too great an influence on the cabinet even after he had resigned his office. With the outbreak of the Quasi-War in 1798, President Washington was called from retirement to lead an expanded American Army. Washington made it a condition of his appointment that Hamilton be named second-in-command. Adams reluctantly had to agree.

For his part, Hamilton believed that Adams was too emotionally unstable to be the commander-in-chief. As a result, during the presidential campaign of 1800, Hamilton was involved in a number of schemes to replace Adams as the nominee of the

Federalist party and substitute another candidate in his place. Hamilton ultimately authored a pamphlet that was highly critical of Adams during the course of the campaign. The publication of the pamphlet caused a split in the party, which probably damaged Adams' chances of re-election.

With Thomas Jefferson's election to the presidency in 1800, Hamilton continued his involvement in New York state politics. Sometime in 1804, Hamilton was confronted by Vice President Aaron Burr and accused of having made defamatory statements about the vice president. Although representatives of both Burr and Hamilton met to try to defuse the controversy, Burr and Hamilton ultimately met in a duel along the banks of the Hudson River in Weehawken, New Jersey, on July 11, 1804. Hamilton was mortally wounded in the duel and died the following day.

## Jacobin

The term "jacobin" originally referred to the Jacobin Club in France, the most famous of the various political clubs that arose in the aftermath of the French Revolution. The club was formed at Versailles by a group of Breton deputies to the Estates General of 1789, and thus was originally called the Club Breton. Among its most prominent members were Jean-Paul Marat and Robespierre.

At its foundation, the club was originally marked by some degree of moderation, but in time, it began to be the centre of a more extreme brand of radical politics. During the Reign of Terror, the Jacobin Club became one of the most powerful institutions in revolutionary France, boasting a membership of almost 500,000 in at least 5,500 branches throughout the country.

With the end of the Reign of Terror in 1794, the club was closed and some of its most famous members, including Robespierre, were executed.

The excesses of the revolution supported by the Jacobin Club eventually led to the coining of a new pejorative. By the end of the 1790s, the term "jacobin" was used to refer to radical politicians of all stripes. In the United States, Federalists often accused Republicans of supporting "jacobinism."

## Jay's Treaty

Throughout the early 1790s, it looked as though war between the United States and Great Britain was imminent. In the United States, a certain degree of resentment remained after the Revolution, which was exacerbated by Britain's practice of stopping American ships on the high seas and occasionally detaining or impressing American seamen. For its part, the British government repeatedly complained that Americans were actively engaged in supporting the French in the war with England that had raged throughout the early part of the 1790s. Various British officials had long complained that French privateers appeared to be using American ports as a base of operations to attack British shipping. Great Britain thus justified the stopping of American ships on the grounds that America had violated its own neutrality by assisting the French.

In an effort to avoid war, President Washington decided to send a mission to Great Britain to negotiate a treaty of "amity and commerce," and chose Chief Justice John Jay to serve as "minister plenipotentiary." Jay's nomination was somewhat controversial since he was the sitting Chief Justice of the United States at the time of his nomination. At the same time, Jay was had a great deal of experience in diplomatic affairs. During the Revolution, Jay had served as minister to Spain and was named as one of the commissioners to negotiate a peace treaty with England. After the war, Jay served as secretary of foreign affairs in the Confederation Congress. The Senate approved Jay's nomination, and Jay set sail for England in the spring of 1794.

Washington hoped that Jay might be able to negotiate a treaty that would open the British West Indies to American ships and resolve several issues left over from the Revolution. These included getting the British to evacuate forts on the frontier, obtaining compensation for American planters whose slaves were taken by the British, and compensating Americans whose ships had been confiscated by the British on the high seas.

In the end, Jay was unable to deliver on all these issues, although he did achieve some success. The British agreed to evacuate the forts on the frontier and to provide some compensation to American ship owners. However, England refused to open the ports in the West Indies to Americans. The British also refused to provide compensation to Americans whose slaves were taken by the British army unless the United States agreed to compensate Loyalists for property confiscated by the various states during after the Revolution.

"Jay's Treaty" was submitted to the Senate on June 8, 1795, and was ratified a few months later on a largely party-line vote. Within a short time, however, the provisions of the treaty were made public, and many of those who had earlier supported war with Great Britain condemned the treaty as a "sell out" to British interests. John Jay was vilified in speeches and demonstrations around the country, so much so that he later commented that he could have found his way home to New York by the light of his burning effigies.

### Jefferson, Thomas (1743–1826)

Thomas Jefferson was born on April 13, 1743, in Albemarle County, Virginia, the son of Peter Jefferson and Jane Randolph Jefferson. His mother was a member of one of the first families of Virginia, while his father was a wealthy landowner in his own right. Jefferson was educated at the College of William and Mary, and then studied law under

George Wythe. In January 1, 1772, Jefferson married Martha Wayles Skelton, and together they had six children, only two of whom survived into adulthood.

In 1769, Jefferson was elected a member of the House of Burgesses, where he served for six years. In 1774, he authored a pamphlet entitled, *A Summary View of the Rights of British America,* in which he argued that Americans' allegiance to the British Crown was essentially voluntary. The pamphlet helped earn Jefferson a reputation as a novel political thinker with the result that he was eventually elected to the Second Continental Congress, then meeting at Philadelphia.

On June 11, 1776, Jefferson was appointed to a committee of five to draft a Declaration of Independence. Although Jefferson was the primary drafter of the Declaration, both Benjamin Franklin and John Adams assisted him in various drafts. The final draft was then thoroughly revised by the full Congress. Jefferson's authorship of the Declaration brought him international fame, although he himself later admitted that it was merely intended to be "an expression of the American mind."

Jefferson left Congress in late 1776 and was elected to the House of Delegates, where he served until 1779. In June 1779, he introduced a bill providing for religious liberty, which created a firestorm of controversy because until this time, no state had provided for religious liberty. The text of the bill provided that "all men shall be free to profess, and by argument to maintain, their opinions on matters of religion, and that the same shall in no wise diminish, enlarge, or affect their civil capacities." The bill was so controversial that it did not pass until 1786.

In June 1779, Jefferson was elected governor of Virginia, although his tenure as governor was marked by controversy. He was criticized for failing to provide adequate defenses for the city of Richmond, which fell to the British in 1780. He was also accused of cowardice when he fled the city shortly before a British patrol attempted to capture him. Jefferson resigned as governor in 1781, and the Virginia legislature ultimately appointed a committee of enquiry into his conduct while as governor. In the end, Jefferson was exonerated, but the episode left a bitter taste in his mouth, so much so that he seemed to harbor resentments about his treatment for many years after.

Jefferson returned to Congress in 1783. The following year, he prepared his Notes on the Establishment of a Money Unit and of Coinage, in which he proposed the use of a decimal-based system. Although his proposal was not acted on immediately, Jefferson's recommendations were ultimately adopted in 1792, when Congress instituted a system based on the dollar, rather than the pound.

Jefferson also served as chairman of a committee charged with administering the western lands. This committee drafted a proposal for government that espoused a liberal attitude toward the new territories. Jefferson's ordinance proposed that each of the territories be self-governing and allowed entry to the union on the same basis as the original thirteen states when they reached a certain level of population. Although

Congress adopted this particular proposal, it was not actually put into effect. It did, however, form the basis for what was to become the Northwest Ordinance of 1787.

In 1785, Jefferson succeeded Benjamin Franklin as minister to France, where he remained until 1789. Jefferson was originally charged with negotiating commercial treaties with European nations, although he achieved little success in that regard. Most European countries had little interest in commercial relations with the new republic, although he did help prepare a draft treaty that was eventually signed with Prussia.

Jefferson remained in Paris during the Constitutional Convention of 1787, and thus had no part in the actual drafting of the document. He did, however, keep up with the progress of the ratification debates through an active correspondence with fellow Virginians, James Madison and James Monroe. He expressed doubts about a number of the Constitution's provisions and was especially critical of the fact that it lacked a bill of rights. In general, however, Jefferson appears to have largely supported the new plan of government.

In September 1789, President Washington nominated Jefferson to be the new nation's first secretary of state. Jefferson was reluctant to assume the position, preferring to return to Paris instead, but he accepted the post in deference to Washington's wishes. In time, however, Jefferson regretted his decision. He consistently clashed with Treasury Secretary Alexander Hamilton, and became a vigorous opponent of Hamilton's fiscal program. Jefferson originally opposed the assumption and funding plans, although he eventually struck a deal to allow the assumption bill to pass in exchange for Hamilton's agreement to locate the new federal capital on the Potomac River on the border between Virginia and Maryland. He also led the opposition to Hamilton's proposed Bank of the United States, although he failed to convince Washington to veto the bank bill. In foreign affairs, Jefferson generally believed that the United States should support France in its war with Great Britain, while Hamilton tended to urge that America adopt a pro-British position. (Neither Hamilton nor Jefferson believed that the United States should abandon its position of neutrality, however.) As the years went by, Jefferson became convinced that Hamilton and the Federalists were engaged in a plan to create a monarchy in the United States. Jefferson became increasingly frustrated as Washington sided with Hamilton on these and other policy matters. As a result, he resigned as Secretary of State on December 31, 1793, and returned to his home at Monticello.

Jefferson spent the next three years rebuilding his home and working on a variety of agricultural experiments. Although he repeatedly disavowed any interest in returning to politics, he kept abreast of developments at home and abroad. More often than not, Jefferson was disappointed in what he heard. He opposed Washington's military expedition to suppress the Whiskey Rebellion, and he joined those who condemned Jay's Treaty.

Upon Washington's retirement in 1796, he became the Republican party's candidate for the presidency, losing to John Adams in the electoral by a three-vote margin. Under the system then in use, Jefferson became the vice president. Thrown together by the political system, Jefferson and Adams soon clashed. As war with France loomed in 1798, Jefferson worried about the increasingly authoritarian tone of the national government. He deplored the passage of the Alien and Sedition Acts and opposed what he believed was Adams' provocative stance toward France.

In 1800, Jefferson defeated Adams for the presidency after a long and bitter campaign. Upon assuming office, set out to reverse what he believed were he worst excesses of the Federalist program. With the help of the new Republican majority in Congress, Jefferson reduced internal taxes, cut the military budget, and allowed the Alien and Sedition Acts to expire. Perhaps his greatest achievement was his successful negotiation of the Louisiana Purchase in 1803. Jefferson was re-elected in 1804. He then sponsored Lewis and Clark's expedition and succeeded in bringing an end to the war with the Barbary pirates.

Upon leaving office in 1809, Jefferson retired again to his home at Monticello. He devoted the final seventeen years of his life to helping establish the University of Virginia. He died on July 4, 1826, the fiftieth anniversary of the Declaration of Independence.

## Judiciary Act of 1789

The Judiciary Act of 1789 is the first judiciary act passed by the U.S. Congress. It was designed to implement Article III of the Constitution, which provided for the establishment of a judiciary with power over cases important to the national interest. In drafting the Constitution, however, the delegates to the Philadelphia Convention could not agree on the precise nature or extent of the national judiciary and so they determined to leave it to the first Congress to determine whether and what type of lower courts might be needed. As a result, the judiciary article merely provided that there should be a Supreme Court and "such inferior courts as Congress may from time to time ordain and establish."

The Judiciary Act provided that the Supreme Court would be composed of a Chief Justice and five associate justices. The Supreme Court would meet in the seat of government twice each year, on the first Monday in October and February. The act also provided that the Supreme Court would have original jurisdiction over suits between states, between a state and the United States, and cases involving ambassadors of foreign governments. The Supreme Court was given appellate jurisdiction over decisions of the circuit courts in civil cases and cases in which a state court invalidated a treaty or state or federal law on the grounds that it was inconsistent with the federal Constitution. The Supreme Court was not given any jurisdiction in criminal cases.

The Judiciary Act also created thirteen judicial districts, one for each of the states as well as one for Kentucky (then part of Virginia) and Maine (then part of Massachusetts). Each district was given a district court, which was to have jurisdiction over minor criminal cases, revenue cases, and suits in admiralty. A circuit court was also created for each state. (The districts of Maine and Kentucky which were not expected to have much business so the district court in these districts was given circuit court powers.) The circuit court was given jurisdiction over civil cases involving citizens of different states or aliens where the amount in controversy exceeded $500 as well as major criminal cases. The circuit courts were to be presided over by two justices of the Supreme Court and the district judge for the district in which the circuit court was sitting.

The act also created the office of Attorney General as well as other court officials, including a U.S. Attorney and a U.S. Marshal for each district. The Judiciary Act was amended several times during the course of the 1790s to allow for additional courts in North Carolina and Rhode Island after those states ratified the Constitution, as well as to make minor changes in the system of circuit riding.

## Maclay, William (1737–1804)

William Maclay was born in Chester County, Pennsylvania, in 1737, and was educated at the classical school of the Reverend John Blair. In 1758, he served as a lieutenant in George Washington's ill-fated expedition to Fort Duquesne, and then went on to serve with distinction in a number of campaigns during the Seven Years War. He studied law and was admitted to the bar in 1760. His practice did not flourish and so, in time, he became a surveyor of land in the employ of the Penn family. He was later served as prothonotary of the courts in Northumberland County in the 1770s, but left that position to serve in the Continental Army during the Revolution. After the war, Maclay was repeatedly elected a member of the Pennsylvania General Assembly. He was also appointed a commissioner to negotiate with the Indians, a judge of the court of common pleas, and a member of Pennsylvania's executive council.

After ratification of the Constitution, the Pennsylvania legislature determined that in order to ensure that its senators would have staggered terms in the U.S. Senate, it would elect two members who would then choose lots, with the loser having a two-year term and the other a six-year term. Maclay lost the lottery, and was thus, appointed to serve from March 4, 1789, until March 3, 1791. Robert Morris, the so-called "financier of the Revolution," received the six-year term. Maclay was one of the most radical members of the Senate, and remained a determined opponent of George Washington's administration. He was a frequent critic of both Washington and Adams, as well as other members of the government and Senate. Maclay was offended by the trappings of ceremony that accompanied Congress's communications with the president, and even went so far as to object to President Washington being present in the Senate while business was being conducted.

While in the Senate, however, Maclay kept a journal of the proceedings and debates. This record turned out to be of vital importance to historians because, unlike the House of Representatives, the U.S. Senate did not permit in-depth reporting of its debates. In spite of its partisan tone, *Maclay's Journal* is thus one of the most important contemporary records of congressional proceedings.

Maclay was unsuccessful in being re-elected to the Senate when his term expired in 1792. He, therefore, retired to his farm in Dauphin County, Pennsylvania, although he was elected a member of the General Assembly several times in the ensuing years. He died in Harrisburg, Pennsylvania, on April 16, 1804.

## Madison, James (1751–1836)

James Madison was born to a wealthy planter family in Port Conway, Virginia, in 1751. He studied at the College of New Jersey (now Princeton University), competing a four-year course of study in two years.

Madison's public career began in 1774, when he was appointed a member of the King George County (Virginia) Committee of Public Safety at the age of 23. Two years later, he was elected a member of Virginia's constitutional committee, a body charged with drafting a constitution for the state of Virginia.

In 1779, Madison was appointed one of Virginia's delegates to the Continental Congress. He soon became a leading member of Congress and consistently advocated for a close union between the states. In 1785, along with George Washington, he helped organize the Alexandria Conference, called to settle a boundary dispute between Virginia and Maryland. The convention successfully resolved a number of commercial issues between the two states, and Madison's success there helped convince him that a larger gathering of states might help resolve some of the commercial difficulties facing the nation. Consequently, Madison and others called for a convention to meet at Annapolis in 1786 to consider these issues. Only five states sent representatives to the Annapolis Convention and little of substance was accomplished. Nonetheless, Madison used this gathering as a springboard for an even grander project. With the help of Alexander Hamilton, Madison convinced the Continental Congress to call for a convention of the states to meet at Philadelphia in the spring of 1787 for the purpose of considering amendments to the Articles of Confederation.

The Philadelphia Convention opened on May 25, 1787, with delegates from eleven of the thirteen states in attendance. (New Hampshire's delegates arrived later, but Rhode Island did not participate.) Shortly after the Convention began, Virginia's Richard Henry Lee presented what has since become known as the "Virginia Plan." This plan largely abandoned any attempt to amend the Articles of Confederation, and instead called for a radical restructuring of the government of the United States. Madison was a tireless advocate in the Convention for a stronger central government, helping to generate support for the Virginia Plan and iron out disagreements between large and small states over representation, the powers of the presidency, and the shape of the judiciary. It is with no little justification, therefore, that Madison is sometimes regarded as the architect of the Constitution. During the ratification debates, Madison joined with Alexander Hamilton and John Jay in writing approximately one-third of the essays now known as *The Federalist.*

Madison was elected a member of the first Congress in 1789. On June 4, 1789, he introduced a list of amendments to the Constitution that were to become the Bill of Rights. Thereafter, he became a bitter opponent of Alexander Hamilton's economic program. Indeed, one of the more puzzling aspects of this part of Madison's career is his apparent desire to limit federal power. After having labored so long and hard in bringing about a stronger central government, Madison became concerned about the scope of that government, at least as envisioned by Hamilton and the Federalists. Madison, thus, became something of a strict constructionist, insisting on a relatively restrictive reading of the Constitution, especially with respect to the "necessary and proper" clause.

Madison retired from Congress in 1797 and returned to Virginia. From there, he became an ardent opponent of John Adam's administration. In 1798, Madison worked with Thomas Jefferson to draft the Virginia and Kentucky Resolutions (1798), which condemned passage of the Alien and Sedition Acts. After Jefferson's election to the presidency in 1801, Madison was appointed Secretary of State. He and Jefferson now set about the work of implementing a program of reform, which resulted in dismantling much of the Federalist program. As Secretary of State, Madison became embroiled in controversy with the Federalist-dominated judiciary when he refused to deliver a commission as justice of the peace to one William Marbury. Marbury's suit for a writ of mandamus compelling Madison to deliver the commission elicited John Marshall's now-famous opinion affirming the Supreme Court's power of judicial review in *Marbury v. Madison* (1803).

Madison succeeded Thomas Jefferson as President in 1808. His decision to go to war with Britain in 1812 was exceedingly unpopular, although he achieved a reasonable settlement of several important areas of dispute with England. In spite of the unpopularity of the war, Madison was elected to a second term. He then retired to his home, Montpelier, in Virginia, where he assisted Thomas Jefferson in founding the University of Virginia. He died on June 28, 1836.

## Monroe, James

James Monroe was born on April 28, 1758, in Westmoreland County, Virginia. He was the son of Spence Monroe, a carpenter and middling tobacco planter, and Elizabeth

Jones. Like many farmers of the period, the Monroes might have been described as "land poor," having extensive holdings of property but with very little cash on hand. Young James received his early education at Campeltown Academy and later attended the College of William and Mary. After graduation in 1776, he joined the Continental Army where he served with distinction.

Monroe embarked upon a career in the law, and developed a thriving practice in Fredericksburg, Virginia. He soon entered politics and was elected to the Virginia House of Delegates in 1782. The following year, Monroe was elected as one of Virginia's representatives to the Continental Congress, where he served until 1786.

Monroe opposed ratification of the proposed federal Constitution in the Virginia ratifying convention of 1788, but that did not prevent him from being elected to the Senate in 1790. While in Congress, Monroe was an ardent opponent of Hamilton's economic program and soon became a leading spokesman for Jeffersonian republicanism.

In 1794, his fellow Virginian, President Washington, appointed Monroe to serve as the American minister to France. He served in Paris for two years, but was recalled by President Adams in 1796. Like Jefferson, Monroe evidenced a great deal of sympathy for the French cause, although he often expressed revulsion at its excesses.

Upon returning to the United States, Monroe served as governor of Virginia from 1799 until 1802. The following year, he was again appointed as ambassador to France, where, with Robert R. Livingston, he helped negotiate the Louisiana Purchase. A short time later, Monroe was appointed ambassador to Great Britain, where he served until 1807.

Monroe returned to Virginia upon Jefferson's retirement from the presidency. He served in the Virginia House of Delegates, and served a second term as governor in 1811. He resigned the governorship in 1811 to become President Madison's Secretary of State. He held that post from 1811 until 1814, when he was appointed Secretary of War at the end of the War of 1812. Monroe went back to the State Department for three more years, serving as secretary from 1815 until 1817.

James Monroe was elected the fifth president of the United States in 1816. His tenure has often been known as the "Era of Good Feelings," because the long years of partisan wrangling that had been so much the hallmark of national politics in the preceding twenty years had dissipated. By this time, the Federalist party had crumbled as an effective opposition, becoming a mere shadow of its former self and confined almost exclusively to parts of New England. At the same time, the controversy between the Whigs and the Democrats was a few years off, so that, at this point, almost every national politician was a member of the Democratic-Republican party.

Sectional differences did remain, however. With the settlement of the territory acquired by the Louisiana Purchase, the slavery question came to the fore. Proslavery southerners battled with abolitionists and northerners over whether slavery ought to be permitted in the western lands. These divisions were exposed in 1819 when Missouri's first application for admission to the Union as a slave state was rejected. The following year, the Missouri Compromise engineered by Henry Clay, preserved the balance of power in Congress by permitting the admission of Maine as a free state and Missouri as a slave state. Deep divisions remained, however, as proslavery forces soon came to realize that most of the new western states would be free states and that their "peculiar institution" would eventually come under full-scale assault.

No doubt, President Monroe is best known for his 1823 address to Congress in which he announced a policy that has since become known as the "Monroe Doctrine." Fearful of the consequences of continued European interference in the Americas, Monroe declared that the western hemisphere was to be off-limits to future European colonization and that the United States would oppose European attempts to influence in the affairs of sovereign governments in North and South America. Monroe declared that the United States would regard any attempt to plant new colonies or interfere in otherwise interfere in the western hemisphere as hostile acts against the United States. Monroe further declared the United States's intention to remain neutral in future European wars.

Monroe retired from the presidency upon the expiration of his second term in 1825. He returned to Virginia for a few years, but later moved to New York upon his wife's death to live with his daughter. He died in New York on July 4, 1831.

## Northwest Ordinance (1787)

The Northwest Ordinance is arguably the single-most important piece of legislation passed by the Continental Congress. Officially known as the Ordinance for the Government of the Territory of the United States, Northwest of the River Ohio, the Northwest Ordinance was passed on July 13, 1787.

The peace treaty, which marked the end of the Seven Years War in 1763, provided that France would cede to Great Britain all its territory on the North American continent. This territory included France's extensive holdings in what is now modern-day Canada, as well as portions of the Ohio, Illinois, and Mississippi River valleys. Upon taking possession of this territory, Great Britain declared in the Proclamation Act of 1763, that the lands of the Ohio River valley were reserved to the Indians and prohibited settlement by the American colonists.

Despite the restrictions of the Proclamation, numerous colonies made conflicting and overlapping claims to the western lands. Among these were Massachusetts, Connecticut, New York, and Virginia, most of whom asserted rights to the Ohio territory by virtue of royal charters granting them title to lands "from sea to sea." Except perhaps for Virginia, these states did not necessary view the western lands as future territory to be incorporated into their boundaries. Instead, most saw these lands as a source of monetary gain. The sale of these lands to speculators, who would pay large sums of money, was especially attractive to governments always in need of new sources of revenue.

These lands changed hands again in the 1783 peace treaty between Great Britain and the United States. The terms of the treaty required England to cede the lands of the Ohio and Illinois River valleys to the United States and to vacate the forts in that region. Although Britain delayed evacuation for many years, the collapse of British rule in the west precipitated a rush on the part of the states to assert claims to the newly opened lands. States such as Virginia and Connecticut chartered land companies and attempted to sell large sections of the west to speculators who would, in turn, resell the lands at profit. In addition, a number of states granted land warrants to revolutionary era soldiers and officers in lieu of pensions or pay.

This frenzy of speculation created the potential for conflict between the states themselves. Consequently, Congress decided to develop some scheme by which the sale of lands could be confirmed and some government for the territories be created. The Ordinance contained several important provisions.

First, it provided for the abolition of state claims. In so doing, the Ordinance ensured that the existing states would not be increased, thus allaying the fears of smaller states without legal claims to the lands. These states often feared that states with claims to western lands would increase in size, gaining power in Congress, and eventually upsetting the balance of power between the northern and southern states. Eliminating state claims allowed the national government to take control of the territories and administer them free of state interference.

The Ordinance established a government in the territory under the control of Congress. It provided for a governor appointed by Congress and judges appointed with no fixed term of office. The territory was permitted to form a territorial legislature once the population reached 5,000.

Perhaps the most important part of the Northwest Ordinance was its provisions concerning the admission of new states to the Union. The act provided that new states would be carved out of the territory and would be admitted on an equal footing with the original thirteen states once their population reached 60,000.

Finally, the Northwest Ordinance declared that slavery would be prohibited in the territory. The fact that the Ordinance applied to lands above the Ohio River meant that the Ohio was to serve as the effective boundary between free and slave states in the region between the Appalachians and the Mississippi. This theoretical boundary was extended into the lands west of the Mississippi by the Missouri Compromise of 1820. The result was that the delicate balance of power between free and slave states could be preserved until the opening of the mountain west made the compromise untenable.

### Paine, Thomas (1737–1809)

Thomas Paine was born in Thetford in East Anglia in 1737. He grew up in an impoverished farm family and left school at the age of 12. The following year, he was apprenticed to a corset-maker, but was dismissed sometime later. He went to sea at the age of 19 but soon returned to England where he set up a corset shop in Kent. In 1762, Paine was appointed a customs officer, serving in various seaports in eastern and southern England. In 1772, Paine led a movement among customs officers agitating for higher salaries, publishing his first political work entitled, *The Case of the Officers of Excise*. He was ultimately dismissed for his efforts.

Jobless and without prospects, Paine met Benjamin Franklin, who was then serving as Pennsylvania's colonial agent, in 1774. Franklin advised Paine to move to the colonies to seek his fortune and gave him letters of introduction to certain associates in Philadelphia. Once in Philadelphia, Paine became active in the revolutionary movement. Within a year of his arrival, he anonymously published a pamphlet called *Common Sense*, (January 1776), in which he argued that the colonies had outgrown the need for dependence on England and ought to be free and independent states. In it, Paine appears to have been the first person to suggest the name "United States of America" for the new nation. *Common Sense* was wildly successful in bolstering the forces of independence. Later that same year, Paine published a series of essays under the title, *The Crisis*, designed to further the revolutionary cause. The first essay so impressed General Washington that he ordered it read to the troops in its entirety.

After the Revolution, Paine went to England where he wrote *The Rights of Man* (1791–92), in response to Sir Edmund Burke's *Reflections on the Revolution in France* (1790). Paine argued that there were certain fundamental rights that could only be guaranteed by democratic institutions. His critique of the monarchy and English political and legal institutions aroused the ire of government authorities. Paine was, thus, forced to flee to France and was subsequently tried *in absentia* for seditious libel. While in France, Paine became actively involved in French politics. Although not a French citizen, he was elected to the National Convocation. During the Reign of Terror, Paine was imprisoned for almost a year, and narrowly escaped death on the guillotine. While in prison, however, Paine authored *The Age of Reason*, (1794–95), which was largely an attack on organized religion.

Paine returned to the United States in 1802, but was largely derided as an atheist and malcontent. He died in largely friendless and in poverty in 1809. It is said that only six mourners came to the funeral.

### Peters, Richard (1744–1828)

Richard Peters was born just outside Philadelphia, Pennsylvania on June 22, 1744. He was the son of William Peters, a large landowner with extensive holdings in both

Pennsylvania and England, who was also a successful lawyer and sometime judge of the Court of Common Pleas in Philadelphia. His uncle Richard, for whom he was named, was rector of Christ Church, Philadelphia.

Young Richard graduated from the College of Philadelphia (now the University of Pennsylvania) in 1761, and then read law. He was admitted to the bar in 1763, and built a successful law practice. He held a number of posts in the colonial government, among which was registrar of the admiralty court. During the Revolution, Peters was appointed by Congress to be the secretary to the Board of War from 1776 until 1781. He was later appointed one of Pennsylvania's delegates to Congress in 1782.

After the war, Peters visited England with a view toward reconciling the now-divided Anglican Church. His efforts were ultimately rewarded when Parliament passed the act for the Consecration of Bishops Abroad, allowing for the consecration of bishops for New York and Philadelphia and the subsequent creation of the Episcopal Church in the United States.

On his return to America in 1786, Peters was elected to the Pennsylvania General Assembly, where he served from 1781 until 1790. In 1792, President Washington named Peters as judge of the U.S. District Court for the District of Pennsylvania to succeed Francis Hopkinson. He remained on the bench until his death in 1828.

# *Chronology*

**1787**  September 17  Constitutional Convention meeting in Philadelphia since May adjourns. Proposed Constitution sent to Congress for transmittal to the states.

**1788**  June 21  New Hampshire becomes the ninth state to ratify the Constitution, bringing the new frame of government into force.

October 10  Continental Congress adjourns sine die.

**1789**  February 4  Presidential Electors meeting in the various state capitals unanimously elect George Washington as the first President of the United States. John Adams is elected vice president.

March 4  The first Congress convenes in New York City.

April 30  Washington inaugurated as the first president of the United States in New York City.

May 4  Congressman James Madison of Virginia introduces amendments to the Constitution in the House of Representatives.

June 8  The House begins debate on Madison's proposed amendments.

September 24  President Washington signs the first Judiciary Act.

Washington nominates John Jay to be the first Chief Justice of the United States. John Rutledge, William Cushing, Robert Harrison, James Wilson, and John Blair, Jr. are nominated as associate justices.

September 25   Congress approves ten amendments to the Constitution and forwards them to the states for ratification. These amendments become the Bill of Rights.

September 26   The Senate confirms Washington's Supreme Court appointments.

Robert H. Harrison declines appointment as associate justice.

**1790**   January 9   Treasury Secretary Alexander Hamilton submits his Report on the Public Credit to Congress recommending that the federal government assume the states' revolutionary war debt and urging that all such debts be paid by the federal government without discrimination between original and subsequent holders.

January   Spanish naval forces seize two British merchant ships in Nootka Sound (later Vancouver Sound) precipitating the Nootka Sound Crisis.

February 8   President Washington nominates James Iredell as associate justice, replacing Robert Harrison.

February 10   Senate confirms nomination of James Iredell.

July 16   Congress passes the Residence Act, providing for the relocation of the national capital to a new "Federal District" along the banks of the Potomac River by the year 1800. The act also provided that the capital move to Philadelphia for a period of ten years.

July 26   Congress passes the Funding and Assumption bills.

August   The national capital relocates to Philadelphia.

December 13–14   Treasury Secretary Hamilton submits a Second Report on the Public Credit and a Report on the National Bank. The first of these recommended a new schedule of taxes on whiskey, the fund of which were to pay the public debt. The second recommended the creation of a national bank.

**1791**   February 25   President Washington signs legislation creating the Bank of the United States.

February 26   Congress passes the Excise Bill imposing taxes on whiskey and other products, thus providing a permanent revenue to pay government debts.

March 5   Associate Justice John Rutledge resigns.

August 3   *West v. Barnes* holds that writs of certiorari must issue from the clerk of the Supreme Court and not lower courts.

August 23   Public meetings in western Pennsylvania denounce the excise law and call upon citizens to treat revenue offices "with contempt."

August 5   President Washington appoints Thomas Johnson associate justice replacing John Rutledge. First recess appointment of a Supreme Court justice.

September 22   Republic of France Republic after monarchy is abolished.

October 31   Washington nominates Thomas Johnson as associate justice.

November 7   Senate confirms Thomas Johnson as associate justice.

December 5   Treasury Secretary Hamilton submits his Report on the Subject of Manufactures to Congress recommending extensive action by federal government to stimulate commerce.

**1792**   August 11   In *Georgia v. Brailsford*, Supreme Court grants injunction on behalf of Georgia to restrain payment of debt claimed by the state.

In *Hayburn's Case*, the Supreme Court declines to comply with federal statute requiring circuit courts to hear pension claims.

**1793**   January 16   Associate Justice Thomas Johnson resigns.

January 21   King Louis XVI of France executed.

February 1   France declares war on England.

February 13   Presidential electors unanimously re-elect George Washington as President of the United States. John Adams is re-elected as vice president.

**February 19**   *Chisholm v. Georgia* holds that states can be sued by citizens of other states in federal courts.

**February 20**   In *Oswald v. New York* Supreme Court orders state to appear or suffer default judgment.

**March 11**   William Paterson takes the oath as associate justice of the Supreme Court replacing Justice Thomas Johnson.

**April 8**   Citizen Edmond Charles Genet, France's new minister plenipotentiary, arrives in Charleston, South Carolina, and shortly begins to issue commissions to privateers to prey on British shipping.

**April 22**   President Washington issues the Neutrality Proclamation declaring America's intention to remain neutral in the war between France and England and forbidding American citizens from giving aid to either of the warring powers.

**July 18**   President Washington requests an advisory opinion from the Supreme Court on the implications of the Treaty of Alliance with France.

**July 29**   Circuit Court of Pennsylvania acquits Gideon Henfield of violating Washington's Neutrality Proclamation thus casting doubt on the ability of federal courts to prosecute nonstatutory crimes.

**August 8**   Supreme Court declines to give advisory opinion on the neutrality question.

**October 11**   France's Committee of Public Safety determines to recall Citizen Genet as minister to the United States and take steps to preserve American neutrality.

**November 6**   A secret Order in Council issued by the Privy Council in London expands the definition of "contraband goods" and authorizes British ships to prey on American vessels trading with the French West Indies. In response, British vessels begin to seize American ships in large numbers.

**December 16**   Secretary of State Thomas Jefferson issues his Report on the Privileges and Restrictions on the Commerce of the United States in Foreign Countries recommending steps that would amount to the beginning of a trade war with Great Britain.

**1794**    January 3    Congressman James Madison introduces resolutions in Congress to increase duties on British goods.

February 7    Supreme Court holds first jury trial in *Georgia v. Brailsford*.

February 18    *Glass v. The Sloop Betsey* holds that federal district courts possess jurisdiction over prize cases and declares that French consular courts cannot function on American soil.

April 15    President Washington nominates to Chief Justice John Jay as minister plenipotentiary to Great Britain to negotiate a commercial treaty and a resolution of American claims.

April 19    Senate confirms John Jay's appointment as minister plenipotentiary to Great Britain.

June 8    Chief Justice Jay arrives in England.

July 16    Armed mob attacks the U.S. marshal and an excise officer in Allegheny County, Pennsylvania.

August 1    Six thousand men convene at Braddock's Field in Pittsburgh, Pennsylvania, to plan opposition to the whiskey tax.

August 4    Justice James Wilson certifies that judicial process in western Pennsylvania had broken down, paving the way for the federal government to take military action against the whiskey rebels.

August 7    President Washington issues a proclamation ordering the militia to put down the rebellion in western Pennsylvania.

September 25    Militia from Pennsylvania, Maryland, Virginia, and New Jersey begin to march on western Pennsylvania to suppress the whiskey rebellion.

November 19    Chief Justice Jay concludes a commercial treaty with the British government.

**1795**    February 24    *Penhallow v. Doane's Administrators* holds that federal district courts have the power to put into effect decrees of the former congressional Court of Appeals in Prize Cases, even though that court has ceased to exist.

March 2    In *Bingham v. Cabot* the Supreme Court attempts to ascertain the limits of admiralty jurisdiction and to resolve several novel issues of evidence and procedure.

March 3    *United States v. Lawrence* holds that Supreme Court will not compel issuance of a writ by a lower court where the judge does not believe the evidence is sufficient.

March 7    Copies of Jay's Treaty arrive in Philadelphia.

June 8    Jay's Treaty is presented to the Senate for ratification.

June 24    Senate provisionally ratifies Jay's Treaty.

June 29    Chief Justice John Jay resigns.

July 1    John Rutledge receives recess appointment as Chief Justice succeeding John Jay.

July 16    Chief Justice Rutledge makes speech in South Carolina attacking Jay's Treaty.

August 14    President Washington signs Jay's Treaty.

August 22    *Talbot v. Jensen* holds that the capture of a neutral vessel made by a privateer illegally fitted out in the ports of the United States is unlawful.

August 24    *United States v. Peters* holds that federal district courts have no jurisdiction to review determinations of foreign prize courts.

October 25    Associate Justice John Blair resigns.

December 15    Senate rejects nomination of John Rutledge to be Chief Justice.

**1796**    January 26    William Cushing nominated Chief Justice to succeed John Rutledge.

January 27    Cushing declines nomination.

February 4    Samuel Chase takes oath as associate justice replacing John Blair.

February 17    *McDonough v. Dannery* affirms federal district courts' jurisdiction over salvage cases in admiralty.

February 26    *Hills v. Ross* holds that a circuit court's failure to cause the facts on which it based its decree to appear fully in the record as required by the Judiciary Act is not a sufficient grounds for reversing the judgment.

March 7    *Ware v. Hylton* holds that state laws impairing the collection of debts due British creditors arising the revolution violate the terms of the treaty of peace and are, therefore, of no effect.

March 8    Oliver Ellsworth becomes the third Chief Justice of the United States.

*Hylton v. United States* declares carriage tax is not a direct tax and thus does not violate provisions of the Constitution requiring direct taxes to be apportioned according to the census.

March 25    House of Representatives passes resolution demanding that President Washington turn over all papers relating to the negotiation of Jay's Treaty before it would agree to appropriate funds to put the treaty in force.

March 30    President Washington declines to provide the House with papers relating to the Jay Treaty.

April 30    House of Representatives votes funds to implement Jay's Treaty.

July 2    French government issues decree authorizing French vessels and privateers to confiscate neutral vessels trading with British ports.

August 9    *Cotton v. Wallace* disallows damages for delay occurring between judgment and final appeal.

*Moodie v. The Ship Alfred* declares that the use of a vessel built in the United States but outfitted in another country for privateering does not violate the Neutrality Act.

*Moodie v. The Ship Phoebe Anne* allows French privateers to put into American ports for repairs.

**August 11**    *United States v. LaVengeance* declares that the trial of seizures of ships or cargo made under the revenue laws are "civil cases of admiralty and maritime jurisdiction" and thus do not require juries.

*Olney v. Arnold* holds that the Superior Court of Judicature of Rhode Island is the highest court of the state for purposes of appeals to the Supreme Court even though Rhode Island law allows for appeals of judicial decisions to the state legislature.

*Del Col v. Arnold* decrees that privateers are liable for damage to ships taken as prize until they are brought into port for adjudication.

**August 12**    *Arcambel v. Wiseman* refuses to allow counsel fees to be included as damages recoverable in a civil action.

*Wiscart v. Dauchy* holds that statement of facts found by circuit court in equity and admiralty cases is conclusive and that Supreme Court will not rehear facts on appeal.

*Grayson v. Virginia* orders that process against a state be served upon the governor and the attorney general of the state.

**September 19**    Washington's Farewell Address published.

**1797**    **February 10**    *Huger v. South Carolina* asserts that delivery of a subpoena to the state attorney general and the leaving of another copy "at the governor's house" is sufficient service against the state.

**February 13**    *Jennings v. The Brig Perseverance* holds that the failure of the decree for error in fact.

**March 4**    John Adams inaugurated as President. Thomas Jefferson becomes vice president.

**March 25**    President Adams calls a special session of Congress to address French depredations on American commerce.

May 16    President Adams announces intention to send diplomatic mission to France.

Elbridge Gerry, John Marshall, and Charles Cotesworth Pinckney appointed commissioners to negotiate resolution of disputes between France and America.

August 15    *Hamilton v. Moore* requires that writs of error bear the date of the term immediately preceding the one at which it is returnable.

October 22    In Paris, John Marshall drafts dispatch to President Adams detailing approaches by emissaries of the French government, which he identified as "X," "Y," and "Z," demanding bribes and loans before American diplomats would be received.

**1798**    February 9    *Jones v. Le Tombe* dismisses a suit against the French consul for repayment of a loan given to the government of France

February 14    *Emory v. Grenough* dismisses diversity action because the original process did not clearly state that the parties are citizens of different states.

*Hollingsworth v. Virginia* declares that the Eleventh Amendment prohibits private citizens from suing the states in federal courts.

*Bingham v. Cabot* requires that the diversity of citizenship be apparent on the face of the record in order for federal courts to exercise diversity jurisdiction.

March 4    Dispatches arrive from France describing the "X,Y,Z Affair." Adams decides to keep the details secret.

April 2    House of Representatives demands access to the "X,Y,Z" papers.

April 23    John Marshall departs France, bringing an end to the peace mission.

June 18    Naturalization Act imposes restrictions on American citizenship.

June 24    Congress authorizes the creation of the Department of the Navy and appropriates funds for strengthening American defenses. USS *Constellation* puts to sea.

June 25   Alien Act allows the president to expel any alien whom he deems "dangerous to the peace and safety of the United States."

July 6   Alien Enemies Act authorized the president to detain aliens of nations with whom the United States is at war.

July 14   Sedition Act makes it a crime to publish "false, scandalous and malicious writing or writings against the government of the United States."

August 7   *Wilson v. Daniel* holds that the jurisdictional amount be determined by the value of the object in controversy, rather than the plaintiff's demand.

August 8   *Calder v. Bull* declares that the Constitution's prohibition on "ex post facto" laws applies to criminal statutes and does not prevent states from retroactively altering private rights.

August 21   Justice James Wilson dies.

September 29   Bushrod Washington receives recess appointment as associate justice replacing James Wilson.

**1799**   February 5   In *Dewhurst v. Coulthard*, Supreme Court refuses to take cognizance of a "case stated," holding that appeals are limited to actual cases proceeding according to the regular process of law.

February 18   President Adams announces intention to send peace mission to France.

February 19   *Fowler v. Lindsey* declares that a state is not a party to an action merely because it might be substantially affected by the outcome. States must be "nominally or substantially" parties to the case.

*Sims' Lesee v. Irvine* holds that legal and equitable rights vested in private parties prior to the Constitution remain enforceable notwithstanding changes in government or judicial system.

August 9   *New York v. Connecticut* rejects attempt by New York to intervene in ejectment actions brought in Connecticut courts where neither state was a party to the original action.

*Turner v. Enrille* requires that alienage be apparent on the face of the record in order to invoke the jurisdiction of the federal courts.

October 20   Justice James Iredell dies.

November 9   Napoleon Bonaparte takes power.

**1800**   March 8   Chief Justice Oliver Ellsworth, William R. Davie, and William Vans Murray, American peace commissioners, meet Napoleon Bonaparte in Paris.

February 6   *Rutherford v. Fisher* allows writ of error only after final judgment.

February 8   *Blaine v. The Ship Charles Carter* holds that writ of error is the only way to bring a case before the Supreme Court.

*Course v. Stead* allows the laws of the several states to be introduced before the Supreme Court without having been proved as fact below.

February 13   In *Cooper v. Telfair*, the justices disagree on whether the Supreme Court has power to declare that a Georgia state law violates the state constitution.

*Blair v. Miller* holds that a writ of error not returned at the proper term is void.

April 21   Alfred Moore replaces James Iredell as associate justice.

August 15   *Talbot v. The Ship Amelia* allows salvage award in admiralty to a vessel that retakes a prize from a privateer.

*Bas v. Tingy* holds that limited hostilities are sufficient to constitute a state of war thereby allowing an American vessel the right to salvage when it recaptures a ship from a privateer.

October 30   Convention of Mortefontaine ends hostilities between America and France.

December 15   Chief Justice Ellsworth resigns.

December 18    John Jay nominated to be Chief Justice a second time.

December 19    Jay declines nomination.

**1801**    February 4    John Marshall takes the oath of office becoming the third Chief Justice of the United States.

March 4    Thomas Jefferson becomes President of the United States.

# List of Cases

*Arcambel v. Wiseman*, 3 U.S. (3 Dall.) 306 (1796)

*Bas v. Tingy*, 4 U.S. (4 Dall.) 37 (1800)

*Bingham v. Cabbot*, 3 U.S. (3 Dall.) 19 (1795)

*Bingham v. Cabot*, 3 U.S. (3 Dall.) 382 (1798)

*Blaine v. Ship Charles Carter*, 4 U.S. (4 Dall.) 22 (1800)

*Blair v. Miller*, 4 U.S. (4 Dall.) 21 (1800)

*Brown v. Van Braam*, 3 U.S. (3 Dall.) 344 (1797)

*Brown v. Barry*, 3 U.S. (3 Dall.) 365 (1797)

*Calder v. Bull*, 3 U.S. (3 Dall.) 386 (1798)

*Chisholm v. Georgia*, 2 U.S. (2 Dall.) 419 (1793)

*Clarke v. Russel*, 3 U.S. (3 Dall.) 415 (1799)

*Clerke v. Harwood*, 3 U.S. (3 Dall.) 342 (1797)

*Cooper v. Telfair*, 4 U.S. (4 Dall.)14 (1800)

*Cotton v. Wallace*, 3 U.S. (3 Dall.) 302 (1796)

*Course v. Stead*, 4 U.S. (4 Dall.) 22 (1800)

*Del Col v. Arnold*, 3 U.S. (3 Dall.) 333 (1796)

*Dewhurst v. Coulthard*, 3 U.S. (3 Dall.) 409 (1799)

*Emory v. Grenough*, 3 U.S. (3 Dall.) 369 (1798)

*Ex Parte Hollowell*, 3 U.S. (3 Dall.) 410 (1799)

*Fenemore v. United States*, 3 U.S. (3 Dall.) 357 (1797)

*Fowler v. Lindsey*, 3 U.S. (3 Dall.) 411 (1799)

*Georgia v. Brailsford*, 3 U.S. (3 Dall.)1 (1794)

*Georgia v. Brailsford*, 2 U.S. (2 Dall.) 402 (1792)

*Georgia v. Brailsford*, 2 U.S. (2 Dall.) 415 (1793)

*Geyer v. Michel*, 3 U.S. (3 Dall.) 285 (1796)

*Glass v. Sloop Betsey*, 3 U.S. (3 Dall.) 6 (1794)

*Grayson v. Virginia*, 3 U.S. (3 Dall.) 320 (1796)

*Hamilton v. Moore*, 3 U.S. (3 Dall.) 371 (1797)

*Hayburn's Case*, 2 U.S. (2 Dall.) 409 (1792)

*Hazlehurst v. United States*, 4 U.S. (4 Dall.) 6 (1799)

*Hills v. Ross*, 3 U.S. (3 Dall.) 184 (1796)

*Hills v. Ross*, 3 U.S. (3 Dall.) 331 (1796)

*Hollingsworth v. Virginia*, 3 U.S. (3 Dall.) 378 (1798)

*Huger v. South Carolina*, 3 U.S. (3 Dall.) 339 (1797)

*Hunter v. Fairfax's Devisee*, 3 U.S. (3 Dall.) 305 (1796)

*Hylton v. United States*, 3 U.S. (3 Dall.) 171 (1796)

*Jennings v. Brig Perseverance*, 3 U.S. (3 Dall.) 336 (1797)

*Jones v. Le Tombe*, 3 U.S. (3 Dall.) 384 (1798)

*McDonough v. Dannery*, 3 U.S. (3 Dall.) 188 (1796)

*Moodie v. Ship Phoebe Anne*, 3 U.S. (3 Dall.) 319 (1796)

*Moodie v. Ship Alfred*, 3 U.S. (3 Dall.) 307 (1796)

*Mossman v. Higginson*, 4 U.S. (4 Dall.) 12 (1800)

*New York v. Connecticut*, 4 U.S. (4 Dall.) 3 (1799)

*New York v. Connecticut*, 4 U.S. (4 Dall.) 1 (1799)

*New York v. Connecticut*, 4 U.S. (4 Dall.) 6 (1799)

*Olney v. Arnold*, 3 U.S. (3 Dall.) 308 (1796)

*Oswald v. New York*, 2 U.S. (2 Dall.) 401 (1792)

*Oswald v. New York*, 2 U.S. (2 Dall.) 401 (1793)

*Oswald v. New York*, 2 U.S. (2 Dall.) 402 (1792)

*Penhallow v. Doane's Administrators*, 3 U.S. (3 Dall.) 54 (1795)

*Priestman v. U.S*, 4 U.S. (4 Dall.) 28 (1800)

*Rutherford v. Fisher*, 4 U.S. (4 Dall.) 22 (1800)

*Sims Lessee v. Irvine*, 3 U.S. (3 Dall.) 425 (1799)

*Talbot v. Janson*, 3 U.S. (3 Dall.)133 (1795)

*Talbot v. Ship Amelia*, 4 U.S. (4 Dall.) 34 (1800)

*Turner v. Enrille*, 4 U.S. (4 Dall.)7 (1799)

*Turner v. Bank of North-America*, 4 U.S. (4 Dall.) 8 (1799)

*United States v. Hamilton*, 3 U.S. (3 Dall.) 17 (1795)

*United States v. La Vengeance*, 3 U.S. (3 Dall.) 297 (1796)

*United States v. Peters*, 3 U.S. (3 Dall.) 121 (1795)

*United States v. Lawrence*, 3 U.S. (3 Dall.) 42 (1795)

*Vanstophorst v. Maryland*, 2 U.S. (2 Dall.) 401 (1791)

*Ware v. Hylton*, 3 U.S. (3 Dall.) 199 (1796)

*West v. Barnes*, 2 U.S. (2 Dall.) 401 (1791)

*Williamson v. Kincaid*, 4 U.S. (4 Dall.) 20 (1800)

*Wilson v. Daniel*, 3 U.S. (3 Dall.) 401 (1798)

*Wisecart v. Dauchy*, 3 U.S. (3 Dall.) 321 (1796)

# *Glossary*

**admiralty**  A system of law that relates to maritime commerce and navigation or ships and shipping. Among the subjects of admiralty are collisions involving ships, injuries to seamen, damage to cargo, and contracts of carriage. Federal courts are given admiralty jurisdiction by virtue of Article III of the U.S. Constitution, although that jurisdiction is not entirely exclusive. State courts have power to hear maritime cases where the common law might otherwise provide a remedy.

**advisory opinion**  An opinion of a court indicating how it would rule on an issue if the issue were presented in an actual case—although no real case exists to present the legal question; an interpretation of law without binding effect.

**alien**  A foreign-born person who has not met the requirements for citizenship.

**appeal**  A process by which a final judgment of a lower court ruling is reviewed by a higher court.

**appellate jurisdiction**  Authority of a superior court to review decisions of inferior courts. Appellate jurisdiction empowers a higher court to conduct such a review and affirm, modify, or reverse the lower court decision. Appellate jurisdiction is conveyed through constitutional or statutory mandate. Federal appellate jurisdiction is granted by Article III of the Constitution, which says that the Supreme Court possesses such jurisdiction "both as to law and fact, with such exceptions and under such regulations as the Congress shall make."

**Appellee**  The party who prevails in a lower court and against whom an appeal of the judgment is sought; in some situations called a "respondent."

**Argument**  An address by an attorney to a judge or jury on the merits of a particular case. A "closing argument" contains the remarks of an attorney to a jury in an effort to convince it of the merits of the case. "Appellate argument" is an oral presentation to an appeals court on the matters covered in the brief.

**"arising under" jurisdiction**   The common name for the federal courts' jurisdiction to decide questions raised by the federal Constitution, statutes or treaties. The term derives from the wording of Article III. Also called "federal question jurisdiction."

**Article III**   The third article of the U.S. Constitution that defines the limits of federal judicial power. It contains three sections. The first section of the article ensures judicial independence by providing life tenure and fixed salaries for federal judges. The second section specifies the types of cases federal courts may decide. The third section defines the crime of treason against the United States.

**Articles of Confederation**   The compact established between the thirteen original American states and formalizing the relationship between them. It provided a framework for creating a national government and was operative between March 1, 1781, and March 4, 1789.

**associate justice**   A justice of the Supreme Court other than the Chief Justice.

**Assumpsit**   Literally, "he undertook" or "he promised." An action at common law for damages for breach of contract.

**Attachment**   The legal process of seizing a person or property in accordance with a judicial writ for the purpose of securing either an appearance in court or the payment of a money judgment.

**attorney general**   The head of the U.S. Department of Justice and the chief law enforcement officer of the federal government. With other heads of department, such as the Secretary of the Treasury and the Secretary of State, the attorney general is part of the president's cabinet.

**bar**   The collective membership of the legal profession as distinguished from the judges of the courts who are referred to as the "bench." The term also refers to the boundary of the courtroom that separates the attorneys and court officers from the general public.

**Bill of Attainder**   A legislative enactment that imposed the death penalty upon persons suspected of committing treason or sedition against the government. Such penalties were imposed regardless of whether the person was convicted in a court of law. Congress is prohibited from passing bills of attainder by virtue of Article I, section 9 of the Constitution.

**Bill of Rights**   A formal declaration of popular rights and liberties traditionally promulgated by the legislature or the people upon a change of government. In the United States, the first ten amendments to the federal Constitution are commonly regarded as the American bill of rights.

**brief**  A document containing arguments on a matter under consideration by a court. A brief submitted to a court by an attorney typically contains, among other things, points of law from previous rulings.

**cabinet**  A board or counsel that advises a king or chief executive. In the United States, the president's cabinet consists of the heads of the various executive branch departments.

**case**  An action, cause, suit, or controversy brought at law or in equity; a judicial proceeding commenced to determine a legal controversy between parties.

**case law**  Precedent created as courts resolve disputes. Judges make case law as they rule on a specific set of facts. Common law is similar to case law but judicially incorporates accepted traditional community values, usages, and customs into court decisions. Statutory law, by contrast, is enacted by a legislative body.

**case or controversy**  A constitutional requirement that disputes or controversies be definite and concrete and involve parties whose legal interests are truly adverse. This requirement, contained in Article III of the Constitution, establishes a bona fide controversy as a precondition for adjudication by federal courts.

**certiorari**  Literally "to be informed of" or "to be made certain in regard to." A writ or order to a court whose decision is being challenged on appeal to send up the records of the case to enable a higher court to review the case. The writ of certiorari is the primary means by which the U.S. Supreme Court reviews cases from lower courts.

**chancery**  A court of equity.

**charter**  A grant from the sovereign to a person or group of persons granting certain rights, liberties, or powers.

**charter party**  A contract by which a ship is let to a merchant for the carriage of goods. The term is often shortened to "charter."

**Chief Justice**  The presiding or most senior justice of a court.

**circuit court**  Lower court established by the first Judiciary Act having both trial and appellate jurisdiction. Originally, there were three circuit courts, each having the power to hear cases from several states. Sessions of the courts were held in the states at different times and were conducted by one or more members of the Supreme Court along with the district court judge of the district in which the court met.

**civil action**  An action brought to enforce or protect private rights in law or equity.

**civil law**   The legal tradition derived from Roman law that serves as the basis of the legal system in most European countries. The civil law is distinct from the common law in its modes of proceeding and substantive content.

**clerk**   Officer of the court who files pleadings and motions and keeps records of court proceedings.

**commerce clause**   Provision found in Article I, section 8 of the U.S. Constitution that empowers Congress to "regulate commerce with foreign nations, and among the several states, and with the Indian tribes." Since the 1930s, the commerce power has been the basis for extensive federal regulation of the economy and, to a limited extent, federal criminal law.

**common law**   That body of judge-made law administered by the royal courts of justice in England and distinguished from the system of law utilized by the courts of equity and admiralty. The common law is also that body of law that is distinguished from statutory law created by the acts of legislatures. It generally comprises the principles of law relating to the rights of persons and the protection property.

**common law crime**   A crime punishable by the common law as distinguished from one punishable by statute.

**complaint**   The initial pleading in a lawsuit that sets forth the plaintiff's claim for relief.

**concurrent jurisdiction**   The authority of a two or more courts to hear the same cause of action.

**concurring opinion**   An opinion written by a judge who agrees with the outcome or decision in a case but disagrees with the logic or reasoning used by the majority.

**confederation**   A league or compact of states or nations; the government created by the Articles of Confederation existing between 1781 and 1789.

**consul**   An officer appointed by a foreign government to watch over its commercial or maritime affairs in a foreign port or city.

**consular court**   A court held by a consul of one country within the territory of another for the settlement of disputes involving matters of interest to the consul's nation. Such courts are generally erected pursuant to a treaty between the two nations.

**contraband**   Property that is unlawful for a citizen to possess. During time of war, contraband includes certain classes of merchandise, such as ammunition or weapons, which cannot be furnished by a neutral nation to one of the belligerent powers.

**contracts clause**   Provision found in Article I, section 10 of the Constitution, which prohibits the states from enacting "any Law impairing the Obligation of Contracts." The Contracts Clause was included in the Constitution to prevent the states from attempting to redistribute wealth or alter established commercial relations.

**creditor**   A person to whom a debt is owed.

**damages**   A sum of money awarded by a court as a remedy for breach of contract or for a tortious act.

**decree**   A judgment or order of a court, especially an equity court.

**de facto**   Literally "in fact" or "in deed." A phrase used to describe an action that must be accepted as done, but that may have been illegal or illegitimate when undertaken.

**defendant**   The party who is sued in a civil action or charged in a criminal case; the party responding to a civil complaint. A defendant in a criminal case is the person formally accused of criminal conduct.

**de jure**   Literally "by right." A de jure action occurs as a result of law or official government action.

**demurrer**   An allegation by a defendant that even if the facts alleged were true, their legal consequences are not such as to require an answer or further proceedings in the cause. Under contemporary rules of civil procedure, a motion to dismiss a case for failure to establish a claim is more commonly used to accomplish the same objective.

**dictum**   An abbreviated form of "obiter dictum," that is an observation or remark on a principle of law made by a judge in an opinion but which is not essential to the determination or outcome of the case.

**dismissal**   An order or judgment of a court that terminates an action without a formal trial on the merits.

**dissenting opinion**   The opinion of a judge that disagrees with the result reached by the majority.

**diversity jurisdiction**   Authority conveyed by Article 3, section 2, of the Constitution empowering federal courts to hear civil actions involving parties from different states.

**docket**   A record of the proceedings of a court of justice that includes a notation of all the acts or orders in a case from its inception to the conclusion.

**due process** Government procedures that follow principles of essential or fundamental fairness. Provisions designed to ensure laws will be reasonable both in substance and in means of implementation are contained in two clauses of the Constitution. The Fifth Amendment prohibits deprivation of "life, liberty, or property, without due process of law." It sets a limit on arbitrary and unreasonable actions by the federal government. The Fourteenth Amendment contains parallel language aimed at the states. Due process requires that actions of the government occur through ordered and regularized processes.

**ejectment** An action at common law to obtain possession of property.

**Eleventh Amendment** The eleventh amendment to the U.S. Constitution that prohibits federal courts from having jurisdiction over suits brought against states by citizens of another state or foreign country. The amendment was proposed and ratified specifically to overturn the Supreme Court's decision in *Chisholm v Georgia* (1793).

**embargo** A proclamation or order of government prohibiting commercial relations with certain nations or ports. It is usually issued during wartime by a belligerent powers.

**enjoin** To require to perform or refrain from a specified action. A party is enjoined by a court issuing an injunction or restraining order.

**enumerated powers** The powers specifically given by the federal Constitution to the national government that are not reserved to the states or the people.

**equity** A system of remedial justice administered by certain courts empowered to order remedies based on principles of fairness and justice as well as precedent. Equity originated in England to provide alternatives to the sometimes harsh rules of the common law.

**excise** A tax imposed on the manufacture, sale, or use of certain goods, or upon a particular occupation or activity.

**execution** Putting into force a legal order or process. Execution of a judgment is the process by which a money judgment is enforced, usually through the seizure and sale of property.

**executive order** A regulation issued by the president, a state governor, or some other executive authority for the purpose of giving effect to a constitutional or statutory provision An executive order has the force of law and is one means by which the executive branch implements laws.

**ex parte** Literally, "on one side." Done for, on behalf of, or on the application of one party only.

**ex post facto law**   A law passed after a fact or event has occurred that changes the legal consequences of the act. Traditionally, an ex post facto law made an act that was legal when done illegal after the fact.

**federal question**   An issue arising out of provisions of the Constitution, federal statutes, or treaties. A federal court has jurisdiction to hear federal questions under powers conferred by Article 3, section 2 of the U.S. Constitution.

**federalism**   A political system in which a number of sovereign political units join together to form a larger political unit that has authority to act on behalf of the whole. A federal system or federation preserves the political integrity of all the entities that compose the federation. Federal systems are regarded as weak if the central government has control over very few policy questions and strong if the central government possesses authority over most significant policy issues. Authority that is not exclusively assigned may be shared by the two levels and exercised concurrently. The supremacy clause of the Constitution requires that conflicts arising from the exercise of federal and state power are resolved in favor of the central government. Powers not assigned to the national government are "reserved" for the states by the Tenth Amendment.

***Federalist, The***   A series of 85 essays written by Alexander Hamilton, James Madison, and John Jay and published in newspapers between October 27, 1787, and May 28, 1788, discussing the various provisions of the proposed federal constitution. *The Federalist* was designed to persuade the people of New York to vote to ratify the Constitution in that state's state ratifying convention. The essays were eventually reprinted in two volumes and have since become a primary source for judges and legal scholars in interpreting the Constitution.

**Fifth Amendment**   Adopted as part of the original Bill of Rights in 1791, the Fifth Amendment contains a number of important procedural and substantive safeguards against government power. Among these are protections against self-incrimination and double jeopardy, as well as the protections for property rights.

**First Amendment**   Adopted as part of the original Bill of Rights in 1791, the First Amendment contains provisions guaranteeing freedom of speech and of the press, as well as a separation of church and state.

**forfeiture**   A term that denotes a confiscation of property without compensation. Forfeitures are usually imposed by law as punishment for the commission of an illegal act.

**grand jury**   A panel of twelve to twenty-three citizens who review prosecutorial evidence to determine whether there are sufficient grounds to formally accuse an individual of criminal conduct. The charges a grand jury issues are contained in a document called an "indictment."

**habeas corpus**   Literally, "You have the body." Habeas corpus is a procedure designed to prevent the improper detention of prisoners. The habeas corpus process forces jailers to bring a detained person before a judge who would examine the justification for the detention. If the court finds the person is being improperly held, it can order the prisoner's release.

**holding**   A statement of law in a judicial opinion that provides the rule of decision in a case. It is contrasted with dictum.

**impeachment**   The process by which an officer of the government may be removed from office. In the federal system, articles of impeachment, which essentially constitute an indictment, are drafted and passed by the House of Representatives. The Senate then holds a trial, where a two-thirds vote is needed for conviction. The grounds for impeachment are not clearly stated in the Constitution, but most impeachments are the result of criminal conduct or some misfeasance in the conduct of office. Impeachment results in removal from office, but it does not prevent a guilty party from later being prosecuted for violation of the criminal law.

**indictment**   A written accusation presented by a grand jury to a court charging that a person has done some act or omission that by law is a punishable offense.

**injunction**   An order prohibiting a party from acting in a particular way or requiring a party to take a specific action. Injunctions are the traditional form of relief granted by the courts of equity. Once issued, an injunction may be annulled or quashed, and injunctions may be temporary or permanent. Temporary injunctions, known as interlocutory injunctions, are used to preserve the status quo until the issue can be resolved though the normal judicial process. A permanent injunction may be issued upon completion of full legal proceedings. Failure to comply with an injunction constitutes a contempt of court and may be punished by civil or criminal contempt proceedings.

**in personam jurisdiction**   Literally, "against the person." In personam actions seek judgement from a person and are commenced directly against him. Courts have in personam jurisdiction to the extent they have power to compel a person to appear and answer a claim against him. Such power is traditionally based on residence on the fact that a person has conducted business within the jurisdiction.

**in rem jurisdiction**   Literally, "against the thing." In rem actions are commenced against property rather than against a person directly. In rem actions are brought against property that is either "guilty" or "indebted." Thus, an action against a vessel caught smuggling goods into the country is one in rem against the vessel. In such a case, the vessel alone is the defendant regardless of whether an action is ever filed against the owner or crew. In rem actions have traditionally been the primary means by which the customs and revenue laws are enforced. Courts have in rem jurisdiction only to the extent the property in question is actually located in the jurisdiction.

**interrogatories**   A set of written questions presented to a party in a legal action designed to obtain facts or other information about the claims or defences at issue.

**judgment**   The final conclusion reached by a court; the outcome of a case as distinguished from the holding or legal reasoning supporting the conclusion.

**judicial review**   The power of a court to examine the actions of the legislative and executive branches with the possibility of declaring those actions unconstitutional. The power of judicial review was discussed extensively at the Constitutional Convention of 1787, but it was not included in the constitutional text as an expressly delegated judicial function.

**judiciary acts**   One of the several acts of Congress creating the lower federal courts and allocating original and appellate jurisdiction between these courts and the Supreme Court.

**jurisdiction**   The boundaries within which a particular court may exercise judicial power; the power of a court to hear and decide cases. The jurisdiction of federal courts is provided by Article III of the federal Constitution and subsequent acts of Congress. Federal judicial power may extend to classes of cases defined in terms of substance and party, as well as to cases in law and equity stemming directly from the federal Constitution, federal statutes, and treaties. Federal judicial power also extends to cases involving specified parties, regardless of the substance of the case. Thus, federal jurisdiction includes actions where the federal government itself is a party, suits between two or more states, suits between a state and a citizen of another state or foreign county, and suits between citizens of different states. State constitutions and statutes define the jurisdiction of state courts.

**jurisprudence**   A legal philosophy or the science of law; the course or direction of judicial rulings. As a science, jurisprudence draws upon philosophical thought, historical and political analysis, sociological and behavioral evidence, and legal experience. Jurisprudence is grounded on the view that ideas about law evolve from critical thinking in a number of disciplines. Jurisprudence enables people to understand how law has ordered both social institutions and individual conduct.

**jury**   A certain number of citizens selected by law and summoned to determine matters of fact in cases brought in the common law courts.

**justiciable**   Appropriate for a court to hear and decide.

**King's Bench**   One of the superior courts of common law in England having a broad jurisdiction over both civil and criminal matters.

**law of nations**   The rules and principles of law governing relations between nations.

**Letter of Marque**    An authorisation granted by a government in time of war to the owner of a private vessel empowering it to capture enemy vessels and goods on the high seas.

**lex mercatoria**    The law merchant; the commercial law.

**libel**    A publication that is injurious to the reputation of another; a defamatory writing, picture or sign.

**lien**    A claim or encumbrance on property for the payment of a debt. Liens may be created voluntarily, as by contract, or involuntarily, as when property becomes liable for payment of a judgment.

**litigant**    A party to a lawsuit.

**mandamus**    Literally, "We command." A writ issued by a court of superior jurisdiction to an inferior court or governmental official commanding the performance of an official act.

**maritime law**    See "admiralty law."

**merchantman**    A ship or vessel engaged in maritime commerce.

**most favored nation**    The right of citizens or subjects of parties to a treaty to trade the most advantageous terms. The primary result of this right is lower customs duties and tariffs.

**motion**    A request made to a court for a certain ruling or action.

**natural law**    Laws considered applicable to all nations and people because they are basic to human nature.

**naturalization**    Legal procedure by which an alien is admitted to citizenship. Congress is authorised by Article I, section 8, of the federal Constitution to establish uniform rules for naturalization. An individual over eighteen may be naturalized after meeting certain qualifications, including residence in the United States for a term of years; ability to read, write, and speak English; and proof of good moral character. The residence requirement is lowered for spouses of citizens and for aliens who serve in the armed forces. Minors become citizens when their parents are naturalized.

**obiter dictum**    Literally, "something said in passing." Statement contained in a court's opinion that is incidental to the disposition of the case. Obiter dicta often are directed to issues upon which no formal arguments have been heard, thus the positions represented there are not binding on later cases.

**opinion of the court**   The statement of a court that expresses the reasoning, or ratio decidendi, upon which a decision is based. The opinion summarizes the principles of law that apply in a given case and represents the views of the majority of a court's members. Occasionally, the opinion of a court may reflect the views of less than a majority of its members; it is then called a plurality opinion.

**order**   A command issued by a judge.

**originalism**   A method of constitutional and legal interpretation that seeks to determine the original meaning of the words being construed. In applying a legal or constitutional provision, judges are to determine what the drafters of the provision intended when they selected the words in question.

**original jurisdiction**   The authority of a court to hear and decide a legal question before any other court. Original jurisdiction typically is vested with trial courts rather than appellate courts, although Article III of the Constitution extends very limited original jurisdiction to the Supreme Court. Trial courts are assigned specific original jurisdiction defined in terms of subject matter or party.

**patent**   A grant of a privilege, right, or property made by the sovereign to one or more individuals. Examples include a design patent, which is a right to exclude others from making or using one's invention, and a land patent, which is a grant of title in a parcel of land.

**per curiam opinion**   Literally, "by the court." An unsigned written opinion issued by a court.

**petitioner**   The party seeking relief in court. The term is commonly used to denote the party who appeals a judgement below.

**piracy**   The illegal taking of life or property upon the high seas without legal authorization or justification.

**plaintiff**   The party who brings a legal action to court for resolution or remedy.

**plea**   In civil cases, the first factual answer made by a defendant in response to a plaintiff's claim. In criminal cases, the defendant's response to the charge laid by the prosecutor or grand jury.

**pleadings**   The formal allegations of those involved in a lawsuit setting forth their respective claims and defences.

**political question**   An issue that is not justiciable, or appropriate for judicial determination, because it is primarily political or involves a matter directed toward either the legislative or executive branch by constitutional language. The political question doctrine is sometimes invoked by the Supreme Court not because the Court is without power or jurisdiction but because the Court adjudges the question inappropriate for judicial response. In the Court's view, to intervene or respond would be to encroach upon the functions and prerogatives of one of the other two branches of government.

**prayer**    The request contained in a pleading that asks the court to grant the relief desired by the plaintiff.

**precedent**    A decision or order of a court that is considered as settling the legal issues and that serves as an example for future courts and decision-makers in cases with similar facts and issues of law.

**privateer**    A vessel owned or equipped by a private party and commissioned by a government to make war upon an enemy. Privateers were commissioned by letters of marque issued by a government official and were then sent out to "cruise" upon the enemy ships. In most cases, vessels and cargo captured by a privateer were sold and the proceeds shared between the owner and crew. See "prize" below. Having a letter of marque was essential to prevent a vessel from being considered a pirate.

**prize**    A vessel or cargo belonging to an enemy lawfully captured at sea by a naval vessel or privateer during time of war and subject to forfeiture. Captured vessels and cargo were brought within the jurisdiction of a prize court, which would then adjudicate the question of "prize or no." If the captured property was proved to belong to an enemy, the captor was entitled to receive a portion of the proceeds, which depended on whether the captor was a naval vessel or privateer.

**prohibition**    A writ issued by a superior court preventing a lower court from determining cases or matters not within its jurisdiction. It ensures that lower courts are kept within their proper bounds.

**qui tam action**    Literally, "Who sues?" An action brought by a private party on behalf of the sovereign to recover damages due the government. If successful, the plaintiff is entitled to a share of the award. Qui tam plaintiffs are sometimes called "private attorneys general" and are designed to encourage those with information about wrongdoing to come forward and assist the government in protecting its rights.

**quo warranto**    Literally, "by what right?" A common law action brought by the government against a person enquiring into the authority by which he acts. It is used to prevent usurpations of power by office holders and can also be used to question the right of a corporation to undertake a particular action.

**report**    A statement of the facts and opinion reached in a case. Reports are usually published by "reporters" in a series of volumes. Reports can be official or unofficial.

The Supreme Court's official reports are published in *The Supreme Court Reports*, while unofficial versions exist in *The Supreme Court Reporter* and *Supreme Court Reports, Lawyer's Edition*. Early cases are frequently cited by including the name of the official who compiled the report, e.g., 4 U.S. (4 Dallas) ___ or 5 U.S. (1 Cranch) ___.

**respondent**    The party against whom a legal action is filed.

**reversal**    An action by an appellate court setting aside or changing a decision of a lower court. The opposite of an affirmation.

**right**    A power or privilege to which a person is entitled. A right is legally conveyed by a constitution, statute, or common law and may be absolute, such as one's right against self-incrimination or conditional, such as the right to free speech, which is not libellous.

**ripeness**    A condition in which a legal dispute has evolved to the point where the issue(s) it presents can be determined by a court.

**salvage**    Goods or property recovered after a casualty. In admiralty, the amount of compensation awarded to a person or vessel through whose assistance property is rescued. Salvage awards depend on the nature of the peril, the difficulties encountered by the salvors, and the amount of property recovered. Awards are designed to encourage bystanders to assist in rescuing those in peril on the seas.

**saving to suitors clause**    A provision in the first Judiciary Act, and included in subsequent acts, which gives federal district courts jurisdiction to hear maritime claims "saving to suitors in all cases all other remedies to which they are otherwise entitled a common law." The provision allows maritime plaintiffs to bring their action in state courts, although state courts must use the same rules of law that would have been applied if the action had been brought in federal courts.

**sedition**    The act of advocating the overthrow or modification of the government by violence or unlawful means. An association or combination of two or more persons to engage in sedition is a seditious conspiracy. A publication written to incite the people to rise against the government is a seditious libel. The law of sedition in the United States has its roots in English law.

**separation of powers**    The principle of dividing the powers of government among several branches to prevent excessive concentration of power. Separation of powers is designed to limit abusive exercise of governmental authority by partitioning power and then assigning that power to several locations. In distributing powers, the U.S. Constitution functionally distinguishes between the government and the people and between legislative, executive, and judicial branches. Although the Constitution creates three separate branches, it also assigns overlapping responsibilities that make the three branches interdependent through the operation of a system of checks and balances.

**seriatim opinions**    The practice of giving judicial opinions one by one. The justices of the early Supreme Court frequently read their opinions seriatim directly from the bench.

**sovereign immunity**    A judicial doctrine that precludes bringing a suit against the sovereign. It is founded on the principle that "the King can do no wrong," and prevents the government from being liable to answer for damages in any action brought by a private party. The federal government and most states have passed statutes abrogating their sovereign immunity in certain cases.

**sovereignty**    The supreme power of a state or independent nation free from external interference. Sovereignty is exercised by government, which has exclusive and absolute jurisdiction within its geographical.

**stare decicis**    Literally, "to let the decision stand." The doctrine that once a principle of law is established for a particular fact situation, courts should adhere to that principle in similar cases in the future. The case in which the rule of law is established is called a precedent. Precedents may be modified or abandoned if circumstances require, but the expectation is that rules from previously adjudicated cases will prevail, creating and maintaining stability and predictability in the law.

**states' rights**    A political and legal doctrine emphasising the power of the states in opposition to the powers of the federal government. The primary basis of the doctrine was the assertion that upon independence, the powers of the Crown were automatically transferred to the individual state governments. In this view, the states were sovereign and could act much like independent nations, except in those areas specifically reserved to the federal government in the Constitution. The doctrine gained force in the years leading to the Civil War, but has waxed and waned since then.

**stay**    An order to arrest or suspend a judicial proceeding or the execution of a judgment.

**taxing power**    The authority granted Congress in Article I, section 8, of the Constitution to "lay and collect taxes, duties, imposts and excises" and to provide for the "common defence and general welfare" of the United States. The scope of the federal power to tax and spend has depended at least in part on the Court's interpretation of the "general welfare" phrase.

**Tenth Amendment**    Provision added to the federal Constitution in 1791 that retains, or "reserves," for the states powers not assigned to the federal government. The Tenth Amendment has frequently been used to limit the actions of the federal government.

**term**  The time during which a court is in session. The Judiciary Act of 1789 required the Supreme Court to sit on the first Monday in October and February each year. The modern Supreme Court now sits in a continuous term beginning on the first Monday in October and usually concludes its term in June of the following year.

**test case**  A legal action commenced to test the constitutionality of a statute or government practice.

**tonnage**  The capacity of a vessel. A tax laid upon a vessel based on its capacity or weight.

**tort**  A private or civil wrong for which courts will give a remedy in damages.

**treaty power**  The power conferred on the national government in Article II, section 2, to enter into treaties with foreign nations. This provision allows the president to make treaties that must then be approved by two-thirds of the Senate. Article VI of the Constitution provides that treaties thus made shall be considered the "law of the land."

**true bill**  The endorsement on an indictment made by a grand jury indicating that the facts are sufficient to support the allegations. The indictment is prepared by a prosecutor and then endorsed as a "true bill" by the members of the grand jury.

**underwriter**  A person or syndicate who agrees to bear the risk in a contract of insurance.

**vacate**  The act of declaring an order or judgement of a court void and of no legal effect.

**venire**  A group of citizens summoned to court from which a jury is chosen. Its name is derived from the writ venire facias, literally cause to come," issued to the sheriff commanding him to summon "twelve good men and true."

**venue**  The neighborhood or place where an injury or crime was committed or done; the geographical area in which a court is authorized to exercise jurisdiction.

**verdict**  The formal decision or finding of a jury in a case. It is distinguished from a "judgment," which is the final determination of the court rendered by a judge. In cases tried to a jury, the jury renders a "verdict" and a "judgment" is entered on that verdict.

**war power**  The power of the national government to wage war on behalf of the United States. The source of the war power is found in the Constitution, and the power is shared by the president and Congress. Article I, section 8, gives Congress the power to declare war, while Article II, section 1, makes the president commander in chief with the authority to conduct military operations.

**warrant**   A judicial order authorising an arrest or search and seizure.

**writ**   A written order of a court commanding the recipient to perform certain specified acts.

**writ of assistance**   A order issued by a court directing a government official to assist a party in enforcing his rights. In colonial times, a writ issued by a court directing officials to assist customs and revenue officers in making searches and seizures of smuggled goods.

# *Annotated Bibliography*

Ackerman, Bruce A. *The Failure of the Founding Fathers: Jefferson, Marshall, and the Rise of Presidential Democracy*. Cambridge, MA: Harvard, 2005.

A study of the election of 1801. The author argues that the Constitution contained a serious flaw in that it did not take proper account of the growth of political parties.

Amar, Akhil Reed. *America's Constitution: A Biography*. New York: Random House, 2005. Billed as a "biography," Amar's book is an attempt to explain the origins of the Constitution and suggest ways in which it ought to be interpreted in light of modern social and political concerns.

Appleby, Joyce Oldham. *Inventing the Revolution: The First Generation of Americans*. Cambridge, MA: Harvard, 2000.

A study of the "first generation" of Americans, those who came of age in the years following the Revolution. Appleby argues that this generation created an ideology of free enterprise and individual freedom that has served as the template for future generations.

Banning, Lance. *The Jeffersonian Persuasion: Evolution of a Party Ideology*. Ithaca, NY: Cornell University Press, 1978.

A revisionist examination of the development of the Jeffersonian ideology and its connection to the party's rise in the 1790s.

Beard, Charles A. *An Economic Interpretation of the Constitution of the United States*. New York: Macmillan, 1913.

The classic economic interpretation of the U.S. Constitution. Beard argues that the structure of the Constitution was motivated by the economic interests of the founding fathers. Beard's interpretation has been challenged repeatedly since.

Beeman, Richard. *Beyond Confederation: Origins of the Constitution and American National Identity*. Chapel Hill: University of North Carolina Press, 1987.

A series of essays exploring the background, writing, and ratification of the federal Constitution.

Bemis, Samuel Flagg. *Jay's Treaty: A Study in Commerce and Diplomacy*. Westport, CT: Greenwood Press, 1975.

The classic study of Jay's treaty and the political aftermath.

Bernstein, Richard B. *Thomas Jefferson*. New York: Oxford, 2003.

An excellent shorter biography of the nation's third president.

Beveridge, Albert. *Life of John Marshall*. New York: Chelsea House, 1980.

A four-volume life of the great chief justice. First published to great acclaim in 1920, it is considered a classic; however, as might be expected, modern scholarship has corrected some of its errors and filled in a few gaps.

Bickel, Alexander M. *The Least Dangerous Branch: The Supreme Court at the Bar of Politics*. New Haven, CT: Yale University Press, 1986.

First published in the wake of the Supreme Court's decision in *Brown v. Board of Education*, the book sets forth a defence of judicial review in light of the "counter-majoritarian difficulty."

Buel, Richard. *Securing the Revolution: Ideology in American Politics, 1789–1815*. Ithaca, NY: Cornell University Press, 1972.

This is a study of the ideology that shaped the partisan divide of the 1790s, rather than an examination of the specifics of party organization.

Caldwell, Lynton K. *The Administrative Theories of Hamilton and Jefferson: Their Contribution to Thought on Public Administration*. New York: Holmes & Meier, 1988.

A study of Hamilton and Jefferson's theories on government. This book was first published in 1944, but some of the insights remain important today.

Chambers, William Nesbitt. *Political Parties in a New Nation: The American Experience, 1789–1809*. New York: Oxford University Press, 1993.

A classic study of the rise of political parties in the early republic.

Chernow, Ron. *Alexander Hamilton*. New York: Penguin Press, 2004.

An exhaustive modern biography that is invaluable to the academic and accessible to the nonspecialist reader as well.

DeConde, Alexander. *The Quasi-War: The Politics and Diplomacy of the Undeclared War with France 1797–1801*. New York: Scribner, 1966.

A diplomatic study of the Quasi-War.

Elkins, Stanley and Eric McKitrick. *The Age of Federalism*. New York: Oxford University Press, 1993.

A complete history of the Federalist era.

Ellis, Joseph J. *Founding Brothers: The Revolutionary Generation*. New York: Alfred A. Knopf, 2000.

Focusing on six events in the early years of the republic, Ellis shows that there was considerable disagreement among the founding fathers on the precise meaning of the Revolution and the best way in which to implement its aims.

Ellis, Richard, E. *The Jeffersonian Crisis: Courts and Politics in the Young Republic*. New York: Norton, 1974.

A sympathetic examination of Jefferson's attack on the national judiciary. It contains an interesting perspective on the relationship between Jefferson and John Marshall.

Estes, Todd. *The Jay Treaty Debate, Public Opinion, and the Evolution of Early American Political Culture*. Amherst: University of Massachusetts Press, 2006.

A study of the debate surrounding the ratification of Jay's Treaty. Shows that the debate helped transform the political sphere from one based on deference to order to a more aggressively democratic one.

Ferling, John E. *Setting the Word Ablaze: Washington, Adams, Jefferson and the American Revolution*. New York: Oxford, 2000.

Ferling offers a "comparative biography" of three of the founding fathers. The author argues that Adams is the most underrated of the three, whereas Jefferson is the most overrated.

Gerber, Scott Douglas. *Seriatum: The Supreme Court Before John Marshall*. New York: New York University Press, 2000.

A series of essays by various scholars on the workings and personnel of the early Supreme Court. Well organized and containing a number of important insights, this book is a good reference for those interested in the Court's early history.

Goebel, Julius. *History of the Supreme Court of the United States*. New York: Macmillan, 1971.

Perhaps one of the most well-known volumes on the history of the Supreme Court, it contains a very heavy focus on the court's antecedents. Unfortunately, it is written in an arcane style that makes much of the subject incomprehensible.

Hogeland, William. *The Whiskey Rebellion: George Washington, Alexander Hamilton, and the Frontier Rebels Who Challenged America's Newfound Sovereignty*. New York: Scribner, 2006.

A lively telling of the Whiskey Rebellion and its aftermath.

Jay, Stewart. *Most Humble Servants: The Advisory Role of Early Judges*. New Haven, CT: Yale, 1997.

Challenges the traditional view that federal judges are barred from giving advisory opinions. Jay shows that 18th-century judges in both England and America often provided advisory opinions. He argues that the justices' refusal to provide an advisory opinion in the neutrality controversy was less motivated by Constitutional theory, than in the practical difficulties such an opinion would create.

Johnson, Calvin H. *Righteous Anger at the Wicked States: The Meaning of the Founders' Constitution*. New York: Cambridge, 2000.

Argues that the primary impetus behind the creation of the Constitution was the desire to pay off the debts arising from the Revolution. Johnson contends that the framers were angry at the states' repeated failure to live up to their responsibilities during and after the Revolution.

Knudson, Jerry W. *Jefferson and the Press: Crucible of Liberty*. Columbia: University of South Carolina, 2006.

Details the coverage given Thomas Jefferson by both Federalist and Republican editors during several important episodes in Jefferson's presidency.

Labunski, Richard E. *James Madison and the Struggle for the Bill of Rights*. New York: Oxford, 2006.

Details the origins, drafting, and eventual ratification of the first ten amendments to the federal Constitution.

Mann, Bruce H. *Republic of Debtors: Bankruptcy in the Age of American Independence*. Cambridge, MA: Harvard University Press, 2002.

Traces the changing attitudes toward debt in the years following the American Revolution. Mann argues that Americans' view of bankruptcy changed as they came to regard bankruptcy as an economic problem rather than a moral failure. This is an invaluable study.

Marcus, Maeva. *The Documentary History of the Supreme Court of the United States, 1789–1800*. New York: Columbia University Press, 1985–2007. A documentary collection containing letters, newspaper articles, and court materials. Perhaps the most valuable resource for study of the Supreme Court's early history.

McCoy, Drew R. *Elusive Republic: Political Economy in Jeffersonian America*. Chapel Hill: University of North Carolina Press, 1996.

Describes the Jeffersonian view that only an agrarian society could foster the sense of virtue and civic-mindedness that would be necessary in a republic. McCoy argues that this view was unattainable given the rapid commercialization of the American economy.

Miller, John C. *Crisis in Freedom: The Alien and Sedition Acts*. Boston: Little, Brown and Company, 1951.

A study of the enactment and aftermath of the Alien and Sedition Acts. Contains a discussion of how the various acts made their way through Congress, as well as a description of the prosecutions that followed.

_____. *The Federalist Era: 1789–1801*. New York: Harper, 1960.

A brief and very readable account of the early years of the new Republic. Although a bit dated and lacking footnotes or good citations, it is still a very good source of information and perspective on the period.

Morgan, Edmund S. *Birth of the Republic: 1763–1789*. Chicago: University of Chicago Press, 1992.

This is Morgan's classic account of how Britain's tax policy forced the colonies to examine the constitutional relationship between Britain and America. Morgan argues that the formulation developed by the newly independent stated were not abstract, but were eventually incorporated into the Constitution.

Morris, Richard B. *The Forging of the Union, 1781–1789.* New York: Harper and Row, 1987. An examination of the "critical period" of American history. Morris examines the difficulties facing the newly independent nation and provides a concise and readable account of the events leading to the calling of the Constitutional Convention.

Nedelsky, Jennifer. *Private Property and the Limits of American Constitutionalism.* Chicago: University of Chicago Press, 1990.

Argues that the federal Constitution was not designed to protect individual rights. Instead, Nedelsky claims that the founders' primary aim was to protect property and that this focus helped shape America's governmental institutions.

Newman, Paul Douglas. *Fries's Rebellion: The Enduring Struggle for the American Revolution.* Philadelphia: Pennsylvania Press, 2004.

An up-to-date telling of the rebellion of Pennsylvania farmers against the 1798 federal land tax.

Newmyer, R. Kent. *Supreme Court Justice Joseph Story: A Statesman of the Old Republic.* Chapel Hill: University of North Carolina Press, 1985.

An important biography of one of the young nation's most important justices. Newmyer attempts to describe the factors that made Joseph Story a giant of his day, while at the same time explaining why Story seems to have faded from popular consciousness.

Pasley, Jeffrey L. *Tyranny of Printers: Newspaper Politics in the Early American Republic.* Charlotte: University of Virginia Press, 2001.

An interesting and intriguing history of the role of the press in the partisan struggles of the 1790s. Beginning with the story of Jefferson's attempt to use the press to discredit Hamilton's policies, the book describes the way in which the press eventually paved the way for the rise of Jacksonian democracy.

Perkins, Bradford. *The First Rapprochement: England and the United States, 1795–1805.* Philadelphia: University of Pennsylvania Press, 1955.

A study of relations between Britain and the United States from the period after the Jay Treaty until the *Essex* decision in 1805. Argues that the two nations experienced a real reconcilliation based on mutual interest, self-restraint, and opposition to France as a common foe.

Presser, Stephen B. *The Original Misunderstanding: The English, The Americans and the Dialectic of Federalist Jurisprudence*. Chapel Hill: University of North Carolina Press, 1991.

An examination of the role of the lower federal courts in the early Republic. The book contains a very interesting discussion of the role of Justice Samuel Chase. It draws connections between Federalist and Republican approaches to constitutional interpretation and shows that both sides' jurisrpudential outlook was well grounded in English tradition.

Schwartz, Bernard. *A History of the Supreme Court*. New York: Oxford University Press, 1993.

A one-volume history of the Supreme Court from its founding to the modern day. As would be expected, it contains a brief analysis of the court's early years.

Sharp, James R. *American Politics in the New Nation: The New Nation in Crisis*. New Haven: Yale University Press, 1993.

Jelswc

Slaughter, Thomas P. *The Whiskey Rebellion: Frontier Epilogue to the American Revolution*. New York: Oxford University Press, 1986.

An excellent study of the Whiskey Rebellion. The author presents a rather fresh, if critical, assessment of Hamilton and Washington's efforts to quell the rebellion.

Sloan, Herbert E. *Principle and Interest: Thomas Jefferson and the Problem of Debt*. New York: Oxford University Press, 1995.

An interesting study of the role of debt in the early Republic. Sloan shows that Jefferson's problems with debt, in particular, helped shape his party's opposition to Hamilton's economic program.

Smith, Joseph Morton. *Freedom's Fetters: The Alien and Sedition Laws and American Civil Liberties*. Ithaca, NY: Cornell University Press, 1956.

One of the most complete studies of the Alien and Sedition Acts. The book is a bit dated as it comes out of the McCarthy era and so is written in the context of those events, but it is invaluable nonetheless.

Stahr, Walter. *John Jay: Founding Father*. New York: Palgrave Macmillan, 2005.

A well-done biography of the nation's first Chief Justice. Shows that Jay was an integral player in the creation and preservation of the new Republic.

Stewart, Donald H. *The Opposition Press of the Federalist Period*. Albany, NY: State University of New York Press, 1969.

A comprehensive study of the Republican press during the Federalist period. Details their opposition to the Jay Treaty, the Alien and Sedition Acts, Assumption and the Quasi-War.

Szatmary, David P. *Shays' Rebellion: The Making of an Agrarian Insurrection*. Amherst: University of Massachusetts Press, 1980.

Discusses the rebellion in terms of its economic origins. Szatmary argues that international economic factors produced a chain reaction that ultimately destabilized the economic structure of the American frontier, resulting in a debtors' rebellion.

Walling, Karl-Friedrich. *American Empire: Alexander Hamilton on War and Free Government*. Lawrence: University of Kansas Press, 1999.

A revisionist account of Hamilton's thoughts on military and political affairs. Challenges the view that Hamilton sought to be an "American Caesar."

Warren, Charles. *The Supreme Court in United States History*. Boston: Little, Brown and Company, 1935.

A classic study of the history of the Supreme Court. Focuses on the political context of the court's decisions, as well as the court's place in the political scheme. Some aspects of its history, particularly with respect to the drafting of the Judiciary Act, have been challenged in recent years.

Weisberger, Bernard A. *America Afire: Jefferson, Adams and the Revolutionary Election of 1800*. New York: William Morrow, 2000.

The title of this book is somewhat misleading, but that's all to the good. A relatively short work, it contains a very readable and exhaustive account of the origins of the party struggle in the early Republic, particularly with respect to Alexander Hamilton and Aaron Burr. It then makes clear how local political differences combined to create the election of 1800.

Wheelan, Joseph. *Jefferson's Vendetta: The Pursuit of Aaron Burr and the Judiciary*. New York: Carroll & Graf, 2005.

A description of the rivalry between Thomas Jefferson and Vice President Aaron Burr. Details Burr's trial for treason, especially John Marshall's role.

White, G. Edward. *The Marshall Court and Cultural Change, 1815–1835*. New York: Oxford University Press, 1991.

Originally published as volumes three and four of the Oliver Wendell Holmes Devise History of the Supreme Court, this book is a monumental study that attempts to reveal the cultural and ideological context in which the Marshall court worked. White asserts that Marshall and his colleagues interpreted the Constitution in such a way as to give the appearance that judicial interpretation was merely an application of timeless legal principles and hid the discretionary elements of judicial action.

Wood, Gordon S. *The Creation of the American Republic, 1776–1787*. Chapel Hill: University of North Carolina Press, 1998. A classic intellectual history of the revolutionary. Wood argues that the original justifications for revolution were found lacking once the colonies gained their independence. He shows that the Constitutional Convention of 1787 grew out of disappointment with the increasing democratization of state governments in the Confederation era.

# Index

# *About the Author*

**Matthew Harrington** is a Professor of Law at the University of Montreal (Canada), where he teaches English and American Constitutional Law, Legal History, and Property. A graduate of McGill University and the University of Pennsylvania, he previously taught at Fordham University, The Catholic University of America, and Rogers Williams University School of Law. He has also served as the Associate Dean for Administrative Affairs at George Washington University. His published work includes articles on judicial review, the history of the civil jury, and the constitutional implications economic expropriations published in *Williams and Mary Law Review, George Washington Law Review, Hastings Law Journal,* and *Wisconsin Law Review.*